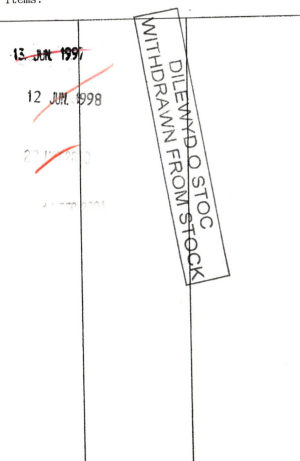

Economic Institutions, Markets and Competition

Economic Institutions, Markets and Competition

Centralization and Decentralization in the Transformation of Economic Systems

Edited by

Bruno Dallago and Luigi Mittone

Edward Elgar
Cheltenham, UK • Brookfield, US

Published by
Edward Elgar Publishing Limited
8 Lansdown Place
Cheltenham
Glos GL50 2HU
UK

Edward Elgar Publishing Company
Old Post Road
Brookfield
Vermont 05036
US

British Library Cataloguing in Publication Data
Economic institutions, markets and competition:
  centralization and decentralization in the transformation
  of economic systems
  1. Money market 2. Financial institutions 3. Competition
  I. Dallago, Bruno, 1950–   II. Mittone, Luigi
  332

Library of Congress Cataloguing in Publication Data
Economic institutions, markets, and competition: centralization and
  decentralization in the transformation of economic systems / edited
  by Bruno Dallago and Luigi Mittone.
    Includes rev. versions of some of the papers presented at the
  fourth Trento Workshop held at the University of Trento, Feb. 28 to
  March 1, 1994
    Includes index.
    1. Comparative economics. 2. Post-communism. 3. Privatization.
  4. Intergovernmental fiscal relations. 5. Competition.
  I. Dallago, Bruno, 1950–   . II. Mittone, Luigi.
  HB90.E274   1995
  330—dc20   96-6436
                                                         CIP

ISBN 1 85898 319 3

Printed and bound in Great Britain
by Hartnolls Ltd, Bodmin, Cornwall

Contents

Preface

Bruno Dallago and Luigi Mittone

Different institutions govern the production and supply of goods to intermediate and final consumers, and their distribution. These institutions were traditionally divided into two groups comprising centralized institutions (the state) and decentralized ones (enterprises, households, non-profit institutions and the like). The nature of institutions has important consequences for the economic system, understood as a set of economic institutions, and for a series of essential variables: the allocation of resources, the efficiency and the continuity of their use, the distribution of income, the nature and origin of important economic information, the motives and incentives for economic activity, the relationships among economic agents.

However, the traditional view based on the antimony between centralization and decentralization is not borne out by the facts, and it is an over-contrivance in analytical terms as well. This point, among others, is clearly demonstrated by the 'laboratory experiment' of the economies in transition. The passage to a market economy does not simply imply the decentralization – though this may be its predominant feature – of a previously centralized economic system. On the contrary, in many fields (taxation, for example), it is necessary to strengthen the role of the central administration. And one should also bear in mind that transition has led to the transfer of some of the important economic competences of the regional apparatuses of the sole party in power to the central government.

There are three reasons why it is necessary to reconsider the nature of the institutions and the relationship among different institutions within a particular economic system. First, centralized and decentralized institutions coexist in all modern economic systems. Although they may differ one from the other according to the role that they occupy in the economy, and according to the relationship between them and the manner in which the decision-making process unfolds, internally to the same economic system both antimony and complementarity hold between centralization and decentralization. Consequently, every move towards decentralization (or centralization) must be accompanied by a move in the opposite direction in order to prevent harmful imbalances from arising within the economic system. Privatization, for example, as one of the most important acts of decentralization, must be accompanied by centralizing measures, such as regulation, in order to forestall negative consequences for the welfare of consumers. These processes can be seen as either institutional innovation, as devices intended to enhance microeconomic efficiency, or as resulting from a competitive process whereby the most efficient institution (in controlling free riding, for instance) emerges.

The same problem arises within individual economic institutions. It has been pointed out that an institution decentralized *per se*, like a market enterprise, is often organized in an extremely centralized manner, to the exclusion of horizontal relationships internally to it. Conversely, an institution traditionally considered to be centralized, like the state, is often organized in a decentralized manner. Even a traditionally centralized function like the collection of taxes, duties and social contributions may be substantially decentralized. The forms differ, though, and range from the federal organization of the state to the development of quasi-markets when for some reason decentralization via privatization is not convenient.

Finally, during the development process, a change takes place in the economic institutions and in their role and weight in the performance of productive and distributive activities, with a concomitant change in the mix between centralization and decentralization. Recent years, in particular since the late 1970s in the Western countries and since 1989 in central and eastern Europe, have witnessed a major and apparently accelerating process of decentralization, of which privatization has been only one, albeit important, component. The aim of this decentralization has been either to reform the economic system or push it towards greater decentralization. However, one may also suppose, following Hirschman and others, that this innovation is (at least in part) only one stage in the historical process of 'shifting involvements' between private interest and public action.

The importance of the topic, the novelty and complexity of the processes involved, as well as the intellectual, scientific and professional interest that they arouse, are the factors that have been responsible for this book, which collects analyses by sixteen different authors from various European countries and the USA on diverse aspects of the centralization and decentralization of the economic institutions. With the exception of the studies by Brosio and Voszka, these are the revised versions of some of the papers presented at the fourth Trento Workshop organized jointly by the European Association for Comparative Economic Studies (EACES) and the Department of Economics of the University of Trento. Other studies published in this book, specifically those by Birner, Coricelli and Egidi, are original works which differ from those presented by their authors at the Trento Workshop – whose theme was 'Centralization and Decentralization of Economic Institutions: Their Role in the Transformation of Economic Systems' and which was held at the University of Trento from 28 February to 1 March 1994, with the participation also by other European and non-European scholars.

The Workshop, and therefore indirectly this book, was made possible by the cooperation of various members of EACES and of the Department of Economics with the organizers (the present writers) and by the sponsorship provided by the Department of Economics of the University of Trento, by the Autonomous Province of Trento, by Tecnofin S.p.A. and by the Cassa Rurale di Villazzano e Trento.

Edith J. Kismarjay, helped by Mariarosa Strafellini, was of invaluable assistance in the organization of the conference. She was also of great help in the preparation of this book, for which Adrian Belton revised and in some cases translated the texts. Erica Franzoi and her colleagues at CRASI have had the patience to prepare the camera-ready copy, carefully following the editors' instructions, and the publishers have provided prompt and valuable assistance in the production of its final version. The editors alone, therefore, are responsible for those errors or omissions that still remain.

List of Contributors

Zoltán BARA

Zoltán Bara is professor of economics at the Budapest University of Economic Sciences, where he is chairman of the Department of Comparative Economics. He was visiting professor at Rutgers University from 1990 to 1992. His research and publications cover the areas of comparative analysis of market structures and of competition regulation, systemic changes in the East-European countries, privatization and foreign direct investment.

Will BARTLETT

Will Bartlett is reader in social economics at the School for Advanced Urban Studies, University of Bristol, researching the effects of market-based reforms in welfare state in the UK and in transition economies in Eastern Europe. He has recently co-edited books on *Quasi-Markets and Social Policy* and *Quasi-Markets and Welfare State: the Emerging Findings*.

Jack BIRNER

Jack Birner teaches economics, the history of economics, and methodology in the Department of Economics of the University of Maastricht. He was visiting professor in the department of economics of the University of Trento in 1993–94. Among his research interests are social amplifiers, the logic of scientific problem-solving, and the role of mathematics in science. His publications include *Hayek, Co-ordination and Evolution; His Legacy in Philosophy, Politics, Economics, and the History of Ideas*, jointly edited with Rudy van Zijp.

Carlo BORZAGA

Carlo Borzaga is associate professor of macroeconomics and policy and of labour economics at the University of Trento. His present fields of research include the features of unemployment in developed countries, employment policies, and non-profit organizations and social cooperatives. He has published on these topics, labour economics and regional economics.

Giorgio BROSIO

Giorgio Brosio is professor of public economics at the Faculty of Political Science of the University of Turin. He has been professor of public finance at the Universities of Camerino, Bari and Geneve. He has authored articles and books covering various topics in the field of public economics.

Fabrizio CORICELLI

Fabrizio Coricelli is currently associate professor of monetary economics in the Departments of Economics of the University of Siena. He holds a PhD in economics from the University of Pennsylvania, Philadelphia. He has worked at the International Monetary Fund and at the World Bank. He is also associated with the Central European University in Prague and is a research associate with CEPR for its programme on economies in transition. He has published widely on issues related to economic tranformation in previously centrally planned economies.

Bruno DALLAGO

Bruno Dallago is associate professor of economic policy and comparative economic systems at the University of Trento and president of the European Association for Comparative Economic Studies. He has been visiting scholar at the University of California at Berkeley and the University of Illinois at Urbana-Champaign. His research interests and publications cover comparative economic systems, privatization in the East and the West, transition in Central-Eastern Europe, the economics of nationalism, institutional economics, the irregular economy.

Massimo EGIDI

Massimo Egidi is professor of economics and chairman of the Department of Economics at the University of Trento. He has been visiting scholar and professor at the Washington University of St. Louis, the Santa Fe Institute, the University of California at Berkeley, the IIASA. He has published various books and articles on organization theory, industrial economics and experimental economics. His research interests cover these same fields.

Ruud KNAACK

Ruud Knaack is associate professor of comparative economics in the Economics Faculty of the University of Amsterdam. He has written extensively on the reform process in the former East-European socialist countries and China. More recently, he has been conducting research on the problems of the Dutch welfare state, from both an empirical and a theoretical point of view.

Jenö KOLTAY

Jenö Koltay is professor of economics and Director of the Institute of Economics, Hungarian Academy of Sciences. His area of research activity is labour economics and industrial relactions, fiscal policy and local governments. He teaches at ELTE University Budapest and College Budapest and has been visiting professor at French and German universities. His most recent publications include *Tax Reform in Hungary* and *Innovation et emploi a l'Ouest et a l'Est*.

Luigi MITTONE

Luigi Mittone is assistant professor of economis at the University of Trento. He is currently studying for a PhD in economics at the University of Bristol. He has published books and articles on health economics, public economics and consumer theory.

Svetozar PEJOVICH

Svetozar Pejovich is professor of economics at Texas A&M University. He also sits on the Advisory Board of the Capitol Research Center and the Washington Legal Foundation. His research interests include the economics of property rights, institutional economics, and comparative economic systems, and he has published various books and articles on these topics.

Jana SEREGHYOVÁ

Jana Sereghyová works at the Institute of Economics of the Czech National Bank and teaches at two Western European universities. She is also vice-president of the Euro-Czech Foundation for Economic Research. Her research activity covers international economic relations of countries in transition and entrepreneurship in international economic relations, topics on which she has published various books and articles.

Pekka SUTELA

Pekka Sutela is Special Adviser in Soviet and East European economic affairs at the Bank of Finland. He was Visiting Research Fellow at the Centre for Russian and East European Studies of the University of Birmingham, and Volkswagen Visiting Fellow at the Federal Institute for Soviet and European Studies in Cologne, Germany. He is Chairman of the Scientific Advisory Board of the Finnish Institute of Foreign Affairs and Deputy Chairman of the Board of the Institute for Russian and East European Studies, The Finnish Ministry of Education. His publications include the co-authored standard Finnish University textbook on economics, and books and articles on Soviet and East European economics.

Wim SWAAN

Wim Swaan is senior research fellow at the Institute of Economics of the Hungarian Academy of Sciences, Budapest, and one of the founding members of the Center for Institutional Studies at that institute. He holds a PhD from the University of Amsterdam and has published in the Cambridge Journal of Economics, Comparative Economic Studies and Soviet Studies as well as other journals. He received the 1994 Award of the European Association for Comparative Economic Studies for the best dissertation in the field covered by the association.

Éva VOSZKA

Éva Voszka is senior researcher at Financial Research Ltd., Budapest and associate professor at the University of Economics in Budapest. She is also economic advisor to the President of Hungary. Her research activity covers government enterprise relations, changes in organizational and ownership structures, the economic and sociological aspects of privatization. On these topics she has published various books and articles.

Hans-Jürgen WAGENER

Hans-Jürgen Wagener was previously professor of economics at the Rijksuniversiteit Groningen, The Netherlands. In 1933 he moved to the newly-founded Europa-Universität Viadrina at Frankfurt/Oder. In 1933–4 he served as president of the European Association for Comparative Economic Studies. Its recent publications include *On the Theory and Policy of Systemic Change* and *The Political Economy of Transformation.*

1. The State and the Firm: the Centralization and Decentralization of Economic Institutions: an Introduction[1]

Bruno Dallago and Luigi Mittone

1 INTRODUCTION

The neoclassical economists developed an idea of an economy based on individual and perfectly rational producers who establish exclusively market, and therefore horizontal, relationships among themselves; that is, among entities at the same level and perfectly decentralized. This is possible because these producers are perfectly equivalent one with the other, except for their endowment of resources (which are anyway equivalent) and their capacity to combine them. They are, moreover, all in possession of complete and identical information which flows through the prices formed in the market. Hence the problem of centralization and decentralization, of hierarchies and market, does not exist. It does arise, however, when one passes from the level of partial equilibria to that of general equilibrium. In this case the intervention is required of the Walrasian auctioneer, who, by virtue of his role assumes central, although impersonal, authority and thus introduces an element of centralization into the economy.

In reality, however, one realizes immediately that this model does not have sufficient interpretative power for an economy as a whole, not so much because of its extreme simplification as because it ignores components of great importance in the real world. The presence of these factors produces substantial changes in the relationships among economic agents, since they themselves are generated by the fundamental variables neglected by the neoclassical account. Thus the problem of centralization and decentralization

1

and more generally of relationships among economic agents acquires central importance in explanation of the working of the economy. This is a first way to address the problem: by examining, that is, the structure of the economic system.

In a world of limited knowledge, specialization, differing initial endowments of individuals and asymmetries of other kinds, increasing returns, public goods and externalities, the problem of centralization and decentralization arises at another level, that of the different ways in which the internal relationships of complex agents, i.e. organizations, are defined.

2   ORGANIZATIONS AND ECONOMIC SYSTEMS

According to Simon's definition,[2] an organization is a complex set of communications, power relationships and relationships of other kinds within a group of human beings pursuing one or more common goals. Internally to this organization, information is produced and exchanged, and goals and attitudes are formed which influence its decisions and give predictability and uniformity to behaviour within it. In short, routines are established which create stable and reasonably sure expectations concerning behaviour internal to the organization.

By virtue of these features, organizations are not solely the entities which incorporate the institutions, defining and concretizing their role in society and in the economy. They also perform an essential function in the formation, growth and change of the institutions. They are therefore the fundamental constitutive component of the economic system. This latter, in fact, is the set of all the major institutions in an economy which pursue, in a socially coordinated manner, the ends of economic activity. All these factors have an important part to play in the decision process, but what is decisive is the presence of authority relationships. And this denotes the existence of at least two functional levels in an organization:

a.   the managerial level, which has authority to take decisions and to check their implementation; this level is the control sphere;
b.   the operational level, where the decisions taken by the control sphere are enacted; this is the real sphere.[3]

This configuration of organizations and of economic systems means that, in extreme cases, the organizational structure of the decision process – and as we shall see, of the information process – may be vertical or horizontal, and that power may be centralized or decentralized.[4] Hence, by analogy, one may speak of a centralized or decentralized organization or economic system.

An organization and an economic system are perfectly centralized if all decision-making authority is concentrated into a single centre. This latter constitutes the control sphere and may consist, in the case of an organization, of a single individual (the owner of a small firm) or of a small group of people (the managers of a large firm). In the case of an economic system, the control sphere may consist of a single body (for example, the secretariat or the political office of the sole party in power), or it may be a collegial body (a government, for example). In a less extreme case, the centre may be a set comprising different bodies with different competences (for example the party in power, the government and the central bank). In the cases of both organizations and economic systems the decisions taken by the central authority (the control sphere) must be implemented by lower-level units, which together constitute the real sphere. The relationships between the centre and the subordinate units are wholly vertical in character.

An organization and an economic system are perfectly decentralized if decision-making authority lies entirely with its individual components, be these the organizations of an economic system or the individual productive units or people of an organization. There is no higher-level central unit and the control sphere is virtual in the sense that it consists of a myriad of mini-control spheres scattered among all the units engaged in economic activity. The decision process is perfectly horizontal and both the organization and the economic system are unstructured. The best example of a perfectly decentralized economic system is a perfectly competitive economy constituted by individual producers and with no complex organizations.

In the real world, organizations and economic systems display characteristics that are intermediate between these two ideal types. In all real cases there is both a centre which takes general decisions and peripheral units, at least partially independent, which take specific decisions. Pure centralization would be impossible for various reasons. For example, in the case of the economic system management of a modern economy requires macroeconomic decisions, while no central body can effectively influence individual agents in taking specific decisions. Moreover, individual economic agents – to which production must be delegated for technical reasons – would eventually achieve substantial autonomy in any case by various means, such as bargaining and the irregular economy. Pure decentralization, in its turn, would be impossible because it would presuppose the permanence, over time and under any circumstance, of relationships of absolute parity among economic agents and a capacity to coordinate economic activity and to control free riders entirely by means of a perfectly competitive market. As we know, the former condition cannot come about because of the widespread presence of increasing returns and of natural monopolies in non-contestable markets, and because of the other economic (of a financial nature, for example) and extraeconomic motivations which generate monopolies and coalitions among agents. The latter condition instead cannot come about because of the presence of public goods and externalities and because of the importance in the economy of forms of coordination other than the market.[5]

3   INFORMATION AND INCENTIVES

This distinction between levels in organizations and economic systems affects the flow of information according to whether it takes place between the managerial staff and the rank-and-file, or between members at the same level. More specifically, the information signals exchanged by lower-level members are almost entirely routine in nature and are aimed not at the development of new strategies (either individual or collective) but at the operational coordination of the production process. They are repetitive signals of a nature known to their recipient agents and which consequently do not raise problems of transmission. They are therefore able to meet most of the exigencies typical of large organizations (the rapid execution of pre-established actions, the implementation of models of complex coordination), thereby freeing the agents from the need to understand rationally the details of the entire production process. Very dissimilar, though, are the information signals exchanged by the members of the managerial staff, since these are strategic in purpose and are designed to enable the development of new decisions and routines. Here the problems of transmission may be very complex, and the signal-elaborating capacity required of agents may be very high. The most common organizational solution to this problem is the creation of a restricted managerial staff, i.e. the creation of an elite of specialized agents.

In the real world, such a rigid division of roles within organizations is very rare and usually occurs outside the economy: it is to be found, for example, in the army, especially in peacetime. It presupposes an unchanged environment external to the organization, which cannot be the case of an economy in which the market has some role to perform, even if it is only in foreign (international) relationships. In these circumstances, perfect and detailed specification and implementation of the terms of the contract between the two levels is impossible, because, amongst other things, it would lead to the rapid demise of the organization, which would be too inflexible to adapt efficiently to changes in the environment.

The perfect centralization of organizations, as well as of the economic system, is the central principle of *dirigisme*[6] enacted through centralized planning, which is the material form assumed by this type of contract.

Consequently an economic system of this kind must eliminate all horizontal relationships within and among organizations. All the managerial functions are concentrated into a centralized control sphere. For the system to work, the environment must be controlled and organizations must be insulated against the non-controllable world. The economy must be autarkic, and technical progress, too, must be planned and centrally implemented.

This kind of world is difficult to create: every attempt to approach it entails strains, loss of effectiveness by organizations and above all their inefficiency. The same obviously applies to the economic system. A world such as this becomes perfectly predictable, but this predictability, although highly advantageous, entirely eliminates endogenous stimuli to innovation and change. The discovery of new solutions to problems as and when they arise is entirely delegated to the centralized control sphere, which however lacks the necessary dataile knowledge. In this situation, moreover, change is exclusively a public good and this converts the real sphere into a potential or actual free rider, thereby rendering change slower and more difficult, or indeed impossible. It is worth dwelling for a moment on dynamic efficiency, returning to the various aspects of static efficiency below.

Innovation is a crucial variable in dynamic efficiency,[7] but perfect centralization, as we have seen, hampers innovation and institutional change. However, also the perfect atomistic decentralization of the neoclassicals creates an environment unfavourable to innovation, because agents have a short time-horizon, because the necessary resources may be lacking (although they are available to complex organizations), and because the instability and unpredictability of relationships among agents means that those who invest in innovation cannot be guaranteed an adequate return on their investment after an acceptable lapse of time. By contrast, it is only the existence of an environment which is sufficiently stable and predictable, but open to change, of prolonged inter-organization relationships based on competition but also on cooperation, of intra-organization relationships based on a non-unilateral division of roles defined by a contract (or a series of contracts), that can create an environment favourable to innovation.

An economic system should therefore be viewed as a network of social relationships among economic agents[8] – the most important of which are organizations – which is more successful (from the point of view of innovation, for example) the more these relationships are stable and spur agents into action (innovation), and the more roles are diversified (see Hodgson, 1988). This gives flexibility to the system, which is able to react promptly and successfully to external and internal changes. At a lower level, this also applies to the relationships and roles internal to organizations.

The foregoing discussion points to two crucial variables in relationships between the two spheres, both in organizations and economic systems: motivations and incentives. The former pertain essentially to the control sphere, in that they presuppose decision-making autonomy. However, it also follows from what has been said that organizations and economic systems are more successful, the more the units that make up the real sphere, for all their autonomy, have motivations which are coincident or compatible with those that guide the decisions taken by the control sphere. This compatibility can be ensured by incentives, which are the variables used by authority to induce those subordinate to it to undertake actions which will achieve a certain outcome (Olson, 1965; Pryor, 1973). They take concrete form in rewards for the achievement of the goal, in punishments for failure, and in coercion.

When the real sphere has no freedom to take the initiative, as in perfectly centralized systems and organizations, incentives become orders – that is, brief messages which indicate to the real sphere which tasks it must perform and how. Although the reverse flow of information – i.e. from the operational body to the managerial body – still predominantly consists of brief messages (types and quality of inputs used, level of production achieved, etc.), it must also serve the purposes of strategic coordination and therefore be as detailed as possible. As we shall see, the difficulty, if not the impossibility, of governing local information encountered by those who elaborate routines[9] – that is, those responsible for allocating the factors – is a problem typical of both planned economic systems and large firms.

As already mentioned, the structure of the economic system and of the organizations which belong to it is closely influenced by the nature of the information exchange process. In centralized economic systems, as in strongly verticalized organizations, one of the most effective reinforcements to the exercise of authority by the centre is the exclusive possession of information about economic macro-events. The decision centre may in fact base the authority of its orders on the fact that peripheral agents, whether these are members of an organization or the production units of an economy, do not possess aggregate-level information and therefore cannot develop coordinated strategies. A classic example of this use of information control as an instrument to govern an organization, and at the same time an entire economy, is provided by the Soviet economic system. In an economic system of that kind individual production units are unable to make correct assessment of their productive capacity in relation to demand and to the productive capacities of other similar production units. The unavailability of this information, in fact, precludes the possibility of rational management by an individual economic agent. In this regard, note that information asymmetries of the type just described may be generated in non-planned economies as well, because control over information about macro-events becomes an instrument of power wielded by an extremely small number of agents or even by a single organization.

Exclusive control over knowledge about the macroeconomic results deriving from the individual behaviours of agents therefore provides crucial backing for the exercise of economic authority in both a market and a *dirigist* system. This strategic advantage, however, is accompanied by a cost in terms of loss of efficiency in the system; a cost which, in this case too, links closely with the nature of the information circuit. It is, in fact, relatively easy for a central authority to exercise control over information as far as aggregate results are concerned, but it is practically impossible as regards micro-events, or knowledge about decisions taken by individual agents. This impossibility is due to the enormous amount of cognitive-computational resources required of anyone who wishes to assess the consequences of changes made to the behaviour of the individual agents which make up a complex organization or indeed an entire economy. The loss in terms of efficiency by the economic system or organization, however, is not due solely to the impossibility of assessing the consequences on output of actions by those who allocate the factors; it also stems from the impossibility of imposing by fiat an adequate system of incentives for the efficient use of these factors.

Even if we grant that it is possible to govern rationally all the local information relevant to the efficient operation of a large organization or an economic system, there still remains the problem of fixing a factor exchange ratio which can be realized, though only theoretically, through linear planning. This is a problem which necessarily entails knowledge of the objective-functions of each individual possessor of factors. Only by knowing individual objective-functions, in fact, is it possible for the central planner to fix, in abstract, an efficient system of rewards and punishments for each possessor of the factors (down to the individual worker) able to promote their efficient use. This, however, is an operation which is simply impossible, unless free bargaining is allowed among the agents possessing the production factors, thereby contradicting the principle of centralized decision-making. It is a process, in fact, which takes place in a decentralized way and thus undermines the centralization of the economy. This outcome may be achieved by defining the objective-function of the centre and imposing it in disaggregate manner on each peripheral agent.

The operation can only be successful if the sole objective-function of the peripheral agents of the real sphere is the fulfilment of orders received. For this system to work, it must be materially impossible for the peripheral agents to evade or avoid the system imposed by the control sphere (for example, by terror in a police state); or else incentives must be more attractive than alternative sources of remuneration (from the underground economy).

Whatever the case may be, this is a situation of scant efficiency because it imposes major transaction costs and because it eliminates the Hayekian role of discovery fulfilled by economic coordination, without it being replaced by the improbable omniscience of the control sphere. Alternatively the centre may take on the suitably weighted objective-functions of organizations, thereby (as in Japanese planning) acting as the clearing house for relationships among organizations and encouraging the dissemination of macroeconomic information.

Of course, in the case of the free exchange of the factors the problem arises of the broadcasting of information on the macro-results of such exchange, which, as we have seen, is not necessary in the perfectly centralized system because its place is taken by orders and by the exercise of authority over peripheral units. The problem is solved, of course, by the competitive market, which, following Hayek, is the information medium appointed to ensure the diffusion of information on the economic results generated by comparison among the individual preferences of agents. This function is performed by the price system, a device which serves as a 'concentrator' of local information (see Egidi, 1992). However, it is an imperfect mechanism hampered by asymmetries of various kinds (information and bargaining power asymmetries especially), by the nature of goods (public goods and merit goods) and of production processes and markets (externalities and increasing returns), by the limited nature of the time-horizon, which leads to underestimation of the discounting of the results actualized in processes which affect the future, and of the social opportunity set of individuals and organizations, which restricts their capacity and reduces competition.

Moreover, if the exchange process is extended to include all the agents in the economic system, this may trigger an explosion of transaction costs; a phenomenon, at least according to Coase's celebrated thesis, which is principally responsible for the birth of firms. The restoration of centralized decision-making within the market is therefore mediated by the creation of firms and it is motivated by same efficiency considerations – although now defined as a reduction in transaction costs – that caused the broader-context failure of the centralized economic system.

Evidently, the nature of the information diffusion system is closely connected with the problem of incentives for the efficient use of the factors, which in its turn is connected with assessment of the individual preferences of agents or with the ability of the control sphere to align them with its objective-function. Real economies therefore comprise a complex interweaving of decentralized informational and structural processes (as in the case of industrial districts, networks of firms and cooperatives) – sometimes the outcome of occasional and unconstrained relationships between individuals and organizations, but sometimes deriving from structured and permanent ones – on the one hand, and the existence of organizations and centralized processes on the other (as in the case of large organizations and monetary variables). The forms in which information is broadcast are not restricted to the price mechanism alone; they are instead managed by a set of central and peripheral bodies which are both public (like the state) and private in nature. The distribution of role and competences in the information sphere between public and private agents, the effective degree to which the allocation of the factors is decentralized, the quality and efficacy of inventive systems, the diffusion of different models of firms' organization: these are the principal factors differentiating among what may appear to be very similar economic systems.

4   CENTRALIZATION AND DECENTRALIZATION VERSUS STATE AND MARKET

The topic of centralization and decentralization has traditionally coincided to a large extent with analysis of the relationship between centralized macroeconomic planning and the market, and with study of the formation of the institutions. However, apart from this line of inquiry, there are a number of other important approaches to the effects of differing degrees of decision distribution in the economy. The function of the state as an institution and its relationships with the economic system and with firms, in fact, is only one aspect of the problem of decentralization. Another crucial issue is the organizational form of the state itself; by which is meant the degree of decentralization of the levels of government and the type of hierarchical relationship established among them. Given the importance of the public sector in determining gross domestic product in Western countries, it is evident that decisions concerning the extent to which the state is to be decentralized have enormous economic importance. And there still remains the issue, already mentioned in previous sections, of the centralization of decision processes in firms. Examination of the various aspects of economic decentralization must begin with the first of the topics just mentioned.

The relationship between plan and market has been a theme central to comparative examination of economic systems, and much has been written about their incompatibility or possible coexistence. This debate – namely the debate on economic calculation in socialism – was conducted mainly in the 1920s and '30s.[10] The Austrian school (in particular von Mises and Hayek) stressed in different ways that the centralized planning of the economy was suboptimal and irrational. According to the traditional interpetation of von Mises' theory, socialism is theoretically impossible. In fact, rational economic calculation can only come about if prices reflect relative shortages, but these types of prices did not exist under socialism, because in the investment goods market both demand and supply derived from the state, which arbitrarily fixed prices and thereby prevented the economically rational (efficient) allocation of resources (von Mises, 1920, 1922).

The proponents of planning and socialism responded to these charges by stressing the ability of planning (implicitly centralized, but in a sense different from that employed by the Austrians) to imitate the working of a market with free competition. It was principally Lange[11] who showed that under socialism it was possible to imitate the functioning of the market in the allocation of resources. The central planner was able to determine equilibrium prices by means of a 'trial and error' process in which the market is reduced to a mere instrument of calculation, similar to a computer, in order to solve a system of simultaneous equations. It is instead the central plan office which fixes prices, including wages and interest rates, adjusting them in order to equalize the demand and supply of each good, thus performing a role similar to that of Walras' auctioneer. The plan office, moreover, dictates rules of behaviour to the economic agents – specifically to the directors of the socialist enterprises. These rules minimize the average cost of production by utilizing that combination of production factors which permits the equalization, for every factor, of the value of its marginal product with its price. Furthermore, economic agents must set the quantity produced of each good to the level at which the marginal cost of the product equals the price fixed by the plan office.

Although he accepted the theoretical feasibility of socialism, Hayek[12] denied that it was viable in practice, because it was a system based on centralized planning. This renders the management of information inefficient. A centralized system, in fact, is unable to gather and to collate – even less to replace – knowledge and information scattered among an extremely large number of individuals (and organizations). This system, moreover, eliminates the incentives which induce the individuals (and organizations) in a decentralized system to search for new opportunities, thereby reducing the social opportunity set available to the economy. Finally, Hayek argued that the rational use of resources was in practice impossible under socialism because the central planners had to gather and process an enormous quantity of information, which no office would be able to handle.

According to Lange, by contrast, the market mechanism, with its complicated bargaining processes (and therefore high transaction costs), can be considered a calculation instrument belonging to the pre-electronic era.

The use of computers gives the central plan office a crucial advantage over the market as far as information is concerned, enabling it to accelerate information processing enormously and to streamline the decision process (Lange, 1967). A further contribution to solving the problem of economic calculation, and therefore of the allocation of resources, in centralized socialism was made in the 1960s by the Soviet school of linear planning (see for example Kantorovich, 1965; Novozhilov, 1969). This technique was applied not only to the problem of combining the resources available in a production unit in order to maximize production, but also to the problem of optimal macroeconomic planning in a socialist economy. According to the linear planning school, if economic planning was to be successful, it had to employ a system of prices – so-called 'shadow prices' – derived from the solution to the problems of linear planning and comprising a social discount rate similar to an interest rate.

The merit of Hayek's position compared with that of von Mises was that it shifted the focus to a very different set of questions: the institutional structures of a socialist economy, systems of information and control, motivations and incentives to economic activity (Dobb, 1969); problems left largely unresolved by centralized planning. As Hayek stressed (see Hayek 1935b), the practical feasibility of socialism was not a purely technical issue; it was a genuine political–economic problem tied to the nature itself of the motivations of individuals and organizations. These are often reluctant to cooperate with the central plan office and they transmit false or erroneous information in order to avoid risks and to defend their autonomy and their pursuit of specific interests. Centralized planning, in fact, eliminates rivalry among economic agents – rivalry, that is, as a dialectical and dynamic form of competition distinct from the static notion of the neoclassical economists (Lavoie, 1985). This has negative consequences on both the transmission of information and on the efficiency of production because it eliminates the decentralized processes of new opportunity discovery typical of the market. And it creates coalitions among economic agents which not only oppose the central government but also and especially damage collective welfare by protecting their specific interests. Centralized planning is intrinsically incompatible with the competitive market: they are alternative coordination devices and any attempt to combine them provokes breakdown in each of them.

Moreover, a centralized system lacks an efficient system for the resolution of conflicts of interest at the centre (government), and between the centre and individual agents, and it also lacks incentives to economic activity (Sik, 1967). The absence of risk to agents because of the institutional solutions adopted may enable them to obtain additional advantages in ways not envisaged by the plan (for example by bargaining with the ministry concerned or through the activity of pressure groups). The flow of information from enterprises to the central planners is thus distorted or incomplete.

Hayek's view of the relationship between centralization and decentralization is very persuasive, especially when one considers the case of a developed economy in which major changes are incremental and therefore continuous in nature. Hayek's interpretation does not envisage other forms of planning, given that – as he stressed (1945) – all economic agents draw up plans, and what distinguishes among different systems is the level at which planning takes place. Equally decisive, one might add, are the relationships established among the various levels of planning. In reality, other types of macroeconomic non-centralized planning (regulative or indicative) may be useful in that they do not conflict with, but are indeed complementary to, the decentralized planning of economic agents. They may in fact help to coordinate the activities of the latter and may stimulate cooperation between them and the central government, thus decreasing transaction costs and opening up new opportunities.

Also still unresolved in economic theory is the problem of the role of centralization in the case of underdeveloped economies operating in a world market dominated by more developed economies; and also in the case of economic changes which are discrete and rapid, as for example in the countries in transition of Central-Eastern Europe.

A further problem of planning was indirectly highlighted by Schumpeter (1942) when he stressed the importance of entrepreneurship and predicted the fall of capitalism and the rise of socialism – defined as a centrally-directed society (Vercelli, 1989) – because of the reduction of innovation to routine; a process which entails the progressive disappearance of the entrepreneur. Following Schumpeter, the role of the entrepreneur is to seek non-routine solutions in an environment of high structural instability. The entrepreneur is an inventor not only of strictly technical solutions but also, and especially, of organizational ones. Given that centralized planning tends by its nature towards equilibrium, it follows that for the state-planner the role of the entrepreneur is no longer necessary and may even be counter-productive. However, the elimination of the instability provoked by market competition also eliminates the decentralized motivation to innovate, thereby removing an important incentive for individual economic agents to search for more efficient productive solutions. The process itself of innovation becomes centralized and reduced to a routine, so that its very essence is denied and its crucial role in economic development is thwarted or erased.

A second definition of the role of the entrepreneur shifts the focus from innovation to that of information gathering and processing. Coase's (1937) entrepreneur is the agent appointed to perform two principal functions. First, within the firm s/he must perform the role of resource management that the price system fulfils in the market. Second, s/he must seek out the best prices by processing information external to the firm. Evidently, if we accept this definition, the entrepreneur is redundant in planned economies because macroeconomic information is perfectly known to the state-planner and the tasks of coordinating the resources internal to the enterprise can be delegated to a manager. In this case too, the immediate consequence is the disappearance of the entrepreneur; but it also means that the enterprise is unable to process micro–macro information autonomously, and this has predictably damaging effects on the efficient use of local information.

Whichever of these two definitions is chosen, there still remains the problem of the institutional specificity of the entrepreneur's role: that is, his/her twofold nature as coordinator of the production process and as owner (sole or partial) of the results achieved by the firm in terms of profits or losses. The apparent non-substitutability of the entrepreneur by a manager (who only owns his or her labour) stems from the difficulty of creating a valid system of incentives for this role; a system, that is, which is at least as efficient as that implicit in the recognition of property rights over profits and losses. We shall return to the efficacy of the decentralization of property rights over the outcomes of production choices – as the engine which drives the search for efficiency within firms – in the next section, drawing on Milgrom and Roberts (1992).

While stressing the crucial role of the entrepreneur in economic development, and therefore the negative role of centralized planning in this respect, it is also necessary to point out that not every entrepreneurial activity is desirable and positive for effectively utilizable production and for economic well-being (see Baumol, 1993). If it is true that the ratio between useful and useless entrepreneurial activities depends on the institutional structure of the economy, macroeconomic planning may play a positive role in curbing useless entrepreneurial activities and promoting useful ones. Planning may in fact prove extremely useful in publicizing macroeconomic information, in reducing uncertainty, in extending the time-horizons of economic agents, and in reducing rent-seeking and opportunistic behaviour.

In truth, a number of authors[13] have stressed that even greater dangers may derive from the fact that planning often leads to the formation of a group of specialists and bureaucrats which may grow extremely powerful and whose democratic control may prove difficult. Should this situation arise, this group may impose its allocation, production and consumption preferences on the rest of society. However, the possibility of this happening does not depend on planning *per se* but on prevailing social relationships. If the institutions and the circumstances are favourable, planning is an instrument which may enhance freedom and democracy by rendering choices transparent and social preferences explicit.

The final outcome therefore depends less on the technical characteristics of planning than on the institutional (and political) framework in which the planning takes place. Moreover, the force of the criticisms set out above varies according to the type of planning considered. They are lethal when directed at centralized planning because it eliminates the market and replaces it with the administrative management of the economy. But in cases where planning does not replace the market, but is instead utilized to resolve problems that the market is unable to handle efficiently or equably, these criticisms lose their impact. Furthermore, examples of the failures of planning can be matched by others in which planning has achieved considerable success.[14]

We may therefore conclude that, in various circumstances, cooperation between plan and market is not only possible but indeed desirable,[15] even if their mix cannot be freely exchanged.[16] The true problem, therefore, is not that of determining whether the market is better than the plan or vice versa, but which combination of the two is more efficient in particular circumstances and what specific features this combination should possess.[17]

5   CENTRALIZATION AND DECENTRALIZATION OF THE FIRM AND OF THE STATE

In the previous section we examined the problem of the appropriate combination of central planning and the market, weighing their roles according to the dichotomy between the centralization – in its extreme form of centralized planning – and decentralization – in its extreme form of perfect competition – of economic decisions. However, both the market and the state may assume highly decentralized forms, or alternatively they may take on the characteristics of absolute centralization. Some of the functions proper to the liberal state – for example the supply of money or national defence, but often also taxation or at least some of its essential components – are performed according to a model which resembles that of centralized planning. Other functions, and here the most interesting case is provided by the British quasi-markets, are carried out by applying supply models which imitate those of market competition. In parallel, the vast range of types of imperfect competition – which often take the form of highly restricted oligopoly or even monopoly – demonstrate the existence of markets with a pronounced vertical integration of decision-making.

The birth of the institutions, their relationship with the market and the state, and the extent of their political and administrative decentralization, have provided the subject matter for two debates which have been traditionally kept separate but nonetheless overlap. Beginning with the first and following Menger (see Wagener, 1993b), we may distinguish between two approaches: one pragmatic–constructivist, the other organic–evolutionist. The former is based on the Enlightenment idea that the institutions can be shaped by the will and intervention of man. Thus institutional engineering by specialized organizations is both conceivable and feasible; and especially by those specialized organizations headed by the state, of which centralized planning is certainly the most complete and extreme, but not the only, accomplishment. This approach has recently come back into fashion as transition in Central-Eastern Europe proceeds, and it has been propounded by those – generally of *laissez-faire* leanings (however contradictory this may appear) – who propose and seek to actuate the 'building' of a market economy in the place of the previously centrally planned economy.

The second approach is based on the conviction that the institutions can only be the result of the action, usually unwitting, of all the individuals and organizations in a society, who seek by trial and error to find the most satisfactory (optimal? best?) solutions to problems as and when they arise. The institutions thus come about slowly, with imperceptible modifications, and spontaneously. Only those that withstand the test of everyday facts manage to reach maturity, because they are able to solve problems and because they correspond to the preferences of individuals and organizations.

This distinction between the different ways in which the institutions originate, and thus between the ways in which organizations are generated by them, is of great heuristic value in explanation of the complex interweaving between centralization and decentralization in different economic systems. However, before we can draw up a systematic picture of these problems, it is necessary to outline the principal features of the second debate, which has centred on the reasons for the distinction between the two fundamental economic institutions: the state and the firm.

An important feature shared by firm and state[18] is that they are both non-market institutions, since internally to them the exchange of goods and services among their members does not involve bargaining; or if it does, this bargaining is informal, and above all it is not mediated by the price system. The coordination of the decisions taken by different individuals on the basis of scattered knowledge and differing skills takes place directly through the issue of orders and control over their execution. Since there is also a division of labour and a hierarchical structure within the two institutions, internal cooperation and authority relationships forcefully simplify the behaviour of the agents belonging to them. This reduction in the space allotted to individual behaviour by the members of the firm and/or citizens of the state (Ullman and Margalit, 1977) can be viewed as a function which simplifies the complexity of decision processes in a manner similar to that achieved spontaneously via the market. If we accept, as we did at the outset, that the market price system is a device which diffuses and synthesises local information and which imposes economically more efficient behaviour on individuals and organizations, then, in the absence of a price system, this simplification may come about by a reduction in the range of behaviours permitted to agents when their relationships are stable over time. It is in fact the variety of strategies available to each agent and the relationships that this agent may establish with others which principally determines the degree of complexity of the islands of local information. More specifically, if just one behaviour and just one relationship existed, it would make no sense to speak of local information (Heiner, 1983). Thus the chief problem of economic agents is closing the gap between the complexity of their various choice problems – complexity considered to be exogenous and therefore as included in the 'environment' – and their decision-making capacity. It is the size of this gap that determines the degree of behavioural rigidity. By assigning the task of producing norms for economic interaction to a social pact (the state) or to a private contract (the firm), agents can reduce the distance between the complexity of the decision environment and their abilities to choose; thereby ensuring greater flexibility in the use of strategies which are effectively utilizable because their outcomes are more predictable.

In every economic system, the firm consists of a network of social relationships based on explicit or implicit contracts among those who possess property rights over different goods (the production factors). The aim of the firm is to coordinate the activity of its components so that it can obtain a certain quantity of goods and services to place on the market or, in the case of planned systems, to consign to the state, which decides their use and distributes them in order to obtain remuneration on their constituent factors. In a pure market economy, production takes place autonomously and for the firm's own purposes: in this case, it is the firm itself (or better the individual or group controlling it) which decides how and how much to produce, and at what price to sell its output on the market, or whether to accept the current market price. However, the coordination impersonally implemented by the market imposes efficient allocative and productive behaviour on enterprises in the short run, and it determines which adaptive strategies will be successful in the long run.

In a *dirigiste* economy, by contrast, property rights over the firm (or more precisely over output) and over the factors are not distributed among agents, and the firm does not autonomously decide its production but fulfils targets fixed externally to it, usually by the state. In this case it is the state which decides the allocation of resources, what, how much and how the firm must produce and to whom or to what organization the firm must consign the goods and services that it has produced, and at what price. The firm's goal in this case is to execute the orders issued by the state, obtaining in return incomes for its workers, including productivity bonuses, and the resources necessary for future production.

Finally, neither the planned firm nor the public agency producing services for individual consumers in a tariff regime (i.e. not at market prices) is subject to consumer scrutiny. In the case of centrally planned economies consumers have no viable alternative choice and therefore cannot express appreciation or criticism of the good supplied through their consumption decisions. In market economies, public services are normally supplied at prices lower than market ones, and therefore under conditions which tend to distort consumption behaviour and hence also assessments of the service. In both cases, this annulment of the consumer assessment mechanism and the lack of effective alternatives also eliminates an important incentive to quality improvement; an incentive which cannot be replaced by production targets set by the centre, because these can only be made efficient if individual evaluations of the product are known.

The different aims of firms in market and planned economic systems, and especially the differing extents to which they are allowed autonomous control over production, are widely cited in explanation of the greater efficiency of the market model. More specifically, the non-definition of property rights and the consequent elimination of both 'residual returns' (Alchian and Demsetz, 1972) and 'residual control' (Grossman and Hart, 1986) account for the inability of a planned or even public firm to compete with a private one (Milgrom and Roberts, 1992).

Residual returns are the result of incomplete definition of the contract that binds the agents which participate in the firm, or better of the impossibility of defining such a contract. This incompleteness is more marked, the greater the internal variety of the firm and the greater the variety or variability of its environment. Note that residual returns cannot be governed by a contract because they are not definable a priori by the parties owing to the inadequacy of the cognitive resources available. The enormous number of possible exchange plans which would have to be discussed by the members of a firm in order perfectly to cover all possible contingencies – deriving from production arrangements and from market results – make rational implementation of such a contract impossible. This entails the existence of an entirely specific type of incentive to the efficient use of resources which arises from the profit space left free by the imperfect contractual rationalization of the relationships among the members of the organization–firm. In other words, the failure of the market regime within the enterprise, due to the bounded rationality which governs contractual relations among agents, provides the best impulse to efficiency, the pursuit of which is left to those who possess property rights over the residual returns.

Equally important is residual control over production choices. This equips the entrepreneur–owner with the maximum possible flexibility of response to the evolution of the market, given the technological constraint. As in the case of residual returns, it is the poor definition of the terms of the contract which creates a space – this time for manoeuvre in decisions concerning the use of resources – which is entirely to the advantage of efficiency. The non-attribution of the right to exert residual control – or more precisely the non-perfect coincidence between possession of this right and property rights over residual returns in firms run by managers – reduces the flexibility of production decisions, which must adhere rigidly to the array of behaviours allowed by the contract. Unlike the entrepreneur–owner, the manager has decision-making autonomy which is constrained by the ownership, or by the state in the case of the centrally planned or public firm. The entrepreneur–owner is instead free to exploit any room for manoeuvre made available by the imprecise definition of the contract stipulated with other agents (who may also be shareholders in the firm, i.e. owners themselves), and the coincidence of this right with ownership of residual profits ensures that it will be used to achieve greater efficiency. This does not happen in the centrally planned or publicly-owned firm, either because the manager is not authorized to use this residual power of choice or because s/he will use it for his/her own purposes and not to enhance efficiency.

It is quite obvious that the importance of both residual control and residual returns must not be over-evaluated. In particular, it is important to stress that efficiency is not mechanically related to these factors, in the way that an increase in the discretionary space of the entrepreneur must become *ipso facto* an increase in efficiency. On the contrary, too much latitude in the contractual definition of the entrepreneur's decision-making sphere and of his/her property rights may reduce efficiency, due to the fact that the agents involved in the production process will perceive the poor contractual arrangement not as a consequence of their cognitive limitations, but as an unfair imposition. In this situation the incentive mechanism for the entrepreneur conflicts with the general incentive system of the organization as a whole.

It should be stressed that the limitations of centrally planned or public firms are also to be found in large private firms, since these are also afflicted by problems of motivation among the managerial staff, and more in general among the entire workforce, which are entirely similar to those of public firms. The boom in studies, both theoretical economic and business in orientation, on incentivating contracts is evidence of this problem.

One of the reasons for this need to improve incentive systems within firms is a phenomenon which explains the existence itself of firms in market economies: the endeavour to create stability over time by attenuating the effects of uncertainty by means of an institutional framework. The firm, in fact, can be viewed as a social institution which, with respect to market relationships, reduces the role of rational economic calculation internally to it, and instead generates agreements and rules resting on a more permanent basis comprising loyalty relationships, professional ethics, routines and cooperation.[19]

The firm may enhance its stability in various ways. It may increase the variety and diversification of its internal structure, both by creating an internal hierarchy with a further division of responsibilities, and by diversifying production. The firm may also expand its area of control by increasing its size, thereby directly strengthening its control over the market. Or it may stipulate enduring agreements and create closer cooperation with other firms. Or it may resort to takeovers and mergers.[20] Finally, the firm may seek to alter the relationships between individuals and itself, both by increasing the flexibility and specialization of its workforce (by providing incentives for training and reskilling) and by encouraging workforce commitment to the life and results of the firm.

The stability of the firm's institutional structure may also create a suitable internal environment for the wide range of specializations and technologies on which its productive capacity is based. The transmission of skills and therefore production is constantly threatened by the corrosive effect of competition and exchanges on the habits and routines that transmit these skills, and on cooperation. Thanks to their stable institutional framework, the existence of firms instead protects and expands these routines. All firms promote trust and loyalty among their members and stimulate internal cooperation, but those that do so more vigorously are precisely those that are more likely to be efficient.[21]

Under the pressure of market competition, the stability of the firm's structure is indispensable for the actuation of innovations and the development of entrepreneurship. The firm in fact provides a sheltered environment in which research and development, especially if they require a long-term perspective and a large quantity of resources, can take place. The firm is therefore able to handle and to compensate for its lack of knowledge concerning the future results of research and innovation, and it thus constitutes the institutional basis for technical progress. These processes could not be promoted and sustained by the market, except in the very early stages of technological development. When high levels of technological specialization in production processes have been achieved, the search for innovation requires proportionally increasing investments which market competition may preclude.

The case of a *dirigiste* economy is different. In this case stability can only be ensured by the state, which may resort to centralized planning. This strategy annuls the autonomy of the firm, which becomes the executor of decisions taken elsewhere (by the state), and it eliminates the market, thereby removing endogenous stimuli to technical progress.

Although formally similar to a market firm, by virtue of its structural resemblance and insofar as it comprises the same functions and skills, the firm of the *dirigiste* system differs profoundly from the former because it is an incomplete institutional structure incorporated into a larger one, namely the state. In a *dirigiste* economy, the firm necessarily becomes highly specialized and often monopolistic: production standardization is taken to its extreme, competition is abolished, technical progress is imposed from above, entrepreneurship is absent, and rational calculation is abolished. All these functions are concentrated into the state, while the firm becomes a place in which only routines and hierarchical and cooperative relationships survive. The firm becomes a mere component of the state – one not developed from below but defined from above – and it is an organizational form which the state creates to carry out specific productive tasks.[22]

Firms consequently exist because technically production can only be organized in this way. Technically, in fact, the inputs to production must be concentrated on one site, in a single installation, because people and goods must be in physical proximity if production is to take place. And this is a further fundamental difference between firms in *dirigiste* economies and market economies: in *dirigisme* the base unit is not the firm proper, but the factory. The firm is simply the sum of one or more factories which have been aggregated for bookkeeping purposes or to exert control, but which could perfectly well be free-standing entities. The firm as an aggregate of installations is therefore simply an intermediate structure between the base unit, the factory, and the government of the economy.

The other institution crucial for economic activity is, as we have seen, the state. The state can be defined as the institution which encompasses and performs legislative, executive, judicial and administrative functions – i.e. those that produce pure public goods. It is the sole entity empowered to create and cancel general norms and rules on property rights which apply to all the citizens and organizations. It is therefore the only institution which is potentially universal in character, since it may extend its jurisdiction to the whole of the economic sphere as well as to all the other sectors of social life. The government is the entity which materially exercises such power and therefore incorporates both a country's formal government and other forms of substantive power such as those exercised by the political party or parties in power.[23]

The distance that separates the state from the firm can only be measured by examining the various administrative–political arrangements that modern societies have created. It seems rather reductive to assert that the fundamental, if not the sole, difference between state and firm is that participation in the former is obligatory while membership of the latter is voluntary. This distinction holds only as long as we restrict ourselves to a high abstract concept of the state, while examination of the concrete forms assumed by this institution counsels caution. Consider, for instance, the diverse degrees of decentralization exhibited by public administrations, or the wide range of goods and services produced by the public sector in most of the Western European countries. It is evident that the amount of coercive pressure applied to an agent is closely tied to its concrete possibility of 'exit' from the normative system, and on its effective capacity to influence the nature and structure of the rules. A good degree of decentralization of the state *qua* institution guarantees the possibility of exit from one system of rules (for example those applied by a given local administration) and entry to another one which more closely matches individual preferences (Tiebout's famous model of 'voting with the feet'). And at the same time it enables greater participation in effective decision-making.

Dwelling for a moment on this latter point – i.e. the institutional form of the state – and referring to the two models analysed here (free market system and centrally planned system), one may first point out that the Western nations have been modelled on a version of the concept of democracy which has abandoned Aristotle's original definition of 'government by the poor' (see Bobbio and Matteucci, 1976) and has come to coincide with Rousseau's idea of the social contract. That is, it matches the republican form of the state, the choice of which form in market economies – most commonly as a representative regime with the separation of legislative and executive power – is antithetical to the institutional structure of the state in Soviet-type systems. At the same time it marks the extent of the differences between firms in their respective economic systems. As we have just seen, in fact, the firm in centrally planned economies is an institution which displays features very similar to those of the state, while in market economies the difference is more marked.

Second, the communist model – at least in its theoretical definition that emerged from the debate which began in the 1920s with Rosa Luxemburg and

Antonio Gramsci (amongst others) and concluded in 1940 with Anton Pannekoek – envisaged the firm, or better the factory, as a site of political decision-making, indeed as *the* site of political choice. Factory councils were therefore to be the institutional instrument by which both the Aristotelian idea of democracy and the decentralization of economic decisions was realized. The state as institution would therefore be embodied also and especially in firm-factories, achieving through them its structural and functional identity. However, and paradoxically, this fusion between the factory-firm and the state instead came about by virtue of the absence of a macroeconomic arena – the competitive market – appointed to test and select among the microeconomic decisions taken by the factory councils. Note finally that the elimination of the market and the assimilation of the two institutions also generated a system of centralized decisions and resources allocation which was entirely at odds with the above-mentioned aim of extending the effective base of political and economic decision-making.

Returning to the apparently greatly degree of heterogeneity of firms *qua* institutions compared with the state in market economies, the organizational structure of the latter has grown increasingly fragmented with time. The liberal state has in fact followed a pattern whereby a strongly centralized democratic arrangement has given way to an increasingly diffuse and close-knit organization of the institutional forms of power. This process began with the universalization of the right to vote and therefore with the broadening of the decision-making base and the propagation of political representation from solely national seats to local ones. This increase in the number of institutional arenas of political decision-making was thereafter typically accompanied by an expansion in the number of collective – non-state – institutions competing for control of political power (political parties, trade unions, sectoral organizations, etc.) which fragmented the structure of the state and opened the door for forms of voluntary, and therefore not coerced, participation in collective decisions. Of course, the degree of autonomy of these subsystems from the institutional structure of the state varies from country to country, and hence the degree of fragmentation in access to collective decision-making may also vary.

6   CONCLUSIONS

The discussion conducted in previous sections has sought to clarify the institutional reasons for the centralization and decentralization of institutions, and the consequences thereof on the economic system. However, it has not addressed a topic of crucial importance: possible degrees of freedom in choosing between centralization and decentralization. After all, the different combinations to be found in the real world suggest that this freedom is considerable. At the same time, each economic system displays relatively similar combinations in its essential components and this suggests that the matter is decided by the type of economic system in force. More careful observation, moreover, reveals the same combinations in different circumstances: monetary functions (under normal circumstances) are everywhere centralized, while industry and agriculture are often decentralized.

These observations imply extremely wide-ranging analysis. Here we can only briefly mention a number of points which are developed elsewhere in this book. First of all, there are the restrictions imposed by the characteristics of goods (in the case of public or merit goods) and of markets (in the case of externalities and of increasing returns). If these restrictions are to be resolved, a certain amount of centralization, though within a broad spectrum, is necessary. These problems can in fact be dealt with by the extreme centralization of the economic institutions and property rights, by resorting to quasi-decentralization, as in the case of quasi-markets, contracting-out and franchising, and by resorting to Pigouvian measures.

Other restrictions derive from the goals pursued by economic systems. The minimum degree of freedom arises in the perfectly competitive market system, in which the economic system can be envisaged as the simple aggregation of the individuals operating within a certain economy coordinated by impersonal and spontaneous factors. In this case, it is not possible to speak of goals pursued by the economic system, only of the goals pursued by individuals, each of whom is unable to exert an appreciable influence on the fundamental variables of the economy, whence necessarily derives perfect decentralization. The case is different when the economic system is more structured and pursues active governance of the economy, in both the short and the long run. Fulfilling this collective preference function presupposes some degree of centralization, although it is one which is not necessarily (and hopefully) extreme.

A further problem of major economic importance, but even greater political and social relevance, is the position taken up by individual people and organizations regarding the choice between centralization and decentralization. For perfect decentralization to give rise to socially desirable results, perfect equality among individuals and among organizations is necessary. But individuals and organizations do not start from equivalent positions, which restricts the social opportunity set available to the majority of them, with major consequences for equity, freedom, justice, and also the social and economic efficiency of the institutional solutions adopted. There therefore exists a substantial problem of asymmetry in initial positions, of knowledge, of the distribution of resources and of preferences. In this situation, perfectly decentralized processes easily lead to the overwhelming of the weak by the strong, with no guarantee that the strong are such because they pursue socially more desirable goals on account of of their superior knowledge or ability. Moreover, initial disparities may not only be self-perpetuating but also self-reinforcing, and lead to monopoly if one advantageous position makes it possible to achieve others. In this manner perfect decentralization assuredly does not lead to the socially better and economically more efficient choices, in that the criterion governing selection of the institutions may be distorted. By reducing social mobility, it may further restrict the social opportunity set for the majority of the populace.

Finally, an interesting and highly topical case is change in the economic system. Perfect decentralization leads to solutions via incremental processes. This outcome may be feasible in an efficient market economy (with suitable institutions), but it is certainly not so in the transition countries, where changes are at least in part discrete and many institutions are lacking. The result of a perfectly decentralized institutional change is the creation of a largely incomplete 'market of institutions'[24] and a decision process in certain respects similar to voting: the new institutions will be accepted when the majority agrees. As demonstrated by Arrow's impossibility theorem, although this ensures that decisions are taken, in contrast to decision processes based on unanimity, there is no majoritarian voting system which guarantees efficiency, which respects individual preferences, and which does not depend on the agenda, i.e. on the way in which the specific actions leading to the development of the institutions are effectively undertaken. Moreover, the majority rule does not only introduce a cyclical trend into the decision process; it may also yield results contrary to the interests of the minority insofar as it does not take the intensity of preferences into account. This may engender redistributive processes to the disadvantage of the minority. A further consequence in legislative assemblies, but also in society at large, is that the intensity of preferences may be expressed through an exchange of favours. Although this may be viewed as similar to the exchange of goods in the private sector, and can therefore bring improvements by moving the economic system closer to the frontier of utility possibilities, it may also give rise to perverse results. In this case, a privileged minority may exchange favours with other interest groups, thereby implementing redistributive processes harmful to other groups and individuals. The privatization of state property in the countries in transition provides numerous examples. These aspects of the dichotomy between centralization and decentralization, as well as others, inevitably point to the conclusion that contrasting the two options fails to yield any solution. In reality, the problem is not the choice between one or the other but deciding under which circumstances one is more efficient than the other, to what extent it is advisable and right to decentralize (or centralize), and how decentralization (or centralization) can be best implemented. Hopefully, this book provides some answers to these questions.

NOTES

1. This introduction results from a study conducted as part of the research project 'Privatization: an economic analysis of motivations and consequences', financed by the Department of Economics of the University of Trento. Although a joint undertaking by the authors, parts 1, 3 and 5 were written by Bruno Dallago and parts 2, 4 and 6 by Luigi Mittone.
2. See Simon (1961), in particular the introduction to the second edition.
3. The concepts of control sphere and real sphere were first introduced by Kornai (1980).
4. See Haitani (1986), although he classifies these two aspects differently.
5. See on this, for instance, Breton's (1989) interesting idea of the competitive state
6. On *dirigisme* see the classic works by Grossman (1963) and Kornai (1959). See also Kornai (1992).
7. There is no definition of dynamic efficiency acceptable to all economists. According to Balassa (1973, p. 21), dynamic efficiency 'may be defined as that hypothetical rate of development of the national income obtained in different economic systems using identical resources and with an identical propensity to save'.
8. On this see in particular Granovetter (1982).
9. The assumption here, of course, is that routines are not solely the outcome of spontaneous coordination among agents but require the exercise of authority by at least one agent appointed to undertake the process – also evolutionary in nature – of experimentation and imitation which produces routines (Nelson and Winter, 1982).
10. On this debate see Bergson (1967), Jossa (1975, 1978), Keizer (1994), Lavoie (1985).
11. See Lange (1936). See also Dickinson (1933, 1939); Taylor (1929).
12. See Hayek (1935a, 1935b, 1945). See also Chapter 3, this volume.
13. See for example Bettelheim (1975), Hayek (1944, 1960), Ricossa (1989).
14. The most notable cases being Scandinavia, France and Japan. See Kovács and Dallago (1990) which examines various national cases of planning.
15. This point has been recently stressed by several authors. See for example Dietz (1989) and Hodgson (1988).
16. During the 1970s, the possibility of a free exchange – though within certain limits – between plan and market was the dominant issue in East European debate on economic reforms. See the classic work by Brus (1961).
17. Different criteria have been used to decide which is the most appropriate combination of

plan and market. According to Kornai (1971), for instance, the most favourable conditions for macroeconomic planning arise when there is industrial concentration, indivisibility in essential factors, increasing returns and long time-horizons, and when decisions are involved which require wide-ranging structural changes. When these conditions are lacking, the market is instead more efficient and advantageous. In like manner, Nove (1983) stresses the existence of 'planability' in cases where output is measurable and homogeneous. Various institutionalist authors, like Hodgson (1988), point out that something more than a simple technical issue is involved. Only a combination of different methods of action and intervention, of different coordination mechanisms, can yield solutions which grant ample space not only to the market but also to non-centralized planning.

18.   On the firm see especially Coase (1937), Eggertsson (1990), Hodgson (1988) and Williamson (1986). In his pioneering work, Coase compared firm and market and argued that both institutions pursue the same objective – of coordinating decisions taken by different individuals – in different ways: the former by means of orders and control, the latter by means of the price mechanism. On the state see Stiglitz et al. (1988). In the discussion that follows we assume the traditional neo-institutionalist standpoint which takes the large firm and the Anglo-Saxon liberal state as its points of reference. Recent developments in the organization of the firm (for example, the production islands introduced in Sweden, the decentralized organization of the Japanese multinationals, or alternative forms of firms' organization like the networks of firms and industrial districts in Italy) or of the state (for example, fiscal federalism) have brought substantial changes to this traditional pattern, although it still predominates.

19.   On these topics see for example Hodgson (1988), Simon (1961), Williamson (1986).

20.   Note that these are only partial measures which, as is well known from studies of monopoly and oligopoly, if successful may insulate the firm against market stimuli and therefore heighten the rigidity of its responses.

21.   This conclusion can also be derived from Axelrod's (1984) argument on the advantage of cooperation when relations among agents are stable or repetitive through time. Of great interest in this regard is the case of Japanese firms. See Dore (1987) and Fodella (1989).

22.   The Soviet-type economy can be represented – with the exception of the consumption sector – as a single large firm internally to which market relationships have been removed. See Wiles (1977), Kornai (1992).

23.   As the neo-institutionalist approach has shown, the distribution of political power and the structure of power organizations are crucial factors in the economic development whenever transaction costs are positive.

24.   On the market of institutions see Chapter 5, in this volume.

REFERENCES

Alchian, A. and H. Demsetz (1972), 'Production, Information Costs, and Economic Organization', *American Economic Review*, 62, pp. 777–97.

Axelrod, R. (1984), *The Evolution of Cooperation*, New York: Basic Books.

Balassa, B. (1973), 'Indici di successo per i sistemi economici', in M. Bornstein (ed.) (1973), pp. 17–36.

Baumol, W.J. (1993), *Entrepreneurship, Management, and the Structure of Payoffs*, Cambridge: The MIT Press.

Bergson, A. (1967), 'Market Socialism Revisited', *Journal of Political Economy*, 5, pp. 655–673.

Bettelheim, C. (1975), *Economic Calculation and Forms of Property: An Essay on the Transition between Capitalism and Socialism*, New York: Monthly Review Press.

Birner, J. and R. van Zijp (eds.) (1994), *Hayek, Co-Ordination and Evolution. His Legacy in Philosophy, Politics, Economics and the History of Ideas*, London: Routledge.

Bobbio, N. and N. Matteucci (1976), *Dizionario di politica*, Torino: Routledge.

Bornstein, M. (ed.) (1973), *Economia di mercato ed economia pianificata*, Milan: F. Angeli.

Breton, A. (1989), 'The Growth of Competitive Governments', *Canadian Journal of Economics*, November, 4, pp. 717–50.

Brus, W. (1961), *The Market in the Socialist Economy*, London: Routledge and Kegan Paul.

Coase, R. (1937), 'The Nature of the Firm', *Economica*, 4, pp. 386–405.

Dickinson, H.D. (1933), 'Price Formation in a Socialist Community', *Economic Journal*, June, pp. 237–50.

Dickinson, H.D. (1939), *Economics of Socialism*, Oxford: University Press.

Dietz, R. (1989), 'The Reform of Soviet Socialism as a Search for Systemic Rationality: A Systems Theoretical View', *Communist Economies*, 2, 4, pp. 419–39.

Dobb, M. (1969), *Welfare Economics and the Economics of Socialism*, Cambridge: Cambridge University Press.

Dore, R. (1987), *Taking Japan Seriously. A Confucian Perspective on Leading Economic Issues*, London: The Athlone Press.

Eggertsson, J. (1990), *Economic Behavior and Institutions, Cambridge*: Cambridge University Press.

Egidi, M. (1992), 'Organizational Learning and the Division of Labour', in H.A. Simon, M. Egidi and R. Marris (eds.), *Economics, Bounded Rationality and the Cognitive Revolution*, Aldershot: Edward Elgar.

Feinstein, C.H. (ed.) (1967), *Socialism, Capitalism and Economic Growth: Essays*

Presented to Maurice Dobb, Cambridge: Cambridge University Press.

Fodella, G. (1989), *Dove va l'economia giapponese*, Rome: La Nuova Italia Scientifica.

Gomulka, S. (1986), *Growth, Innovation and Reform in Eastern Europe*, Brighton: Wheatsheaf.

Granovetter, M. (1982), 'The Strength of Weak Ties: A Network Theory Revisited', in P. Marsden and N. Lin (1982), pp. 105–30.

Gregory, P.R. and R.C. Stuart (1980), *Comparative Economic Systems*, Boston: Houghton Mifflin.

Grossman, G. (1963), 'Notes for a Theory of the Command Economy', *Soviet Studies*, **XV**, (2), pp. 101–23.

Grossman, S.J. and O.D. Hart (1986), 'The Costs and Benefits of Ownership: A Theory of Vertical and Lateral Integration', *Journal of Political Economy*, 94, pp. 691–719.

Haitani, K. (1986*), Comparative Economic Systems: Organizational and Managerial Perspectives*, Englewood Cliffs: Prentice–Hall.

Hayek, F. (1935a), 'The Nature and History of the Problem', in F. Hayek (1948), pp. 119–47.

Hayek, F. (1935b), 'The Present State of the Debate', in F. Hayek (1948), pp. 148–80.

Hayek, F. (ed.) (1935c), *Collectivist Economic Planning: Critical Studies on the Possibilities of Socialism*, London: Routledge & Sons.

Hayek, F. (1944), *The Road to Serfdom*, Chicago: University of Chicago Press.

Hayek, F. (1945), 'The Use of Knowledge in Society', *American Economic Review*, **35**, September, pp. 519–30, reprinted in F. Hayek (1948), pp. 77–91.

Hayek, F. (1948), *Individualism and Economic Order*, Chicago: Univeristy of Chicago Press.

Hayek, F. (1960), *The Constitution of Liberty*, Chicago: University of Chicago Press.

Heiner, R.A. (1983), 'The Origin of Predictable Behaviour', *American Economic Review*, 83, pp. 560–95.

Hodgson, G. (1988), *Economics and Institutions. A Manifesto for a Modern Institutional Economics*, Cambridge: Polity Press.

Jossa, B. (1975), *Lezioni sulla teoria economica del socialismo*, Napoli: Cooperativa editrice di Economia e Commercio.

Jossa, B. (1978), *Socialismo e mercato. Contributi alla teoria economica del socialismo*, Milan: Etas Libri.

Jossa, B. (ed.) (1989), *Teoria dei sistemi economici*, Turin: UTET.

Kantorovich, L.V. (1965), *The Best Use of Economic Resources*, Cambridge, Mass: Harvard University Press.

Keizer, W. (1994), 'Hayek's Critique of Socialism', in J. Birner and R. van Zijp (1994), pp. 207–31.

Kornai J. (1959), *Overcentralization in Economic Administration*, Oxford: Oxford

University Press.

Kornai, J. (1971), *Anti-Equilibrium: On Economic Systems Theory and the Tasks of Research*, Amsterdam: North-Holland.

Kornai, J. (1980), *Economics of Shortage*, Amsterdam: North-Holland.

Kornai, J. (1992), *The Socialist System*, Princeton: Princeton University Press.

Kovács, J. and B. Dallago (ed.) (1990), *Economic Planning in Transition. Socio-Economic Development and Planning in Post-Socialist and Capitalist Societies*, Aldershot: Dartmouth.

Lange, O. (1936), 'On the Economic Theory of Socialism', *The Review of Economic Studies*, October 1936, 1, pp. 53–71 and February 1937, 2, pp. 123–42, reprinted with some changes in B.E. Lippincott (1938), pp. 55–143.

Lange, O. (1967), 'The Computer and the Market', in C.H. Feinstein (1967), pp. 158–61.

Lavoie, D. (1985), *Rivalry and Central Planning. The Socialist Calculation Debate Reconsidered*, Cambridge: Cambridge University Press.

Lippincott, B.E. (ed.) (1938), *On the Economic Theory of Socialism*, New York: McGraw–Hill.

Marsden, P. and N. Lin (eds.) (1982), *Social Structure and Network Analysis*, Beverly Hills: Sage.

Milgrom, P. and J. Roberts (1992), *Economics, Organization and Management*, New Jersey: Prentice Hall.

Mises, L. von (1920), 'Die Wirtschaftsrechnung in sozialistischen Gemeinwesen', *Archiv für Sozialwissenschaft und Sozialpolitik*, **47**, April, pp. 86–121; English translation: 'Economic Calculation in the Socialist Commonwealth' in F. Hayek (1935c), pp. 87–103.

Mises, L. von (1922), *Die Gemeinwirtschaft*, Jena: G. Fischer (English translation: *Socialism: An Economic and Sociological Analysis*, London: Jonathan Cape, 1936; 2nd ed., New Haven: Yale University Press, 1951).

Nelson, R.R. and S.G. Winter (1982), *An Evolutionary Theory of Economic Change*, Cambridge, Mass: The Belknap Press.

Nove, A. (1983), *The Economics of Feasible Socialism*, London: George Allen & Unwin.

Novozhilov, V.V. (1969), *Problems of Measuring Outlays and Results under Optimal Planning*, New York: International Arts and Sciences Press.

Olson, M. (1965), *The Logic of Collective Action*, Cambridge, Mass: Harvard University Press.

Pryor, F.L. (1973), *Property and Industrial Organization in Communist and Capitalist Nations*, Bloomington: Indiana University Press.

Ricossa, S. (1989), 'Socialismo, liberalismo e liberismo', in B. Jossa (1989), pp. 53–76.

Schumpeter, J.A. (1942), *Capitalism, Socialism and Democracy*, New York: Harper

& Brothers.

Sik, O. (1967), *Plan and Market under Socialism*, White Plains, N.Y.: International Arts and Sciences Press.

Simon, H. (1961), *Administrative Behaviour*, 2nd ed., New York: Macmillan.

Stiglitz, J.E. et al. (1988), *The Economic Role of the State*, edited by A. Heertje, Oxford: Basil Blackwell and Bank Insinger de Beaufort NV.

Taylor, F.M. (1929), 'The Guidance of Production in a Socialist State', *American Economic Review*, March, reprinted in B.E. Lippincott (1938), pp. 41–54.

Ullman, L. and E. Margalit (1977), *The Emergence of Norms*, Oxford: Oxford University Press.

Vercelli, A. (1989), 'Un riesame critico della teoria schumpeteriana della "transizione" al socialismo", in B. Jossa (1989), pp. 265–93.

Wagener, H-J. (ed.) (1993a), *On the Theory and Policy of Systemic Change*, Heidelberg: Physica-Verlag.

Wagener, H-J. (1993b), 'Some Theory of Systemic Change and Transformation', in H-J. Wagener (1993a), pp. 1–20.

Wiles, P.J.D. (1977), *Economic Institutions Compared*, Oxford: Basil Blackwell.

Williamson, O. (1986), *The Economic Institutions of Capitalism. Firms, Markets, Relational Contracting*, New York: The Free Press.

PART ONE

Institutions and Markets

2.   'Creative Destruction' in Economic and Political Institutions

Massimo Egidi

1   WHY REVISIT 'CREATIVE DESTRUCTION'[1]

One of the analytical advantages brought by transaction costs is that it provides a general framework within which one can consider all economic organizations as displayed in a 'space' of different contractual forms between the two extreme situations of pure markets and pure hierarchies. Even though this approach is still incomplete and characterized by unresolved problems,[2] it has consolidated the idea of market and hierarchical organizations as alternative devices with which to coordinate economic activities. This idea originates from the debate on socialist planning to which during the 1930s Lange (among socialists) and Hayek (among Austrians) made the most outstanding contributions. The Austrian claims concerning the inefficiency of planning created a dilemma in the neo-classical camp because capitalistic business firm are basically planned organizations, and therefore large and giant firms should be expected to be poorly efficient. Coase's notion of transaction costs can be considered a reply to the dilemma raised by the Austrians: in fact, in his view planned organizations exist because the costs of coordinating economic activities via markets are positive and can be higher than the costs of coordinating them via plans and orders.

Transaction costs are therefore introduced as the costs of 'running the market', and the limit on the expansion of planned organizations is reached when the costs of organizing economic activity by orders within a plan become equal or superior to the costs of organizing the same activity via transactions on the market (the so-called make-or-buy decision).

In its earlier versions, by consequence, transaction costs economics focused on vertical integration as the basic mechanism with which to explain the shift among different organizational forms. In current debate the

perspective has widened: markets, firms and hybrid forms which characterize
economic activity are considered to be different 'governance structures of
transactions' (Williamson and Winter, 1991) and the differences among
different forms are analysed by comparing the attributes of transactions with
the features of the governance structures, and also the costs involved. Yet,
even in this more sophisticated version, this approach requires precise
definition and operationalization of the concept of transaction costs: a task
which, despite the large amount of theoretical and empirical work devoted to
it, still has not been fully accomplished.[3]

One of the reasons for this difficulty seems to be incomplete analysis of
the nature of the human decisions involved in the make-or-buy choice: in fact,
the contours of the areas of economic activities covered respectively by
markets and by hierarchies depend on the outcome of decisions 'rationally'
taken by managers of the firm: but managerial decisions may have unintended
consequences because of the limits on the human rationality. Analysis of
alternative possible lines of action and the computation of costs involved
(whatever their definition) are normally largely incomplete, and this feature is
amplified when decisions are innovative. In consequence, since managerial
activities display unintended effects in the long run, we cannot take it for
granted that the level of transaction costs will perfectly discriminate between
market and planned activities.

Therefore, it is possible that an institution (market, hierarchical
organization or hybrid) will remain locked in a highly sub-optimal
configuration without the 'spontaneous' rise of an alternative institution to
render coordination more efficient. This suggests a vision of the economy
which is somewhat more pessimistic, but also more realistic, than that
entailed by full use of transaction costs theory: this approach in fact implies
that the distribution between economic activities undertaken respectively via
markets and via planned organizations is optimal, thereby coming
philosophically close to Spinoza's thesis that we live in the best of the
possible worlds.

The suspicion that institutions are not perfectly self-regulating clashes with
a long-standing tradition in economics. Since the parable of the Invisible
Hand, the market has been depicted as a self-regulating institution, efficient
by virtue of competition, which allows social benefits to be achieved despite
individual egoism.

Smith' evocative image fails to take account of the possibility of the long-
run undesired effects of boundedly rational egoistic behaviour on economic
institutions. Even though a glance at any historical example of the economic
redistribution of wealth and resources confirms the existence of negative
effects, only recently, with the rise of the theory of adverse selection and

market failure, has the myth of the market as a mechanism which *always* leads to optimal resource allocation been seriously challenged. The idea of the possible failure and decadence of markets has been advanced in works by Arrow (1971) and Akerlof (1970). The former points out that in economic contexts characterized by systematic innovative (inventive) activity, conditions of the imperfect appropriability and appraisability of new goods hold, and in consequence the market fails to achieve optimal resource allocation. Imperfect appraisability, as Akerlof showed, is also the key condition which can lead to the decline of a market and its disappearance.

The point is that the decline of the market, and eventually its disappearance, does not automatically lead to the rise of an alternative institution which enables the system to achieve optimality. Akerlof's analysis suggests that the mechanism of competition, which is expected to select 'virtuously' the most competent behaviours, may be superseded by a 'vicious' mechanism of adverse selection which discourages the emergence of efficient and competent behaviours. My contention is that if a contractual system does not allocate optimally, this does not imply that it will be possible for an alternative contractual system to emerge, consequently the economy may remain trapped in a highly sub-optimal condition.

To verify the implications of this assumption, the first step is to examine under what conditions the forces fostering or preventing the efficient working of market are active, and if they work in different institutional contexts. To do this we must establish whether it is possible to transfer the idea of the virtuous effect of competition from its natural environment, the market, to hierarchical systems. And secondly we must clarify whether the same holds for 'adverse' mechanisms, i.e. whether corresponding to market failure mechanisms there is some form of organizational failure within hierarchies.

We must first revisit the notion of competition, in order to clarify the conditions for the failure of its virtuous effects. How competition works, in fact, is not fully agreed upon by the different schools of economic thought. The notion has been formulated in at least three different ways. First we have the standard neo-classical description of competition as leading the economic system to equilibrium and allowing optimal resource allocation.

Beyond this view, which addresses the question of computability, stability and Pareto optimality in conditions of perfect knowledge, a more subtle issue is raised by the Austrian approach to competition: that of the emergence of markets as institutions in conditions of dispersed and divided knowledge. Hayek attributed a quite different feature to competition than did standard neoclassical theory: namely its capacity to discover better ways to use economic resources by allowing the more competent and efficient behaviours to prevail.

A third description of competition is offered by Schumpeter's 'Creative Destruction'. Even though couched in terms very similar to the Austrians', by emphasizing the emergence of innovative behaviours as individualistic, 'heroic' actions, Schumpeter suggested that also these behaviours could be standardized, that competition could consequently decline and be replaced by bureaucratic planned activity. For reasons I shall explore later, Schumpeter's prophecy of an historical, long-run decline of market competition was not borne out; one reason for this failure being that, while he suggested that the incentives of market competition were destined to weaken, he assumed it as natural that bureaucratized organizations would be able to create a system of incentives more effective than the market's; which historically did not happen.[4]

Although Schumpeter's predictions have not been fulfilled, his analysis conducts important historical comparison of the relative performances of two economic institutions which sheds light on the possibility that competition can fail and market system can disappear.

For reasons which I will clarify later, Creative Destruction is not a simple extension of the Austrian's view of competition as a virtuous mechanism; it also contains also the idea of adverse selection. Competition, in Shumpeter's view, is primarily a process of the creation and diffusion of new knowledge within the economic system under conditions of rivalry; a process which has important re-allocative effects and, reinterpreted with current analytical tools, presumes conditions of market failure. The argument set out in the following pages, therefore, is that this process works in an environment of market failures and externalities where Hayekian 'virtuous' selection *and* adverse selection operate jointly in dynamic equilibrium.

Confirmation of this feature of Creative Destruction is provided by the theory of democracy expounded in the second part of *Capitalism Socialism and Democracy*. Schumpeter did not provide explicitly micro-foundations for his analysis of Creative Destruction, but most of the essential elements for a micro-foundation of human behaviour in economics and politics are contained in his theory of democracy.

This part of his analysis is in fact based on the idea of bounded rationality, cognitive inertia and the limited ability of humans to evaluate information relevant to *political* decisions. On the one hand these assumptions are crucial to Schumpeter's theory insofar as they permit the representation of political institutions as based on delegation, trust and leadership; on the other, they are strikingly 'Austrian' and easily extended to economics. It is important to note that the assumption that human decisions are affected by limits in using rationality and processing information cannot be restricted to the context of political institutions; and in fact Schumpeter points out that the only difference between the nature of decisions in political and economic contexts is the extent of the knowledge base, i.e. the competence area of consumers and producers, which in economics is normally broader than in politics.

In his theory of democracy Schumpeter describes a process which in modern terms can be called a process of 'adverse selection in politics', based on the assumption that bounded rationality, asymmetry of information and opportunism characterize human behaviour.

As I have suggested, these three features are not specific to human behaviours in politics; they are valid in economic contexts as well. Therefore Schumpeter's theory of democracy and his theory of Creative Destruction can be regarded as based on a unified theoretical background. At the same time his theory of democracy allows us to explore to what extent the modern idea of adverse selection can be used beyond its original sphere of application, the economic theory of market failure, to describe organizational and political failures and to gain better understanding of the limits of hierarchical organizations.

Summing up, we started from the observation that if markets are trapped in a sub-optimal configuration, an alternative, more efficient way to coordinate economic activities will not necessarily emerge. One possible reason is that transaction costs are not fully computable, because of the unintended effects of economic decisions, and therefore a more efficient contractual set-up may fail to emerge. Instead of appealing to transaction costs, this paper suggests a different approach to the problem based on identification of the forces which lead to the rise and the fall of the different coordination devices. It explores the possibility of re-interpreting the meaning of competition on the one hand, and that of adverse selection on the other, as selective mechanisms which give rise, respectively, to the prevalence of competent and loyal behaviours over opportunistic ones, or vice-versa, in markets and within hierarchical organizations. Schumpeter's theory of democracy and his theory of Creative Destruction can be used as benchmarks with which to verify the appropriateness of this approach and as a suitable basis for analysis of the rise and the fall of different organizational and contractual contexts.

The paper is organized as follows: the different features of competition are analysed and compared, beginning with the debate on planning and socialism, in the first three sections.

Then the possible extension of adverse selection to hierarchies, and its relation to Schumpeterian Creative Destruction are discussed (sections 4, 5, 6). In the last sections Schumpeter's theory of democracy is revised in relation to adverse and virtuous *political* selection, and links are examined with Creative Destruction.

2   WALRAS–BARONE: COMPETITION AS THE COMPUTABILITY OF EQUILIBRIUM IN PLANNED AND MARKET ECONOMIES

The debate on the feasibility of a collectivist planned economy began in the early years of this century with the appearance on the European political scene of parties inspired by socialism as an ideology and a political Utopia. The problem was to answer to the question whether a socialist (collectivist) economic system based on the public ownership of the means of production and on planning could work.

The controversy in part took the form of a clash between the two rival economic camps of neoclassical theory and Marxian theory, but this contrast seemed to lose much of its relevance when it was claimed by Pareto first, and then definitively by Barone, that a planned economy can be treated with the analytical tools of general economic equilibrium theory, and in consequence that it was possible formally to prove the workability of a planned economy; that is, the viability of the 'pure logic of socialism' and particularly the existence of equilibrium in planned economies.

Barone employed the Walrasian model to give a formal demonstration of the fact that equilibrium can exist in a planned economic system. However, he failed to show how this equilibrium could be computed in the absence of the market.[5] His position therefore implicitly assumes that the distributed and unconscious computation of equilibrium performed in the markets by the 'invisible hand' can be replaced by a calculation performed directly and consciously by some alternative institution within planned organizations; that is, by what we may call the 'Central Planning Office'.

This raises the question of whether a (presumably huge) bureaucracy can replace market mechanisms and perform the calculation required to establish the levels of supply and demand for all goods and services, by planning their production.

Transfer of the Walrasian model to the context of planning is not 'natural'. Assuming that it is possible to prove the existence of an equilibrium in a planned economy with the same analytical tools that general equilibrium theory provides for market economies, it is not clear what will substitute for competition mechanisms within planned economic systems, in relation to the degree of decentralization of information, knowledge and computation, and the incentives system.

This issue – whether or not a planned system could be made to work – provoked heated debate in the neoclassical school. The Austrian branch of the marginalist school, Menger in particular, argued that planning was theoretically impossible, and claimed that the Plan Office could never possess all the knowledge and information required to calculate artificially what the market calculated 'naturally' via price movements.

In the opposite camp, O. Lange (1937) responded to the impossibility argument with a model of socialist planning based on decentralized decision-making which seemed to settle the question in favour of the socialist position (Keizer, 1994). And, in fact, some years after in *Capitalism Socialism and Democracy*, Schumpeter argued that not only was an *artificial* calculation entirely feasible, but the introduction of an extensive bureaucracy (apart from the problem of the degree of centralization) would render it more straightforward than was the case in a market economy. It would eliminate the decisional uncertainty created in market systems by the existence of a large number of subjects deciding independently (for example, small entrepreneurs competing in the same industry) and reduce unpredictability in managerial decisions (Schumpeter, 1942: 175).

Hayek wrote a critical rejoinder to Schumpeter's position (Hayek, 1980: 90) in which he noted that Pareto himself, while suggesting that the problem of calculation was essentially the same in socialist and market economies, had sustained the *practical* impossibility of socialist calculation, due to the astronomically high number of equations that must be computed.

The point at issue here is that Hayek's polemic against the possibility of a planned system to work as a market economy was not based solely on the complexity of economic calculation; he contended that, since a planned system lacked competition, the incentives that would ensure its efficient functioning were absent.

To assume that it is possible to create conditions of full competition without making those who are responsible for the decisions pay for their mistakes seems to be pure illusion. (Hayek, 1980, p. 186)

The crucial point is therefore that Hayek viewed the role of competition very differently from Walras, and he raised reasons for the inefficiency of planning (as defined by Barone) that were much more relevant than the question of calculation complexity.

3   HAYEK: COMPETITION AS A VIRTUOUS MECHANISM OF SELECTION

Walras' model of competition as the equilibrium adjustment mechanism captured only some aspects of competition, a shortcoming of which the late-nineteenth-century economists were well aware. His model was contested by the Austrian school, which – mainly through Hayek – propounded a version of the notion of competition very different from the Walrasian one, by emphasizing two very different features of competition: selection and learning.

The Austrian school's point of departure was a profound analysis of the nature of human reason and of its relationship with the social institutions; analysis which has no equivalent in Walrasian theory. Mises and Hayek stressed that human rationality and intelligence are characterized by strong cognitive limitations, and that individual knowledge is highly idiosyncratic. Individuals, they contended, develop skills, abilities and experience which are specific and personal; the role of the institutions is therefore to enable individuals with different skills and knowledge systems to interact, helping them to accomplish tasks which they would otherwise find impossible.

Hayek criticized the economists of the Walrasian school because they took for granted what should instead be explained. They considered, that is, of secondary importance, the problem of knowledge by assuming relevant information and knowledge as available to everybody.

> Clearly there is here a problem of *division of knowledge* which is quite analogous to, and at least as important as, the problem of the division of labour. But, while the latter has been one of the main subjects of investigation ever since the beginning of our science, the former has been as completely neglected, although it seems to me the really central problem of economics as a social science. The problem which we pretend to solve is how the spontaneous interaction of a number of people, each possessing only bits of knowledge, brings about a state of affairs in which prices correspond to costs, etc., and which could be brought about by deliberate decision only by somebody who possessed the combined knowledge of all those individuals.
>
> Experience shows us that something of this sort does happen, since the empirical observation that prices do tend to correspond to costs was the beginning of our science. But in our analysis, instead of showing what bits of information the different persons must possess in order to bring about that result, we fall in effect back on the assumption that everybody knows everything and so evade any real solution of the problem. (Hayek, 1980, pp. 50–1)

Since knowledge is idiosyncratic and personal, a key problem is determining how individuals discover the 'relevant information'. Hayek argued that it is not necessary for producers to conduct an exhaustive search for the knowledge they require, because the economic system provides signals which induce them only to seek the relevant knowledge. These signals are emitted by markets and are transmitted through prices. What markets do is to signal, through variations in costs and prices, the existence of inefficiencies within the economic system. This image of competition seems tailored to capture processes of distributed micro-innovation and innovation diffusion. If, for example, a group of innovators reduces the price of a certain good because they are able to produce it more efficiently, this price modification provides other producers with a very clear signal, and exerts strong pressure on them to adjust rapidly to the new mode of production.

This is therefore a view – one shared by all the Austrians – which regards competition as a form of natural selection from which the best technologies, behaviours and organizational forms emerge.

4   SCHUMPETER: COMPETITION AS CREATIVE DESTRUCTION

Schumpeter extended the Austrian argument to include the problem of the division of knowledge within the economy, and to suggest a model which combined selection and innovation. He argued that the engine of the (cyclical) process of development is the innovative activity undertaken by entrepreneurs when economic conditions are favourable (the low interest rates and low production factor costs which characterize depressions). Successful innovation activity reduces the costs and prices of goods and hence obliges all producers to adjust rapidly. Otherwise they are negatively selected and forced out of the market.

In his view too, economic development proceeds through a sequence of innovation–imitation in which competition acts selectively. This Schumpeter called the process of 'Creative Destruction':

> Economists are at long last emerging from the stage in which price competition was all they saw. As soon as quality competition and sales effort are admitted in the sacred precincts of theory, the price variable is ousted from its dominant position. However, it is still competition within a rigid pattern of invariant conditions, method of production and forms of industrial organization in particular, that practically monopolizes attention.
>
> But in capitalistic reality as distinguished from its textbook picture, it is not the kind of competition which counts but the competition for the new commodity, the new technology, the new source of supply, the new type of organization (the largest-scale unit of control for instance) – competition which commands a decisive cost or quality advantage and which strikes not at the margins of the profits and the outputs of the existing firms, but at their foundations and at their very lives. (Schumpeter, 1942, p. 85)

This position reverses the order of the Walrasian account. The convergence of prices to levels which ensure equilibrium between supply and demand – the central component of Walras' theory – is regarded as of secondary importance. The main problem, Schumpeter contends, is that of competition as a selective procedure which singles out the best mode of production.

So, even if declaredly a great admirer of Walras' general equilibrium approach, Schumpeter fully incorporated into his theory the competition features focused upon by the Austrians: learning (innovation), selection and (profit) incentives play a fundamental role in the picture. What was not clear in Hayek's vision, namely the fact that competition does *not* lead to (static) optimal resource allocation, but to a dynamic re-allocation of resources, becomes evident in Schumpeter's analysis: he views competition as giving rise to the continuous redistribution of resources and wealth among individuals, expelling those found to be unfit from the market. Competition creates and destroys fortunes, jobs and wealth, and therefore it is the fundamental source of the rise and decline of economic institutions.

In contrast to this clear statement of competition's features within markets, Schumpeter did not attribute any particular importance to the existence of similar features within bureaucratic organizations. Unfortunately, this is one of the central points for comparison between the performances of market and planned organizations, and ultimately with which to respond to the historical debate with which we started: whether a collectivist economic system, in which competition has been eliminated and replaced by planning, can achieve the same performance and the same results as a market economy.

Central here are the two functions of competition: market clearing, the function stressed by the Walrasian school, and that of giving producers incentives to be as efficient as possible, the Austrian school's thesis. If the price mechanism is replaced by a hierarchical command system by means of which bureaucrats implement their centralized plan, what happens to the two functions fulfilled by competition in markets?

Regarding the first function, that of market clearing, Schumpeter asserted that it is highly likely that bureaucrats can perform the calculations required for planning, thereby substituting for the perfect competition mechanism and proving in practice that it can be done. He paid scant attention to competition's second function, that of producing a system of incentives able to reduce opportunistic behaviour; or at least he assumed that a change of mental habits would be possible in a bourgeois environment which generated symbolic incentives (like the rewards and honours in the army) able to produce efficiency within a bureaucracy in the same way that economic incentives do in market economies.

5   ADVERSE SELECTION, VIRTUOUS SELECTION : IS THE MARKET A SELF-REPAIRING INSTITUTION?

According to the Austrian school, it was competition that gave efficiency to the economic system through a process of selection. What seems to have escaped their analysis are the limits of competition, and the consequences which arise when competition fails to have beneficial effects. This happens, as adverse selection and moral hazard analysis illustrates, when the appropriability and appraisability of assets and goods traded does not hold.

Let us examine these two concepts, beginning with appraisability. To be certain that a new good satisfies their requirements, purchasers must be able to evaluate its possible uses, but this they can only do once they have purchased the good. This entails that purchasers are unable to know the uses of, and therefore to attribute a value to, the good that they buy, except *ex post*. Moreover, appraisability requires competence, which is not uniformly distributed among consumers. This is particularly evident with innovations and inventions, which, like all goods containing knowledge, are not perfectly appraisable.

As regards appropriability, a good is said to be appropriable when it is possible to make exclusive use of it. The reasons why inventions are largely non-appropriable rest on the particular features of knowledge as a good: despite the division of labour, there is a broad overlapping of knowledge and competences among producers in the same industry. They all share a common knowledge base which makes it possible to imitate inventions, by reproducing them, without incurring all the costs of research and development that the first inventor has sustained.

The weakness or absence of these two characteristics – appropriability and appraisability – may markedly reduce the size of the market of inventions (Arrow, 1983). As a consequence, resources may be allocated non-optimally and the economic system may grow at a rate less than its potential.

Inappropriability and non-valuability are key factors in enabling selection to function in an either favourable or adverse manner. The reasons for this I now examine.

If we assume that the appraisability of a good is imperfect, the buyer may be 'sold a lemon' by the seller, who may assure him that the good possesses the desired qualities although this is not actually the case. Opportunistic behaviour arises which may discourage or prevent the transaction. The certainty that the good's declared qualities correspond to its actual ones is only guaranteed by the fact that there exist *endogenous* conditions which motivate producers not to behave opportunistically. These conditions have been highlighted by game theory: if the two parties to a contract expect the exchange to be repeated in the future, for a large number of times which are not known *a priori*, each of them will be motivated to behave correctly, thereby acquiring a good reputation.

In this case it becomes *convenient* to keep to agreements; otherwise it is always possible that those who have been dissatisfied with their partner's behaviour will turn to a more able and more honest one. Hence Hayekian competition is effective in the case of 'large numbers' and low barriers to entry in which the selection process favours the best.

When this does not happen, opportunistic behaviour may appear, and as consequence a process of adverse selection may arise. In examination of how virtuous Hayekian and adverse selection are interrelated, I cite, as a celebrated example, Akerlof's analysis (1970) of the market for lemons.

Let us suppose that there is a used-car market in which every individual seller wishes to sell his car privately. In order to evaluate the quality of the good correctly, the buyer must consult an expert mechanic, and therefore sustain what may be high costs. The buyer may have to pay for the mechanic's expertise several times before he finds a car of good quality. This means that the average cost to be borne in finding the desired car may exceed the difference between the value of a well-maintained car and the value of one in an average state of repair; and this is a cost which no buyer is willing to sustain. Consequently, since the buyer is uncertain of the quality of the good, he tends to value it cautiously and offers a price appropriate to an average-quality car, although the car is actually of good quality. The dealer offering the best good, i.e. the well-maintained car, is discouraged because he is unable to obtain a price that matches the quality of the good. This is therefore a process of adverse selection in which the best commodities are forced out of the market and the more able producers are disincentivated.

A 'negative externality' effect also arises. If, despite everything, the sellers of good-quality cars remain in the market, resources are redistributed in favour of sellers of 'lemons', because they are able to earn more than the real value of the good, while the honest dealers earn less than this value. This is therefore a process of adverse selection which eliminates the good 'well-maintained car'. There is consequently a strong incentive against the habit of maintaining one's car in good condition.

What, then, are the conditions which give rise to adverse selection, and those which lead to Hayekian selection?

The key point in the above example is the possibility that the less well-informed parties to the contract may correctly evaluate, directly or indirectly, the quality of the good that interests them, and at reasonable cost.

If, in the market described above, in which one private individual sells to another, there appears a dealer who manages to build up a large clientele by providing car appraisals backed by guarantees, this sets up a virtuous circle again. Knowing that buyers are willing to pay an above-average price for good-quality cars, and that this quality can be guaranteed by a reputable dealer, car-owners are once again incentivated to keep their cars in good condition. The dealer in this case is an innovative entrepreneur, who may assume the costs of hiring an expert mechanic to appraise cars because he divides these costs among a large number of cars bought and sold. This the private buyer is unable to do.

Note that a new institutional figure – namely the dealer – is required in order to restore the virtuous mechanism of favourable selection which the market alone could not guarantee. This figure arises 'spontaneously' because the conditions are right for him to do so. In fact, adverse selection prevails over favourable selection because of the high cost of appraising goods. The trader's solution is to distribute these costs among a large number of goods sold.

The question therefore becomes the following: is it always possible for institutions 'spontaneously' to arise – and permit Hayekian competition to exert its virtuous effect – or are there situations in which the forces of competition are unable to accomplish their favourable effect and the economic system remains trapped in an sub-optimal configuration?

The case of the market for inventions examined by Arrow provides an outstanding example of a situation in which the market is unable to self-regulate itself through the 'spontaneous' emergence of the institutions necessary to ensure its efficient functioning.

In contrast to Akerlof's example, in this case it is impossible for a new institutional figure to emerge spontaneously; i.e. a new agent able to resolve the problem created by the failure of the market for inventions. Let us imagine that a private individual, an agent, assumes the task of selling inventions; to do this, he must defend the interests of inventors and purchasers. However, although he can protect purchasers by guaranteeing the quality of the invention that they buy, he cannot with the same means protect the inventors. In fact, he cannot prevent the onset of opportunistic behaviour – that is, the appearance of copiers or imitators – unless he decides to resort to coercive measures against imitators. For this to happen, every individual must be able to enforce respect for agreements by the *private* use of violence; only in this case can agents spontaneously arise to protect inventors against violations, by means of a private police system, mercenaries or the like. However, the fact that it is possible to make private use of violence in order to enforce agreements implies that there is the possibility to use private violence to enforce any kind of right: by consequence there does not exist a system of universally shared and accepted laws protecting rights by means of a legitimate Central Government with the monopoly of coercive measures. Hayekian competition may therefore function to its fullest extent only in the absence of a legitimate monopoly of violence able to enforce a set of universally accepted human rights.

Therefore, if there exists a Central Government which is the legitimate monopoly-holder of violence, and which is assigned the role of enforcing respect for the rules ensuring that markets function (all the rules, not just those which concern respect for commitments undertaken in relation to exchange but also those protecting property rights), this means that there are breaches of the rules of the market which are not corrected by Hayekian competition. The market is therefore not a self-enforcing institution able autonomously to generate all the forces necessary for its efficient functioning.

This is especially apparent in the defence of property rights on assets and goods which are only partially appropriable or valuable, and in particular inventions. In order to protect inventors, the guarantee of an authority external to the market, namely the state, is required. The patents office is an economic institution whose existence rests on a force *external* to the market: the guarantee offered by the state that it will enforce the law. Its failure to do so will allow opportunism and adverse selection to prevail, thereby severely restricting the size of the inventions market.

6 THE CREATIVE DESTRUCTION AND MISSING MARKET

I have stressed the phenomenon of market failures and in particular of situations in which, because competition cannot operate virtuously, some markets disappear and the market system is therefore unable to allocate resources optimally.

Interestingly, this phenomenon arises within the process of 'Creative Destruction'. In fact, as this process unfolds, the innovations market is not created to its fullest extent. In Schumpeter's description, after the success of the first inventors, a swarm of imitators arises to diffuse innovations throughout the system. There is nothing to say that these imitators will purchase patents from the innovators; indeed, opportunistic behaviour will predominate because most innovations cannot be easily protected. This gives rise to the transfer of unpaid-for resources from the innovators to the imitators. The cyclical process of development is therefore highly sub-optimal, because it cannot ensure full recompense for innovators. Nevertheless, sub-optimal recompense is sufficient to trigger the process and to finance the growth of innovative firms. Here, favourable selection and adverse selection operate simultaneously, and the former dynamically prevails over the latter.

'Creative destruction' is a virtuous process of competition because it improves the economy by enabling the best modes of production, the best working practices, etc., to emerge. But innovators are discouraged by the difficulty of protecting the results of their efforts, and by the impossibility of earning long-term profits from their innovations. If they were able to prevent their rivals from gaining access to their innovations, they could secure a permanent source of profits (technically, a rent) for themselves. But this privileged situation might become permanent, thereby eliminating the key element of competition.

In competitive capitalism, innovators are only temporarily successful in this endeavour: when innovations are first introduced, innovators are monopolists, because they are sole possessors of the innovation, but they are unable to prevent entry to the sector by imitators and hence the resurgence of competition.

The outcome is therefore a paradoxical situation in which the easier it is for a swarm of imitators to appropriate the secrets of innovators without paying for them in full, the less costly becomes entry to the market and therefore the larger the number of competitors. This enables competition to deliver its beneficial effects: the diffusion of the innovation and the consequent improvement in the quality or price of goods.

Schumpeterian competition operates so rapidly and effectively precisely because there exists a situation in which opportunistic behaviour can arise. However, such behaviour cannot exceed certain limits, for if innovators are unable to earn sufficient profits from their efforts, they are subject to a process of adverse selection which, by discouraging them, progressively reduces the size of the innovations market.

To conclude: the market of innovations cannot develop as a self-regulated institution because it is governed by an unstable dynamic relationship between the two processes of virtuous and adverse selection. Therefore if we move out of the comparative static context and assume evolutionary conditions, i.e. if we assume, as the natural environment of our discussion, Hayekian–Schumpeterian conditions in which the most important way to recreate profits and re-allocate resources is the distributed creation of new knowledge, we must recognize that the dynamic relationship between virtuous and adverse selection characterizes all innovative economies. From this viewpoint, asset specificity helps to explain the preference for long-term contractual forms when a new innovative project has to be realized: new firms created to realize innovative investments allow the growth of internal competences in a network of idiosyncratic knowledge, without requiring the full appraisability and valuability of the individual contributions to growth of common knowledge.

7   VIRTUOUS AND ADVERSE SELECTION WITHIN HIERARCHICAL ORGANIZATIONS

I have outlined some features and limits of the idea of innovation as a distributed process of creation and diffusion of knowledge via markets characterized by Creative Destruction. These limits suggest that a similar process (the creation and diffusion of knowledge) may occur within firms, perhaps in a more efficient way.

A pre-condition for examination of the possible extension of Creative Destruction mechanisms within organizations, is to provide a definition of competition – which is a typical feature of the firms in the market – also within firms. Put otherwise, we must establish whether the rivalry among individuals that typifies their unconscious and unplanned cooperation behaviour in the market still survives when individuals consciously cooperate within the same firm.

The contractual approach helps us answer this problem. Relationships among firms are regulated and limited by contracts which restrict the rights of individuals and their range. Williamson's fundamental transformation is a very clear and vivid illustration of this phenomenon: consider the situation that arises when several firms enter a joint agreement to develop different parts of an innovative project. In this case, long-term joint investments are established and constitute sunk costs which prevent the partners from breaking the contractual relationship. The more the joint relationship among partners is improved by the creation of complementary competences, the more difficult it becomes for rival competitors to enter the relationship and substitute for pre-existing partners. The same happens within large firms: the more workers, employees and managers develops idiosyncratic competences within the internal knowledge network of the organization, the more difficult it becomes for external competitors to substitute for them. Therefore we may suggest that to 'residual rights' – i.e. to the power of decisions not involved in the contractual relationship – there corresponds a 'residual power of competition'.[6]

It follows that as assets specificity increases – within organizations or among firms involved in a lock-in process – so 'residual rights to compete' become increasingly restricted. In the extreme case, in a pure theoretical world of complete long-term contracts, we will arrive at null competitive power because the vertical relationship is entirely reduced to bilateral monopolies. But this limiting case presumes full knowledge and unlimited computational power (to calculate rationally all contingencies of the contracts).

Therefore, assuming a context of bounded rationality, we may say that to whatever extent vertical relationships are strengthened, some residual rights to compete still remain. This suggests that the features of the competitive process, which constitute the regulatory mechanism of the market, can be transferred from their 'natural' environment to the opposite economic context, the firm, and used to explain the mechanisms governing large bureaucratic organizations. In fact, rivalry among individuals within economic organizations is regulated by an internal system of incentives (deliberately or unconsciously) designed to support the working of an internal competition. What I shall maintain in the following pages is therefore that competition within organizations and competition across markets are basically the same phenomenon, i.e. two different ways of converting rivalry into 'virtuous' economic effects. Yet these effects differ between the two institutions because of the large difference in their abilities to compensate people damaged by the reallocative effects of shirking and innovation.

The foregoing discussion suggests that if we represent the market realistically, i.e. as a device for realizing plans and projects in a distributed way[7] (a major implication of which is that prices are signals not sufficient to coordinate the plans of different firms: the transfer of knowledge and information among them is needed), we can compare the two ways to innovate – the distributed and the centralized – in terms of the relative advantages that competition and adverse selection bring in the different contexts.

A crucial point is the limits to the efficiency of planned systems in realizing projectual activities. Projecting is in fact essentially a high-level problem-solving activity which normally require a top-down process of division of labour and delegation, and for this reason it is highly conjectural and uncertain. It therefore can be realized only if it is complemented by a bottom-up distributed micro-innovative activity, i.e. by the 'local' activity of adaptation and micro-innovation activated by the individuals cooperating in the realization of the project.

In his pessimistic description of the declining opportunities for the bourgeoisie, Schumpeter attributed major importance to technological innovations by downgrading organizational adaptive innovations and imagining a future in which almost all innovative activity would be conducted in large laboratories within great planned firms.

Schumpeter omitted to take serious account of organizational innovations because his image of entrepreneurial activity was essentially that of an individualistic 'heroic action'; not a distributed and competitive projecting activity. Innovation is a necessarily diffused process because of the distributed nature of knowledge creation, and organizational micro-innovations are the normal by-product of everyday activity within organizations. The division of knowledge, as Hayek stressed, is a phenomenon which derives inevitably from the limits of human intelligence and rationality; and it is precisely these limits which make the full prediction and planning of discoveries and inventions impossible. Hence it follows that opportunities to innovate cannot be fully controlled by a centralized system, nor can their development be fully planned.

These limits on centralized planning reduce the advantages of great hierarchically-planned firms over networks of small firms, from the point of view of their capacity to react to change and to external challenges. This helps explain why Schumpeter's prophecy has not been fulfilled, taking into account the cognitive aspects of economic organizations.

A complementary explanation requires consideration, one based on the observation that adverse selection can also operate within organizations.

Schumpeter underestimated the fact that when planning replaces the market, the place of Creative Destruction he envisaged as the fundamental mechanism in the competitive struggle *among* firms in the market is not replaced by a selective process operating with equally brutal efficiency *within* organizations, by motivating managers and bureaucrats to direct their action efficiently and creatively towards achievement of the organization's goals.

If we accept that the relationships within a large economic organization are regulated by internal competition, we must admit not only that a conflict of interests may arise among individuals but also, as Marris and Mueller (1972, 1980) suggests, that the interests of a hierarchy of managers, bureaucrats and office-workers do not normally coincide with the interests of the owners, nor with those of the shareholders.

Were competition to operate efficiently, the managers of a large firm would introduce appropriate organizational innovations, change procedures, methods and organizational rules, promote the most able workers up the hierarchy to achieve unanimously shared goals. But any 'efficient' restructuring of the organizational set-up may alter the internal distribution of resources and power, by reducing managerial attributes and their discretionary power.

There therefore may be strong resistance within a bureaucratized large firm against the rapid redefinition of its managers' roles and against change to the organizational procedures involved. This resistance may be viewed as one of the principal sources of inefficiency in large organizations, and interpreted in terms of the adverse selection mechanism. Following Hirschman (1970) and Simon (1991), loyalty is a crucial element in the improvement of organizational compactness. Opportunism is not a 'natural' trait of human behaviour uniformly shared by individuals; it is a habit which can be reinforced or discouraged by the working of the institutions themselves. One way of discouraging opportunistic behaviour is to improve loyalty, which can be done by creating incentives within hierarchical systems, for example by guaranteeing career advancement and rewarding competent behaviour. But if individuals, employees and managers, are to be rewarded by a mechanism of competitive selection within an organization, their ability and fitness must be evaluated by able superiors; and evaluation is effective only if it is performed by an authority which is 'accepted' by inferiors in the hierarchy, in the sense that they recognize the competence of their superiors. To some extent, this operates bottom-up control within hierarchies, insofar as inferiors evaluate the appropriateness of their superiors' decisions and commands. This happens mainly when cognitive and reallocative conflicts arise from an internal innovation – even micro innovation during everyday adaptive activity. Conflicting opinions must find room for expression: 'voice' (Hirschman) enables the most competent opinion to emerge. The parties involved can better establish their reciprocal competences by using voice; and in consequence their decisions reinforce loyalty and identification. Only on this basis – the possibility of taking the voice option – can conflicts of opinion and interest be resolved, with the the most competent position prevailing, and only thus can loyalty overcome opportunism. If, on the contrary, voice fails to command attention, loyalty is not sufficiently improved, and the virtuous effects of competition may be overwhelmed by adverse selection, which may lead the organization into a highly sub-optimal 'order' characterized by a strongly authoritarian and poorly competent hierarchy (Egidi). This explanation was not considered by Schumpeter in his discussion of the features of planned economies: however, if it is transferred to a different context, the political one, it largely fits with Schumpeterian analysis of democracy.

8   THE COGNITIVE FOUNDATIONS OF CREATIVE DESTRUCTION: LEADERSHIP AND THE MANIPULATION OF PREFERENCES

I argued at the outset that one of the most important features of the theory of Creative Destruction is that it can be transferred from analysis of the economic institutions to that of the political ones. Schumpeter accomplished this transfer by revising – in a manner as radical as it was surreptitious – the neoclassical theory of decision-making and of the formation of supply and demand.

Mainstream microeconomics views the formation of supply and demand as the effect of the rational behaviour of perfectly informed and independent economic agents. No explicit hypotheses are formulated on the costs that sellers and buyers must sustain in order to acquire information. Without specifying who must pay information costs, it is assumed that consumers possess a complete picture of the goods available and that, moreover, they are able to evaluate their uses in a perfectly competent manner.

How do consumers react in an environment with a constant stream of innovations, and in which they are confronted by goods whose features they can only imperfectly know? The answer provided by the standard analyses of comparative statics is the following: as new goods enter the market, consumers develop new preference structures which were entirely unknown to them before these new goods appeared; on the basis of these new preferences, certain of these new goods are selected and are successful. It is not deemed important to study how new preferences are formed, the assumption being that it is a transitory and costless process.

In reality, and in the Schumpeterian account, matters are rather different. Consumers possess neither complete information nor sufficient knowledge for perfectly competent decision-making. And nor do they individually possess sufficient resources with which to conduct exhaustive research on existing goods and their quality, and thereby mitigate their ignorance.

This is a typical case of appraisal difficulty which exposes buyers to the risk of opportunistic behaviour. The price system is unable to transmit sufficient signals for consumers to be able to orient their choice (a consumer will not purchase a good offered by a producer at a lower-than-normal price unless he is able to ascertain that the quality of that good is at least equal to that of its competitor goods). Producers and consumers must therefore directly exchange the information about goods that the price system is unable to furnish.

For reasons that I shall not examine here, in the real world there do not normally exist sufficient sources (newspapers, magazines, catalogues, etc.) of information which enable complete and detailed assessment of quality. That is to say, the market system is unable to generate internally to itself – unlike the used-car market – a new market, that of information about goods. Essentially, the emergence of this market is prevented by (a) the difficulties faced by experts in evaluating new goods, since they are ignorant of innovations which are protected by patent or may even be secret; (b) the fact that, whereas competition among sellers is virtuous, because it forces them to improve their expertise in sectors in which they are already specialists, to be 'experts' buyers must be knowledgeable about the whole range of goods on offer. Consequently, there cannot exist that powerful mechanism of competition which obliges consumers to conduct ever more accurate appraisals of the goods that they purchase. This is because, given the limited nature of their knowledge, they would have to undertake processes of learning and information-gathering on an enormous scale. Consumers are therefore forced to delegate appraisal to experts, to opinion leaders, or simply to rely on the word of the seller.

The crucial point is that consumers lack not only information but also expertise. They are therefore obliged to accept external and 'pre-packaged' judgements and evaluations. This is the most insidious aspect of delegation, because it induces consumers to accept and internalize judgements and evaluations which have not been objectively elaborated and tested. The word 'persuasion', indeed, signifies inducing others to accept one's assessments, and in an innovative context this means that the seller of a new good will seek to impose assessment criteria on potential buyers which work in his favour.

The massive growth of the advertising sector in the course of this century clearly testifies to the crucial nature of information and of the persuasion of consumers by producers. Schumpeter highlights this phenomenon in the second part of *Capitalism, Socialism and Democracy*. He points out that advertising does not merely convey information to a public perfectly able to discriminate and choose; it is intended to persuade. Firms do not restrict themselves to providing information. They augment their knowledge of the real or potential needs of consumers by conducting market surveys so that they can induce them to buy their products.

Contrary to the neoclassical model, in which supply and demand are formed entirely independently of each other, in Schumpeter's view, therefore, the formation of demand is influenced by the mechanisms of persuasion deployed by producers. Although consumers possess decision-making autonomy, it is restricted by the persuasive action of firms, which are able to orient buyers' choices by focusing their attention on specific products and by exaggerating their qualities.

Schumpeter adopted a cautious position regarding the autonomy of the consumer; nevertheless it was a position directly at odds with traditional theory. He advanced the hypothesis that the cognitive and decisional autonomy of consumers is limited, and that its 'range of action' depends on the opportunities available to them to appraise the quality of goods directly, on their familiarity with the goods that they intend to purchase. This provided Schumpeter with the link between his analyses of economic choice and of political choice. As we shall see, whereas he attributed a substantial amount of autonomy to consumers, given that they can personally and directly appraise the quality of goods, he attributed much less autonomy to electors when they must decide which party or candidate to support.

In making this assertion, Schumpeter anticipated many of the conclusions reached thirty years later by cognitive psychology in its analysis of consumer behaviour. Empirical studies of consumption and decisions under conditions of uncertainty show that bounded rationality, attention focusing, cognitive frame dependence (see in general the works of Kahnemann and Tversky) play a systematic and crucial role in the formation of preferences. This provides strong *a posteriori* confirmation for the validity of Schumpeter's theory.

However, in the 1940s, economists were entirely unaware of this line of analysis. The gulf between the experimental psychological study of consumer behaviour and the economic theory of consumption decisions was (except in the works of Katona) total. Schumpeter's analysis was therefore interpreted solely as an attempt to introduce realism into the description of economic facts, and its powerful innovative potential in the theoretical field was ignored.

With the recent development of the theory of bounded rationality (Herbert Simon), and the consequent intellectual alliance between cognitive sciences, psychology and economics, it is now clear that Schumpeter's assumptions can be used to conduct a radical revision of the theory of consumption. If one assumes that individuals act on the basis of limited rationality and competences, the consequence is that the formation of consumer choices and preferences is affected by external agents which provide or suggest the criteria for assessment: the expert, the opinion leader, or the producer exert a decisive influence on the collective formation of new systems of opinion and therefore of preferences.

I do not consider this phenomenon – the fact that it is possible to create new needs 'artificially' to 'manipulate' consumer preferences – as intrinsically negative, for it is the inevitable consequence of the cognitive and rational limitations of human beings. All needs, with the exception of the most basic ones, are eminently cultural in nature (anthropological in the broad sense), and the incessant creation of new needs by competitive capitalism has undeniably increased the sum of human well-being. The fact that needs are 'artificially' created and re-created has therefore had both positive and negative consequences for economic and civil progress. It all depends, of course, on the institutional framework within which the phenomenon unfolds, and of the level of awareness of those involved. One may choose to accept the assessments proposed by others; but this choice is freer, the more it is based on knowledge and awareness. This is the key component of Hirschman's (1984) analysis of changes in preferences.

Hirschman draws on the approach developed by the philosopher Harry

Frankfurt to distinguish between 'wanton' and non-wanton' changes in preferences. The former are simple, random and induced by fashion; the latter are deliberate, complex and the outcome of an often arduous process of introspection ('wanton', Hirschman reminds us, means 'frivolous', 'vacuous' but also 'unpremeditated'). He proposes that the capacities attributed to an economic agent should also include an ability to make non-wanton choices; that is, the ability to reflect on previous choices and, if necessary, change the criteria on the basis of which those choices were made.

The problem is establishing whether there are elements endogenous to the market which induce consumers to make non-wanton choices; that is, whether there are forces which prompt consumers to make competent and informed choices, although most appraisals must nonetheless be delegated because of the rational and cognitive limitations of human beings.

Now it is a commonplace experience that this is not what actually happens: systematic rivalry exists among competing firms. Firms do not have a common interest which induces them faithfully and impartially to inform consumers about the characteristics of their new products; on the contrary, it is in their interest to advertise their products and to persuade consumers that they are better than those of their competitors.

Accordingly, and given the 'cognitive laziness' of the mass of consumers, advertising techniques manipulate the unconscious and irrational elements that determine consumer choices. The advertiser who based his campaign on the rationality of choice and on the transparency and completeness of information would encounter serious problems with his client, and, by subjecting the consumer to high cognitive overload, he would probably fail to sell the product.

The crucial point is that producers have no interest in providing consumers with the means to make a free, informed and conscious choice. On the contrary, the knowledge that a choice is 'wanton' substantially reduces the producer's uncertainty, because in this case the choice is subject to advertising and fashion, and therefore to a certain amount of control and influence exercised by the producer himself. This is exactly the opposite of what should be guaranteed to the consumer, namely the provision of every incentive to choose with the maximum amount of knowledge and competence.

This phenomenon is a very subtle form of market failure. The market is blind, in the sense that it does not possess the power to force consumers to adopt entirely rational behaviour, to undertake 'virtuous' competition similar to the competition among producers. This may set a trap for the economic system as a whole, which becomes unable to force its components to express their needs and interests with a high degree of rationality.

This phenomenon is driven by an element closely associated with the difficulty of appraisal analysed by Arrow: namely the fact that the transfer and modification of preferences is largely the result of exogenous factors. Schumpeter was fully aware of the great significance of this phenomenon – which lies at the basis of delegation mechanisms and therefore of the emergence of leadership – but, as we have seen, he believed it to be of limited importance in the economic field. By contrast, he argued that it had a crucial impact in the political arena.[8]

9   DEMOCRACY AND COMPETITION

The above discussion of the limits of competition links directly with the last part of *Capitalism, Socialism and Democracy*, which contains what was certainly Schumpeter's most innovative contribution to the history of thought. The aim of this section is not to conduct a critical reading of Schumpeter's views on democracy, but, more simply, to show how his original conception of human economic behaviour was naturally extended, in this part of his book, to social and political behaviour.

Schumpeter suggests that the struggle for power is a process entirely analogous with the competition for profit. Democracy is therefore a system of rules ensuring that the contest for power takes the peaceful form of the political election.

This analogy between market and democracy holds true because Schumpeter developed a set of postulates which enable political and economic behaviour to be treated in unitary fashion.

Schumpeter's analysis was based on the following three principles: (i) the limited ability of individuals to reflect, to form independent opinions and to decide (an assumption of 'Austrian' stamp, which was given its first thorough formulation in the modern theory of bounded rationality); (ii) the fact that evaluation of goods requires knowledge and expertise; (iii) the principle of delegation, which enables leaders to rise to power. Let us examine the connections among these three principles.

Human cognitive difficulties and bounded rationality are of especial significance when one moves from the economic sphere to the world of politics.

> However, when we move still further away from the private concerns of the family and the business office into those regions of national and international affairs that lack a direct and unmistakable link with those private concerns, individual volition, command of facts and method of inference soon cease to fulfil the

requirements of the classical doctrine. What strikes me most of all and seems to me to be the core of the trouble is the fact that the sense of reality is so completely lost. ...

Thus the typical citizen drops down to a lower level of mental performance as soon as he enters the political field. He argues and analyzes in a way which he would readily recognize as infantile within the sphere of his real interests. He becomes a primitive again. His thinking becomes associative and affective. (Schumpeter, 1942, pp. 260–1)

The phenomena of advertising and fashion, which as we have seen subtly pervade the economic system, find their maximum expression in politics. They are phenomena which render the criteria and motives for decision-making even less transparent, when they instead require rationality and expertise, and subject the citizen to the decisive influence of political groups and parties. These latter create opinions and ideas with which they persuade citizens to change their attitudes and criteria of choice.

The only point that matters here is that, Human Nature in Politics being what is, their are able to fashion and, within very wide limits, even to create the will of the people. What we are confronted with in the analysis is not a genuine but a manufactured will. And often this artefact is all that in reality corresponds to the volonté générale of the classical doctrine. So far as this is so, the will of the people is the product and not the motive power of the political process. (Schumpeter, 1942, p. 263)

This position should not be interpreted as an Orwellian prophecy. Schumpeter realistically acknowledges that the degree of cognitive and decision-making autonomy of the 'average' citizen as regards political choice is very low. Consequently, the chief problem is to establish whether there exist institutional mechanisms which exert a virtuous effect by enabling citizens to make their political assessments and choices in a more rational manner.

This may happen if the political institutions permit the leaders of new groups and parties to emerge, and if they ensure that conflictual political rivalry is resolved peacefully through elections. This for Schumpeter is the function of democracy: to guarantee the proper working of a process of political competition so that leaders enjoying broad consensus may assume power.

Of course, operating in harness with the virtuous process of competition is adverse selection. In fact, the winners of the competitive struggle, those who manage to form majority coalitions on the basis of the rules of democracy, must fulfil their promises. But verifying that pledges have been maintained, using the power assigned to him to fulfil pre-announced plans, is very difficult for the average citizen.

This evident difficulty also stems from the fact that the good promised to the citizen at the moment of voting is, by the very nature of things, extremely generic. The vote is in a certain sense a blank cheque issued on the basis of an extremely ill-defined agreement between voter and candidate. When the deal is struck, it is of sufficient vagueness to give the future leader broad margins of discretionality.

Precisely because of the extremely generic definition given to the good, it is not possible to conduct fully rational appraisal of its nature and its consequences: the vote is therefore a radical act of delegation, and as such presupposes a high degree of trust in the potential leader.

This is therefore a situation which faithfully replicates the mechanism of 'market failure' discussed in the case of the economic system. The good that the electors evaluate is a good for which neither appropriability nor full and rational appraisability exist; it may therefore lead to the emergence of opportunistic behaviour.

In previous sections I have argued – on the basis of the non-appraisability and the non-appropraibility of innovations – that the market is unable to develop into a fully self-regulated institution, but requires rules guaranteed by an external power – state power – if it is to maintain its competitive mechanisms. What happens in the case of the institutions of democracy?

There is a distinct possibility that the world of politics dupes citizens, that voters are systematically sold 'lemons' by leaders who make vague promises, who make massive use of covert methods of persuasion, who substitute advertising for political debate. This, to continue with the analogy, induces citizens to withdraw from the electoral market; that is, participation dwindles to the point where democracy as an institution collapses.

Are there remedies? If so, what are they? As in the market, so in democracy opportunistic behaviour can be unmotivated with the threat of loss of reputation, of the trust placed in the leader. The problem once again is whether there exist mechanisms which can bring this about.

Schumpeter suggests – as we have seen – that adverse selection can be combatted by a system which ensures that groups and parties embracing different political positions emerge and can assume power by winning elections. If the competition is effective, leaders are provided with an incentive to keep their promises and to define their policies unambiguously. Since there nonetheless remains a broad margin of non-appraisability of the good, due to its very nature, the rise of institutions which enable citizens to form opinions on, and assessments of, the policies proposed by the leaders in the most informed manner possible is a key factor in the 'virtuous' working of political competition. The mass media may perform this function by furnishing information and evaluations, and by enabling the citizen to assess the leader's performance as a non-wanton good. However, as in the economic system, so in the political arena the markets of information and knowledge are not complete.

10   FINAL REMARKS

With its conceptual unification of economic and political behaviour, Schumpeter's analysis warns us that virtuous selection and adverse selection are ever-present in the market and in politics. Democracy is therefore a vulnerable institution. The limitations of Schumpeter's analysis, as discussed in previous sections, do not blunt the powerful thrust of his ideas, which even today have still to find full development. He suggests that cooperation and conflict in society are resolved by much more sophisticated and complex mechanisms than those denoted by the Smithian metaphor of the 'invisible hand'. It is not sufficient for everyone to pursue their interests for advantages to accrue – without those involved in the process being aware of it – to all other individuals and with the overall enhancement of the economy and society. There exist, as the consequence of the pursuit of individual interests, also perverse mechanisms. And since these mechanisms are not imposed from outside but are born of the limitations on human behaviour in the political and economic institutions, there is no guarantee that market and democracy will function in a virtuous manner.

NOTES

1.   A preliminary formulation of the ideas discussed in the present paper was presented to a meeting of the EAPE association in Florence, where I benefited from comments by J. Hodgson, E. Screpanti and K. Dopfer. I then sent a second version of the paper to friends and colleagues, some of whom answered with careful written comments. Among these, I am particularly indebted to M. Balconi, M. Franzini, G. Lunghini, R. Marchionatti, L. Mittone, S. Rizzello, E. Screpanti, S. Zamagni for the precision of their comments and the strength of their criticisms, which induced me largely to revise of the paper. After the final revision of this paper I have received comments from R. Langlois and M. Messori. While unfortunately I cannot make a further remake of this paper, I am very grateful for their suggestions, from which I have largely benefited. Of course responsibility for the final result is mine.

2.   See for example Demsetz 's oservations in Williamson and Winter (1991, pp. 159–178)

3. See the contributions of Williamson and Demsetz in Williamson and Winter (1991, pp. 90–116 and pp. 159–178).
4. He transposed to the long run and extended to the entire economic system what in capitalist economies happens as an everyday 'local' and possibly temporary phenomenon: the reduction of competitive opportunities produced by the rise of vertical integration. But even though Schumpeter's epochal predictions have not been fulfilled, his analysis contains in nuce some important elements with which to regard the shift from market to hierarchical organizations as resulting from the reallocation of resources in conditions of market failure.
5. See Hayek (1980, p. 90, note 1) and more generally 'Socialist Calculation III: the Competitive "Solution"' (pp. 181–208).
6. See Hart, in Williamson and Winter (1991).
7. An important implication of this statement is that prices are not sufficient signals to coordinate the plans of different firms; a transfer of knowledge and information among them is normally needed.
8. See his brilliant exposition of the problem in Schumpeter 1942, pp. 242–51.

REFERENCES

Arrow, K.J. (1971), 'Economic Welfare and the Allocation of Resources for Invention', in G. Lamberton (1971) (ed.), *Economics of Information and Knowledge*, London: Penguin Books.

Arrow, K.J. (1983), 'Innovation in Large and Small Firms', in J. Ronen (ed.) (1983), *Entrepreneurship*, Lexington (Mass): D.C. Heath.

Akerlof, G.A. (1970), 'The Market for "Lemmons": Quality Uncertainty and the Market Mechanism', *Quarterly Journal of Economics*, **84**, pp. 488–500.

Barnard, C. (1962), *The Function of the Executive,* Cambridge: Harvard University Press (first printing 1938).

Barone, E. (1908), 'Il Ministro della Produzione nello Stato Collettivista', *Giornale degli Economisti,* reprinted as 'The Ministry of Production in the Collectivistic State' in F.A. Hayek (1935) pp. 245–90.

Coase, R. (1937), 'The Nature of the Firm', *Economica,* **4**, pp. 386–405.

Egidi, M., 'Virtuous and Adverse Selection within Economic Organizations. (A comment)', in *Simon. Mattioli Lecture,* Cambridge University Press, forthcoming.

Hayek, F.A. (1935), *Collectivistic Economic Planning: Critical Studies on the Possibility of Socialism*, London: G. Routledge.

Hayek, F.A. (1952), *The Sensory Order*, London: Routledge & Kegan Paul.

Hayek, F.A. (1945), 'The Use of Knowledge in Society', *American Economic Review,* **35**, (4), pp. 519–30.

Hayek, F.A. (1980), *Individualism and Economic Order* (reprinted from the 1948 original printing), Chicago: The University of Chicago Press.

Hirschman, A.O. (1970), *Exit, Voice and Loyalty: Responses to Decline in Firms, Organizations and States,* Harvard: Harvard University Press.

Hirschman, A.O. (1984), 'Against Parsimony: Three Easy ways of Complicating Some Categories of Economic Discourse', *Bulletin of the American Academy of Arts and Science.*

Kahneman, D. and A. Tversky (1986), 'Rational Choice and the Framing of Decisions', in R.M. Hogart and M.W. Reder (eds.), *Rational Choice – The Contrast between Economics and Psychology,* Chicago: The University of Chicago Press.

Keizer, W. (1994), 'Hayek's Critique of Socialism' in J. Birner and R. van Zijp (eds.), *Hayek, Co-ordination and Evolution,* London: Routledge.

Lange, O. (1936–37), 'On the Economic Theory of Socialism: Part One/ Part Two', *Review of Economic Studies,* **4**, (1), pp. 53–71 and **4**, (2), pp. 123–42, reprinted in B.E. Lippincot (ed.) (1964), *On the Economic Theory of Socialism,* New York: McGraw Hill.

Loasby, B.J. (1989), 'Herbert Simon's Human Rationality', in W. J. Samuels (ed.), *Research in the History of Economic Thought and Methodology,* volume 6, A Research Annual, Greenwich: Conn. and London: JAI Press, pp. 1–17.

March, J.G. (1988), *Decisions and Organizations,* Oxford: Basil Blackwell.

March, J.G. and H.A. Simon (1958), *Organizations,* New York: John Wiley.

Marris, R. (1964), *The Economic Theory of Managerial Capitalism,* London: Macmillan.

Marris, R. (1972), 'Why Economics Needs a Theory of the Firm'. *Economic Journal,* **82** (325).

Marris, R. (1984), 'A New Model of the Process of Business Concentration', in C. Levicki (ed.), *Small Business: Theory and Policy,* London: Croom Helm.

Marris, R. and D.C. Mueller (1980), 'The Corporation, Competition, and the Invisible Hand', *Journal of Economic Literature,* **18** (1).

Nelson, R.R. and S. Winter (1974), 'Neoclassical vs. Evolutionary Theories of Economic Growth: Critique and Prospectus', *The Economic Journal,* **4** (336), pp. 886–905.

Nelson, R.R. and S. Winter (1982), *An Evolutionary Theory of Economic Change,* Cambridge (Mass): The Belknap Press of Harvard University Press.

Newell, A. and H.A. Simon (1972), *Human Problem Solving,* Englewood Cliffs, N.J.: Prentice Hall.

Polanyi, M. (1958), *Personal Knowledge: Towards a Post-Critical Philosophy,* London: Routledge & Kegan Paul.

Robertson, D.H. (1930), *Control of Industry,* London: Nisbet & Co.

Schumpeter, J.A. (1942), *Capitalism Socialism and Democracy,* New York: Harper & Brothers.

Simon, H.A. (1957), *Models of Man*, New York: Wiley.

Simon, H.A. (1972), 'From Substantive to Procedural Rationality', in C.B. McGuire and R. Radner (eds.), *Decision and Organization*, Amsterdam: North-Holland.

Simon, H.A. (1991), 'Organizations and Markets', *Journal of Economic Perspectives*, **5** (2), Spring, pp. 25–44.

Simon, H.A. (1993), 'Altruism and Economics', *American Economic Review*, **83** (2), May, pp. 156–61.

Simon, H.A and A. Newell (1972), *Human Problem Solving,* Englewood Cliffs, N.J: Prentice-Hall.

Singley, M.K. and J.R. Anderson (1989), *The Transfer of Cognitive Skill*, Cambridge, Massachusetts: Harvard University Press.

Williamson, O.E. (1975), *Markets and Hierarchies: Analysis and Antitrust Implications,* New York: Free Press.

Williamson, O.E. (1985), *The Economic Institutions of Capitalism,* New York: Free Press.

Williamson, O.E. and S.G. Winter (eds.) (1991), *The Nature of the Firm: Origins, Evolution and Development*, New York: Oxford University Press.

Winter, S.G. (1982), 'An Essay on the Theory of Production', in S.H. Hymans (ed.), *Economics and the World Around It,* Ann Arbor: Michigan University Press.

3. Decentralization as Ability to Adapt

Jack Birner

1 INTRODUCTION

The issues of centralization and decentralization are not new in the history of economic and social theory, but lessons from the past tend to be forgotten. I will here discuss some insights of one of the greatest economic and social theorists of this century, F.A. Hayek. Until quite recently, Hayek's work was almost completely unknown, and those few who were aware of it were only acquainted with his later writings on social and political philosophy. Hayek's economics remained in the shadow cast by the prominence of his former opponent Keynes during the quarter-century following publication of the *General Theory* in 1936. In this contribution I shall seek to show that Hayek's work contains the resources with which to address the problems of centralization and decentralization now confronting the ex-socialist societies in Eastern Europe. Hayek's technical economics of the 1920s, '30s and '40s will be discussed first. I will then summarize his arguments in the debate on a socialist economy, and show how they were generalized into a theory of society. Decentralized decision-making occupies a central position in Hayek's later work on the emergence and evolution of social institutions and their relations within society as a whole. His ideas in this domain were shaped by his cognitive psychology, which was his earliest contribution to the sciences of man. I shall link various Hayekian ideas to those in other domains, my purpose being to examine how further light can be shed on some pressing problems of social organization.

2 ECONOMIC PLANNING

2.1 Planning versus the market?

The difference between socialist and capitalist economies is usually discussed in terms of planning versus the market. However, as early as the first half of the 1930s Hayek was arguing that this is a false dichotomy. Hayek discussed planning in terms which lead us directly to the issues of centralization and decentralization. He observed that in the analysis of an economic system the relevant question is not whether or not planning takes place. This question is misguided, for planning takes place in every economic system. All economic agents make plans. The relevant question is who is in effective control of the process of making and carrying out the plans. Is it a central planning bureau or individual decision-makers? Economic systems differ according to the extent to which the planning process is centralized (see Hayek, 1945, para. 2). This manner of formulating the problem has far-reaching consequences which if they had been recognized fifty years ago might have turned economics into an entirely different discipline. Instead of limping along on the crutches of static models when pursuing dynamic paths, economists might have developed dynamic models much earlier; they might have recognized the role of expectations much earlier; and instead of dealing with representative agents they might have started analysing coordination problems. All these elements are closely related to the way in which Hayek modelled the planning process.

2.2   Plan, equilibrium and time

Starting from the idea of a plan, Hayek constructs a dual concept of equilibrium (Hayek, 1928) which comprises both the equilibrium of the individual and that of the economic system as a whole. For the individual, Hayek defines equilibrium as the state in which the data of his economic plan correspond to his expectations (ibid., pp. 38–9). The data are the individual's own preferences and the plans of other individuals; or rather the actions undertaken as a consequence of these plans and as perceived by other individual planners. When the perceived actions are in accordance with the actions as expected by everybody, nobody's expectations are falsified. Hence no-one has an incentive to change his plan. The plans of all individuals are consistent with one another. In other words, they are coordinated, and the economic system as a whole is in equilibrium. This dual formulation of equilibrium applies both to a centrally-directed economy and to a market system.

Equilibrium is a relation among actions, and the actions of an individual follow one another in time. Every individual compares the actual level of the satisfaction of his needs with the desired one. In his evaluation he includes the means available to satisfy his needs. Time separates the actual state of affairs from the desired one. Hence every plan involves a time interval, and there is no plan without time (Hayek, 1937, pp. 36–7). Hayek's modelling of equilibrium entails that equilibrium analysis is not restricted to a static or a stationary system. Whether an economy is stationary, grows, or shrinks depends on the expectations of the individuals of which the system is made up (ibid., p. 41). If every economic agent expects a particular rate of growth, equilibrium is preserved as long as there are no signals that are inconsistent with these expectations. Equilibrium means not the immutability of objective data but the fulfilment of subjective expectations.

2.3 Disequilibrium

Plans are based on knowledge and expectations. A change in the expectations of a planner will induce him to change his course of action. This will generate signals which change the informational input of other planners. A dynamic theory is needed to describe the processes that operate in the system after the state of equilibrium has been disturbed. During the 1930s, Hayek developed such a theory to explain business cycles. Individuals base their actions on perceived prices, that is, money prices. If, however, changes in the money supply do not exactly keep pace with changes in the real relative scarcities of goods and services, perceived money prices do not correspond to real relative prices. According to Hayek, credit money is a systematic source of disturbances, and these may be aggravated by occasional monetary interventions by governments. As a consequence of these disturbances, individuals take the wrong consumption and investment decisions. This causes changes in the structure of capital and production that do not correspond to changes in real intertemporal relative scarcities. It is not until the output produced by the changed production structure is confronted with demand by consumers that the mismatch is discovered. The structure of production is re-adapted, which involves capital destruction and unemployment. The result is a series of cyclical movements in the level of investment. Hayek spent most of the 1930s working the capital–theoretical foundations of his theory of industrial fluctuations; work which culminated in the publication of *Pure Theory of Capital* in 1941.[1]

Implicit in Hayek's business cycle theory is a theory of social learning. Changes in the structure of production impose constraints on the ability of individuals to realize their plans. When encountering these constraints they learn that their plans cannot be realized the hard way.[2] Owing to the locality of individual perception (or the existence of distributed, limited knowledge), a learning process is required to force individuals to do what they would have chosen to do had they been in a position to take the correct decisions to begin with. This process is a social learning process in that the constraints that emerge from the interaction of individuals force them to adapt their plans. It is in this sense that the system 'knows' more than the individuals of which it consists.

2.4 Socialism

After the resounding success of Keynes's *General Theory*, Hayek withdrew from analytical economics. In so far as he was still remembered, it was for his contributions to the debate on the feasibility of socialism. Even so, his arguments did not play a part in the analysis of centrally-planned economies until recently. In joining the debate of the 1930s Hayek defined socialism as central planning by the government.[3] He criticized a socialist economy as being informationally inefficient in three ways. First, the millions of individuals who together constitute an economy know their own specific circumstances in quite some detail. However, a centrally-planned economy lacks the means to collect all these individual items of information. Second, under a system of centralized decision-making there are no incentives for individuals to discover new opportunities. And third, even if a central planning bureau had the means to collect all relevant information, the computational demands on it would exceed the capacities of even the fastest computer. Although Hayek concentrated on economic arguments in the debate, he made it clear that this was too narrow a perspective. His subsequent work may be seen as an attempt to supplement the economic arguments against a socialist economy with arguments about the social framework of an economy.

3 FROM ECONOMICS TO THEORY OF SOCIETY

Although neglected, the basic thrust of Hayek's economics was not lost forever. After Keynes' victory, Hayek proceeded to develop a theory of society and of social institutions which is both a generalization and an elaboration of his ideas on the mechanisms that regulate an economy. Even though these later theories never achieve the heights of analytical sophistication displayed by his economics, they contain elements of considerable interest for the study of centralization and decentralization today. In a series of books and articles, Hayek developed his ideas on social learning and the evolution of institutions and on the manner in which markets and competition function.[4]

Hayek's article 'Individualism True and False' published in 1945a (ITF)[5] represents a key moment in the generalization of his thought from the domain of economics to that of social theory. ITF examines the consequences of the theory of society developed by the philosophers of the Scottish Enlightenment. According to Hayek, 'its basic contention is ... that there is no other way toward an understanding of social phenomena but through our understanding of individual actions directed toward other people and guided by their expected behavior' (ITF, p. 6).

The individualism of the Scottish philosophers must be distinguished from the alleged individualism of the Cartesian school, which is usually referred to as rationalism. This is why Hayek calls the true individualism of the Scottish Enlightenment 'anti-rationalist'.

> The antirationalistic approach, which regards man not as a highly rational and intelligent but as a very irrational and fallible being, whose individual errors are corrected only in the course of a social process, and which aims to make the best of a very imperfect material, is probably the most characteristic feature of English individualism. (ITF, pp. 8–9)

Hayek owed this insight to Mandeville. True individualism is closely connected to classical political economy, and the great discovery of the classical economists was that 'many of the institutions on which human achievements rest have arisen and are functioning without a designing and directing mind ... and that the spontaneous collaboration of free men often creates things which are greater than their individual minds can ever fully comprehend' (ITF, p. 7).

Contrary to the pseudo-individualism of the rationalists and social engineers, 'true individualism is the only theory which can claim to make the formation of spontaneous social products intelligible' (ITF, p. 10), and it 'believes ... that, if left free, men will often achieve more than individual human reason could design or foresee' (ITF, pp. 10–11).

These ideas were applied to the domain of politics, where they were used to design 'a system under which bad men can do least harm' (ITF, p. 11).[6] But true individualism is more than a political doctrine. It is a theory of society as a whole.

Underlying this theory of society is

> a view which in general rates rather low the place which reason plays in human affairs, which contends that man has achieved what he has in spite of the fact that he is only partly guided by reason, and that his individual reason is very limited and imperfect ... One might even say that the former is the product of an acute consciousness of the limitations of the individual mind which induces an attitude of humility toward the impersonal and anonymous social process by which individuals help to create things greater than they know. (ITF, p. 8)

A theory of this kind must provide an answer to the question of what it is that binds a society together. The answer is that social cohesion is a matter of an adequate institutional framework; one, moreover, which does not rely for its operation on the application of outside force: 'The great concern of the great individualist writers was indeed to find a set of institutions by which man could be induced, by his own choice and from the motives which determined his ordinary conduct, to contribute as much as possible to the need of all others' (ITF, pp. 12–13).

Two central ideas mark Hayek's transition from economics to the theory of society. One concerns 'the constitutional limitation of man's knowledge and interests, the fact that he *cannot* know more than a tiny part of the whole of society and that therefore all that can enter into his motives are the immediate effects which his actions will have in the sphere he knows' (ITF, p. 14). The other idea is the description of social institutions as problem-solvers. Social institutions solve the problem of complexity, a problem that Hayek came to address in more general terms in his philosophy of science of the late 1950s and early 1960s.[7] The philosophers of the Scottish Enlightenment had argued that institutions are capable of performing tasks that are far too complex for individual human minds. Hayek adopted these ideas to view social institutions as undesigned, spontaneously evolved interaction patterns, or rules, which by discovering and coordinating dispersed knowledge reduce the complexity faced by individuals with limited knowledge and thereby enable them to coordinate their actions. These rules are largely implicit in that they contain the accumulated tacit knowledge of past generations.

4   COGNITIVE AND SOCIAL SYSTEMS

4.1   Learning and rationality as social phenomena

That the transition of Hayek to social philosophy involves a generalization of his ideas on economics is confirmed by what he writes in ITF:

> What the economists understood for the first time was that the market as it had grown up was an effective way of making man take part in a process more complex and extended than he could comprehend and that it was through the market that he was made to contribute to 'ends which were no part of his purpose'. (ITF, pp. 14–5)

Hayek acknowledges that these economists had found a theory of social learning. The belief in a theory of social learning is consistent with the idea that rationality is a social phenomenon.

> The true basis of [the individualist's] argument is that nobody can know *who* knows best and that the only way by which we can find out is through a social process in which everybody is allowed to try and see what he can do. The fundamental assumption, here as elsewhere, is the unlimited variety of human gifts and skills and the consequent ignorance of any single individual of most of what is known to all the others members of society taken together. Or, to put this fundamental contention differently, human Reason, with a capital R, does not exist in the singular, as given or available to any particular person, as the rationalist approach seems to assume, but must be conceived as an interpersonal process in which anyone's contribution is tested and corrected by others. (ITF, p. 15)

This process generates the tacit knowledge that enables society to function, and this tacit knowledge is embodied in a particular institutional structure. Obstructing the spontaneous interaction of individuals hampers the growth of this type of knowledge:

> [The] desire to make everything subject to rational control, far from achieving the maximal use of reason, is rather an abuse of reason based on a misconception of its powers, and in the end leads to a destruction of that free interplay of many minds on which the growth of reason nourishes itself. (Hayek, 1964, p. 93)

4.2   Cognitive psychology and social theory

In 1920, at the age of 21, Hayek had written a manuscript that contains a theory of cognitive psychology which was not published until 1952, in an extended version, as *The Sensory Order* (SO).[8] I will discuss Hayek's psychology because his later theory of society bears many traces of it.

Hayek assumes that there are two 'orders' into which the human mind arranges the objects in the world: the physical order, which classifies external events as similar or different according to whether they produce other similar or different external events; and the sensory order, which classifies events according to their sensory properties. In contrast to Ernst Mach, Hayek holds that there is no simple one-to-one correspondence between the elements of these two orders. It was this criticism of Mach that prompted Hayek to develope his own cognitive psychology (see de Vries, 1994). Events which appear to our senses to be of the same kind may be different in the physical order, and the other way around. The relation between the sensory order of the human mind (the 'microcosm') and the physical order of external events (the 'macrocosm') is the central problem addressed by SO.

The principal tenet of the book, which also constitutes its main difference with respect to contemporary psychological theories, is that

> the sensory (or other mental) qualities are not in some manner originally attached to, or an original attribute of, the individual physiological impulses, but that the whole of these qualities is determined by the system of connexions by which the impulses can be transmitted from neuron to neuron; that it is thus the position of the individual impulses or group of impulses in the whole system of such connexions which gives it its distinct quality; that this system of connexions is acquired in the course of the development of the species and the individual by a kind of 'experience' or 'learning'; and that it reproduces therefore at every stage of its development certain relationships existing in the physical environment between the stimuli evoking the impulses. (SO, 2.49)

There are no pure sense data or facts; instead, all facts are embedded in a complex of relations with other facts which we may call, in the terminology of SO, a 'map'. From this map, which serves as a kind of first approximation, more permanent sets of classifications are formed. Hayek calls these 'models'.

> It is ... the process of multiple classification which builds the model. What we have before called the 'map', the semi-permanent apparatus of classification, provides the different generic elements from which the models of particular situations are built. The term 'map', which suggests a sort of schematic picture of the environment is thus really somewhat misleading. What the apparatus of classification provides is more a sort of inventory of the kind of things of which the world is built up, a theory of how the world works rather than a picture of it. It would be better described as a construction set from which the models of particular situations are built. (SO, 5.89)

These models are not complete representations of the world.

The mind's ability to build representations of the physical order from a necessarily set of models stems from the accidental fact that the structure of the world is 'redundant', to use Herbert Simon's term (Simon, 1969): 'It is ... no more than a fortunate accident that the different events in the macrocosm are not fully interrelated to any significant degree, but that as a rule it is possible to base predictions of certain kinds of events on a mere selection of a totality of events' (SO, 5.90).

Hayek's psychology is an evolutionary theory. The idea that the human mind evolves as part of man's struggle for survival dictates the problem:

> Our task is ... to show in what sense it is possible that within parts of the macrocosm a microscosm may be formed which reproduces certain aspects of the macrocosm and through this will enable the substructure of which it forms part to behave in a manner which will assist its continued existence. (SO, 5.78)

The mind works through a continuous process of classification and reclassification of sense impressions and of the classifications formed from them. This takes place in the central nervous system, which engages in a constant process of self-organization. This give rise to an ever more complex set of classifications in the shape of increasingly intricate patterns of connections among neurons. It is this evolutionary process which constitutes the working of the mind. To perceive is to classify sense impressions along neural routes which become more and more firmly established, and which in the end require no further adaptation. To use a term that has become familiar with the work of Simon, we may call them 'routines'.

This argument in Hayek's cognitive psychology has a parallel in his theory of society. A developed society has to a large extent become 'routinized'. This is a characteristic of what Hayek calls the 'extended order' of society. The spontaneously evolved social institutions contain a surplus of tacit over explicit knowledge. As Keizer writes: 'Civilization advanced by increasing the number of operations mankind performs without thinking about them' (Keizer, 1994, p. 216). This, however, is a mixed blessing. On the one hand, the advanced level of routinization frees a great deal of social energy for the creative innovation of the institutional structure. On the other hand, the progress of routinization makes it ever harder to change what has grown. Hayek argues that any intervention in these institutions may have unintended consequences, ones that may eventually lead to their total destruction.[9]

This parallel between Hayek's psychology and his theory of society is not an isolated instance. There are many more homeomorphisms. But this is not as strange as it might appear if one bears the following in mind. In Hayek's work, the theme of communication is a crucial intermediate step between his economics and his later theory of society as a whole developed in 'Economics and Knowledge' (1937) and then further elaborated in 'The Use of Knowledge in Society' (1945) and 'Competition as a Discovery Procedure' (1968). Communication failures are just as crucial in Hayek's contributions to the debate on socialism as they are in his business cycle theory. The response of an economy to these communication failures constitutes a process of social learning.

Also of relevance is the fact that for most of his active intellectual life,

Hayek endeavoured to solve the problem of explaining collective effects from individualist premises. Thus a large part of Hayek's effort in developing his economics during the 1930s was devoted to reducing the macro-economic phenomenon of the business cycle to the micro-economic theory of rational choice. The same type of problem is central to his investigations in psychology, viz. establishing the relationship between the microcosm of the human mind and the macrocosm of external events. Hayek's resumption of work on his cognitive psychology made him see the role of collective effects, and more in particular of social institutions, in a new light.

> When I look back, it seems all to have begun, nearly thirty years ago, with an essay on 'Economics and Knowledge' in which I examined what seemed to me some of the central difficulties of pure economic theory. Its main conclusion was that the task of economic theory was to explain how an overall order of economic activity was achieved which utilized a large amount of knowledge which was not concentrated in one mind but existed only as the separate knowledge of thousands or millions of different individuals. But it was still a long way from this to an adequate insight into the relations between the abstract rules which the individual follows in his action, and the abstract overall order which is formed as a result of his responding, within the limits imposed upon him by those abstract rules, to the concrete particular circumstances which he encounters. (Hayek, 1965, pp. 91–2)

And in the third volume of *Law, Legislation and Liberty* (1979) Hayek remarks:

> The work on it [SO] has helped me greatly to clear my mind on much that is very relevant to social theory. My conceptions of evolution, of a spontaneous order and of the methods and limits of our endeavours to explain complex phenomena have been formed largely in the course of the work on that book. As I was using the work I had done in my student days on theoretical psychology in forming my views on the methodology of the social science, so the working out of my earlier ideas on psychology with the help of what I had learnt in the social science helped me greatly in all my later scientific development. (Hayek, p. 199, n. 26)

4.3   A reliable system from unreliable parts

Hayek's argument that rationality is the property of a social system, and that a system is more stable and reliable than a collection of atomistic rational individuals is reminiscent of Simon's remark concerning the reliability of computers: 'The question is how to build a reliable system from unreliable parts. ... We can cope with unreliability only by our manner of organizing them' (Simon, 1969, p. 19). If we do not read Simon's 'organize' in the sense of consciously creating a system, Hayek's and Simon's ideas amount to the same thing. This is no coincidence. Simon is a cognitive psychologist and a pioneer in linking the analysis of human cognition and computer science, a field in which neural network theory plays a prominent part. Hayek's SO was one of the sources from which the neural network theory was developed.[10] These common roots account for the frequently striking resemblances between neural networks and Hayek's spontaneous-order model of society. To give just two instances, McClelland et.al. (1986, p. 3) answer the question 'What makes people smarter than machines?' by observing that 'people are smarter than today's computers because the brain employs a basic computational architecture that is more suited to deal with a central aspect of the natural information processing tasks that people are so good at.' Hayek's answer to the analogous question in the domain of society is that it is the social *structure* that is important; that is, the interaction patterns which make markets so much more efficient than the essentially sequential and hub-like processes and structure of central planning.

Another instance is the modelling of learning in neural networks as the strengthening of connections between neurons. This has its counterpart in Hayek's idea that successful interaction rules will be repeated more often than less successful ones, and become embodied in the tacit knowledge of social institutions. Another connection–strength model is to be found in sociological network theory, which will be discussed below.

4.4 Incentives

In his contribution to the debate on socialism, Hayek did not elaborate the problem of incentives as requisites for the working of the market. Ludwig von Mises, however, did, so he defined socialism as state ownership of the means of production, and focused his criticism on the absence of private property rights in a socialist society. Under this regime, individuals neither gain nor lose as a direct consequence of their own decisions, and therefore they have no incentives to balance costs and revenues optimally. This entails that under socialism real scarcity prices are not established, although they are a necessary ingredient for rationally calculating decision-makers. Without private property there is no rational calculation.

At the level of the social system, incentives play a part which is not related to rational calculation but to the cohesion of a social system as a whole in the face of opposing interests. Adequate incentives are required to maintain social cohesion; individuals in a society must be motivated to cooperate. For a particular institutional framework to be stable, a mechanism is needed whereby it reproduces itself over time. Bianchi has formulated the problem as the following paradox: when interests are opposed 'private interests cannot be generalized without losses, and what can be generalized (moral codes) does not obey private motivations' (Bianchi, 1994, p. 243). Neither Mises nor Hayek explain how opposing interests can be reconciled. Unless this problem is solved, a system in which individual knowledge and actions are coordinated and rational calculation takes place is not likely to arise, or if it does, it is not likely to be stable. The analysis of prisoner dilemma situations has made it clear that in situations in which everyone rationally pursues his own private interests and searches for personal gain, no social rules may arise without generating mutual losses. Even in the situation of a repeated prisoners' dilemma there is no guarantee of a cooperative outcome, i.e. a stable system of social rules. And even if an agreement to cooperate should arise spontaneously, enforcement rules have to be discovered if the interaction pattern is to be stable: 'without an evolved and continuously adjusting system of enforcement rules, conflictual interests will prevail' (ibid., p. 244).

Bianchi argues that Hayek's theory of competition as a dynamic discovery procedure contains elements for an explanation of the both coordination and incentive effects. Hayek conceives of competition as a discovery process which is instrumental in coordinating individual actions. However, competition has another function as well. It provides the incentives for outcompeting rivals, and this may have positive external effects.

> Competition is not only the place for arbitrage gains, for 'stepping in' and grasping first an opportunity ..., but also searching for, and the means of rewarding, new forms of gain. ... Vices are not replaced by virtues; they remain vices, only they become more sociable in their effects. Nothing guarantees that this form of socialization proceeds steadily and irreversibly ... But the learning procedure that is implied in the process will provide the flexibility for adjustments and corrections. The meaning of 'order' changes; it is not a state of affairs, but a process; not a correct state, but a corrigible one. (ibid., p. 245)

The appropriate institutional framework for the market is as much the object of continuous discovery as market opportunities themselves:

> On the one hand, a complex system of moral codes, rules of fairness, as well as an articulated system of punishments for the violators, has to be continuously discovered and adjusted. On the other hand, the search for competitive gains must always find new channels. In this different setting the market game, Hayek's game of catallaxy, not only teaches the players how to transform the enemy into friend ..., it also provides the incentive structure to discover and reward more social ways of 'defection'. (ibid., p. 246)

5 SYSTEM AND INDIVIDUAL

5.1 Levels of analysis

In the foregoing discussion the possibility was mentioned that an entire social structure is more reliable than the individual units of which it is made up. Closely related to this scientific question is the methodological problem of the basic unit of analysis, or the correct level of aggregation. In his early work Hayek was a staunch defender of methodological individualism. However, he gradually abandoned the individualist methodology for a holistic one, probably under the growing influence of evolutionary ideas in his social theory. After *The Constitution of Liberty* (1960), he no longer described the evolution and selection of institutions in terms of a mechanism consistent with methodological individualism. Hayek became alienated, so to speak, from the individualism of the Scottish philosophers which he had held up as a shining example. His later theory of the evolution of institutions relies on the holistic concept of group selection. This vague notion prevented Hayek from solving the problem of what incentives would be required to induce individuals to adopt rules that, though conflicting with their self-interest, had survival value for the social order as a whole.

Bianchi returns to Hayek's former individualism. She retains the core of his evolutionary ideas on social institutions without the conservative conclusions that Hayek himself drew from them. She shows that there is no need for holistic elements such as group selection. She also improves on Hayek in several other respects. She explains learning behaviour, which Hayek had not addressed, in terms of the incentives provided by the prospect of competitive gains. Moreover, she proposes a more satisfactory criterion for measuring the selective evolutionary advantage of a particular social system. It is the ability to learn which constitutes a selective evolutionary advantage of a society, rather than the criterion that Hayek proposes in his *Fatal Conceit*, namely the number of people that a society can keep alive. Bianchi's is a process criterion which is more consistent with Hayek's rejection, in his earlier work, of end-state criteria. But the main advantage of Bianchi's proposal of linking social selection to learning is that it may assist us to find ways of implementing a selection mechanism that benefits all members of a society. This will be elaborated below.

5.2 Social learning

There are two main aspects to the ability to learn in a social structure. One is discovery, the other is the transmission of knowledge. Theories on these aspects come in two varieties: there are those that emphasize structural mechanisms, and others that analyse these aspects in terms of the actions of individuals.

A 'structural' theory of discovery is to be found in Mises's discussion of the role of the entrepreneur in his contribution to the debate on socialism. Mises stresses the importance of positions in a social structure: 'Like Plato's philosophers, the directors so appointed [i.e. in public enterprises] may well be the wisest and best of their kind, but they cannot be merchants in their posts as leaders of a socialist society, even if they should have been previously' (Mises, 1920, p. 121). This is because '[a] merchant's qualities are not the property of a person depending on inborn aptitude, nor are they acquired by studies in a commercial school or by working in a commercial house ... The entrepreneur's commercial attitude arises from his position in the economic process and is lost with its disappearance' (ibid.).

In a more sophisticated form, we find a similar structural view of entrepreneurship in Ronald Burt's *Structural Holes; The Social Structure of Competition*. Burt models the economy as a network of agents who are linked to one another. There may be connections that are possible but which have yet to be realized. Burt calls these 'structural holes'. In this analysis,

> competition is a matter of relation, not player attributes. The structural hole argument escapes the debilitating social science practice of using player attributes for explanation. The relations that intersect to create structural holes give a player entrepreneurial opportunities to get high rates of return. The player in whom the relations intersect – black, white, female, male, old, young, rich, poor – is irrelevant to the explanation. Competition is not about being a player with certain physical attributes; it is about securing productive relationships. Physical attributes are a correlate, not a cause, of competitive success. Holes can have different effects for people with different attributes or for organizations of different kinds, but these differences in effect occur because the attributes and organization forms are correlated with different positions in social structure. The manner in which a structural hole is an entrepreneurial opportunity for information benefits and control benefits is the bedrock explanation that carries across player attributes, populations, and time. (Burt, 1992, p. 4)

Notice that Burt adds the concept of control to the Hayekian theme of information.[11] This opens the way for an analysis of dominance and power in markets which is lacking in Hayek.

The transmission aspect of social learning involves the ability of that structure to transmit information efficiently and without distortion. This is a topic that has been studied extensively in sociological network theory, and more in particular in the tradition of which Mark Granovetter is a prominent theorist. What is known as the strength-of-weak-ties argument contains an elaboration of the idea to be found in Hayek, namely that the transmission of information has to do with the overlapping domains of perception of individuals (see Hayek, 1945, p. 86). In network theory this is known as connectivity. I derive the following version of the argument from Flap (1976).

The basic assumption of the argument is that differences in communication behaviour are caused by differences in social networks. In their turn, the characteristics of networks are defined in terms of the attitudes of the individuals of which the network is made up. Individuals have various types of ties with one another. The intensity of the ties determines both the nature and the frequency of the interactions. Ties are distinguished in terms of the differences between individuals as similar or homophilous and dissimilar or heterophilous. It is assumed that homophily is correlated positively with strong ties and heterophily with weak ones. Another dimension of interactions or relationships is their multiplicity, i.e. the number of different social roles in which individuals interact. Multiplicity is positively correlated to strength. Hence we arrive at the hypothesis that the greater the number of social roles in which agents interact, the stronger their ties.

Flap then introduces the notion of cognitive dissonance, with intensity and frequency as its dimensions. These are linked to the strength of ties as follows. The stronger an individual's emotions, the stronger the dissonance; the stronger the dissonance, the more will information be distorted; the stronger the ties, the stronger the emotions; hence, the stronger the ties, the more information becomes distorted. The frequency with which information is distorted is introduced in a similar way. The more often new information is offered, the more often does cognitive dissonance arise; the more frequently dissonance arises, the more often will there be distortion of information; the stronger the ties, the less often will there be dissonance; hence, the stronger the ties, the less frequently will information be distorted.

Taken all together, these steps lead to the prediction that in the case of homophilous or strong ties, more limited information which is strongly distorted will be distributed less frequently over fewer agents. Finally, the openness of a network (i.e., the extent in which it consists of elements with weak ties) is linked to the open-mindedness of agents (agents are more tolerant of cognitive dissonance). Thus one arrives at the following theoretical prediction. The more a society consists of networks that are characterized by weak ties, the faster will more comprehensive and less distorted information be distributed over more agents who are more tolerant. Conversely, the more a society is characterized by closed or strong-tied networks, the more slowly will less comprehensive and more distorted information be distributed over fewer agents and agents who are less tolerant.

The above version of the strength-of-weak-ties argument offers a fruitful generalization of Hayek's argument on markets and the price system as communication mechanisms. This warrants more detailed comment than is possible here; I merely draw attention to the element of cognitive dissonance. Hayek defines the equilibrium of the individual as the state of affairs in which the individual's expectations are not falsified. This can straightforwardly be reformulated as the absence of cognitive dissonance. The strength-of-weak-ties argument was originally developed for labour markets. It is strange that with one recent exception it has never been generalized to an analysis of the functioning of all markets.[12] What it has been applied to, in sociology, are matters of social stability. Under the Granovetter approach, social relationships become more stable if individuals enter into multiple and weak social relationships with one another. This would explain why the communist societies of Eastern Europe, long after they went bankrupt in the accounting sense of that word, continued to function tolerably well. Their citizens entertained many more relationships with one another than the official blueprint of society envisaged and allowed.

5.3   Structure versus individual?

Both Burt and Bianchi describe a social discovery process, but the objects of discovery differ. Burt emphasises the purely structural phenomena of missing links or 'holes' which are bridged by entrepreneurs. Bianchi speaks of new forms of interaction. These have to do with the rules and motivations governing the behaviour of individuals, from which Burt abstracts on purpose (Burt, 1992, p. 35). In explaining competition it does not seem necessary to make this mutually exclusive choice between individuals' characteristics and their structural position. As Hayek observes in his writings on rule-guided behaviour, individuals have certain dispositions which must be activated. A rule is a disposition (Hayek, 1969, p. 43), a 'movement pattern ..., ordering principle' (Hayek, 1963, p. 45), 'a statement by which a regularity of the conduct of individuals can be described' (Hayek, 1967a, p. 67). A rule can be conceived of as a model of behaviour or a law of individual behaviour (cf. also Hayek, 1963, p. 37). Rules are not sufficient conditions for behaviour; they must be activated by 'a particular external stimulus or ... an internal drive' (Hayek, 1963a, p. 69). The behaviour stops when the stimulus ceases to be operative. In a social system the original stimulus may be deactivated by coordination.

> The orderliness of the system of actions will in general show itself in the fact that
> actions of the different individuals will be so coordinated, or mutually adjusted to

each other, that the result of their actions will remove the initial stimulus or make inoperative the drive which has been the cause of activity. (Hayek, 1963a, p. 69)

When one realizes that the sort of stimulus an individual receives will be largely dependent on his location in the social structure (which influences his perception of signals), this seems like a perfectly satisfactory way of integrating (individual) function with (position in a) structure. This is consistent with the methodologically individualist Granovetter tradition.

6 PAST BEFORE PRESENT

6.1 Prediction and stability

Bianchi's account of social order as the ability to learn is reminiscent of the pre-conservative Hayek of *Constitution of Liberty* (1960), who argues that social innovation is necessary for a social order to survive. The creation of new rules competing for the favour of society prevents that society from becoming fossilized in its old ways when the environment changes and requires new ways to cope with problems of complexity. But how can the conditions that favour competition be created? Or, more generally, how can we implement the idea of social order as the ability to learn? It would be contrary both to the nature of the competition process and to the evolutionary spirit of Hayek's social theory to presume that this can be achieved by imposing a detailed set of conditions.

Hayek's methodology offers some guidance. In the 1950s and 1960s he explicitly dealt with problems of complexity, both as a phenomenon in the social world and as a problem for the theory of science. He argued as follows. Even if we, as social scientists, know the laws that are relevant for predicting social situations, we cannot know all the relevant initial conditions. Therefore, detailed predictions are beyond our reach. This implies that detailed social engineering is out of the question. The most we can achieve is that sometimes, when we know the relevant regularities, we may predict that particular global situations cannot occur together. Particularly in his later work after 1960, Hayek gives a rather radical interpretation of this idea. Instead of thinking in terms of trade-offs, for example between more and less centralized planning, he constructs pairs of mutually exclusive states of the world. This is related to the fact that Hayek conflates the notion of unintended with that of unpredictable. This has been noticed by Plant (1994), who argues that whereas income redistribution may have unintended consequences for the functioning of the market, these consequences are not necessarily unpredictable. This is all for the better, because it may be necessary for the introduction and the stability of a market system to 'buy the loyalty' of those who are dissatisfied with the outcome of the market process. Predicting the consequences of redistribution may help us determine the extent to which incomes can be redistributed without destroying the system. The 'solution' Hayek offers is a moral one. The only thing we can do to preserve the market in the face of demands for redistribution is to educate the individuals within a market society into accepting that the outcomes of market processes may not be just.

It is much more fruitful to formulate problems such as these in more general terms. Constructing a theory that takes possible trade-offs into account is an advance from a scientific point of view as it leads to non ad-hoc explanations. For instance, instead of asking why the introduction of some central planning leads to complete centralization, one may ask if there exists a stable mix between centralized and decentralized decision-making. If one reads Hayek's work in this way, several other trade-offs may be found which are of relevance to transition problems, such as individual planning as compared to central planning, changing a social structure according to a blueprint as compared to change by spontaneous evolution. Underlying the latter is the more general problem of the correct mix of conservatism and innovation. Another possible trade-off may concern dispersed knowledge which must be coordinated, as compared to knowledge which is more generally available and needs less coordination

Let me return to prediction and stability. There is a different level at which predictability matters. For the participants in social processes predictability is an important condition for stability. To a certain extent this can be furthered by legal measures. The coordination of knowledge without the resulting 'contracts' being enforceable would not work. The crux of small-units capitalism is that there is a great deal at stake for all decision-making units when they enter into relationships with others. The situation is typically *not* one of a one-shot prisoners' dilemma (even though many small entrepreneurs behave this way). Under the Granovetter approach, relationships become more stable if units enter into multiple relationships with one another. This is another feature of a social framework that might conceivably be enhanced by ensuring that people encounter each other in as many different roles as possible. This makes for more tolerance, more stability and more open networks, hence for more opportunities for social learning.

6.2 Myths about markets

Discussion on the desirability and the feasibility of introducing a decentralized market society in Eastern Europe has been marred by the habit of comparing actual centrally-planned economies with an idealized market economy. Unfortunately, however, this idealized picture is about all we have. We just do not know how markets really work. The analysis of markets as conducted by traditional mainstream economics is a travesty of understanding. To begin with, they drew any teeth their theory might have by defining equilibrium tautologically as a state of perfect information (see Hayek, 1937, p. 42). They ignored the essentially dynamic character of competition by searching for static conditions under which particular market forms (misleadingly referred to as various types of competition) might exist. And they built models that claimed to give an individualist behavioural foundation to an analysis of a market system which centred on a representative individual, thus precluding any role for information, coordination, communication or the organization of the economy. There is even no exchange.[13] However, the feature of neoclassical Walrasian general equilibrium theory that probably renders it most useless for understanding markets is that it is based on the assumption of an interaction structure that does not fit a market economy. As Kirman observes (Kirman, 1983), the structure of a Walrasian economy is star-shaped. All transactions are modelled as being conducted via a central auctioneer. This is the structure of a centrally-planned economy, and it is paradoxical to apply this structure to a market economy, which has the structure of a network of multiple relations among individuals. Equally paradoxical is the fact that the only economy to which the standard neoclassical model applies straightforwardly is a centrally-directed dictator economy. It is only in a centrally-planned economy, where allocation and price formation is centralized, that the neoclassical allocation mechanism applies in its full force.[14] But 'once we break away from the "star-like" structures of a classical economy with central auctioneer, who trades with whom, and who passes information to whom becomes very significant' (Kirman, 1983, p. 107).

Paradox turned into scandal when the millions of dollars made available by the West to help the former communist countries create a market society were spent in the same West on hiring the preachers of this sterile mainstream economic doctrine.

The centralized star structure of a Walrasian or a socialist economy, is tantamount to a network in which individuals are connected by non-multiple, strong ties. The work of Granovetter and others teaches us that, from a communication viewpoint, a social structure of this kind 'will be fragmented and incoherent. New ideas will spread slowly, scientific endeavors will be handicapped, and subgroups that are separated by race, ethnicity, geography, or other characteristics will have difficulty in reaching a modus vivendi'

(Granovetter, 1982, p. 106). This is in stark contrast to the virtues that the neoclassical defenders of a market society claim for it.

The weak-ties analysis also suggests an explanation for the recent upsurge of ultra-nationalism in Eastern Europe. In the absence of a network consisting of weak ties, the central authority of the communist societies required a strong repressive apparatus with which to suppress the forces counteracting cohesion. As soon as that authority lacked the means for repression, many societies in the East fragmented into warring atoms.

In the foregoing discussion, I have defended the view that markets should be considered as social networks. I now wish briefly to draw attention to two other aspects of markets. First, markets, like other social networks, are constructs. They are social constructions in two senses. The first is that markets only exist by virtue of the beliefs of individuals; this directly relates to the fact that the perception by an individual is partly a result of his or her development, which in turn incorporates a learning process. Hence, whether a particular market exists and is stable (i.e. reproduces itself[15]) depends on learning processes. This is of direct relevance to Eastern Europe. Unless people are given a chance to learn how to play the social roles of which market relations consist, no market society will be established. The second sense in which markets are social constructions is that they are the result of a historical process of development which is in large part unplanned or spontaneous.[16] The fact that this process may have comprised episodes of deliberate intervention does not contradict this argument.[17]

The other feature of markets that I wish to mention involves the idea of collective or public goods. Markets rely for their functioning and stability on the existence of public goods such as money and a legal framework (see for instance Desai, 1986). Defenders of the idea that markets arise out of the perfectly free pursuit by individuals of nothing but their self interest are defending a myth. In so far as they invoke Adam Smith as their patron saint, they should know better. True, in *The Wealth of Nations* Smith focuses his analysis on self interest as motivating human action. But he is also the author of an earlier book, *The Theory of Moral Sentiments*, whose first sentence runs:

> How selfish soever man may be supposed, there are evidently some principles in his nature, which interest him in the fortune of others, and render their happiness necessary to him, though he derives nothing from it, except the pleasure of seeing it. (Smith, 1759, p. 47)

Smith develops the theory that disrespect for one's fellow citizens renders a society unstable.

Society may subsist among different men, as among different merchants, from a sense of its utility, without any mutual love or affection; and though no man in it should owe any obligation, or be bound in gratitude to any other, it may still be upheld by a mercenary exchange of good offices according to an agreed valuation. Society, however, cannot subsist among those who are at all times ready to hurt and injure one another. (Smith, 1759, p. 166)

In some former communist countries there are currently many signs of a form of pirate capitalism whereby partners in market transactions only seek their own short-term gain. This evidence suggests that Smith's important lesson has still to be learned. Smith is opposed to the idea, which he attributes to Mandeville, that man only heeds his self interest in his relationships with others. Clearly, there is a tension between Smith's criticism of Mandeville's idea of competition and Bianchi's interpretation. According to Smith, a society could not persist on the basis of a Mandevillean motivation of individuals. Bianchi, on the other hand, stresses the discovery aspect of this behaviour and argues that the learning process engendered by it makes for a dynamic type of social stability. One way to resolve the tension is to attribute to competitors the awareness that they all benefit from keeping intact the broad institutional framework which enables them to compete and benefit from others.

We have thus arrived at the second way in which collective goods are involved: markets themselves are collective goods. Markets emerge because at least two individuals find it in their interest to undertake an exchange. Whereas it is usually in the interest of the original market partners to exclude others from entering their own side of the market, it is equally in their interest to invite others to enter the opposite side. Suppliers will try to keep other suppliers out but they like to be faced by more demanders, and the same is true of the demand side. This is so provided those engaging in exchange understand that it is in their interest to keep a particular market in existence. Or, as Loasby observes: 'Arrangements which facilitate transactions often create externalities. They will almost always do so when the arrangements are designed to create a continuing transaction capability – in other words a market – which is accessible to many' (Loasby, 1994, p. 9). This is part of the mechanism whereby increasingly more individuals become involved in the market. The external effect of a newly-established market may consist of the fact that it serves as an example to be imitated by others. Once individuals stop behaving as one-shot maximizers, a market infrastructure may establish itself where there was none before. These external effects are a type of social amplifier, a mechanism that acts as a generator of value. Not only will needs be satisfied that could not be satisfied before the emergence of a market system, new needs will be created as well. And whatever one's subjective opinion of the intrinsic value of such newly-discovered needs, they provide opportunities for an increasing number of other individuals to participate in the social game of value creation.

6.3   Stability and the past

A system in transition needs both change and stability. Social institutions and the texture of the institutions that make up a society are such a complex whole of relationships and processes that we are only just beginning to understand how they work. Hayek argues that evolved institutions constitute a stock of social capital which took a long time to accumulate. Applied to the former communist societies this means that the eradication of the habits and other institutions that have evolved over the last seventy-five years is a destruction of social capital which may have (and already has had) disastrous consequences. The results of such a long evolution cannot be abolished from one day to the next. Doing so would leave a society bereft of any kind of stability: a highly dangerous situation. This is the mistake that Gorbachev made. Under the old structure there was at least some knowledge of the sort of behaviour patterns that could be expected. This explains why in almost every formerly communist country ex-communists were re-elected in the first free elections to be held. It was not because the voters wanted to reinstate communism; all they wanted was some stability. Given the alternatives, their voting behaviour was entirely rational. Having some structure, however unsatisfactory, is better than having no structure at all.

The history of a society matters for its future development. There is a division between, on the one hand, countries that have within living memory had an entrepreneurial tradition and, on the other, those that have been centrally ruled for much longer. Transplanting a social system which has evolved and been proven satisfactory in one culture to another may have disastrous consequences. The underlying traditions must match. If we had the time to introducing changes in Eastern Europe at a more cautious pace, we would first have to apply historical analysis in discovery of what may be called the social constants of the various societies. Social constants may be defined as behaviour patterns that are resistant to change, except perhaps in the long run. In Russia, for instance, the revolution of 1917 did not so much change the social structure (which had long been centralist under the czars) as the ideology. Of course, over time, this ideology helped to create a social structure that might not have evolved under the czars, but this is something that we will never know for certain.

7 CONCLUSION: FINDING THE BOUNDARIES OF THE CONTROLLABLE

If one wants to change, one must start somewhere, and even in an evolutionary framework respect for stability must go hand in hand with a vision of the goals to achieve and the means to apply in doing so. It lies within the nature of the complex evolutionary mechanism of society that the number of detailed measures to be taken, the number of variables that can be controlled, is limited. The problem is establishing the boundaries of the controllable. Hayek is certainly right to draw attention to the fact that what enters into this complex of problems is the notion of unintended effects. But as we have seen, unintended effects may to a certain extent be predictable. This creates room for social engineering. The conservative radicalism of Hayek's later work is unfounded, and an approach such as the gradualism of Popper's *Open Society* is defensible in Hayekian terms. It is in this light that one may try to implement Bianchi's proposal and introduce a type of social framework which favours the ability to learn. The creation of conditions under which this becomes, most probable may benefit from the type of empirical research conducted in sociological network theory. Enhancing the probability that individuals will establish and maintain weak ties will be conducive to the 'amendable society' that Bianchi advocates. Such an open society has to be supported by an adequate legal and political framework. In the end, for the former communist countries it is not the introduction of the market that is of the highest importance but finding a system which is both better adapted to each country's specific history and more adaptable to unforeseeable future developments. It is likely that this will be a decentralized system, but the insistence that it must be an exact copy of the market society of the West is as dogmatic as the one-time defence of centralized planning by Marxists.

NOTES

1. His other main contributions to business cycle theory can be found *in Prices and Production and Profits, Interest and Investment.*
2. Thus Hayek uses the term 'forced saving' to indicate a situation in which consumers cannot fulfil their plans.
3. For a detailed discussion of the contributions by Hayek, and of those by Mises, to the debate on socialism see Keizer (1994).
4. The most important early publications are the collection of essays in Hayek (1949), and Hayek (1960). In his later work Hayek is markedly more conservative in his conclusions.

See Hayek (1973), (1967), (1979) and (1988).

5. The references in the text are to the edition in Hayek (1949).

6. This is very similar to Popper's approach to social science. Watkins has coined the term 'negative utilitarianism' for this.

7. See for instance Hayek (1955a), (1963), (1964) and (1967).

8. Since the published version of 1952 contains the basic ideas of the manuscript of 1920, all references will be to the book.

9. Up to and including *The Constitution of Liberty*, Hayek is more open to the possibility of intervening in social institutions than in his later work. I will return to this topic in section 6.1.

10. See for instance George (1961, p. 112): 'The idea that the human senses worked on a classification principle had previously been suggested by Hayek (1952), and Uttley was able to build a simple classification system in hardware'. See also ibid., p. 319, and Rosenblatt (1958, p. 92).

11. Burt does not refer to Hayek (or to Mises).

12. Granovetter has concentrated on the labour market.There have been few attempts to describe the functioning of markets in general in network models. Some of the exceptions are the work of Burt, Morrison White and Mattson. See for istance Burt (1992), White (1988) and Mattson (1987). The present author is engaged in a research project with that scope.

13. See Kirman (1983). See also Garretsen (1994) and van Zijp and Visser (1994).

14. See Robinson (1956), and also Hayek (1941). This criticism is a variant on the criticism of the representative-individual model. Hayek starts with an idealized dictator-led economy and then subsequently introduces more decentralized decision-making. This makes the book compulsory reading for all those interested in issues of economic decentralization.

15. The problem of the reproduction of markets in a subjectivist context is analysed in White (1988).

16. The word 'construction' should not be taken to refer to a deliberate action; this also applies to the first sense. Contrary to the views of Mises and Hayek, it is not necessary for networks to exist that actors be aware of their attitudes.

17. Desai even argues that the free market society was the deliberate creation of the English state. Less controversially, he observes that, at the time when the philosopher now almost universally hailed as the theorist of the free market was writing, market society had not yet come into being. Smith's arguments in favour of such a society were as theoretical as are the arguments by Arrow and Debreu for the invisible hand theorem. See Desai (1986).

REFERENCES

Anderson, J.A. and E. Rosenfeld (1988), *Neurocomputing. Foundations of Research*, MIT Press.

Arts, W., S. Lindenberg and R. Wippler (eds) (1976), *Gedrag en Struktuur, De relevantie van microtheorieën voor de verklaring van macroverschijnselen*, Special issue of *Mens en Maatschappij*, Universitaire Pers Rotterdam.

Bianchi, M. (1994), 'Hayek's Spontaneous Order: The "Correct" versus the "Corrigible" Society', in Birner and Van Zijp, 1994.

Birner, J. and R. van Zijp (eds) (1994), *Hayek, Co-ordination and Evolution. His Legacy in Philosophy, Politics, Economics and the History of Ideas*, Routledge.

Burt, R.S. (1992), *Structural Holes. The Social Structure of Competition*, Harvard University Press.

Desai, M. (1986), 'Men and Things', *Economica*.

Flap, H.D. (1976), 'De kracht van zwakke bindingen of de zwakte van sterke bindingen', in Arts, Lindenberg and Wippler, 1976.

Garretsen, H. (1994), 'The Relevance of Hayek for Mainstream Economics', in Birner and Van Zijp, 1994.

George F.H. (1961), *The Brain as a Computer*, Pergamon Press.

Granovetter, M. (1982), 'The Strength of Weak Ties: A Network Theory Revisited', in Marsden and Lin, 1982.

Hayek, F.A. (1928), 'Das intertemporale Gleichgewichtssystem der Preise und die Bewegungen des "Geldwertes"', Weltwirtschaftiches Archiv.

Hayek, F.A. (1931), *Prices and Production*, Routledge & Kegan Paul.

Hayek, F.A. (ed.) (1935), *Collectivist Economic Planning. Critical Studies on the Possibilities of Socialism by N.G. Pierson, Ludwig v. Mises, Georg Halm & Enrico Barone*, edited with an introduction and a concluding essay by Friedrich A. Hayek, Augustus M. Kelley, 1975.

Hayek, F.A. (1937), 'Economics and Knowledge', in Hayek, 1949.

Hayek, F.A. (1939), *Profits, Interest and Investment and Other Essays on the Theory of Industrial Fluctuations*, Routledge.

Hayek, F.A. (1941), *The Pure Theory of Capital*, Routledge & Kegan Paul.

Hayek, F.A. (1945a), 'Individualism, True and False', in Hayek, 1949.

Hayek, F.A. (1945), 'The Use of Knowledge in Society', in Hayek, 1949.

Hayek, F.A. (1946), 'The Meaning of Competition', in Hayek, 1949.

Hayek, F.A. (1947), '"Free Enterprise" and Competitive Order', in Hayek, 1949.

Hayek, F.A. (1949), *Individualism and Economic Order*, Routledge & Kegan Paul.

Hayek, F.A. (1952), *The Sensory Order. An Inquiry into the Foundations of Theoretical Psychology*, Chicago University Press.

Hayek, F.A. (1955), *The Counterrevolution of Science*, The Free Press.

Hayek, F.A. (1955a), 'Degrees of Explanation', in Hayek, 1967a

Hayek, F.A. (1960), *The Constitution of Liberty*, Routledge & Kegan Paul.

Hayek, F.A. (1963), 'Rules, Perception and Intelligibility', in Hayek, 1967a.

Hayek, F.A. (1964), 'The Theory of Complex Phenomena', in Hayek, 1967a.

Hayek, F.A. (1965), 'Kinds of Rationalism', in Hayek, 1967a.

Hayek, F.A. (1967), 'Notes on the Evolution of Systems of Rules of Conduct', in Hayek, 1967a.

Hayek, F.A. (1967a), *Studies in Philosophy, Politics and Economics*, University of Chicago Press.

Hayek, F.A. (1968), 'Competition as a Discovery Procedure', in Hayek, 1978.

Hayek, F.A. (1969), 'The Primacy of the Abstract', in Hayek, 1979.

Hayek, F.A. (1973), *Law, Legislation and Liberty. Volume 1, Rules and Order*, Routledge & Kegan Paul.

Hayek, F.A. (1976), *Law, Legislation and Liberty. Volume II, The Mirage of Social Justice*, Routledge & Kegan Paul.

Hayek, F.A. (1978), *New Studies in Philosophy, Politics, Economics and the History of Ideas*, Routledge & Kegan Paul.

Hayek, F.A. (1979), *Law, Legislation and Liberty. Volume III, The Political Order of a Free People*, Routledge & Kegan Paul.

Hayek, F.A. (1988), *The Fatal Conceit. The Errors of Socialism*, Routledge.

Keizer, W. (1994), 'Hayek's Critique of Socialism', in Birner and Van Zijp, 1994.

Kirman, A. (1983), 'Communication in Markets: A Suggested Approach', *Economic Letters*.

Loasby, B.J. (1994), 'Understanding Markets', unpublished paper.

Marsden, P. and N. Lin (eds) (1982), *Social Structure and Network Analysis*, Sage.

Mattson, L.G. (1987), 'Management of Strategic Change in a "Markets-as-Networks" Perspective', in Pettigrew, 1987.

Mises, L. von (1920), 'Economic Calculation in the Socialist Commonwealth', in Hayek, 1935.

McClelland, J.L., D.E. Rumelhart and G.E. Hinton (1986), 'The Appeal of Parallel Distributed Processing', in Rumelhart and McClelland, 1986, vol. I.

Pettigrew A.M. (ed.) (1987), *The Management of Strategic Change*, Blackwell.

Plant, R. (1994), 'Hayek on Social Justice: A Critique', in Birner and Van Zijp, 1994.

Popper, K.R. (1945), *The Open Society and its Enemies*, Routledge & Kegan Paul.

Robinson, J. (1956), *The Accumulation of Capital*, Macmillan.

Rosenblatt, F. (1958), 'The Perceptron: A Probabilistic Model for Information Storage and Organization in the Brain', in Anderson and Rosenfeld, 1988.

Rumelhart, D.E., J.L. McClelland and the PDP Research group (1986), *Parallel Distributed Processing. Explorations in the Microstructure of Cognition*, 2 vols., MIT Press.

Simon, H.A. (1968), *The Sciences of the Artificial*, MIT Press.

Smith, A. (1759), *The Theory of Moral Sentiments*, with an introduction by E.G. West, Liberty Classics 1976.

Vries, R. de (1994), 'The Place of Hayek's Theory of Mind and Perception in the History of Philosophy and Psychology', in Birner and van Zijp, 1994.

Wellman, B. and S.D. Berkowitz (eds) (1988), *Social Structure: A Network Approach*, Cambridge University Press.

White, H.C. (1988), 'Varieties of Markets', in Wellman and Berkowitz, 1988.

Zijp, R. van and H. Visser (1994), 'Mathematical Formalization and the Domain of Economics: The Case of Hayek and New Classical Economics', in Birner and Van Zijp, 1994.

4. What Type of Capitalism is Produced by Privatization?

Hans-Jürgen Wagener

1 CAPITALISM: THE MARKET AND PRIVATE PROPERTY

Capitalism is a systemic paradigm which can be described from a Marxian as well as from an Austrian point of view. The Marxist would see its constitutive features as lying in the market and private property, meaning by the latter particular interests which govern the production process via property rights. (Whether 'really existing socialism' was indeed socialism in the sense that the common interest predominated in the production process through communal or state property rights is not at issue here.) An Austrian economist would likewise stress the market and private property as constitutive features of capitalism, meaning by 'private property' effective control over the allocation of scarce resources by means of property rights. The neoclassical mainstream has been rather indifferent to the matter until recently because of its lack of interest in institutions (see Wagener, 1992).

An Austrian and mainstream economist would argue that even if particular interests are the motive force of capitalism, they cannot govern the production process as long as there is sufficient competition in the market, which is the old Mandeville theme of 'private vices – public benefits'. The Marxist argues that sufficient competition is structurally impossible in the capitalist set-up. Hence corporate control is biased in favour of the possessing class, which is the old Marxian theme of 'structural vices – private misery'.

All three schools of thought agree on the dynamic properties of capitalism arising from private property rights. The Marxist, however, sees this growth as a process of permanent harmful disequilibria (business cycles, unemployment). The Austrian considers these disequilibria to be less grave or even functional (creative destruction). The mainstream adheres to the (rather utopian) view of equilibrium growth. To avoid misunderstandings, it should be remembered that in Marx's historical analysis capitalism is a 'progressive' economic system for a certain slice of historical time. The other two schools make no attempt at historical analysis and apparently view capitalism as a final state (see for instance Mises, 1949).

When the post-communist economic systems strive to institutionalize markets and private property, it should be clear from any point of view that what they are striving for is capitalism. Yet this word is often studiously avoided in that region, almost as if it had obscene connotations. Of course, since capitalism is a rather abstract system paradigm, it cannot constitute a concrete programme for the transformation of the former communist planned economies. There are numerous models of capitalism – historical (early, high, late) as well as national (the Swedish, the Japanese, the American model, and so on). This is not the place to analyse how these models have evolved over time; my interest focuses instead on the institutional means whereby the main functions of private property, static and dynamic efficiency are set in motion and on how the dysfunctional features of unemployment and alienation are checked.

A distinction is commonly drawn among three levels of decision-making in any modern economic system with the firm as its central production unit. These levels are determined by position within the organization (the shop floor, the intermediate operative, the strategic operative), by endowment with property rights (worker, management, owner), and sometimes also by socio-political stratification (worker/capitalist, worker/*nomenklatura*). The *differentia specifica* among economic systems are property rights. Hence, from a decision-making point of view, the real problem of transformation in Central and Eastern Europe is the privatization process. What I shall seek to establish is the foreseeable outcome of this process and why a concrete strategy has been chosen.

Before I address the central topic of privatization, however, three short sections deal with the governance implications of the three-level structure of decision-making. From this it follows that the most interesting aspect of privatization is the privatization of large-scale enterprise, since it is here that management and ownership are clearly separated, thereby giving rise to a control problem which is solved in different ways in actually existing capitalism. This is the active versus passive (or internal versus external) control examined in sections 5 and 6. However, as argued in section 7, the efficiency properties of capitalism cannot be separated from the market or competition. Section 8 examines privatization in Central and Eastern Europe in general. The Polish project (paragraph 9) may be characterized by the model of political control, while the Czechoslovak project (paragraph 10) tends more towards the bank-centric control model. Finally, some conclusions are drawn.

2   GOVERNANCE: PRINCIPALS AND AGENTS

Any modern economic system can be described as consisting of three main actors: workers, managers and owners. Systems differ as to legally admissible ownership forms (with socialism excluding almost all forms of private ownership and appointing the state as owner) and methods of coordination (with markets assuming the firm as their basic economic unit, while central planning subordinates the firm to a central authority, the state). This gives us three possible principal–agent relations which the state must manage in order to achieve efficiency (see de Kort, 1994):

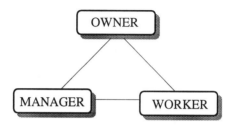

The (neo)classical assumption concerning markets was that with perfect knowledge and under perfect competition, classes or groups of actors did not matter: the optimal allocation of resources would be achieved independently of the internal organization of firms and of concrete owner–manager relations. There are three flaws, however, in the ideal neoclassical world: non-convex technologies, asymmetric information and positive transactions costs. This opens up a vast field of organizational alternatives, each of which must be evaluated according to its efficiency performance and equity properties. Above all, the question 'who hires whom?' is no longer irrelevant. Alternatives to the capitalist mode of the market economy may be fruitfully discussed (see Bonin and Putterman, 1987; Atkinson, 1993).

The original socialist assumption was that under communism there was no difference or conflict of interests among the three groups of actors; and that this, indeed, would cause them to disappear as distinct groups. The abolition of private property constituted organizational unity where the interests of all three groups coincided with the common weal. This assumption later proved to have been a fatal error, since their mutual relations were in fact of the ordinary principal–agent type. It thus became necessary to design appropriate mechanisms which would bring divergent interests into line.

3 THE MANAGER–WORKER RELATION

At first sight one might conjecture that the manager–worker relation does not differ greatly between the two systems. Although socialist managers directly monitored worker performance, they lacked the effective means to sanction performance.

Under classical capitalism, managers could wield the stick (dismissal) and the carrot (wages). Under ideal communism neither need be applied as an incentive: a communist, the theory ran, knew what was to be done and got it done. Under transitional socialism, the carrot was accepted by Marx, but the stick was banned.

The workers' quasi-property rights of guaranteed employment left the manager with only piece rates, bonus schemes, and non-work related perks – the famous material incentives – with which to stimulate effort. The system managers resorted to these incentives when it became clear that communist conscientiousness did not evolve instantaneously.

The socialist expectation may have been utopian, like many of the models of the labour–capital partnership. However, Japanese labour relations show that classical adversarial capital–labour relations are by no means inevitable or inherent to human nature. We should, of course, be careful not to idealize Japanese cooperative capitalism. Social dividing lines in Japan seem not to run between capital and labour (and whether they do in modern Western capitalism can also be questioned). They instead separate different groups of workers and, as under socialism, they relate to property rights, since the core employees of the large Japanese firms also possess quasi-property rights in their jobs and receive a sizeable share of the residual income (Aoki, 1988). Non-core employees of large corporations and workers in medium and small enterprises are in a much less privileged position. It could be argued that the position of the core employees depends upon the existence of non-core workers.

That is to say, it is not generalizable in a capitalist setting because market flexibility excludes universal and strong employee property rights.

However, for the moment we may accept the possibility of a non-hierarchical solution to the manager–worker principal–agent relation. The institutional features of this solution – leaving the Confucian ethic aside – are small work teams with decentralized management functions, the long-run material interest of employees in the performance of their firm, firm-specific skills, large conglomerate corporations allowing for internal flexibility, market assessment of the firm's results, and a sufficient degree of competition.

In the 1970s, the Soviet system managers tried to institutionalize a rather similar solution to their manager–worker principal–agent problem: the so-called 'new brigade' (Lane, 1987). Obviously lacking, however, was market assessment of the firm's results and competition, which also reduced the significance of the employees' material interest in their firm's performance and flexibility in reaction to structural change.

It is perhaps to be regretted that the central focus of the privatization debate in Central and Eastern Europe is on the ownership position or the property right to receive the residual income. All other property rights, especially those linked to labour organization, receive less attention and are left more or less to spontaneous evolution. It would be wrong, however, to hold that Western experience enables concrete recommendations to be made with respect to filling the ownership position, whereas with respect to labour organization it has nothing to say.

The owner (planner)–worker principal–agent relation is a feature somewhat peculiar to a planned economy. Although the planner is unable to monitor the performance of individual workers, he can stimulate them as a group by allocating means to the consumer goods sector and by regulating the distribution of income. It can be argued that there are two basic decision-makers in a socialist planned economy: the planner and the worker (de Kort, 1994).

The planner decides on allocation and distribution and the workers decide on effort, thus determining the volume of output to be distributed. This raises the question of the position of the manager in the planned system.

4   THE OWNER/MANAGER RELATION

In terms of his decision-making power, the manager occupies a rather weak position between the planner and the worker. But when his information capacity is taken into account, the manager plays a crucial role in the system. This is what makes the planner–manager principal–agent relation so important. It is a relation that has been studied sufficiently as far as static efficiency is concerned (see Weitzman, 1980, for example); but much less satisfactory in theory and in reality have been results with respect to dynamic efficiency or innovation (see Berliner, 1976). The lack of market test and competition have enabled the planner–manager relation to develop in an idiosyncratic and inefficient way.

We reach the conclusion that despite its hierarchical structure the planned economy has organized the relation between the three main actors in an incoherent or rather fragmented way:

Total control has to be exercised discretely. There is no automatic and constantly operating economic feed-back mechanism, like competitive market prices and capital markets, which controls either the managers' or the planners' performance.

The only control is political control by the Party. The Party leadership, however, is not distinct from the owner–planner. It has usurped this position and administers it by means of the *nomenklatura* system. Control by the Party leadership is manifest only in discrete events – either internal reform (cf. the demise of Kruschev) or political revolt (cf. the events of 1989) – both of which are dangerously destabilizing.

The situation under capitalism is entirely different. And this entails that the role of the planner under socialism cannot be compared to the role of the owners of productive resources under capitalism. The difference lies precisely in the control mechanism and in the motivation structure.

The capitalist owner is interested in more or less long-run profits. It will be seen later that there may be a difference between strategic interest and control deriving from a long-run engagement in a business and speculative interest and control deriving from a short-run engagement.

Simplifying, one may say that the capitalist manager has discretionary power over all strategic and operative decisions; while the owner tries to control only the use of this power and to ensure that it works to the benefit of the firm's survival and profitability. That is to say, his interest lies in the preservation and increase of the capital value. Welfare and economic optimality hinge upon prices and competition. There is no actor in the system who deliberately and directly takes system-optimality into consideration. (It will be recalled that the state is not treated in this paper other than in the owner position.)

The capitalist firm seems to be even more hierarchical than the socialist one:

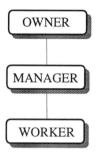

The crucial point is that parallel to the two principal–agent relations – that is, parallel to the internal structure of the firm – there exist markets which provide information and exert control: the capital market, the market for management services, the labour market and, of course, the goods market. Control is exerted continuously and it does not destabilize the system: bankruptcy may ruin an individual owner (and eventually the workers dependent upon him) but it does not rock the boat.

It has been frequently observed that the socialist planner's central interest is the maintenance of his position or, more generally, the Party's power. This does not distinguish him greatly from the capitalist owner, who is also loath to lose his position: the essential difference, in theory, is that the latter's power, or the value of his capital, depends exclusively on market performance. He cannot regulate and guide the entire economic system in order to preserve his power. The socialist planner never restricted his influence to monitoring the managers' performance measured in terms of profitability, since this, of course, would have presupposed a socialist market economy. The socialist planner's degrees of freedom, however, seemingly had a price in terms of efficiency.

5 PRIVATE PROPERTY IN LARGE ENTERPRISES

According to the conventional view of the market order, private property is a necessary condition for the efficient allocation of resources. One may nevertheless enquire whether the satisfactory performance of developed capitalism is due to corporate control by means of private property rights or to assessment of its results in more or less competitive markets, goods markets and capital markets (Dallago, 1994). There is Mises's old (1935) hypothesis that competitive market exchange presupposes private property rights – that is, distinct economic actors with full rights of *usus fructus* and *abusus* – which would make the question redundant. But this is not the practice of large-scale enterprises, which constitute the component of modern capitalism which is my sole concern in this paper. Besides, Mises's hypothesis does not imply individual private ownership, but only independent economic units together with freedom of contract.

The majority of firms engaged in large-scale enterprise are stockholding companies. Hence, formally, it is the stockholders' concern to control the managers. But are they able and willing to do so? There are personal stockholders and institutional stockholders. Personal stockholders, as a rule, have negligible stakes in a large firm's equity. Organizing themselves into an interest group to control management involves considerable transactions costs and creates principal–agent problems of their own. Personal stockholders consequently tend to be passive owners. In some countries, Germany for instance, they may delegate their control rights to financial intermediaries, thereby bringing personal ownership close to institutional ownership.

There are numerous variants of the institutional stockholder: other manufacturing firms, financial institutions (banks, insurance companies, investment funds, mutual funds, pension funds), public authorities. In most advanced countries, institutional ownership is the predominant form of 'private' property, with mutual funds and pension funds – where pension payments are capitalized – acquiring great importance. These institutions exert their ownership rights in quite different ways. Institutional ownership, however, only multiplies the principal-agent problem: who, one asks, owns and controls the institutions which own the large corporations? There seems to be the danger of a *reductio ad infinitum* here.

Generally speaking, however, this problem dos not arise. Apart from public authorities (the state and local government), the controlling institutions themselves are normally share companies controlled either by interlocking institutional ownership or by personal ownership. While mother companies, holding companies, and banks tend to exert active ownership control, mutual funds, investment trusts, and pension funds are, as a rule, passive owners. The purpose of the latter group of financial companies is not to exercise economic control over the companies in which they have invested. Their aim is instead risk diversification, which is sometimes reflected in regulations. German law, for instance, does not allow an investment company to hold more than 5 per cent of voting shares in a single company. And, most interestingly, the investment company's managers cannot be bound by a mandate from their formal owners in the exercise of their voting rights. Since there is freedom of trade, this causes little concern. Quite different, however, is the case of pension funds.

American pension fund trustees, for instance, are obliged to act in the interest of their members. (This regulation is reminiscent of Lange's behavioural rule that market socialism's managers should act in accordance with social welfare maximization.) The members, however, are unable to control the trustees' activities (see Alexander, 1994). Neither are they free to trade their pension fund rights. Yet pension funds hold considerable ownership positions in many sectors of the American economy.

The following table shows the huge differences among Western capitalist countries with respect to the distribution of 'private' property (Kester, 1992[1]).

Table 4.1   Ownership of shares of companies first quoted on the stock exchange, 1990–91 (in percentages of market value)

	Germany	Japan	UK	US
Financial sector				
Banks	8.9	25.2	0.9	0.3
Insurance	10.6	17.3	18.4	5.2
Pension funds	–	0.9	30.4	24.8
Investment and mutual funds	–	3.6	11.1	9.5
Non-financial sector				
Firms	39.2	25.1	3.6	n.a.
Households	16.8	23.1	21.3	53.5
Government	6.8	0.6	2.0	–
Foreign	17.7	4.2	12.3	6.7

There may be some statistical divergences among the individual countries. Nor does the table depict the situation of ultimate control, especially in the countries where the share of firms is high. In addition, the influence of banks in Germany is considerably enhanced by the practice of proxy voting, that is, voting rights attached to depository shares administered by the banks. This results in the fact that German banks control about one-half of all voting rights.

6   ACTIVE AND PASSIVE CONTROL

The problem of control thus comes down to the question: what are the practices and mechanisms of passive ownership and of active ownership? It has become commonplace to distinguish between two basic models: the Anglo–American market for corporate control and the German–Japanese model of bank-centric control. (It can be questioned whether the Japanese model of active ownership is correctly described as bank-centric. But since the Japanese model boils down to a similar result, oligarchic control, we may skip the details.) I should like to add as a third basic type the Italian model of political control. It should be clear that neither model is applied exclusively and in pure form in its respective region.

Where passive ownership prevails, capital market control is the only possible form of corporate control. A precondition for its effective functioning is that managers must react with their goods market decisions on the capital market performance of their firms. Appropriate reward schemes can be devised. There are, however, two problems connected with this arrangement: short-termism and imperfect knowledge.

It is said that fixation on the capital market performance of the firm induces managers to look for short-run success. (A similar argument was was advanced regarding the planned economies, where short-run plan performance targets impeded the development of long-run innovative strategies.) Empirical evidence does not always corroborate this hypothesis.

The problem of imperfect information has been addressed in the vast body of literature on the efficient market hypothesis (Malkiel, 1992). If capital markets were immediately to reflect all possibly available information on performance, neither market analysts nor active ownership control could rationally outperform the market. This does not exclude the possibility that they may successfully anticipate yet unknown future developments and become active as entrepreneurs.[2] Investment fund managers, for instance, sell a product whose quality depends not so much on their entrepreneurial effort to control actively and effectively the managers of the firms in which they work – which they simply do not do – as on their entrepreneurial ability to monitor the market instantaneously and to select the future winners.

There is only one minor problem with the efficient market hypothesis: if superior knowledge cannot outperform the market and hence cannot exist, how does the market do what it does? A tentative answer might take the following form: by nonetheless trying to outperform the market using any available information, all market participants work together to instantly diffuse all available information and transform it into perfect prices. By implication, any information imperfection must spoil the perfect market hypothesis. And indeed, its strong version is not generally accepted. Weaker versions of the hypothesis allow monopolized, non-publicized information to exist which is not immediately transformed into perfect prices. It makes insider trading possible and worthwhile while at the same time leaving scope for active ownership control.

In the context of the bank-centric control model, ownership is only part of the story. The other part consists of property rights based on credit contracts. In Germany and Japan the banks play a different role from their counterparts in the Anglo–American environment. Firms are financed to a greater extent by debt than by equity, which already gives the banks more knowledge and more influence.[3] Moreover, firms cooperate predominantly with one bank. Banks also hold the equity of large enterprises and they administer the ownership rights of their personal clients. And finally, investment funds and mutual funds, which are formally independent firms owned by their shareholders, are more often than not bank-centred and belong to the financial family of a bank. Japanese conglomerates are probably less bank-centric, as already said, but are instead characterized by cross-ownership. Yet it seems quite logical for the conglomerate bank to be the place of information gathering and evaluation.

The rationale behind the German bank-centric model is said to rest on the following principles (Walter, 1993, p. 22):

- the orderly restructuring of enterprises: the banks take over firms in trouble, restructure them, and then sell them to new shareholders;
- support for poorly capitalized medium- and small-scale enterprises through direct bank participation and credits that otherwise would not be granted;
- the efficient privatization of state-owned firms;
- the introduction of privately held firms to the capital market.

If this were true, the bank-centric model would be the ideal solution for the problems of privatization and restructuring in Central and Eastern Europe. However, Edwards and Fischer (1994) have carefully analysed the workings of the German system of corporate finance and do not find conclusive evidence for its alleged merits.

The Italian model of active control seems now to have been dismantled. It is, however, not solely a historical curiosity. Since it was based upon a sizeable share of state ownership in large enterprise and state property rights in the prevailingly public banking sector, it must be of interest to countries which, even after privatization, will have to live with similar shares of state ownership for a long period. The characteristic feature of the Italian model is the involvement of political institutions in the control of large enterprises. It should, however, be stressed, without going into detail, that the Italian model of corporate control has operated in a world of keen international competition, not equally in all branches of the economy.

What both models of active control, the political and the bank-centric, have in common is that a group of, say, two to five hundred senior managers cooperatively guide and control the large enterprise of the country. It can therefore be called the oligarchic model. In the bank-centric case the state is an independent regulatory authority which can resist rent-seeking activities. In the political case, rent-seeking should be rather easy: the oligarchic group is not controlled directly, apart from internally by its own members. Here, too, performance in the goods market and in the capital market is of major importance. This influence, however, works in the longer run, and this implies the alleged possibility of longer-view strategies under the bank-centric model. The growing internationalization of both markets probably enhances the influence of the market and reduces the scope for autonomy.

7   EFFICIENCY: PERFECT OR IMPERFECT COMPETITION

It is very difficult to assess the effectiveness of either approach. There seems to be no sound economic argument in defence of the Italian model (and its political support has broken down). There are indications that it has considerably distorted the price system away from the competitive ideal (Seton, 1985). Nevertheless, Italy has experienced remarkable post-war growth (Maddison, 1991). So too have Germany and Japan, and also in these countries the price system seems to deviate to a significant degree from the theoretical point of reference (one must admit that Seton's calculations are far too tentative to allow firm conclusions). Britain and the USA have been the slow growers, but approach the competitive price system fairly closely.

Under the accepted view, the bank-centric and the political control models produce long-run interests and control relations. Passive control is inclined instead to short-termism. It could be argued that enhanced stability as to expectations, rules, and personal relations has a positive effect upon motivation, risk assessment and risk bearing, and, in the end, upon innovation.

Another very preliminary hypothesis in explanation of this apparent contradiction with the received competitive market view links the control models of private property to the new paradigm of trade and growth theory: imperfect competition (see Romer, 1986; Helpman and Krugman, 1985; Porter, 1990). Under conditions of perfect competition, capital markets should be efficient in dynamic terms as well. Hence there is no reason why a market for corporate control could be improved by discrete active intervention, although this is by no means certain under conditions of non-convex technologies and imperfect competition. It is, however, not so much the active exercise of private property rights in the owner–manager principal–agent relation which can be held directly responsible for growth performance as the cooperative approach to growth and trade strategies which active

control allows as long as it works in an oligarchic context.

This uncomfortable conclusion immediately raises, of course, the question why the socialist planning system was unable to exploit the opportunities of non-convex technologies and imperfect competition. A tentative answer might be that imperfect competition is still competitive. The exclusion of all competition and risk of failure under socialism deprived the price system of any welfare-related content and produced a motivation structure which did not support welfare growth and innovation.

8   PRIVATIZATION IN CENTRAL AND EASTERN EUROPE

I now turn to various privatization projects in Central and Eastern Europe in order to establish the type of capitalism implied by them. Privatization in Central and Eastern Europe is characterized by a plurality of projects and a multiplicity of methods (ECE, 1993).

As said, this paper is only concerned with the large enterprise segment. It thus omits medium and small enterprise and with it bottom-up or evolutionary privatization. Of course, this segment should not be underrated as a source of innovation, as a training ground for managerial abilities and as the social basis for the capitalist system as a whole.

The ex-GDR constitutes the most straightforward case. By selling the large firms almost exclusively to Western, predominantly West German, investors, the *Treuhandanstalt* incorporated East German large enterprise into the West German property system. West German bank-centric control and West German codetermination now also govern enterprise in East Germany. Nothing new or unforeseen has arisen. This result has been condemned as colonization by some quarters. One can understand this resentment, given the extreme asymmetry involved, but if one takes the process into account, there is nothing unfair about it. If a Stuttgart-based corporation with equity spread around the world and control rights concentrated with a Frankfurt-based bank buys an ailing firm in Frisia, nobody mentions colonization. The asymmetry is implied by the decision to sell East German property. The organizational structures are the result of the adoption of West German law.

Nothing of the kind could happen in any other country of Central and Eastern Europe. There, the privatization of large enterprise must necessarily be innovative (which the *Treuhandanstalt* approach was only by virtue of its sheer size), and the resulting system of governance is by no means evident. Let us take the examples of the Polish and the Czechoslovak mass privatization projects. The Russian case might also be of interest, although the situation is still so chaotic that very little can be said about the intended or the resulting governance structure (see Meyer, 1993; Malle, 1994).

It is not the procedure that interests us here, only the possible functioning of private property as envisaged as the final outcome. The procedure adopted reflects the different starting conditions in both (or now all three) countries: a mixed system of sorts in Poland with state ownership and employee self-management, and more or less orthodox state ownership in the former Czechoslovakia. These different starting conditions are also responsible for the differing speeds of implementation. The Polish project was mapped out in 1991 and, in a slightly revised version, passed into law in 1993 (see Blaszczyk and Dabrowski, 1993; Chilosi, 1994): it has not yet been put into practice, however. The Czechoslovak project is already partly realized, with a first round completed and a second one well under way.

The core feature of both projects is the distribution of ownership rights to the total population for free. Formally, people must acquire coupons or vouchers at a nominal price which should cover the transactions costs of the procedure. However, once they realize that something is to be had for nothing, almost everybody will take advantage of the opportunity. In Czechoslovakia, however, the unplanned emergence of investment funds and their publicity was required before this news filtered through to the population.

9 POLAND: POLITICAL CONTROL

In the Polish case these coupons will be used when the National Investment Funds (NIFs) are privatized. One coupon will yield the same as shares in each of these funds, the number of which has not yet been definitively determined but will be between ten and twenty. Yet privatization of the NIFs is the final stage in the process. Prior to it, the privatization of state enterprises must takes place.

Again, owing to the procedural peculiarities, the number of firms to be privatized is not yet known. The equity of state enterprises will be distributed as follows:

- 33 per cent to one NIF;
- 27 per cent distributed more or less evenly among all other NIFs;
- 15 per cent distributed for free to the enterprise's employees;
- the remaining 25 per cent will stay with the treasury.

The obvious intention is for the leading NIF to exert active control rights, while the other owners, including the treasury, remain passive. It should be clear that the employees' share of 15 per cent has nothing to do with any form of employee capitalism, since these 15 per cent ownership rights are not structurally reserved for the firm's employees. They are distributed to the present population of employees in order to buy their consent to the privatization project (after all, they are losing self-determination property rights). But these shares will most probably be dissipated in due time.

The centrepiece of governance for each newly privatized firm is its leading NIF. The denomination 'investment fund' is therefore somewhat misleading. Unlike their Western counterparts, these investment funds are not pure risk diversifiers. Such might be their behaviour with respect to their minority stakes, but regarding the major engagements allotted to them, they act like holding companies; that is, as said, they are intended to exercise active control. The question is how they will manage to combine the tasks of risk diversifier and holding company. As the leading owner, each NIF will control twenty or more privatized firms. It may be assumed that, for reasons of anti-monopoly policy, competitors will be placed in different NIFs. This can be effective only if the NIFs do not collude but effectively compete.

The portfolio of a NIF closely resembles that of a conglomerate. This need not give rise to a tightly knit *keiretsu*-like conglomerate, but it should also be different from the ordinary Western holding of the kind typified by Nestlé or Unilever. Regulation of cooperation among NIFs or portfolio swaps has yet to be seen. But the idea that privatized firms will maximize their profits in competitive markets, and that NIFs will act as umpires to ensure that they do so effectively, seems rather naive. Even if the NIFs do not develop a corporate strategy, there will be pressure from below to exploit their linkages and leverage.

It seems almost impossible that the NIFs will become mutual funds with a staff of three to five professional analysts operating in an efficient capital market. This makes the question of who controls the NIF of paramount importance. The idea of hiring foreign expertise unaffected by any interest bias seems to have been dropped. In the first instance, fund managers are appointed and controlled by a supervisory council which is itself nominated by a government-dominated commission. This boils down to the Italian model of political control enhanced by the state's 25 per cent direct stake. After the privatization of the NIFs, their shareholders ought to control them; but since shareholders of investment funds exert, as a rule, their ownership rights only passively, there is a positive chance that the NIFs will remain government-centred.

Of course, it is envisaged that a capital market will develop which will make passive control more effective. But, first, the existence of a capital market does not exclude the oligarchic governance model, as evidenced by the case of Germany, Italy and Japan. And second, it remains to be seen whether the emerging capital market can be efficient. Assume that the NIFs stick to their majority engagements, which they may even enlarge by buying errant shares from the employees' stake. Assume further that the NIFs cooperate in the utilization of their minority voting rights and that they do not use these stakes for speculative purposes. The treasury more or less by definition does not speculate. So the capital market will be extremely thin, and there will be no professional expertise trying to outperform the market and thus contributing to its efficiency.

10   THE FORMER CZECHOSLOVAKIA: BANK-CENTRIC CONTROL

The original idea behind the Czech and Slovak privatization project was to create some sort of people's capitalism: the shares of privatized large enterprise were to be distributed to the population at large, while vouchers were to be used to buy the shares of privatized companies. Since these vouchers were transferable, they could be transferred to investment funds in exchange for fund certificates or shares. The emergence of investment funds (IFs) has been a largely spontaneous development which the designers of the project did not intend to be its centrepiece. This can, for instance, be deduced from the belated legal regulation of the IFs. This flexibility and openness to evolutionary developments is one of the outstanding features of the Czechoslovak project. On the other hand, this flexibility renders it impossible to specify the equity structure of privatized large enterprise. We know that, of the firms undergoing large scale mass privatization, 77 per cent of their equity was allotted to vouchers in Slovakia and 62 per cent in the Czech republic (Mejstrik, 1993; Schmögnerová, 1993). As for the rest, in Slovakia 3 per cent of shares are sold directly, another 3 per cent go into restitution investment funds, and 17 per cent remain with the treasury, of which 6 per cent are intended for later sale and 11 per cent should belong permanently to the state.

The Czechoslovak IFs are private companies set up by individuals or other firms, most of which are still state-owned financial intermediaries. At the beginning of the privatization process there were some 430 IFs competing in a market for the investment points of the vouchers, of which they collected 72 per cent in total. Public confidence in the IFs was markedly uneven: the ten largest funds – with one exception all bank or insurance controlled – collected about 40 per cent of all investment points. These investment points then were used to bid for the shares designated for mass privatization. Hence neither the destination nor value of the distributed assets was predetermined. The public, the small IFs, and the large professional IFs all competed for them.

In this case too, the IFs seem to be the centrepiece of the governance structure. The small IFs, if they act as risk diversifiers, together with the public and those who acquired shares via direct sale, form a potential for capital market control. But the large IFs most probably perform a dominant role and are liable to exert their control rights actively. The law allows them a maximum stake of 20 per cent in a firm. As Schmögnerová's (1993) empirical research shows, they tend to approach this limit, and would like the law to allow them larger engagements. Harvard IF, for instance, a smaller member of the above-mentioned group of ten and the only non-bank-controlled member, has a stake of 15 to 20 per cent in no fewer than thirty-seven firms, although we do not know the branch affiliation of the latter. But there were no restrictions in the auction process: the IFs were able to pursue a strategic acquisition policy.

Under the law, the IFs are obliged to sever links with their founding organizations within three months. But this requirement does not cover the possibility of networking. The idea that the IFs' shareholders will control them other than passively via the capital market is an illusion. They consequently either operate independently or within a corporate family which, given their founding institutions, could be bank-centred. *Investicná banka*, for instance, has set up sixteen IFs. Should they be expected to operate independently? Coalition forming between individual funds has already started, and interlocking directorates and strategic cooperation are therefore highly probable. As in Central and Eastern Europe in general, Czech and Slovak industry requires a great deal of capital in order to restructure. This, too, places the banks in a central position. The ingredients for the German bank-centred model of corporate control are all present.

11   CONCLUSIONS

We may conclude that Poland and the Czech and Slovak republics show a tendency towards the active mode of corporate control: the former inclines towards the Italian model of political control, the two latter towards the German bank-centric one. The Anglo–American model of passive capital market control can only be of secondary importance in the governance structure. This, of course, does not exclude the possibility that highly speculative capital markets may emerge. But we would not expect capital market performance to become the guiding objective of firm managers.

Assessing the efficiency of these evolving systems is even more difficult than it is in existing systems. We may envisage sectoral or conglomerate clusters of firms belonging to a corporate family with a financial intermediary or a state holding at centre-stage. The bargaining position of big enterprise *vis-à-vis* the state is impressive, more so under the model of political control than under the bank-centric one. In both cases the state has at least a minority stake in strategic enterprises, especially financial intermediaries. Firms' investment policy is coordinated and financed by the banks, whose equity is owned predominantly by the state but also by investment funds, by firms and by the public.

Interlocking directorates create a layer of two to five hundred exceptionally powerful individuals who guide and control the economy. Management skills are a very scarce factor of production, and especially in the transition from socialist planning to competitive markets. It could be argued that the oligarchic governance structure makes optimal use of this scarce factor. As latecomers to international competition, the economies of Central and Eastern Europe need strategic industry and trade policies. Economies of scale and scope must be detected and exploited. Again, imperfect competition prevails, but it is no guarantee of international competitiveness. We could equally well envisage an alternative scenario where competitiveness is provided by the more independent segment of small and medium enterprise, while cartellized big business is a bastion of inefficiency and a drag on development and growth which survives only through state protection and subsidies.

It may seem paradoxical, but there is a good chance that mass privatization will end up with the oligarchic governance structures of finance capitalism or state capitalism. Whether the usufruct part of private property will stay with the people depends on their behaviour as owners. If they seek a quick profit and sell out their portfolio, the concentration of property will rapidly ensue. If they stick to their portfolio and only adapt its composition to capital market performance, some of the traits of people's capitalism will be preserved.

Finally, a warning well known from comparative economic studies is in order. A governance structure that has seemingly led to reasonable efficiency and welfare in a 'Western' country may have quite different outcomes when implemented in Central or Eastern Europe, or anywhere else. The functioning of what I have called the oligarchic governance structure of Germany, for instance, depends on many different factors – political, cultural and historical – and above all on the intense international competition to which (West) Germany has traditionally exposed itself. When transplanted to, say, the Czech Republic one or several of these factors – of which economic analysis may not even be aware – may be absent, and hence performance would differ from the German experience. This is not an argument against learning and imitation; it is, as said, merely a warning against too high expectations.

NOTES

1.   I am indebted to E. Nijsse for this reference.
2.   In this sense, as early as 1902, A. Weber (1922) used the term 'speculation banks' (*Spekulationsbanken*) to refer to the German banks, because they actively engage in entrepreneurial activities with respect to production. Weber's view strongly influenced Schumpeter (1911) and Hilferding (1910) in their interpretation of capitalist development.
3.   Admittedly, this situation prevailed in the period of capital shortage. In the period of high development, large enterprises in Japan and Germany earned their investment funds, and banks had to seek other outlets for their funds. See, for instance, Tsuru (1993) and Edwards and Fischer (1994).

REFERENCES

Alexander, G.S. (1994), 'Pensioners in America: The Economic Triumph and Political Limitations of Passive Ownership', in G. S. Alexander and G. Skapska (eds), *A Fourth Way? Privatization, Property, and the Emergence of New Market Economies*, New York: Routledge, pp. 33–54.

Aoki, M. (1988), *Information, Incentives, and Bargaining in the Japanese Economy*, Cambridge: Cambridge University Press.

Atkinson, A.B. (ed.) (1993), *Alternatives to Capitalism. The Economics of Partnership*, London: St. Martin's Press.

Berliner, J. (1976), *The Innovation Decision in Soviet Industry,* Cambridge Mass.: MIT Press.

Blaszczyk, B. and M. Dabrowski (1993), *The Privatization Process in Poland*, Workshop on 'Privatization Experiences in Eastern Europe', Budapest, 21–22 May 1993.

Bonin, J.P. and L. Putterman (1987), *Economics of Cooperation and the Labor-Managed Economy*, London: Harwood Academic Publishers.

Chilosi, A. (1994), 'Property and Management Privatization in Eastern European Transition: The Economic Consequences of Alternative Privatization Processes', ACES Annual Scientific Meeting, Boston, 3–5 January 1994.

Dallago, B. (1994), 'Some Reflections on Privatization as a Means to Transform the Economic System: The Western Experience', in H.-J. Wagener (ed.), *The Political Economy of Transformation,* Heidelberg: Physica, pp. 113–43.

ECE (1993), *Economic Survey of Europe 1992–93,* New York: United Nations.

Edwards, J. and K. Fischer (1994), *Banks, Finance and Investment in Germany*, Cambridge: Cambridge University Press.

Helpman, E. and P. Krugman (1985), *Market Structure and Foreign Trade*, Cambridge Mass.: MIT Press.

Hilferding, R. (1910), *Das Finanzkapital*, Vienna.

Kester, C.W. (1992), 'Governance, Contracting, and Investment Horizons: A Look at Japan and Germany', *Journal of Applied Corporate Finance*, **5** (2), pp. 83–98.

Kort, J. de (1994), *Interactions between the Planner, Managers and Workers in Centrally Planned Economies*, Tilburg: Diss.

Lane, D. (1987), *Soviet Labour and the Ethic of Communism*, Boulder: Westview.

Maddison, A. (1991), *Dynamic Forces in Capitalist Development: A Long-Run Comparative View*, Oxford: Oxford University Press.

Malkiel, B.G. (1992), 'Efficient Market Hypothesis', in P. Newman, M. Milgate, G. Eatwell (eds), *The New Palgrave Dictionary of Money and Finance*, London: Macmillan, pp. 739–44.

Malle, S. (1994), 'Privatization in Russia: A Comparative Study in Institutional Change', in L. Csaba (ed.), *Privatization, Liberalization and Destruction. Recreating the Market in Central and Eastern Europe*, Aldershot: Dartmouth, pp. 71–101.

Mejstrik, M. (1993), 'Vouchers, Buyouts, Auctions: The Battle for Privatization in Czechoslovakia', Workshop on 'Privatization Experiences in Eastern Europe', Budapest, 21–22 May 1993.

Meyer, M. (1993), 'Vouchers and the Financing of the Russian Economy', *Most*, **3**, pp. 95–125.

Mises, L. von (1935), 'Economic Calculation in the Socialist Commonwealth', in F.A. von Hayek (ed.), *Collectivist Economic Planning*, London: Routledge, pp. 87–130.

Mises, L. von (1949), *Human Action. A Treatise on Economics*, New Haven: Yale University Press.

Porter, M. (1990), *The Competitive Advantage of Nations*, New York: Free Press.

Romer, P.M. (1986), 'Increasing Returns and Long-Run Growth', *Journal of Political Economy*, **94**, pp. 1002–37.

Schmögnerová, B. (1993), *Privatization in Transition. Some Lessons form the Slovak Republic*, Workshop on 'Privatization Experiences in Eastern Europe', Budapest, 21–22 May 1993.

Schumpeter, J. (1911), *Theorie der wirtschaftlichen Entwicklung*, Munich: Duncker und Humblot.

Seton, F. (1985), *Cost, Use, and Value*, Oxford: Clarendon.

Tsuru, S. (1993), *Japan's Capitalism. Creative Defeat and Beyond*, Cambridge: Cambridge University Press.

Wagener, H.-J. (1992), 'System, Order, and Change. On Evolution and Transformation of Economic Systems', in J. van den Broek and D. van den Bulcke (eds), *Changing Economic Order*, Groningen: Wolters-Noordhoff, pp. 23–65.

Walter, I. (1993), 'The Battle of the Systems: Control of Enterprises and the Global Economy', Kieler Vorträge NF 122, Kiel (Institut für Weltwirtschaft).

Weber, A. 1922, *Depositenbanken und Spekulationsbanken. Ein Vergleich deutschen und englischen Bankwesens*, Munich: Duncker und Humblot.

Weitzman, M. (1980), 'The "Ratchet Principle" and Performance Incentives', *Bell Journal of Economics*, **11**, pp. 302–8.

5. The Market for Institutions Versus the Strong Hand of the State: the Case of Eastern Europe

Svetozar Pejovich

1 INTRODUCTION

Judging from the results of recent elections, anti-free market parties (i.e. socialists, former communists and nationalists) are doing well in Eastern Europe, including the former USSR. This paper will argue that the growing strength of those parties is a consequence of people's frustrations with the transition process rather than a rejection of capitalism.

It is clear that in 1989 ordinary people in Eastern Europe wanted the socialist rule to end. Short of risking social breakdown, the new leaders in Eastern Europe could not immediately replace all the institutions and legacies of socialism. The end of socialist rule confronted them with two critical issues: (i) how to choose new institutions, and (ii) at what rate the new rules of the game should replace the old ones.

For several decades East Europeans were forced to live under a system that tolerated neither the free market for ideas at home nor contacts with the rest of the world.[1] As the socialist rule ended, they were certainly in no position quickly to identify alternative institutional arrangements and evaluate their expected consequences. There is, however, enough evidence to assert that ordinary people in Eastern Europe were in favour of capitalism as they perceived the system.

On the other hand, academics, media people and politicians in the West interpreted the end of socialism in Eastern Europe as a vote for capitalism as we understand the system.[2] The new leaders in Eastern Europe were encouraged to use the strong hand of the state to 'build' capitalism in their respective countries. For example, the International Monetary Fund and the

World Bank have been pushing East European countries, which need their good will, in the direction of rapid privatization of state factories and 'macro' stabilization programmes.[3] From the standpoint of ordinary people in Eastern Europe, the transition process appeared to be a substitution of one set of institutions for another, neither of which they chose for themselves.

The first section of this paper will discuss four major sources of pro-collectivist ideas and concepts in Eastern Europe. The second section will address the effects of the transition process on the median voter preference in Eastern Europe. Finally, the paper will outline a legal framework that could help East Europeans to close the gap between their perceptions of capitalism and the system's true characteristics.

2   THE SOURCES OF COLLECTIVISM IN EASTERN EUROPE

Major causes of pro-collectivist attitudes among ordinary people in Eastern Europe are the region's philosophical heritage, the radicalization of nationalism, the way East Europeans perceived capitalism during socialist rule, and investments in system-specific assets.

2.1   The region's philosophical heritage is quite heterogenous. There is more of a Western tradition in the Czech republic, Hungary and Slovenia than in other East European countries. However, the intellectual tradition of classical liberalism and methodological individualism, which is only a part of the Western tradition, has no roots in the region.[4]

The prevailing concept of the community in the region is not a voluntary association of free individuals who join and leave the community in the pursuit of their private ends. The community is seen as an organic collective with common values to which individuals are expected to subordinate their private ends. Over time, this concept of the community has produced a tradition which links ordinary people together through communalism, political hierarchy, shared values, shared tradition and ethnicity. This tradition is conducive to communalism, welfarism, economic controls and political hierarchy but not to methodological individualism, rewards based on performance, the exchange culture of capitalism, and a government under law.

This collectivist tradition affects the behaviour of ordinary people in Eastern Europe. They see the gains from exchange as a redistribution of wealth within the community rather than as rewards that individuals receive for creating new value.[5] State authorities are more likely to exclude those who earn large profits by producing and selling goods whose supplies are low relative to demand than to encourage others to emulate them in open markets. Members of collective farms in Russia are making life difficult for farmers who choose to go private. Small shop owners in Ukraine are treated as second-class citizens. There is also a common conviction in Eastern Europe that resources are found rather than created. Thus, the accumulation of private wealth in many East European communities is suspect.

Capitalism has overcome similar problems in many other countries with strong collectivist traditions. While ordinary people in post-communist Eastern Europe seem to be turning away from capitalism, many other traditional communities around the world have accepted the system. Chile, Japan, South Korea and Taiwan, among others, have permitted their people to experiment with alternative institutional arrangements and adopt those which pass the market test. Eventually, most of those societies have ended up with a blend of capitalist institutions and old traditions. On the other hand, the new leaders in Eastern Europe, with considerable support from the West, have used the strong hand of the state to 'give' capitalism to their people. An implication is that the method of institutional choice matters.[6]

2.2   Nationalism is another major cause of the growing strength of pro-collectivist parties in Eastern Europe. It represents the conviction that the community's common good transcends the private ends of its members. The implication is that the individual can attain his/her greatest potential only through his/her 'nationality'. Nationalism thus suppresses individual liberty and competitive markets.[7]

Nationalism is not the monopoly of Eastern Europe. We observe strong nationalistic movements in Ireland, Canada, Germany and Italy. However, nationalism in Eastern Europe has two specific characteristics which have influenced the transition path in the region.

First, nationalism is specific to a group of people who share the same traditions and values. In Eastern Europe, these groups of people are members of the same ethnic groups.[8] Since the old ethos in most East European communities is a repository of unsettled scores among the region's ethnic groups,[9] an important implication is that interactions within each ethnic group are subject to rules of the game that do not necessarily hold in exchanges across ethnic lines. Nationalism creates incentives for members of each ethnic group to be cautious at best and hostile at worst in dealing with 'aliens'.

Second, as socialist rule ended in Eastern Europe, the ruling elite had incentives to seek ways to maintain its privileges. In order to preserve the value of their human capital, which is specific to a bureaucratic environment, former communists had somehow to maintain a state-centred system. To accomplish this, they had to convince their people that other ethnic groups were either threatening their political independence, or trying to steal their resources, or both. With many unsettled scores from the past, these arguments were rather easy to sell.

In the process, the former 'internationalists' quickly turned themselves into the most zealous nationalists. Many current leaders in Eastern Europe, such as Meciar in Slovakia, Kucan in Slovenia, Milosevich in Serbia and Kravchuk in Ukraine, were loyal communists up to 1989. By using nationalism as a vehicle to preserve their power and privileges, former nomenklaturists are setting back the development of individual liberty in Eastern Europe.[10] The case of Czechoslovakia is a good example. The Czechs, with virtually no former communists in positions of influence on public policy, are treating nationalism as a nuisance. And they are well along the path of economic recovery from socialism.[11] On the other hand, Meciar has remained in power by adroitly exploiting Slovak nationalism. As of late 1993, the Slovak economy is declining and so too is the cause of liberty in that country.

2.3   After half a century (seven decades in the former USSR) of Marxist indoctrination, East Europeans did not and could not see capitalism as a way of life in which each and every individual bore the value consequences of his/her decisions. The prevailing perception of capitalism in Eastern Europe was to identify it with bountiful supplies of goods and equally large incomes to buy those goods. The benefits of capitalism were somehow to be captured with neither a change in work ethic nor a reduction in prevailing welfare benefits.

2.4   East Europeans had no opportunity to save and invest in 'owned' assets during socialist rule. Instead, the state provided them with assets that are specific to a non-private-property economy. Those assets consisted of: (i) a variety of welfare benefits such as job security, allowances for children, medical benefits and subsidized housing, and (ii) the shortage economy. A well-defined group of East Europeans finds the returns from those assets irreplaceable.

Older workers see capitalism as a threat to their current and future benefits from system-specific assets. They fear, and for good reason, that the remainder of their working lives will not be long enough to allow them to replace those benefits with private saving and investments. Retired people have already seen a decline in the value of their pensions and other benefits. In addition, the shortage economy made them an important asset to their families in two ways: first, they had time to wait in line for consumer goods; second, they specialized in knowing what goods would be available, where and when they were going to be available. They thus raised the real incomes of their families. As scarcity prices replace price controls, retired people fear that they will become a liability to their families.

Predictably, older workers and retirees perceive capitalism as a real threat to the value of their assets accumulated during socialist rule. They did not purchase those assets by choice but that is all they got. Thus a major segment of the population in Eastern Europe is hostile to capitalism for reasons of self-interest, whatever their ideological preference might be. The evidence is consistent with this assertion. Young people, who have made no investment in the old system's specific assets, are strong supporters of the transition to capitalism, while older workers and retired people tend to support pro-collectivist parties.

3   THE TRANSITION AND ANTI-FREE MARKET ATTITUDES

The transition process in Eastern Europe has been a heaven-sent gift for academics, media people and politicians in the West. And they have responded by flooding the intellectual market with numerous proposals and schemes advising the new leaders in Eastern Europe on how to use the strong hand of the state to build capitalism. Even many free-market oriented economists have joined in advocating the method of institutional change which they consistently condemn at home. Most of those transition models endorse institutional changes, such as the privatization of state factories[12] and methods for organizing production,[13] which must be introduced by fiat.

Some spontaneous institutional changes have occurred in Eastern Europe. For example, private-ownership firms have emerged in most countries even though private property rights are yet to enjoy credible legal guarantees. However, for reasons discussed earlier in the paper, exogenous institutional changes have dominated the transition from socialism to capitalism. This section of the paper analyses some specific and predictable effects exerted by the transition process via exogenous changes on the preferences of the median voter in Eastern Europe.

3.1   Exogenous changes are outcome-oriented. They require an activist government for their imposition and maintenance. In Eastern Europe, the role of the strong hand of the state in the transition process is usually justified by reference to either the 'public interest' or to the efficiency enhancing consequences of capitalist institutions. Both of these justifications are misleading.

The public interest argument assumes that a social welfare function exists and that public decision-makers know it. Both assumptions depend on a miracle which is not derivable from scientific knowledge. To justify exogenous changes by reference to the maximization paradigm of economic theory conveys a message that capitalism is a 'mechanism' for the allocation of resources which, by implication, may or may not outperform alternative institutional arrangements. This is a harmful message because the critical difference between capitalism and alternative arrangements does not lie in comparative performance.[14]

Capitalism is a process within which individuals voluntarily interact in the pursuit of their own private ends and by so doing create an order. The spontaneous order which the market achieves is a way of life which derives its energies and behavioural incentives from the right of ownership, contractual freedom and a government under law. An important positive aspect of this spontaneous order is that the value of resources in their alternative uses are identified by the only source of value: the individual. Buchanan wrote: 'Economic performance can only be conceived in values; but how are values determined? By prices, and prices emerge only in markets. They have no meaning in a non-market context',[15] where choice-influenced opportunity costs are ignored. Hence, any comparison of capitalism with socialism on the basis of traditional efficiency criteria is devoid of meaning.[16]

3.2   Another consequence of exogenous changes is a contraction in the social opportunity set.[17] Two factors are responsible for this outcome. First, exogenous changes interfere with 'the constraints that are voluntarily arrived at when individuals are free to impose restrictions upon themselves'.[18] The result is a distortion in social benefits and social costs relative to individuals' valuations of resource uses, which in turn encourages economic activities with social benefits lower than their social costs. For example, protectionism requires substantial investment of resources in the political process. 'Social costs of [protectionism are] usually overlooked in the political process whereas some private benefits are much touted as social gains.'[19] The result is a contraction in the social opportunity set.

Second, we live in a world of uncertainty and incomplete knowledge. This means that social engineers and public decision-makers do not and cannot possess reliable information about the economy's dynamic responses to exogenous institutional changes.[20] Individuals do not always behave in ways policy-makers expect them to behave. A dissipation of resources is therefore a predictable consequence of the transition process in Eastern Europe.

3.3   Finally, the people who impose and those who implement exogenous changes are not the same. Local bureaucrats in charge of implementing political and economic reforms have considerable discretionary powers in interpreting the intent of policy-makers. They also have their own incentives and private ends which are likely to differ from those of their superiors. A predictable outcome is a difference between the intended and actual results of the transition process. Responding to a paper presented by Professor Jermakowicz, an 'expert' on privatization in Poland, at the Hayek Symposium in Freiburg, 1992, Naishul, a free-market economist from Russia and a former employee of GOSPLAN, made an interesting observation. He said that the language social engineers use today is the same language that the Soviet planners used yesterday.

To conclude, the transition process via exogenous changes could not and did not deliver the goods. It has also failed to educate East Europeans about the basic characteristics of capitalism. We should not be surprised that they attribute the results of the transition process to capitalism. The growing strength of pro-collectivist parties is thus a predictable consequence of the transition process.

4   AN ALTERNATIVE: THE MARKET FOR INSTITUTIONS[21]

The end of socialism was supposed to bring freedom to East Europeans. And the basic premise of a free society is to let people make their own choices. If a society of free and responsible individuals were genuinely the objective of the new leaders in Eastern Europe they should have accentuated the development of competitive markets for institutions.

The market for institutions is a process which allow individuals to select the rules of the game for their community. Through their voluntary interactions, individuals evaluate the prevailing rules, and identify and test new ones. The critical function of competitive markets is thus to encourage institutional innovations and adaptive behaviours.

The market for institutions accomplishes this function by providing individuals with strong incentives and low transaction costs in seeking contractual agreements which they perceive to be their best options. 'Successes' and 'failures' emerge from these voluntary interactions. The former are copied by others and eventually institutionalized.[22] These institutional arrangements, which are produced within the system, are self-sustaining and in (continuous) competition with alternative rules. Examples of spontaneous institutional changes in the United States are the law of limited liability, stock exchanges and the private-ownership firm.

The market for institutions in Eastern Europe would enhance individual liberty by enabling the preferences of the median voter to determine both the transition path and the rate of institutional change in the region. Instead of being replaced by the strong hand of the state, the prevailing institutions in the region would have to compete with new ones freely chosen by the people. Some old institutions would survive, but many more would expire. A few critical requirements for the development of the market for institutions in post-communist Eastern Europe are:

4.1   A credible and stable legal system. The major function of law is to foster the predictability of behaviour. And the predictability of behaviour requires a set of credible[23] and stable rules.

Legal rules provide people with some specific benefits and impose on them some specific costs. From the standpoint of an individual, the benefit of a rule is the predictability of other people's behaviour. The cost of the same rule is the satisfaction s/he has to forgo by not being able to engage in some specific activities. In general, the flow of benefits from law depends on its stability and credibility.[24] In the passage of time, people learn how to adjust to the rules, identify the opportunities allowed by the rules, and exploit the most beneficial ones.

However, were the rules to change every year or so, the process of 'relearning' the rules would reduce people's ability to maintain and to enhance the flow of benefits from law. Frequent changes in the rules increase the risk and uncertainty associated with exchanges that have future consequences (e.g. the purchase of land, investment decisions, and non-simultaneous exchanges). A stable and credible set of rules removes this bias. Buchanan wrote: '[In a capitalist society] there is an explicit prejudice in favor of previously existing rules, not because change itself is undesirable, but for the much more elementary reason that only such a prejudice offers incentives for the emergence of voluntary negotiated [contracts] among the parties themselves. Indirectly, therefore, this prejudice guarantees that resort to the authority of the state is effectively minimized'.[25]

In Eastern Europe, socialist rule subjugated the rule of law to the will of the ruling elite and totally undermined the people's confidence in enforcement mechanisms. If the objective of new leaders in Eastern Europe IS the development of competitive markets for institutions, one of their top priorities should be to establish the tradition of the rule of law and independent courts in their respective countries. The jury is still out but it is clear that some countries (the Czech Republic and Hungary) are doing better than most others.[26]

4.2   Equal legal protection of all property rights. Property rights are relations among individuals that arise from the existence of scarce goods and pertain to their use. They are not relations between individuals and things. When I say that I own a computer, I am defining the relationship between myself and all other individuals with respect to the right to use that computer.

The effects of the right of ownership on economic behaviour derive from the exclusivity of ownership, the transferability of ownership, and the constitutional guarantees of ownership.[27] These three fundamental components of private property rights provide incentives that have specific and predictable effects on both the terms and extent of individual interactions. Interference with any of them obscures those effects.

In Eastern Europe, private property rights were suppressed during socialist rule. Today, the attitudes of the new leaders in Eastern Europe range from encouraging private property rights in productive assets (e.g. The Czech Republic, Hungary) to tolerating them (e.g. Romania, Serbia). However, credible guarantees[28] of private property rights have yet to be forthcoming in Eastern Europe.[29] This is why the development of private property rights in Eastern Europe has taken two parallel paths. One is privatization of state-owned firms via the strong hand of the state. The spontaneous development of small private firms is the other.

The privatization of large state-owned firms has failed to enhance the appreciation of private property rights in Eastern Europe for several reasons. First, many state-owned firms cannot survive in open-market competition. Unfortunately, ordinary people in Eastern Europeans tend to attribute their failures (bankruptcies, unemployment) to capitalism. It would be quite educational and more efficient to leave the state-owned firms alone to compete with other types of business enterprise, even at a price of subsidizing them over a limited number of years. Second, in many parts of the region, former managers and party leaders have been able to use their positions to profit from privatization. Many East Europeans find economic reforms which reward their former oppressors somewhat distasteful.[30] Third, in many East European countries, a number of restrictions on the right of ownership increases transaction costs of moving resources to their highest-valued. A consequence of those restrictions is to impair East Europeans' perceptions of the benefits of private property rights. Fourth, by relying on the strong hand of the state to change the prevailing ownership rights, privatization does not enhance the stability and credibility of the rule of law.

The development of the market for institutions in Eastern Europe thus requires credible guarantees of: (i) the right of non-attenuated ownership, (ii) equal legal protection of all property rights, (iii) equal fiscal treatment of all sources of income (which is a corollary of ii), and (iv) efficient financial markets. These guarantees would provide East Europeans with strong incentives and low transaction costs in exploring alternative institutional arrangements.

4.3   Freedom of exchange and law of contract. Individuals enter into voluntary exchange because they expect that the exchange will make them better off. The benefit from exchange is the increment in satisfaction a person derives from acquiring a bit of something s/he values.

The costs of exchange is the satisfaction that a person has to forgo. With uncertainty and incomplete information, the benefits and costs of exchange are based on expectations.

The freedom of exchange means that individuals are free to identify opportunities for exchange, seek new ones, and negotiate terms of exchange in accordance with their preferences.[31] However, in the absence of a credible enforcement mechanism, transaction costs of exchange can be substantial. An implication of high transaction costs is a reduction in the extent of exchange, which is not a desirable outcome.

The law of contract reduces the transaction costs of free exchange in several ways. By holding people to their promises, contracts reduce the transactions costs of exchanges which are either non-simultaneous (purchasing a car on credit) or which have consequences that arise after the agreement has been concluded (i.e. investment decisions), or both. With uncertainty and incomplete knowledge, standardized contracts, trade customs, warranties and similar devices reduce the costs of negotiating exchanges by assigning in advance the losses and gains involved by the various contingencies.

The law of contract also reduces transaction costs by preventing opportunistic behaviour.[32] Finally, the law of contract enhances the selection of most efficient types of business firms.[33]

Freedom of exchange and the law of contract combine to encourage individuals to seek and negotiate the most advantageous contracts regardless of the length of time over which their consequences are expected to occur. Some types of contracts pass the market test, while some others do not. Those that are repeatedly observed are eventually institutionalized (i.e. the law of limited liability). Freedom of exchange and the law of contract are thus efficiency-enhancing components of the market for institutions.

The efficiency effects of freedom of exchange and the law of contract depend on the tradition of the rule of law and scarcity prices. Neither condition is fully satisfied in Eastern Europe, although the remaining price controls seem to be on the way out in the region.

5   CONCLUSIONS

The transition process 'imposed' some institutions of capitalism in Eastern Europe with little regard for the region's philosophical heritage, traditions, and the allocation of the costs of transformation. By identifying the results of the transition process with capitalism, East Europeans are voting free-market parties out of power.

An alternative approach to institutional changes in Eastern Europe is to allow people to choose their way of life. Spontaneous institutional changes cannot guarantee that East Europeans will choose capitalism. However, the market for institutions would give them an opportunity to identify alternative arrangements, try them out, adjust to their consequences, and select those they prefer.

Indeed, we already observe thousands of small private firms – mostly kiosks and miniature shops – which have spontaneously emerged throughout Eastern Europe in spite of the absence of credible legal guarantees of private property rights. Many of those shops will not survive, but some will grow. While their economic significance is still modest, private enterprises are the breeding ground for entrepreneurs, for a work ethic, for a capitalist exchange culture and for positive attitudes toward capitalism in general. They educate ordinary people into an appreciation of a way of life which rewards performance, promotes individual liberties and places high value on self-responsibility[34] and self-determination.

I conjecture that, in an environment which guarantees freedom of choice, the institutions of capitalism will eventually win the competition with other types of institutions. In addition to their contributions to individual liberty and to superior economic performance,[35] the institutions of capitalism are also uniquely suited to eliminating the ugly phenomenon of nationalism. 'Driven by their self-interest, people would, sooner or later, learn to judge others on merit and performance rather than on ethnic origin. Thus, the institutions that promote and strengthen a society of free and responsible individuals could spontaneously curb the rise of nationalism in Eastern Europe and reduce nationalism's menace to the transition process.'[36]

NOTES

1. Yugoslavia was the only exception.
2. This paper defines capitalism as a system based on private ownership, contractual freedom, a government under law, and the behavioural principles of self-interest, self-responsibility and self-determination.

3. See Odling-Smee et al. (1992, p. 35).

4. Classical liberalism means individual liberty, openness to new ideas, tolerance of all views, and a government under law. Methodological individualism is a method for understanding social phenomena. The individual is the only decision-maker; that is, corporations, governments and other entities cannot make decisions, only individuals can. To understand the behaviour of any entity, it is necessary to identify the incentives under which its leaders operate. For example, it is meaningless to compare the behaviour of private and public firms using the same objective function.

5. For example, 'The Rumanians clearly resent the fact that some Gypsy groups have rapidly become rich, mainly owing to their activities. Almost every account of clashes between Rumanians and Gypsies includes the list of riches found in the Gypsy houses.' (Ionescu, 1991, p. 25.)

6. Given the importance of the method of institutional choice for the purpose of this paper, let us restate the difference between endogenous (spontaneous) and exogenous institutional changes:

Suppose there is an event that creates new opportunities for individuals to interact. If the prevailing institutional structures are poorly attuned to those opportunities and fail to enforce new interactions, utility-seeking individuals will generate spontaneous pressure to modify the rules of the game to embrace the novelty. For example, technological developments made mass production of goods relatively cheap. However, exploiting new opportunities required a large investment in capital assets. But the rule of unlimited liability made contractual agreements for raising large amounts of capital difficult. A new rule eventually emerged: limited liability. That was an endogenous change that adjusted the rules of the game to the new requirements of the game.

Instead of adopting the rules to the changing requirements of the game, exogenous changes force the game to adjust to the rules. For example codetermination in Germany was mandated by law. However, prior to this law there was no law in Germany that prohibited codetermination. Managers, workers and the shareholders were free to write any contract they chose. Indeed, we observe a large number different types of business firms in the West, including Germany. All these firms have emerged voluntarily and have survived competition from other types of firms. The fact that the German government had to impose codetermination by fiat is evidence that the value to the employees of their participation in management was less than the cost to the owners and managers of providing it. Most exogenous changes in institutional arrangements are brought about by ideologists, pressure groups and bureaucrats in pursuit of their own private ends, while hiding behind the facade of the public interest. (Pejovich, 1993, p. 77.)

7. It is important not to confuse patriotism with nationalism. Patriotism means attachment to a community, and its tradition but does not rule out voluntary associations of diverse people who choose to live together. Unlike nationalism, patriotism is consistent with individual liberty, the pursuit of private ends and cultural diversity. Institutional developments in the United States and United Kingdom are good evidence of this.

8. This is not always the case. For example, the Americans and the British belong to many ethnic groups.

9. Some scholars and opinion-makers claim that these unsettled scores from the past are currently created myths. The evidence is not on their side, however.

10. In August 1993, Kravchuk endorsed 'the proposal that a referendum be held asking Ukrainians to decide whether they wanted to build a capitalist or socialist society' (Linden and Zvyglianich, 1994, p. 24). I conjecture that the leaders of Ukraine are not merely ignorant.

11. Vaclav Klaus will probably be remembered as the best East European leader in the immediate post-communist era.

12. Most state factories in Eastern Europe have no chance of surviving in competitive markets. Yet we already observe that ordinary people fail to attribute the dismal performance of these firms to the decades of communist mismanagement. Instead, they tend to say, 'The free-market, private-property economy is not working either'.

13. For detailed analysis of the effects of exogenous changes on the choice of business enterprises see Pejovich (1994).

14. I strongly recommend Buchanan (1993).

15. Buchanan (1976).

16. See the interesting paper by Chilosi (1993).

17. The social opportunity set is not confined to standard goods and services. It also includes all socio-economic and socio-political institutions. See Jensen and Mecking (1979).

18. Alchian and Woodward (1988, p. 65).

19. Brunner (1987, p. 42).

20. Human interactions continuously create and disseminate new knowledge. The assimilation and interpretation of this knowledge by different individuals keeps changing private opportunity sets and expectations about future. Thus, to assume that individual utility functions are given is meaningless. They are continuously modified in the action-choosing process.

21. Institutions are defined here as the legal, regulatory and customary arrangements for repeated human interactions. The market for institutions means an environment that allows people continuously to try, adopt and replace alternative arrangements.

22. See Alchian (1950).

23. For example, uncertainty about enforcement of contracts increases the costs of exchanges that are not simultaneous.

24. We can think of law as a capital good that, like all capital assets, has to be maintained. Failure to maintain it reduces the flow of benefits. See Pejovich (1978).

25. Buchanan (1972).

26. '[In the Ukraine] government abolished an article in a law passed earlier guaranteeing the rights of foreign investors for ten years. ... In addition, the drafts for a new constitution, a new law on the Ukrainian security service, and other legislation contain 'claw-back clauses' that virtually nullify the efforts of Ukrainian and foreign legal experts to conform

the Ukrainian legislation to the standards of the rule of law' (Linden and Zvyglianich, 1994, p. 24).

27.   The exclusivity of ownership means that the owner has the right to choose what to do with his/her asset (e.g. to speak on a social issue), how to use it (e.g. to oppose abortion), and who is going to be given access to it (e.g. to join an anti-abortion lobby). The owner (or the people s/he appoints) decides what to do with his/her asset, s/he captures the benefits of his/her decisions and bears its cost. The exclusivity of ownership creates strong incentives for the owner to seek the highest-valued use for his asset. The transferability of ownership means that the owner has the right to transfer his asset to others at mutually agreed upon terms. It provides incentives for resources to move from less-productive to more-productive owners. The transferability of ownership and the exclusivity of ownership jointly define the owner's right to bear changes in the value of his/her asset. See Pejovich (1990, p. 28).

28.   Equal legal and tax treatment of all property rights, and stable and predictable tax obligations are important guarantees that are still lacking in Eastern Europe.

29.   Exceptions are the Czech Republic, the former East Germany, and perhaps Hungary.

30.   The author's personal experience is relevant here. My generation in Belgrade was sharply divided between 'us', that is the children of non-communists, and 'them', who were the children of the ruling elite. We were beaten and mistreated for 'loving' the West. Today, I observe the children of our oppressors holding jobs in the West.

31.   It is important to note that we can transfer to others only those rights in a good that we possess. Thus, private property rights enhance the extent of exchange.

32.   In Alaska Packers' Association v. Domenico, the defendant hired a group of workers to fish salmon off the coast of Alaska. The wages and other conditions of work were agreed before the voyage. However, once in Alaskan waters, the employees demanded higher pay. The defendant had no choice but to agree. The case eventually went to court and the defendant won. See Posner (1985, p. 87).

33.   The firms that manage to survive have discovered a set of contractual relations which reduce the transaction costs of ensuring performance and metering rewards. See Alchian (1993, pp. 365–9).

34.   In the late 1980s, a rich Texan made an number of bad investments and lost most of his wealth. He did not run to the government for help, however. Instead he remarked that capitalism is also about growing poor.

35.   The socialist's favourite criticism of capitalism points to the number of people below the poverty line in Western countries. One never hears about the number of people in socialist states who are above the poverty line. Also, socialists always compare the actual results of capitalism with their own models of socialism.

36.   Pejovich (1994, p. 73).

REFERENCES

Alchian, A. (1950), 'Uncertainty, Evolution and Economic Theory', *Journal of Political Economy,* **58,** pp. 211–21.

Alchian, A. (1993), 'Thoughts on the Theory of the Firm: A Tribute to Eirik Furubotn', *Journal of Institutional and Theoretical Economics,* **149,** June, pp. 365–9.

Alchian, A. and S. Woodward (1988), 'The Firm is Dead; Long Live the Firm', *Journal of Economic Literature,* **26,** p. 65

Buchanan, J. (1972), 'Politics, Property and the Law', *Journal of Law and Economics,* **156,** pp. 439–52.

Buchanan, J. (1976), 'General Implications of Subjectivism in Economics', paper presented at the Conference on Subjectivism in Economics, Dallas, Texas, December.

Buchanan, J.(1993), 'Asymmetrical Reciprocity in Market Exchange: Implications for Economies in Transition', *Social Philosophy and Policy,* **10** (2), summer, pp. 51–64.

Brunner, K. (1987), 'The Limits of Economic Policy', in S. Pejovich (ed.), *Socialism: Institutional, Philosophical and Economic Issues,* Dordrecht: Kluwer Academic Publishers.

Chilosi, A. (1993), 'Rules Versus Discretion in Economic Transition', *Revue Europeenne des Sciences Sociales,* **31** (96), pp. 210–15.

Ionescu, D. (1991), 'Violence Against Gypsies Escalates', *Report on Eastern Europe,* 2 June.

Jensen, M. and W. Meckling (1979), 'Rights and Production Functions: An Application to Labor-Managed Firms and Codetermination', *Journal of Business,* **52** (4), pp. 470–2.

Linden, K. and K. Zvyglianich (1994), 'Pushing Ahead, Holding Back', *The World and I,* January.

Odling-Smee, J. et.al. (1992), 'Russian Federation', *Economic Review,* IMF, April 1992, p.35.

Pejovich, S. (1978), 'Law as a Capital Good', in G. Sirkin (ed.), *Lexeconics: The Interaction of Law and Economics,* Boston: Martinus Nijhoff, pp. 257–67.

Pejovich, S. (1990), *The Economics of Property Rights: Towards a Theory of Comparative Economic Systems,* Dordrecht: Kluwer Academic Publishers.

Pejovich, S. (1993), 'Institutions, Nationalism and the Transition Process in Eastern Europe', *Social Philosophy and Policy,* **10** (2).

Pejovich, S. (1994), 'A Property Rights Analysis of Alternative Methods of Organizing Production', *Communist Economies and Economic Transformation,* **6** (2).

Posner, R. (1985), *Economic Analysis of Law,* New York: Little, Brown and Co.

PART TWO

Centralization and Decentralization, Paradigms
and Facts

6. A Presentation of Fiscal Federalism

Giorgio Brosio

1 INTRODUCTION

When referring to the American constitution – the first constitution to introduced a full-fledged federal system – Tocqueville made a remark of fundamental importance: that the federal system was created in order to combine the various advantages that derive from the magnitude and smallness of nations. We may translate Tocqueville's point into economic terms by saying that a decentralized system – that is, a system with different layers of government – offers the opportunity to allocate responsibilities to the layer where it is most advantageous; the layer, that is, where better results can be obtained.

The existence of clear advantages from decentralized government has not been, however, universally accepted by social scientists and politicians. Moreover, the real world displays contrasting trends in the evolution of countries. Although the American example has found many imitators – federal systems abound, especially among former British colonies – centralizing tendencies have been both frequent and marked. Technical and political factors explain this contradictory evolution. For example, developments in communications and transport have had a centralizing impact by increasing the overspill of policies pursued at the local level. Political factors have also been important. For example, the expansion of the welfare state has been a strongly centralizing force, because redistributive programmes are more easily implemented at the national level.

In the last two decades, however, decentralizing tendencies have appeared all around the world. Here I merely mention a few general cases, of which the former communist countries are the first. Nominally federal countries, like the former URSS, were in fact highly centralized countries, where the Communist Party dictated policies that applied to the entire territory. The fall of Communism has triggered demand for autonomy and self-government by

129

linguistic and ethnic minorities. At the same time, the transition to market requires, amongst other things, the restructuring of the entire public sector; that is, the assignment of responsibilities and fiscal powers to different levels of government.

Western Europe also displays a widespread trend towards decentralization. A formerly unitary country, Belgium, has been peacefully transformed into a federal one, in order to accommodate the aspirations to self-government of the various linguistic components of Belgian society. In Italy, Spain and, to a lesser degree, in France there is strong demand for an increase in the powers and responsibilities of the regional governments created during the 1970s, with the transformation of a unitary state into a regional system. In some regions of Italy and Spain political forces are now pressing for the regional system to be transformed into a full-fledged federal one.

Latin America is the third case. Here, decentralization is mainly the outcome of the transition from dictatorship to democracy. Regional and local jurisdictions are now governed by popularly elected bodies, mayors and governors which have replaced officials appointed by the central government. Most of these countries have also adopted a pro-market orientation in their approach to economic policy. Decentralized government allows, to a certain extent, the simulation of the market by reducing the distance between the benefits and the costs of political decisions. A growing number of Asian countries are following a similar path, moving from authoritarian regimes to democratic ones. South Korea, for example, has recently introduced national elections for mayors and local government councils, thereby giving the system a strong impulse towards local autonomy. Whereas in Western Europe, and to a certain extent in the former Communist countries, the principal aim of decentralization is to strengthen regional governments (i.e. the intermediate level of government), in Asia and to some extent in Latin America local governments are the primary beneficiaries of the decentralizing impulse. This paper describes some of the most important features of fiscal federalism, namely the advantages of decentralized government, expenditure and tax assignment, and intergovernmental transfers. Although the focus is mainly theoretical, frequent references to real world experiences will be made.

2 A FRAMEWORK FOR ASSESSING THE ADVANTAGES OF DECENTRALIZATION

Economics is concerned with both equity and efficiency. At the territorial level, efficiency requires the unrestricted and undistorted mobility of labour, capital, goods and services among all regions. In other words, it requires a fully developed common market. Equity rests on the principle that like persons should be treated in a like manner throughout the country (horizontal equity).

A decentralized system assigns certain allocation decisions to sub-national levels of government. It also assigns them with fiscal power. An inevitable consequence of this is that sub-national governmental decisions have an impact on both efficiency and equity. These decisions may improve overall efficiency and equity, but it may also reduce them. Both equity and efficiency judgements are closely influenced by financial arrangements between the national and the sub-national governments. For example, central government grants to poor regions may enable these regions to provide a level of services to their citizens equal to the level of those provided by the rich regions, thereby solving the problem of horizontal equity.

In theory, a national government can provide different services to different areas. If there were no decision-making costs, a national parliament could decide to build, for example, a new airport in Bavaria, to protect animal species in Provence, or to regulate opening hours for shops in Rome. One can imagine, however, the sheer size of this parliament's agenda or the number of members of parliament that would be required to convey the information needed for efficient decision-making. Members of a national parliament vote on both local and national issues, whereas members of local parliaments take decisions on local matters only. The latter therefore have greater incentives than the former to gather and process information on local preferences (see Cremer, Estache and Seabright, 1994). As a result, a centralized decision-making process ends up with a more or less uniform level of services to all jurisdictions.

If preferences are completely uniform across the country, the need for decentralization does not arise. If they are not homogeneous across the country but homogeneous within each local/regional jurisdiction, then decentralization increases the level of welfare of citizens by catering to their preferences. This is the so-called decentralization theorem proposed by Oates (1972). Tocqueville (1833, p. 444) advanced a similar argument by saying that it is not in the nature of things for a central government to be able to cater to the needs of a whole nation. The great advances in civilization and in material progress are preeminently due to decentralization.

A second efficiency argument in favour of the decentralization of public goods and services concerns the evaluation of preferences. In general, rational individuals tend to misrepresent preferences for public goods. Tiebout has argued that when citizens have complete mobility between various jurisdictions, and when these jurisdictions provide distinct tax/expenditure packages, citizens will reveal their preferences for locally provided public goods through the choice of their location. As Tiebout puts it: 'Just as the consumer may be visualized as walking to a private market to buy his goods, the prices of which are set, we place him in the position of walking to community where the prices (taxes) of community services are set. Both trips take the consumer to market ... Spatial mobility provides the local-public-goods counterpart to the private market's shopping trip'. Tiebout's model rests on very restrictive assumptions.[1] When these assumptions are borne out – as in the case of locational choice within a metropolitan area – the result is the efficient provision of public goods, just as it is in the private sector. In addition, the more decentralized the public sector, the more efficient it will be.

A third argument concerns experimentation. Local jurisdictions do not provide local public goods alone: the bulk of their expenditure goes on the provision of goods and services – like education, health and social services – which have a mixed private/public character. Education, for example, has neither exclusion nor jointness of consumption. In fact, private schools thrive in almost all countries. The reasons for the public provision of education, health and social services lie instead in the externalities that these services produce and in equity considerations. Their provision by sub-national governments has the advantage of allowing both greater adaptation to local tastes and experimentation and innovation by distinct jurisdictions. In other words, solutions found in one jurisdiction may be adopted by other jurisdictions when they have proved to be successful.

A fourth, more fundamental, reason for decentralization is that it promotes competition between governments to the advantage of their citizens. The competition I refer to here does not require the mobility of Tiebout's model, and it therefore rests on a more realistic and solid foundation. A decentralized system, especially a federal one, is merely a manifestation of the separation of governing powers. In a decentralized system, citizens with a need to satisfy may apply to the national or the local government of their residence. In other words, they can play off one government against the other to their advantage. It is generally acknowledged that competition is beneficial in the economic sector; but it is evident that competition can be very beneficial in the political arena as well. A few examples will help to clarify the argument. There is no doubt that citizens benefit from competition between political parties and not from their cooperation.[2] In courts of law, the defence is set against the prosecution – that is, it has to compete with the prosecution – in order to ensure the best outcome in terms of justice. The fight against organized crime in Italy has been waged more effectively by the introduction of competition among different public security agencies. And numerous further examples could be cited.

The French economist, Pierre Salmon (1987), has developed an interesting model of horizontal competition: that is, of competition among jurisdictions situated at the same level. In Salmon's model, although citizens do not move there is nevertheless competition, because citizens evaluate the policies implemented in the jurisdiction of their residence and compare them against the performance on the same policies of other reference jurisdictions. These comparisons then shape their decisions at elections. For example, the citizens of Turin compare the performance of their city's administration with that of Milan. If Turin fares better they will continue to support the present governing coalition. If it fares worse, they will vote for other parties or party coalitions. If politicians are aware of this behaviour and seek re-election, this simple mechanism will force them to improve their performance. This model applies not only to local governments but also to higher levels of governments, like national states. It requires only realistic assumptions about the behaviour of citizens and politicians, and the circulation of information on the performance of governments which is not difficult to obtain.

3   THE ASSIGNMENT OF RESPONSIBILITIES

3.1   Broad principles

Richard Musgrave has introduced the notion of fiscal federalism – as the study of economic and financial relationships between various levels of government – and he has given content to Tocqueville's point by proposing a distribution of functions that gives stabilization and redistribution policies to the national government, and allows it to share responsibilities in the production of services: 'The heart of fiscal federalism thus lies in the proposition that policies of the Allocation branch should be permitted to differ between states, depending on the preferences of their citizens. The objectives of the Distribution and Stabilization branches, however, require primary responsibility at the central level' (Musgrave, 1959, pp. 181–2).

Although Musgrave's guidelines have been the subject of some debate in the literature, they remain basically true. There is certainly scope for decentralization in the allocation branch, that is, in the provision of public goods and services. A number of goods provide collective benefits largely in a local or regional dimension, for example, street lighting or control of acoustic pollution. These goods are referred to as local public goods (since they possess jointness of consumption and no exclusion characteristics). To determine the efficient level of provision of these local public goods, only local preferences – that is, the preferences of those who will consume them – should be taken into account. If these preferences vary between different areas, then a decentralized decision-making process will work better than a centralized one. That is, every local/regional government will decide the quality and quantity of goods and services to be provided. Before specifying the criteria for the assignment of specific allocation policies to distinct levels of government, let us briefly examine the broader issues of redistribution and stabilization policies.

There are limits on decentralized redistributive policies. If a local government implements a generous policy in favour of the poor – by increasing money transfers to them and financing the expenditure out of increased taxes on the rich – it risks stimulating an inflow of poor people from neighbouring jurisdictions and an outflow of rich people. There is some evidence of these movements in the USA (see the literature cited by Oates, 1994), but the point should not be exaggerated.

In a persuasive paper, Pauly (1973) has argued that there is room for redistributive policies at the local level. If, in a local jurisdiction, citizens consider that the poor deserve more help than that given to them by the national government, they will press for their local government to implement a redistributive policy. In other words, (a limited amount of) redistribution may be a local public good.

Moreover, one should bear in mind that some degree of redistribution is unavoidable at the local level. Since local governments cannot finance their expenditure on a pure benefit basis, some citizens will pay more than they receive and some will pay less. This distribution will not necessarily be from the rich to the poor; it may also move in the reverse direction, although this is difficult to implement. Municipal governments, especially in Europe, historically helped the poor by means of rudimentary welfare services, such as free medicine, the free distribution of food, shelters for the homeless, and so on.

There is much less scope for local policies in the stabilization branch. The effects of tax cuts, or expenditure increases made at the local level, will flow out of the local economy because of its high degree of openness. Recently, however, some economists have discerned a limited scope for local stabilization policies. In essence they argue that macroeconomic disturbances have differing impacts on different areas and that the instruments used by national governments to correct them may not easily differentiate between the various areas. Moreover, local governments – especially state (in federations) and regional governments – may help to absorb this impact by supplementing national policies with their own.[3]

3.2 The overlapping of responsibilities between governments

Let us return to the allocation branch. Some clarification is in order. Assigning responsibility for the provision of a service to a specific level of government does not imply that this level of government must effectively produce this service. Responsibility in a field includes a wide variety of activities, like fixing policy goals, determining minimum standards and/or ensuring that they are applied. For example, in the health sector in Italy the national government is responsible for medical research, for setting uniform standards throughout the country and for financing health services by means of grants to regional governments. These regional governments in their turn distribute funds to the local agencies in charge of health care provision (*Unità Sanitarie Locali*), coordinate their activities and oversee them. The effective provision of medical and hospital services is organized by the *Unità Sanitarie Locali*.

In most countries, responsibilities are equally sharply divided among distinct layers of government. Each layer of government has a certain amount of responsibility in almost every field of activity. Experts define this institutional model as that of inclusive authority, of which the main features are:

- the national government (even in federal states) extends its powers to almost every field;
- in many fields of activity some responsibility attaches to sub-national governments. This gives rise to an important core of joint intervention;
- small spheres of autonomy are left to sub-national governments;
- a similar pattern applies to revenues as well. National governments have access to the most important tax instruments. Some tax bases are shared between different levels of government. Sub-national governments have rather restricted autonomy in exploiting a particular tax base.[4]

Also to be stressed is that the overlapping of responsibilities – or at least the overlapping of the effects of policies assigned to distinct levels of government – is practically unavoidable in the real world. A simple example may help clarify this point. Imagine a country in which expenditure responsibilities have been assigned following the standard tenets of fiscal federalism theory. That is, redistribution and stabilization powers have been assigned to the central level, while allocation has been assigned to the local level. Some local governments may adopt policies – in areas such as education, or land use – which change the distribution of income in a manner that contradicts the goals pursued in this field by the central government. For example, these local governments may introduce high school fees, thereby reducing access to school by pupils from poor families. The central government may feel itself obliged to implement policies of its own in order to re-establish the distribution of income that it prefers: for example, by giving school grants to poor families (see Breton, 1985).

3.3   The production and provision of services

It is also necessary to distinguish between provision and production. That is to say, assigning responsibility for providing a service to a level of government does not entail that this level must produce it. Production may be sub-contracted to a private firm. For example, solid waste collection and disposal – a typical local government responsibility – is frequently sub-contracted to private firms. Local governments regulate this activity and monitor private contractors. This is a solution which has gained ground in the recent years, and it frequently enables the greater efficiency of private firms to be exploited. It also exerts a major impact on decentralization. Although economies of scale are an important factor in centralization – unit costs decrease with the increase in the producer's size – sub-contracting to private firms allows economies of scale to be exploited while keeping the government providing the service at the lowest layer.

Suppose that the same waste-collecting firm has numerous contracts with different small municipalities. The overall size of its activity may be large enough for all potential scale economies to be exploited. As a consequence, these economies no longer inevitably lead to centralization.

3.4   Specific criteria for the assignment of allocation policies.

There are three main criteria for this assignment. Two of them – spatial externalities (cost-benefit spillovers) and economies of scale – apply on the supply side. The third, homogeneity of citizens' preferences, operates on the demand side.

Spatial externalities arise when the benefits or costs of public services accrue to non-residents. In the case of benefit spillovers, the jurisdiction providing the service does not take account of the benefits deriving to residents of other jurisdictions. The consequence of this is an inefficient under-provision of services; a phenomenon which typically occurs in large urban areas in which a metropolitan authority in charge of the entire area does not exist. In the case of cost spillovers, overproduction is the result: for example, when one municipality dumps its solid waste in another municipality's area. Economies of scale – that is the reduction of unit costs as size increases – require that the local jurisdictions' areas should coincide with the optimum scale of production, unless sub-contracting with private firms is used.

Table 6.1 Examples of expenditure assignment using analytical criteria

Categories	Appropriate Level of Government	
	Policy goals and supervision	Provision/ production
Defence	N	N
Foreign Affairs	N	N
International trade	N	N
Monetary policy	N	N
Immigration policy	N	N
Unemployment insurance	N	N
Subsidies to poor	N,S,L	N,S,L
Environment protection	N,S	S,L
Highways		
inter-regional	N	N,S
regional	S	S,L
local	L	L
Water, sewerage, refuse	L	L
Health	N,S	S,L
Education		
university	N,S	N,S
higher	N,S	S
primary	N,S,L	S,L

Notes:

N = National government

S = State governments

L = Local governments

Although these criteria may suggest which are the appropriate layers of government for distinct services, they may create other problems. Strict adherence to them may imply a distinct layer of government for each public service to be provided. Let us consider only economies of scale. Since every service usually has a different optimal productive size, full exploitation of scale economies would require a different layer of government for each service, causing huge administrative and political costs. As a consequence, these costs must be weighed against the economies of scale and efficiency gains deriving from the elimination of jurisdictional spillovers.

An illustration of the impact of the criteria just mentioned is presented in Table 6.1 (suggested by Shah, 1994), which shows that for many services concurrent assignment to (at least) two different levels of government is possible.

4   FINANCING DECENTRALIZED GOVERNMENTS

4.1   An increasingly difficult problem

The funding of local governments has become increasingly difficult in the recent decades and in every part of the world. There are good reasons for this phenomenon. First, the revenue needs of sub-national governments have increased faster than those of the central government. One should also bear in mind the spread of urbanization and the rapid increase of the costs associated with the provision of urban services. Second, technical progress in transport and communications has constantly increased the mobility of both persons and things. This higher mobility has produced in turn two main effects on local taxes. First, it allows tax exporting; that is it enables a local government to shift the tax burden from its citizens to those of other jurisdictions. This takes place, for example, when a local government is allowed to tax a natural resource sold outside its jurisdiction, or when a city government charges parking fees only on cars from other jurisdictions. Tax exporting is not only unfair, it is also inefficient. Local governments tend to increase their tax revenues to an excessive extent when the tax burden can be exported to other areas.

The second effect is tax competition. Citizens may react to a high level of taxation imposed by their local government by moving to another jurisdiction with lower taxes. For their part, local governments may use tax reductions to attract persons and firms from other jurisdictions. Tax competition is not necessarily evil. It is certainly not evil from the point of view of the tax-payers, but it constrains the choices of local governments regarding their tax instruments. The joint effect of tax exporting and tax competition has been to reduce the number of taxes that can be administered by local governments without creating too many problems and conflicts. These problems have been compounded by the growing spatial unevenness of economic growth, which has exacerbated differences among local jurisdictions in their tax bases and thus their ability to finance expenditures.

Finally, some experts (see for example, Groenewegen, 1990) have argued that tax administration is both more difficult and more costly when performed by lower levels of governments. The empirical evidence does not completely support these claims. It is clear, however, that the broad-based taxes (on income or consumption expenditure, for example), which are the central components of modern tax systems, can be better administered at the central level. In most countries, some of these problems have been solved by reducing the role of sub-national taxes and by increasing the proportion of grants from the central government in the revenues of local governments. Furthermore, local governments have increasingly relied, for their own financing, on 'non-tax' sources of revenue, primarily user charges and fees.

It is important to stress, however, that in most recent years many countries have tried to reverse the trend towards tax centralization: partly as an attempt to trim their central budget deficit and partly to achieve a greater degree of efficiency in the operation of local governments. New taxes have been created, and the role of old ones has been expanded. This latter phenomenon means that practically all the problems mentioned here tend to decrease with an increase in the geographical size of local jurisdictions. For example, they tend to become less acute, if not disappear, as one passes from local governments to regional governments or to states in federal countries. In fact, a number of countries in Europe – the United Kingdom and Belgium, for example – have merged their small local governments in the last two decades, thereby creating more viable units of government, from the point of view of tax policy as well.

4.2   Tax assignment theory

At the theoretical level these problems have been addressed in the literature on tax assignment. R. Musgrave (1983) has used equity and efficiency criteria to formulate the following broad principles:

– taxes suitable for economic stabilization should be left to the responsibility of the central government;
– taxes with a high redistributive potential should be also central;
– tax bases which are very unequally distributed among jurisdictions should be left to the central government;
– taxes on mobile factors and goods are best administered by central governments;
– taxes on immobile (or scarcely mobile) factors and goods should be left to the responsibility of local governments;
– taxes and user charges based on the benefit principle can be

appropriately used at all levels of government, but are especially suitable for assignment to the local level, inasmuch as they are able to capture the benefits of local expenditures.

Table 6.2   Local taxes ranked according to the degree of autonomy that they provide for local governments

1. Own taxes:	the base and the rates of tax are under local control, in other words, local governments can control the burden they impose on their citizens.
2. Overlapping taxes:	the base is determined at the national level but the rates are decided locally.
3. Shared taxes:	the base and the rate are decided nationwide. It is not possibile to control the tax burden locally, although local governments may bargain with the central government over the amount of revenue they receive. Furthermore, as with other taxes, they can stimulate the growth of the tax base with their policies.

These general principles can be translated into more detailed tax policy recommendations:

– personal income tax and corporation income tax should be assigned to the central government: the former for the redistribution and stabilization reasons already given; and both in order to discourage the inter-jurisdictional mobility of factors of production;
– broad-based consumption taxes should be treated differently according to how they are levied: sales taxes levied at the manufacturing level should be assigned to the upper tier of government and to subordinate levels of government only where geographical areas are large (as in the case of the states and provinces of the USA and Canada, respectively); sales taxes levied at the retail level can be given to local governments insofar as it is possible to restrict the tax to residents;
– selective excise taxes should be assigned to central government if they are levied on goods (to avoid tax exporting) or to local authorities if they are levied on services (since much smaller tax exporting is assumed for them);
– land and property taxes are the most suitable for lower tiers of government, especially when they are imposed on residential property, which is the least mobile. Taxing commercial and industrial property, on

the other hand, allows the burden to be exported. This property is therefore a less suitable tax base for local governments;
- benefit taxes, licence fees and user charges have an important role to play at the local level.

5.   THE RATIONALE FOR TRANSFERS

5.1   The inevitable fiscal imbalance

Since spending responsibilities and tax powers are determined separately and with different criteria, there is usually no correspondence between them in a federal/decentralized system. In other words, intergovernmental fiscal relations are characterized by vertical fiscal imbalance. As already mentioned, tax exporting and tax competition place a severe constraint on the assignment of taxes to sub-national governments. On the other hand, responsibilities traditionally (but also efficiently) assigned to these governments involve services that are normally quite expensive to provide, such as health, education, urban transport and social services. The consequence is a fiscal gap for sub-national governments – that is, expenditures tend to exceed revenues from own taxes. This gap is larger, the smaller the size of sub-national governments. For example, in federal systems, state or provincial governments have a smaller fiscal gap than local governments, since capital and labour are less mobile among the former than among the latter. The fiscal gap may be (and indeed is) corrected by the national government[5] by paying transfers. There are two broad categories of transfer: general purpose transfers, and specific purpose transfers.

Whereas the aim of the first category is to reduce (or to eliminate) fiscal imbalance between different levels of government, or to reduce income and revenue disparities between jurisdictions situated at the same level, specific purpose grants are paid in order to correct inter-jurisdictional spillovers, or to implement specific national priorities and policies concerning the lower level of government: for example, to promote preventive medicine, or environmental protection, or to ensure the provision of equal national standards in the provision of certain basic public services, like health or education. As we can easily see in the latter case specific purpose grants may also have an equalization effect. That is, they may work as more or less close substitutes for general purpose grants. Some countries rely mostly on specific purpose grants to correct inequalities in income distribution and poverty problems across their various geographic areas. Latin America countries, like Colombia, have an extensive system of such grants. In these countries, which have a long-standing tradition of centralization, the central government does not trust local officials and politicians. It prefers to distribute specific purpose grants instead of general purpose ones, since the former allow stricter control over the behaviour of beneficiary governments.

5.2   General purpose transfers

The fiscal gap is usually inversely correlated with the level of wealth and income of distinct jurisdictions within the same country. In general, poor jurisdictions have greater than average per-capita expenditure needs because they must cater to a larger percentage of poor households. On the other hand, their tax revenues are lower than the average when all jurisdictions apply the same tax rate.

This is shown graphically in Figures 6.1a and 6.1b, where the per-capita expenditure and per-capita tax revenues of distinct jurisdictions are measured on the vertical axis and the average household income of each jurisdiction is measured on the horizontal one.

Figure 6.1a   A fiscal gap for all sub-national governments

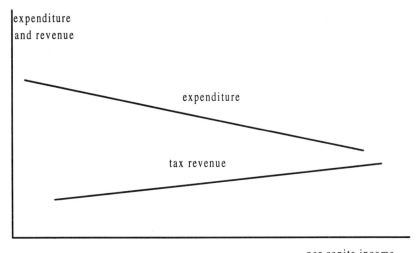

Two cases are considered, assuming that every jurisdiction is financed by an income tax with flat tax rate which is equal across all jurisdictions. In Figure 6.1a, all sub-national jurisdictions experience a fiscal gap, which is represented graphically by the vertical distance between the expenditure and the revenue lines. The lower the per-capita income, the larger the gap.

In the second case, only poor jurisdictions experience a fiscal gap, whereas rich jurisdictions would have a fiscal surplus if they did not reduce their tax rates.

Figure 6.1b   A fiscal gap for poor sub-national governments

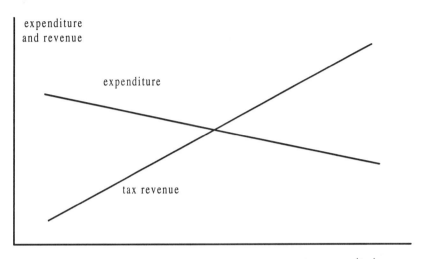

Some degree of vertical imbalance may even be justified in this context. Without a superior revenue capacity, the central government would be unable to make equalization transfers to the poor jurisdictions; nor could it finance the provision of minimum standards across different jurisdictions, if this was the policy that it intended to pursue.

5.3   General transfers and efficiency

The problem may be analysed using a simple model developed by Boadway and Hobson (1993). Let us consider a decentralized system with two sub-national governments: canton A and canton B. Each of these provides a basket of services financed by taxes on residents (tax exporting is excluded). There are no spillover benefits across cantons. Labour and natural resources, the only productive factors, are combined to produce aggregate output in each canton. Labour exhibits decreasing marginal productivity when applied to a fixed quantity of natural resources.

Individuals are homogeneous and are endowed with one unit of labour.

They are perfectly mobile across cantons. In equilibrium, they are equally well-off in each canton. This means that they migrate whenever they see a possibility to improve their welfare. The well-being of each individual is measured by his or her overall income, I_i, which consists of income from labour, w_i, net of personal taxes, T_i, as well of transfers from the national government and implicit income deriving from the provision of goods and services by the cantonal government, G_i.

$$I_i = w_i - T_i + G_i.$$

Migrational equilibrium arises when the overall income is equal across the cantons; that is, $I_a = I_b$. Individual benefits from public expenditure are denoted by (G_i/N^a), where G_i is the expenditure and N the population of each canton. When $a = 0$ we have the case of public, that is not rival, goods. This means that migration from canton A, for example, will not reduce the quantity of public goods consumed by existing residents. When $a = 1$ we have a case of publicly provided private goods, that is, of fully rival goods in consumption. In this case, migration from canton A to B will reduce the quantity of benefits that residents receive from a given level of public expenditure.

It is necessary to introduce an important concept here: net fiscal benefit (*NFB*), which is defined as the difference between the benefits that accrue to individual i from cantonal expenditure and the taxes that s/he pays. Thus $NFB_i = (G_i/N_i^a - T_i)$. We may now analyse efficiency costs, beginning with a pure public good. In this case, each individual benefits from the full amount of expenditure made by his/her canton G. If the budget must be balanced, then $G_i = NT_i$. In this case, $NFB_i = G_i - T_i = (N_i - 1)T_i$.

Someone migrating to a canton will receive a NFB equal to the total cost of public services paid by existing residents. Thus there is an incentive to migrate to the canton with the highest NFB; that is, to the canton with the largest population, or to the canton that applies the lowest tax rate, or both. By migrating, the individual confers an externality on existing residents. By paying his/her amount of local taxes, T_i, s/he will reduce the liability of the other residents, without reducing their public goods consumption. In a sense this externality derives from economies of scale in the provision of public goods. In this case migration is inefficient, since migrants do not take into account the externality they produce in their decisions to move.

Let us turn to the case of a publicly-provided private good, such as education. Here, with a cantonal balanced budget the net fiscal benefit becomes zero. NFB = $G_i/N_i - T_i = 0$. No benefit derives to the individual from migration; nor does his/her move produce an externality for existing residents, since s/he pays T_i. But it reduces the benefit from the expenditure by an equal amount, i.e. G_i/N_i.

In this model migration takes place when local governments produce public goods and are of different sizes. Migration results in an inefficient allocation of labour across provinces. This inefficiency may be corrected with a transfer from the central government which must equalize per-capita revenues from the local tax with the national average. Since individuals and their incomes are equal across the cantons, differences in net fiscal benefit may derive only from the size of canton. The biggest one is able to provide a larger quantity of public goods by charging the same tax price (or, with the same quantity, by charging a lower price). The transfer must originate from the big canton and pass to the small one.

Much more interesting and realistic is the case where individuals are not equal in their abilities to earn income. Let us suppose that there are two types of individual: the Rich and the Poor. The Rich have an income of 4000 the Poor of 1000. The population of canton A consists of two Rich and one Poor, whereas the population of canton B has one Rich and two Poor. Each canton levies a 10 per cent income tax and uses the revenue to finance the provision of a publicly-provided private good which yields equal benefits to all residents. Per-capita income tax revenue in canton A will be 300, while in canton B it will be only 200.

The net fiscal benefit for the same type of individual will now diverge across cantons. The Rich in canton A will have a NFB of $-100 = 300 - 400$, whereas the Rich in canton B will have a NFB of $-200 = 200 - 400$. The Poor in canton A will have a positive NFB of $200 = 300 - 100$ higher than that of the Poor in canton B, $100 = 200 - 100$. In other words, residence is essential in determining the size of NFB. Differences in NFB will induce inefficient migration from canton B to canton A; inefficient because it is dictated only by private benefits. To correct this inefficiency an equalization transfer is needed which equalizes per-capita revenue across cantons. For example, if a transfer of 150 units is made from canton A to canton B, then a Rich will have a NFB of $-150 = 250 - 400$, regardless of the canton of residence.[6]

5.3 General transfers and equity

The strongest case for equalization transfers is based on the premise of fiscal equity. Efficiency problems arise only if individuals do in fact migrate from one jurisdiction to another. Equity problems are always present. For economists, individuals who are equally well-off should be treated equally by government policy. Horizontal equity has an important implication in decentralized systems; namely that the public sector must give equal treatment to persons residing in different localities (states, provinces or municipalities). Equal treatment means in this case equalizing the net fiscal benefit, irrespective of where it is created. The previous example can be used to illustrate this point.

Rich individuals in canton A have an overall income of 3900 = 4000 – 100, whereas the same individuals when resident in canton B will have an overall income of 3800 = 4000 – 200. Analogously, a Poor person in canton A has an overall income of 1200 and a Poor person in canton B of only 1100. There are, in theory, two different ways directly to eliminate these differences by paying transfers to the individuals concerned. The first is to impose a national uniform tax on income of 2 per cent. Its revenue will then be 300 units, which can be distributed on an equal per-capita basis of 100 units each to residents of canton B only. The second method is impose a tax – for example a head tax of 50 units – on residents of canton A only, and to transfer the proceeds of this tax, on an equal per-capita basis again, to residents of canton B only. The result is the same.

Legal and political factors, however, raise a strong impediment against this direct solution. It is rather difficult to impose different rates or different taxes within the same country on persons with the same incomes only because they have a different NFB due to differences in income distribution within local jurisdictions. Governments prefer to tax the generality of tax-payers at the national level and then to pay transfers to sub-national governments. In our example, the national government would impose a 2 per cent income tax, and distribute the proceeds as a general purpose transfer to canton B.

However, the practical result may not be the same as that achieved by means of direct transfers to individuals. This is because of a possible 'fly-paper effect'; a well-known phenomenon in the literature which indicates that 'money sticks where it hits'. That is, officials and/or politicians of the beneficiary canton may keep the transfer for themselves – with legal or illegal means – instead of redirecting it to their citizens through lower taxes or increased expenditure.

5.4   General purpose grants in practice

As we have seen, the main purpose of these transfers is to enable beneficiary governments to provide equal – or at least comparable – levels of public services irrespective of the per-capita income level of their citizens; that is, irrespective of the ability of these governments to fund these services. The capacity to finance equal levels of services does not derive, however, from revenues alone. It may also derive from cost or need differences. In other words, two local jurisdictions with the same per-capita incomes may not have the same ability to finance the services they provide if they incur different costs by providing these services and/or if their populations have different expenditure needs – like, for example, different proportions of a young or elderly population. Different countries address these problems in different ways. Here I present three main cases: Canada, Germany and Australia.

5.4.1 Canada

Canada has a highly decentralized system: almost 60 per cent of total expenditures are undertaken at the sub-national level (by provinces and the local governments).

The Canadian Constitution requires all provinces to provide comparable levels of public service irrespective of their capacity to finance them:

> The Parliament and the Government of Canada are committed to the principle of disbursing equalization payments in order to ensure that the provincial governments have sufficient revenues with which to provide reasonably comparable levels of public services at reasonably comparable levels of taxation. (art.36[2])

There are two features specific to the Canadian equalization system of a federal government.[7] The first feature is that only revenue capacity is taken into account. The second is that tax capacity is equalized and not revenues. As we shall see, this makes a major difference, because the equalizing of tax capacity stimulates provinces to exert a tax effort. More precisely, the equalization payment to each province is calculated with reference to its standardized tax revenue. In turn this standardized tax revenue is the revenue that the province would be able to obtain if it applied to its tax base the average tax rates calculated at the country level.

The consequence is that if a province makes a low tax effort – that is, if its tax rates are lower than the national average – the equalization transfer will not cover the difference. Conversely, if a province applies higher-than-average tax rates, it will not be penalized: the transfer will not be reduced correspondingly. Finally, the aim of equalization transfers is to bring the per-capita tax capacity of every province up to the level of 95 per cent of the tax capacity of a group of five rich provinces which constitute the standard for equalization.

The transfer is calculated separately for 37 different taxes and other revenue sources of the provinces using the following formula:

$$TR_i = [(R_{10}/B_{10} \, xB_5/P_5) - (R_{10}/B_{10} \, xB_a/P_a)]P_a$$

where for revenues source i:

TR is the equalization entitlement from the federal government;
R_{10} is the total revenue obtained in the ten Canadian provinces;
B_{10} is the tax base in the ten Canadian provinces;
B_5 is the tax base in the five rich provinces of reference;
P_5 is the population of these five provinces;
P_{10} is the population of the ten Canadian provinces;
B_a is the tax base of province a;
P_a is the population of province a.

In other words, the formula simply states that the equalization transfer for province a and for revenue source i will be calculated by applying the national tax rate to the tax base of the five provinces of reference and by deducting from this result the standardized revenue of province a.

5.4.2 Germany
Germany has a peculiar horizontal system of equalization whereby the rich *Länder* pay directly to the poor *Länder*; a system which stems from the fact that in Germany taxes are collected by the *Länder* directly, with the sole exception of customs duties. Inter-*Länder* equalization payments operate as follows.

First, the tax capacity (TC) of each *Land* is calculated by summing the revenues from its own taxes, the revenues accruing to it from joint shared taxes,[8] and half of the local tax revenue.

Second, deductions are made for extraordinary expenditures (SE), if any, made by each *Land*. That is, the adjusted tax capacity is $ACT = TC - SE$.

Third, some need factors are considered: that is, population density (PD) and the size of municipalities[9] are taken into account: ($NEED = TC/POP \times PD$).

Fourth, the resulting figure is compared, on a per-capita basis, with the average tax capacity (AVT) of all *Länder*. The equalization transfer, TR, is calculated as follows: $TR = ATC - NEED - AVT$.

5.4.3 Australia
Australia has the most comprehensive system of equalization. The law (ACT 1970 of the States) fixes the guidelines for equalization as follows:

> [The] respective payments to which the States are entitled under this act should enable each state to provide, without imposing taxes and charges at levels appreciably different from the levels of the taxes and charges imposed by other

states, government services at standards not appreciably different from the standards of government services provided by other states.

Illustrating the methods used to calculate these transfers would be too cumbersome. I merely point out that a special public, but independent, body, the Commonwealth Grants Commission, is entrusted with the task of calculating relative indicators of need and tax capacity. These indicators are defended in open adversary proceedings by the Commission and a final report is submitted to the federal cabinet for review.

6   CONCLUSIONS

There is no consolidated theory of fiscal federalism. Even if one did exist, its practical usefulness would be rather limited. Distinct countries have different systems; systems which have also evolved differently over time. There is, however, one general conclusion that can be drawn. Decentralized government is an instrument which may render governments more responsible towards their citizens. To enhance accountability, decentralized expenditure must be financed with decentralized revenues. When this is not possible, intergovernmental transfers must be designed in order to foster responsibility. Equity considerations do not conflict with this approach. In other words, it is possible to construct decentralized systems that are efficient and equitable at the same time.

NOTES

1. In addition to the mobility of citizens between various jurisdictions, the model requires a number of jurisdictions large enough to offer every citizen the expenditure/tax package that s/he prefers, the absence of scale economies in the provision of public services, the absence of externalities in their provision, and so on.
2. The theory of competitive federalism has been developed by Breton (1985).
3. Clearly, as in the case of redistributive policies, one cannot exaggerate the potentialities in this field of local governments.
4. The USA is in some respects an exception.
5. This is the most common case. There are however situations, as in the former Communist countries, where the fiscal gap goes in the opposite direction; that is, sub-national governments are richer in terms of taxes than the central government and are thus forced to transfer some of their tax revenues to it. This was (and still is for some provinces) the case of China.
6. This transfer reduces the per-capita revenue of canton A to 250, and it increases that of canton

B to the same level.

7. Canada also has an equalization system which benefits local governments and operates at the provincial level. Each province has its own system.

8. In Germany, personal income tax is shared among the federal government, the *Länder* and the local government; company income tax is shared between the first two levels only. VAT is also shared between them, but on a per-capita equal share.

9. For all local governments of more than 500,000 inhabitants, the number of inhabitants (used to determine per-capita values) is increased by 2 per cent for those communities with a density of 1500 to 2000 inhabitants per square kilometre and by 6 per cent for those communities with a density of more than 3000 inhabitants per square kilometre.

REFERENCES

Boadway, R. and P. Hobson (1993), *Intergovernmental Fiscal Relations in Canada*, Canadian Tax Foundation, Toronto.

Breton, A. (1985), 'Supplementary Statements', in *Report of the Royal Commission on the Economic Union and Development Prospects for Canada*, Minister of Supply and Services, vol. III, Ottawa.

Cremer, J., A. Estache and P. Seabright (1994), 'The Decentralization of Public Services: Lessons from the Theory of the Firm', World Bank Policy Research Working Paper, Washington D.C., The World Bank.

Groenewegen, P. (1990), 'Taxation and Decentralization. A Reconsideration of the Costs and Benefits of a Decentralized Tax System', in R.J. Bennett (ed.), *Decentralization, Local Governments, and Markets*, Oxford: Clarendon Press.

Musgrave, R. (1959), *The Theory of Public Finance*, New York: McGraw-Hill.

Musgrave, R. (1983), 'Who Should Tax, Where and What?', in C. McLure (ed.), *Tax Assignment in Federal Countries*, Canberra: Australian National University Press.

Oates, W.E. (1972), *Fiscal Federalism*, New York: Harcourt Brace Jovanovich.

Oates, W.E. (1994), 'Federalism and Government Finance', in J. Quigley and E. Smolensky (eds), *Modern Public Finance*, Cambridge Mass.: Harvard University Press.

Pauly, M. (1973), 'Income Redistribution as a Local Public Good', *Journal of Public Economics*, **2**, pp. 35–58.

Salmon, P. (1987), 'Decentralization as an incentive scheme', *Oxford Review of Economic Policy*, **3**, pp. 24–43.

Shah, A. (1994), *The Reform Of Intergovernmental Fiscal Relations in Developing and Emerging Market Economies*, Washington, D.C.: The World Bank.

Tiebout, C. (1956), 'A Pure Theory of Local Expenditures', *Journal of Political Economy*, **64** (Oct), pp. 416–24.

Tocqueville, A. de (1833), 'Voyage en Angleterre de 1833. Carnet Alphabétique', in *Oeuvres*, Paris: Gallimard.

7. Fiscal Federalism in Russia

Pekka Sutela

1 FEDERALISM IN THEORY AND HISTORY

Federalism is about allocating responsibility and authority for certain state functions to various autonomous levels of government. In a confederation, the central government is subordinate to the regional governments and dependent upon them. In a federation, a division of powers implies that the general and regional governments are each, within a sphere, coordinate and independent. The history of federalism dates back a long way, at least to the ancient Israelites of the 13th century BC who endeavoured to maintain national unity by linking their several tribes. The original purpose of federalism was therefore either nation-building or the joining of forces for common defence. Either way, federalism was a way of creating cohesion. In the Russian case, however, federalism is now more appropriately viewed as an attempt to contain at least some of the obvious threats to cohesion.

Defensive purposes were also evident in such other well-known early cases of federalism as the Greek city-states, medieval commercial towns in central Europe and Swiss cantons since 1291. More recent examples of federalism include the relationship between Scotland and England, and also the Netherlands, Italy, France, Germany, Argentina, Brazil, Mexico, Nigeria, India, the United States and Canada. Federalism thus seems to be, or to have been, a crucial feature of the history of many European countries as well as of large heterogenous countries worldwide. Unlike confederations, federations have often proved to be fundamentally stable.

Recent events in Europe and elsewhere have placed the design and working of federal constitutions on the agenda of the general public, decision-makers, constitutional lawyers, political scientists and economists alike. Integration in Western Europe involves questions concerning the form of two- (and indeed three-) tier government. German unification has strained fiscal policy and raised serious issues about budget interaction between central government, different *Länder* and individual citizens. In Italy, Belgium, the United States and Canada perceived problems – especially concerning redistribution, public debt and regional conflict – have led to reconsideration of the relationship between central and local government, all of which has been duly reflected in the scholarly discussion of economists.

Of greater immediate interest for this paper is the existing federalist experience of the former socialist countries. The former Yugoslavia perhaps qualifies as a federalist state, the former Soviet Union does not. Since its independence, Russia has searched for a suitable form of federalism; a search – especially that part of it concerned with fiscal federalism (i.e. the decentralization of fiscal state functions) – which is the topic of this paper.

Scholarly interest in the constitutional design of a federation goes back at least two hundred years to the American Federalist Papers (Madison, Hamilton and Jay, 1982). Important contributions were later made by Musgrave (1959), Riker (1964) and Oates (1972). The recent developments outlined above have revived interest in both normative and positive federalist issues. Unfortunately, no appropriately useful overview of this revival seems to be currently available.

Federalism has three main characteristics. First, a federation should have a written constitution, which can be altered only by extraordinary procedures. Second, non-centralization is required to diffuse power among a number of substantially self-sustaining .centres. Finally, there should be a geographical division of power, preferably including: (a) territorial democracy, (b) the guarantee of neutral and equal representation for various groups and interests and (c) local autonomy and representation for diverse groups.

Federalism often includes a number of further elements. There are those elements which maintain union, such as direct communication between the citizenry and government based on common nationality and common defence against common enemies. There are also elements which maintain non-centralization. Among these, two seem paramount. Constituent polities in a federal system must be fairly equal in population and wealth. If this condition cannot be fulfilled – consider the example of the USA – inequalities must be balanced geographically or numerically. Non-centralization is also maintained by non-centralized political parties with financing and decision-making dispersed across regions. Finally, there are important elements which maintain federal principles. Thus federal and constituent governing institutions should be complete in the sense that they prevent the institutional vacuums that are filled all too easily by monopolistic means, either by the centre or by the constituent polities. The contractual sharing of public responsibilities is also most useful.

Historically, federalism has proved to be among the most stable and most enduring of polities. However, it does seem to require a political environment conducive to popular government and traditions of political cooperation and self-restraint. Federalism probably operates best in societies where there is sufficient homogeneity of fundamental interests to allow substantial latitude to local government and to permit reliance upon voluntary collaboration. Also, relatively abundant human resources are needed competently to fill the many public offices arising from multi-level government.

Federalism can also be viewed as a strategy to protect minorities. In addition to the usual separation of powers, federalism helps to establish checks and balances in two additional ways. In one form or another, there will a division of the legislature into upper and lower houses. There will also be a division of governmental powers between two sets of authorities, those in the centre and those in the regions or localities.

Obviously, any given country will necessarily display the characteristics of federalism enumerated above in an imperfect way. The ideal, however, is so far from contemporary Russian reality that one is left wondering whether Russia, as it withdraws from a unitary state, will really see federalism as its destination, or whether federalism will only prove a way station along the road of further devolution towards something still unknown. In order to make an assessment, we need some idea of the minimum powers of a central government within a federation. Rather obviously, there is no 'scientific' way of deriving such requirements, although Hewitt and Mihaljek (1992) enumerate the following high priority federal functions: promoting internal free trade, facilitating international trade and controlling the exchange rate, maintaining macroeconomic stability, and providing public goods that benefit the whole country. Stabilization policy, which is of central interest to this paper, seemingly presupposes both central money creation, recourse to well-defined revenue sources by the centre,[1] and limitations on both national and subnational budgetary deficits.

2 WAS THE FORMER SOVIET UNION A FEDERAL STATE?

The foregoing discussion – although extremely general – should already make it clear that the former Soviet Union was not a federal state. It is true that the Soviet constitutions paid lip service to many elements of federalism. There were union republics with ministries both at the federal and republic levels and a two-chamber federal Supreme Soviet in Moscow. But the republics' legislative, administrative and financial discretion was always trivial, with the partial exception of 1957–64. Such centralization naturally violated one of the main requirements of a federal state. Furthermore, actual Soviet decision-making powers did not rest with the Supreme Soviet but with the Communist Party. Although all the republics – with the non-trivial exception of Russia – had their own communist parties, for practical purposes the Soviet Communist Party was a unitary establishment from the top down. This, together with the fact that the role of the party was not properly codified in the constitution, further distances the former USSR from federalism.

Finally, one should note that the sheer size of Russia, with three-quarters of the area, three-fifths of the population and at least as much of the production as well as four-fifths of all export revenue of the Soviet Union, would have severely limited prospects for authentic federalism even if the communist system had not.[2]

In principle, however, the USSR had a federal constitution. Union responsibilities included the management of various economic processes and resources; all the diplomatic, military and security functions; the ownership and management of land, mines and agriculture; as well as the maintenance of the judicial system and legal code and social welfare, education, public health and labour legislation. Republics, on the other hand, had the right to establish their own constitutions, legislatures and administrative organs, had guaranteed territorial integrity; and they also had the right to establish diplomatic relations and their own military formations and naturally could, in law, secede from the Union.

The Soviet fiscal structure was also formally federal.[3] The state budget was a consolidation of the Union budget and the state budgets of the Union republics. Similarly, the state budget of a republic was a consolidation of its own budget and the budgets of each level of government under its jurisdiction. In actual fact, however, the budgetary process was highly centralized in order to impose conformity with the relevant plan.

The minimum levels of revenue and maximum expenditure were determined at each level of government for the budgets of the immediately lower level under its jurisdiction, with the global levels set for the state budget by Union authorities. Deficits at any level could be and were covered with transfers from the budget of the next higher level of government. Such transfers could cover substantial proportions of the expenditure of republic budgets, particularly in the case of the Central Asian Republics. Some of these transfers were formally loans, other were openly recorded as gifts. Any surpluses could be transferred to the next higher level or carried over to the following year, upon approval by the central authorities.

This system was highly centralized. The Union authorities had almost total control over taxation at various levels of government. Spending directives were also issued by the Union authorities. To cover expenditure, sub-Union governments were allocated a certain proportion of tax or non-tax revenue in a given category collected within their territory. In 1990, these allocations ranged from 70 to 100 per cent for turnover tax revenue, were raised from 50 to 100 per cent for personal income tax revenue in half of the republics and were kept at 20 per cent or less for the profit tax on Union-subordinated enterprises (except for the Baltic republics where allocations exceeded 50 per cent). Revenues from most other tax and non-tax sources (local charges, the profits of regionally-subordinated enterprises and cooperatives, and the agricultural tax) were allocated fully to sub-Union budgets. The Union budget received all revenue from foreign trade as well as most of the profit tax revenue from Union-subordinated enterprises. As will be shown below, the structure of the Soviet tax sharing scheme had much in common with later Russian arrangements, with Russian regions taking up the position of Soviet republics. There was a significant decentralization of taxation power and responsibility to the *oblast* and city level between 1985 and 1990. This decentralization, accompanied by greater pressure on local organizations to spend, contributed to the breakdown of the all-union fiscal system (Berkowitz and Mitchneck, 1992).

On the expenditure side, fiscal responsibilities were divided along broadly functional lines but under tight central control. The main items financed solely out of the Union budget were defence, justice, internal security, subsidies to the external sector and most budgetary investment in the economy. Local governments were primarily responsible for outlays on health and education. Republics dispersed most price subsidies and the majority of social security benefits.

The picture that emerges is complex. The high degree of centralization should not be underestimated, even if republics were demanding and obtaining a larger share of the resources by the end of the Soviet era. From the Russian point of view the huge budgetary transfers involved – further boosted by the subsidies implicit in the Soviet price system – were a net loss. In this sense the Soviet budgetary system certainly contributed to the collapse of the USSR. In the end, and in spite of the labours of Grigory Yavlinsky and his colleagues in Autumn 1991, there was neither the time nor the will to find a new solution for the reform of intergovernmental fiscal relations. This failure was to haunt Russian fiscal reformers.

Within the Russian Federation, the general picture of the Soviet fiscal system was now replicated in the relations between the Federation and its constituent units, (autonomous) republics, regions and cities.

According to Wallich (1992), an ideal system of subnational government financing would: (a) ensure correspondence between subnational expenditure responsibilities and subnational resources, (b) incorporate the power and incentives to mobilize subnational revenues, (c) not compromise the macroeconomic management policies of the central government, (d) give appropriate expenditure discretion to subnational governments, support public infrastructure development, and improve the accountability of local officials, (e) be transparent, based on objective, stable, non-negotiated criteria, as well as administratively simple, and (f) be consistent with national income-distribution goals. In addition, the intergovernmental system – specifically in Russia – should obviously support the emergence of a governmental role consistent with market-oriented reform.

With these admittedly demanding criteria in mind, we may now turn to examination of Russian experiences and intentions in fiscal federalism.

3   FISCAL FEDERALISM IN RUSSIA, 1992–1993

Under the constitutional regime in force in 1992–1993, the Russian Federation was – and still remains – a three-tiered federal state. This was confirmed in the Federation Treaties of March 1992. Units directly subordinate to the federal government include 16 republics as well as *oblasts*, *okrugs* and *krais*, two metropolitan cities with *oblast* status and national regions. These units are further divided into municipalities, urban districts and *rayons*. To simplify further discussion, this paper adopts the terminological convention of only distinguishing among: (a) the federation, (b) republics and *oblasts* and (c) *rayons*.

In the Federation Treaties, republics and *oblasts* were granted different control over natural resources. Thus, according to the treaty, the land and natural resources of the republics belong to the people living there. This is not true of *oblasts*; an annoying asymmetry which gave rise to two rounds of unilateral declarations of republic status by regions, first in 1992 and again in mid-1993. The asymmetry was only abolished by the Constitution of December 1993. The new constitution also failed to respect the notion of republic sovereignty sanction in 1992. Nor did it mention any right of the republics to secede from the Federation, as had earlier been the case. Nonetheless, the 1993 constitution does not really make republics and *oblasts* equal. The former still have their presidents and constitutions, and the example of Tatarstan in February 1994 (see below) implies that centre-republic relations are to be regulated on the basis of bilateral treaties.

Two simultaneous processes further complicate the picture. First, in addition to the *oblasts* which unilaterally declared themselves republics, there were several republics which declared themselves sovereign or even independent. The exact contents of such declarations remained unclear, but at least they referred to the ownership of natural resources, to the primacy of subnational over national legislation, to sovereign foreign trade rights and to fiscal relations between the federation and the sovereign republics belonging to it. In some cases, republics stopped or interrupted all tax payments to the federal centre. Secondly, a reorganization of the fiscal bureaucracy was also under way. The Russian State Tax Service (STS) was created as an autonomous agency with ministerial ranking in November 1991. This was intended to subordinate *oblast*-level tax authorities directly to the Moscow administration. Earlier, they had dual leadership, both from Moscow and from the *oblasts*. Alhough formal subordination to *oblasts* has gone, much loyalty and dependence still remains (Wallich, 1992, p. 27).

In the USSR, taxation was traditionally based on bargained 'tax sharing'. Sub-Union units collected most taxes and forwarded to Union authorities a share of the tax revenue negotiated for each tax type. As republics became more powerful, they first – and often unilaterally – increased their own share of revenue and in some cases finally stopped forwarding any revenue to Moscow. The danger of this being repeated within Russia after 1992 was all too obvious and indeed it did take place to some extent. Tax revenue sharing between the federation and *oblasts* duly became a complex and non-transparent issue of bargaining, backroom dealing and payment withdrawal. None of the self-evident standard criteria of efficiency, equity, transparency and simplicity seem to have been fulfilled. Both in 1992 and in 1993 general principles solemnly decreed by the federal government were later diluted. Indeed, it would be difficult to argue that the central government had any consistent policy on fiscal (or other, for that matter) federalism.

In an attempt to remedy the situation, Russia enacted a Law on Basic Principles of Taxation in January 1992. This law featured a planned, radical shift from the earlier system of tax sharing to 'tax assignment', whereby different levels of government receive revenue from different tax types. It envisages a unitary system where the tax rates and bases of all major taxes are set by the federal government, but all revenue from individual taxes is dedicated to particular levels. Thus, under the basic taxation legislation, personal income tax (PIT) is decided on the federal level but assigned 100 per cent to *oblasts*. Corporate profits tax (CIT), though federally decided, is subject to *oblast*-level amendments and 100 per cent also accrues by law to *oblasts*. Value added tax (VAT) is assigned 100 per cent under law to the federation, while excise taxes are shared between the federal and subnational governments, with rates varying among commodities. All revenue from taxation on international transactions accrues by law to the federal level. There are also other taxes of lesser importance (for details see Wallich, 1992). According to one count, there are 44 different taxes in Russia (Feldman, 1993).

The 1992 tax legislation assigns increasing official powers to the regions. Thus there is no longer any mandatory return of accumulated surpluses to higher levels of government. Subnational governments may dispose of eventual budget surpluses by channelling them to regional extra-budgetary funds created for the purpose. Such funds are not only dependent on budgetary surpluses; lease payments, privatization proceeds and various other non-tax revenues may also be deposited therein. In the case of budget deficits, Russian legislation – contrary to, for instance, Ukrainian legislation – only allows for short-term borrowing from banks and for the sale of subnational securities. It is not clear whether the limitation on short-term borrowing is binding, since local banks – and enterprises – are often subordinate to regional authorities.

In principle, the shift from tax sharing to tax assignment should have simplified matters and rendered the tax system more efficient and transparent. In practice, transitory regulations for 1992 allowed for continued tax sharing, in particular concerning CIT and VAT. Some *oblasts* also amended VAT rates unilaterally – naturally downwards. Such tax sharing continued into 1993, as shown in Table 7.1. Transitory regulations tend to become permanent.

Table 7.1 The federal government's statutory share of selected taxes (in percentage)

	Basic Legisl.	1992	1993	St. Petersburg 1993
Value-added tax	100	70–80	45–80	50
Personal income tax	0	0	0	0
Enterprise profit tax	0	41	31	31
Export taxes	100	100	100	0
Excise taxes	0–100	0–100	0–100	0–100
Natural resource payments	20–40	20–40	55–75	..
Payroll Tax	n.a.	n.a.	5.6	..

Sources:
Wallich (1992), IMF (1993), Lainela (1993).

For the sake of perspective one should point out that in 1993 (in parentheses the figures for 1992) total tax revenue was divided by tax as follows: enterprise profit tax 35 (29) per cent, value-added tax 25

(38) per cent, foreign trade revenue 9 (9) per cent and excises 4 (4) per cent.

Clearly, the intended shift from tax sharing to tax assignment had not taken place in practice. Nor were all *oblasts* treated similarly. VAT tax rates and natural resource payments varied across regions, and exemptions from export taxes were granted to several regions. No complete picture is available on other exemptions granted on an *ad hoc* basis to these statutory shares, but they were no doubt frequent. Furthermore, some of the *oblasts* accumulated tax arrears while others did not. It was only in Autumn 1993 that subnational governments – with the exception of Chechnya – accepted such arrears as debt to the federal government.[4] This was not a binding promise of payment, but it at least implied acceptance of the legitimacy of the central government's power of taxation.

The fact that the 1992 tax reform failed should come as no surprise. In Russia as elsewhere, the intergovernmental fiscal system is linked closely to political trends and economic developments. The attempted and failed stabilization, together with partial liberalization after January 1992, implied that both government revenue and expenditure were impossible to forecast. An orderly budgetary process simply could not exist, and the *ad hoc* management of state finances became inevitable. At the same time, and especially in 1993, regions became crucial power-brokers among branches of the administration. This inevitably led to widespread bargaining. By 1992, some 20 *oblasts* had reportedly decided unilaterally to determine by themselves the proportion of taxes to be shared with the centre (Wallich, 1992, pp. 34–5). Some *oblasts* had a 'single channel' agreement with the federal government. This meant that the *oblasts* retained all the tax revenue collected and transferred only a fixed nominal amount each month to the federal government.[5] At one point, in mid-1992, some ten of the economically most powerful members of the federation made formal decisions not to contribute any of their revenues to the federal budget. Combining stick and carrot, the central government succeeded in pushing this number down to a reported four – Tatarstan, Sakha, Chechnya and Bashkortostan – in April 1993 (Whitlock, 1993). As already mentioned, in Autumn 1993 all of these units with the exception of Chechnya accepted their tax arrears as debt to the central budget.

Tax arrangements are only one side of fiscal federalism. Expenditure sharing is another. Obviously public expenditures should be assigned to the different levels of government according to 'benefit areas'. This is the principle of subsidiarity in fiscal federalism. If expenditure benefits a subnational unit, it should be correspondingly provided. As far as current expenditure is concerned, this principle seems to be well understood in

Russia, though practical assignment has often suffered from a lack of clarity. Capital investment, on the other hand, was fully centralized until 1992. Another peculiarity is the traditional role of productive enterprises in providing social services. Not all of them should be taken over by local authorities after they have been off-loaded by plants in the name of marketization. Some might properly be assigned to *oblasts* and perhaps even to the national authorities.

Since 1992, much social expenditure and most capital investment has been reassigned from the national to the subnational level. In her thorough analysis Wallich (1992)[6] argues that this has often taken place without a concomitant revenue assignment. The central government has attempted to balance its budget at the expense of subnational units. In so doing, it may have pushed *oblasts* and others into an impossible financing situation, thereby in fact worsening incentives for stabilization. This issue will be addressed below.

4   ISSUES AND CONTROVERSIES IN 1993

Russian fiscal federalism may be approached from several angles, and Wallich (1992) offers an admirable discussion of them, as well as detailed proposals for remedies. This paper concentrates upon the relationship between federalism and fiscal stabilization, which also has several dimensions of especial interest in the Russian context.

First, one should ask whether current Russian arrangements secure sufficient flow of revenue to the federal level. If single channel taxation were to prevail, the federal budget would become dangerously dependent upon subnational discretion.

Second, if federal authorities have indeed delegated expenditure to subnational units without proper revenue, such units will be forced to engage in irregular financing – such as borrowing from enterprises, arrears, credit and additional taxation – that might endanger global stabilization goals.

Finally, there is the fact that the fiscal system has been further eroded and complicated by the creation of various subnational extra-budgetary funds. Easterly and Vieira da Cunha (1994a) argue that these funds may be a crucial source of fiscal instability, but little aggregate information seems to be available on them.

The World Bank has played a central role in the channelling of technical assistance to Russia in intergovernmental fiscal relations. In 1992, the Bank repeatedly[7] diagnosed a tendency to 'push the deficit downward' by shifting the unfunded expenditure responsibilities of both national and subnational importance downward, in the hope that the subnational sector would do the cost-cutting. As already mentioned, instead of cost-cutting the outcome may be recourse to the central government, arrears, borrowing from local banks – though this is only legally possible for short-term purposes – or enterprises, and monetization of the subnational deficit.

To a large extent, these fears apparently failed to materialize in 1992. The tax-collecting ability of the government improved notably during that year, and revenue collection by the state budget increased from an average of 21.5 per cent of GDP in the first half of the year to 39 per cent of GDP in the second half of the year (IMF, 1993, p. 10). In the absence of astronomically high subsidies often channelled outside the budget,[8] such revenue would have easily sufficed to finance normal government operations. Indeed, when the revenues of extrabudgetary social security funds are included, the Russian tax burden was significantly higher than that of the OECD countries in general (see Whitlock, 1993). This was in spite of the well-publicized problems of tax collection.

The elasticity of the tax-sharing schemes described above meant that, contrary to the central government (which had stabilized its expenditure towards the end of 1992), local governments were able to increase their expenditure progressively during the year. As late as the third quarter of 1992, local government expenditure was less than 15 per cent of GDP (and that of the federal government about a third of GDP). By the next quarter, local expenditure had risen to 20 per cent (while that of the central government remained almost constant as a share of GDP) (IMF, 1993, Chart 9). At the same time, the regions continued discussion of further tax sharing, in particular as regards export tax receipts and natural resource payments. In both these ways the policy goals expressed by the federal government suffered. These developments also tended to create tension between regions well endowed with resources and export industries and the others (Tolz, 1993). Overall, however, local governments maintained a surprisingly steady budget surplus of about 2 per cent of GDP throughout the year.[9] To date, the fears of Wallich (1992) and others have seemingly not been borne out. It is unclear, however, whether these figures properly cover the local extrabudgetary funds.

The difference in the budgetary positions of the regions must have been huge, which raised the issue of horizontal equity and income transfers between regions. This issue remains to be tackled with the proper seriousness. On the one hand, there are regions like the Khanty-Mansy autonomous *okrug* which are so well endowed with resources that they are considering the creation of regional financial corporations to handle their revenue (Baranov and Pirozhkov, 1993). Other regions are unable to make ends meet and depend on federal subsidies. Both the Khabarovsk and

Irkutsk regions have recently announced that they will be unable to pay federal taxes in 1994.

In late January 1993, the Russian Supreme Soviet passed a Law on Local Budgets (see Igudin, 1993; 'Byudzhetnaya', 1993) which stated that the federal budget was not responsible for shortfalls in local budgets, but that such shortfalls must be covered by local government bond issues or short-term loans from commercial banks. A Law on Subventions to Local Government was, however, also passed, and this allowed grants from the federal budget to be transformed into specific targeted programmes in regions. These programmes are frequent in areas such as road construction, health care and education, where the division of responsibility for expenditure had been contested in 1992. According to the law, the size of transfers and their destination are determined on the basis of individual circumstances. The law thus sanctioned continuation of individualized bargaining in expenditure allocation among government levels. While the Russian tax sharing system has been plagued with exceptions and arbitrariness, in expenditure allocation exceptions and arbitrariness have been caused more often by the system itself than by deviations from it. The situation was naturally made even worse by the 'War of the Budgets' waged between the government and the Supreme Soviet until October 1993. Even if there had been a sincere desire to meet all the tax and expenditure obligations undertaken, the level of economic and political uncertainty in 1993 would have made it virtually impossible.

The issue of expenditure distribution in Russia is greatly complicated by the existence of economically unviable regions – especially in the north – and endangered company towns. It is therefore not surprising that the issue of subsidizing the northern regions proved to be a highly contested one in the fiscal policy of 1993.

For 1993, Ministry of Finance showed a federal budget deficit of 10.6 per cent of GDP. However, if payments postponed to early 1994 are included, the recorded budget deficit rises to 15.4 per cent of GDP (*Kommersant-Daily,* 12 February 1994; *Segodnya,* 15 February 1994).[10] According to Goskomstat data (*Ekonomika i zhizn,* 1994, p. 6), subnational government ended the year with a slight budget surplus. It is unclear whether these figures include all extra-budgetary expenditure at various levels of government. The information available still indicates that the federal government also failed to push the deficit downwards in 1993.

In 1993 the consolidated budget was, according to incomplete information (*Ekonomika i zhizn,* 1994, p. 6), almost exactly divided between federal and regional levels. As shown in Table 7.2, the share of the federal budget in tax revenue tended to decline during the year. Overall, it dropped from 47 per cent of all collected taxes in the first quarter to 36 per cent in the third quarter

(*Delovoi mir*, 12 November 1993). By the end of August there were already an estimated thirty regions which had unilaterally cut the share of tax revenue handed over to Moscow (*Nezavisimaya gazeta*, 1 September 1993). According to the Russian Tax Administration (*Nezavisimaya gazeta*, 1 September 1993), by the end of September, twenty-nine regions had accumulated value-added tax arrears totalling SUR 400 billion, and enterprise profit tax arrears totalling SUR 200 billion.[11] Bearing in mind the amount of discussion devoted to the issue of regional tax arrears, these totals are not huge. By way of comparison, one notes that, according to the same estimate, unpaid taxes at the same time amounted to SUR 1400 billion, or 7 per cent of all tax revenue.[12] By January 1994 the total sum of tax arrears to the republic budget had reportedly climbed to SUR 1800 billion (*Rossiiskie*, 1994, p. 29). On the basis of these data, regional tax arrears are not the major problem of Russian financial authorities.

Table 7.2 The percentage of the Federation in tax revenue collected in 1993

	Statutory	93/I	93/III	1993
Value-added tax	45–80	66	62	65
Personal income tax	0			
Enterprise profit tax	31	41	31	34
Export tax	100	96		
Excise tax	0–100	53		
Natural resources payment	55–75			
Payroll tax	5.6			

Sources:
Table 7.1 above; *Delovoi mir*, 12 November 1993; *Ekonomika i zhizn*, 1994, p. 6.

Discussion on tax arrears is complicated by the tendency for figures to be announced without care being taken to specify what they actually refer to. Thus, Prime Minister Chernomyrdin (*Rossiiskaya gazeta*, 5 March 1994) and Acting Finance Minister Dubinin (*Moskovskye novosti*, 20–27 February 1994) have recently reported an increase in uncollected taxes to 30 or even 40 per cent of theoretical tax revenue. Presumably this gap is not only due to problems in collection but may also partly derive from a deeper-than-expected recession and other such factors. It is possible that, during the last months of 1993 and early 1994, the Russian problem of tax revenue worsened substantially. This, however, is not self-evidently equal to a deterioration in tax collection ability, and the basic problem may well lie in the tax base.

In the aftermath of the October crisis, President Yeltsin continued his stick-and-carrot approach in his dealings with the regions. Tax arrears by regions were deemed so serious that, on 27 October 1993, he had a decree issued (see *Rossiiskaya Gazeta*, 6 November 1993) which itemized the sanctions impending for regions in arrears; sanctions which included: (i) a withdrawal of state financing from enterprises located in the region; (ii) cancellation of foreign trade licences; (iii) interruptions in centralized supplies; (iv) a corresponding cut in credit granted; (v) confiscation, even, of the region's money from accounts held in the Central Bank. In a wider perspective, although the Sverdlovsk *oblast* may have declared itself to be the Republic of the Urals on 27 October (*Delovoi mir*, 29 October 1993), for practical purposes unilateral declarations of the status of republic lost any meaning they might have had as regional and local soviets were dissolved. New elections were held in most cases, and the December 1993 Constitution finally abolished most of the asymmetry between *oblasts* and republics (see Tolz, 1993). During the last quarter of 1993 and before the December elections, the federal government seemed to have moved into a position of strength *vis-à-vis* the recalcitrant regions.

At the same time, the republic of Sakha, which had remained loyal to Yeltsin, was allowed to retain all federal taxes in 1994 and to finance regional and federal programmes out of its own budget (*RFE/RL News Brief*, 25–29 October 1993).

Nor have privileges previously granted been revoked, or at least not in all cases. The Republic of Karelia, for instance, was granted broad economic powers by a presidential decree of 29 May 1991[13] whereby it does not channel any foreign trade revenue into the federal budget; nor does it contribute to federal extrabudgetary funds, while most of its enterprise foreign exchange revenue is sold to the republic foreign exchange fund, not to Moscow. Overall, according to interview information gathered in June and November 1993, the republic keeps 90 per cent of all tax revenue. Additional money – SUR 43 billion in 1993, SUR 158 billion planned for 1994 – is earmarked for an extrabudgetary Fund for Reconstruction and Investment, and since 1994 has been regarded in principle as concessionary credit issued by the federation to the republic. This arrangement will remain in force until 1999.

Before the elections, the largest Russian republics opposed adoption of the 1993 Constitution primarily because it omitted the principle of republic sovereignty that had been contained in the 1992 Federation Treaty. Although almost 70 per cent of the Karelian electorate voted in favour of the new constitution, it was rejected in nine of the republics and ten of the *oblasts*.

Overall support, however, was sufficient for the constitution to take effect on 25 December 1993. Obviously, as foreseen by article 11, the time had come for negotiations with at least some of the subnational units (*Izvestiya*, 22 December 1993). In the case of Tatarstan, negotiations soon achieved results (see below): in a speech delivered in February 1994 (*Nezavisimaya gazeta*, 16 February 1994), President Shaymiev of Tatarstan calmly announced that, since both the Russian and the Tatar constitutions were in force, agreement between the republic and Moscow must be reached on that basis, although 'it is more complicated than before'. Indeed, according to the Tatar constitution the republic is a 'sovereign state' and 'a subject of international law'.

Only relatively little information is available on the global outcome of tax collection in 1993. According to tax authorities (*Ekonomika i zhizn*, 1994, p. 8), total tax revenue in 1993 was 23.4 per cent of GNP (25.2 per cent if tax arrears are included). This was down 2.7 per cent (1.3 per cent) from the tax share in 1992. The downturn is explained by the decrease in VAT rates decided by the Parliamant in early 1993, by a decline in enterprise profitability, as well as by 'some softening' of tax discipline and increase in tax exemptions. Clearly, these figures do not include extra-budgetary funds and thus cannot convey a complete picture of the *ex-post* Russian tax burden.

Interestingly, enterprises in the energy sector are the biggest violators of tax discipline (*Ekonomika i zhizn*, 1994, p. 8). In some regions tax arrears may almost be equal to actual tax collection. Among the worst offenders in this respect are the Orenburg, Kemerovsk and Tomsk *oblasts*, Krasnoyarsk *kari* and the two West Siberian neighbours, the Khanty-Mansy and Yamalo-Nenetsk autonomous *okrugs*. Khanty-Mansy *okrug*, which – as we have seen – has problems in placing its income flow, alone accounted for 21.2 per cent of total tax arrears in Russia.

Another problem of the December 1993 Constitution is its attempt to put on the same footing, not only republics and *oblasts*, but also *oblasts* on one hand and *krais* and *okrugs* on the other. This is somewhat problematic since the latter belong to *oblasts* as their subregions. Nenetsk *okrug* seems to have been the first to have drawn its own conclusions, and has announced a referendum on eventual secession from the Arkhangelsk *oblast* (*Izvestiya*, 24 February 1994).

5   THE 1994 BUDGETARY SYSTEM

For the 1994 budget, the Russian Ministry of Finance under Boris Fyodorov planned another complete overhaul of intergovernment fiscal relations. The Economics Minister Shokhin also contended that the 1994 budget would indeed be the first to be truly based on the principles of fiscal federalism (*Nezavisimaya gazeta*, 10 December 1993). And, indeed, the start of the budgetary process was promising. According to the incomplete information available (see, for instance, *Sankt-Peterburgskoe Ekho*, 1993, p. 51), the budget proposal establishes unified norms for transfers into subnational budgets by all regions. Simultaneously, a separate regional support fund is to be established in the federal budget. Subsidies would only be given to those regions classified as 'regions in need of support' – those where the revenue earmarked for the subnational budget is less *per capita* than the Russian average – or 'regions in an exceptionally adverse economic situation'.

This system aims to achieve three goals. First, it tries to limit subnational expenditure to revenue. Second, it seeks to establish objective criteria for regional subsidies. Third, it is interpreted as an incentive to broaden the subnational tax base instead of appealing to Moscow for support.

One peculiarity of the proposed system is that the smallest units of local administration – small country towns and villages – are to be separated from the consolidated budget. However, it is unclear how many of them will finance their expenditure.[14]

On 22 December 1993, President Yeltsin signed a decree on intergovernmental financial relations in 1994 (see *Rossiiskaya gazeta*, 6 January 1994). Unless a different decision is adopted by the Federal Assembly, Yeltsin's decree will take effect in April 1994. Among other things, the decree determines tax-sharing ratios for 1994. The differences with respect to 1993 include a minor federal personal income tax – at a rate of 1 per cent, but probably the principle is deemed important – and a reorganization of corporate profit taxation. As detailed by a lower-level decree (see *Rossiiskie vesti*, 10 February 1994), federal profit tax is at a rate of 13 per cent. In addition, regions may establish their own profit tax, with a maximum of 25 per cent for enterprises and 30 per cent for banks and insurance companies (sic!). Until such decisions are made, a regional profit tax rate of 22 per cent will be in effect. This implies a three percentage point increase from the 32 per cent profit tax rate of 1993. For most commodities, only 25 per cent of value added tax remains with the regions, while the crucial issue of natural resource payments is to be determined in later legislation.[15]

Overall, the decree clearly attempts to reverse the long-term trend in central government revenue deterioration described above. It grants subnational units the right to broaden their tax bases by adopting new taxes, but also stipulates that in the case of enterprises such payments should only be made from the income remaining after payment of the federal enterprise income tax. This is also a manifest attempt to strengthen federal priority.

At the time of writing, the fate of the government's tax proposals is still undecided. It is clear, however, that there will be much opposition. One issue already raised – by the Central Mathematical–Economic Institute in the person of Sergey Glaziev, the former Minister for Foreign Economic Relations who is now the potentially powerful Chairman of the Duma Committee for Economic Policy – is to shift emphasis from value added and other current taxes to rent payments for land and natural resources.[16] If implemented, the proposal will be of obvious regional importance. In addition, its other distributional and efficiency properties in a country without a working market in land – and therefore with an essentially arbitrary valuation of land – remain utterly unclear, and it is not obvious if such a shift could be combined with any eventual privatization of land. In any case, the administrative capacity for managing such a tax reform in an orderly way hardly exists.[17]

Equally important is the fact that, although the importance of clear rules in fiscal federalism is widely acknowledged,[18] the possibility of using authority in order to extend subsidies has also been dear to reform-minded governments.[19] One example of this – and others could be added – is a Government decree on supporting the *Primorsk kray* adopted on 8 October 1993 (see *Sobranie aktov Prezidenta i Pravitelstva Rossiiskoy Federatsii*, 11 October 1993, pp. 4328–32), which specifies everything from the price of electricity to the number of locomotives to be allocated. Fortunately for politicians, the Ministry of Finance proposal leaves a door open for deliberation by its reference to 'regions in an exceptionally adverse economic situation'.

The results of the December 1993 parliamentary elections did little to contribute to an orderly solution of the Russian federal crisis. On the one hand, the opposition is dominated by groups evidently supporting a unitary Russia.[20] On the other, the Shakhrai-Shokhin group, now in the government, presents itself as the champion of regional interests against the allegedly Moscow-centred 'Russia's Choice'.[21] From this perspective, it is not surprising that the exit of Deputy Prime Minister Fyodorov from the government seems to have paved the way for the recent treaty between Moscow and Tatarstan.[22] While Tatarstan – contrary to its existing constitution – now seemingly lays claim to independence because the treaty does not contain the magic words 'sovereign state' and 'subject of international law', the question nevertheless concerns a treaty, as if signed between two equal sides. It has been indeed argued that although the magic words are missing, in essence the threaty confirms Tatarstan's *de facto* sovereignty (R. Tuzmukhamedov and V. Pustogarov, *Nezavisimaya gazeta*, 25 February 1994). The ebb of recentralization which led to the December 1993 Constitution has given way to a reflux, reaching at least the level of the 1992 Federation Treaty and quite possibly further.

According to the treaty, Tatarstan does not have the right to decide unilaterally on tax sharing, but in other respects its financial and other powers can only be characterized as being 'extensive'. Only personal income tax, enterprise profit taxes and VAT revenue are shared between Tatarstan and Moscow. Exact tax sharing still remains to be agreed upon (*Segodnya,* 16 February 1994). The share paid by Tatarstan may prove to be small, but on the other hand the treaty seems to be based on the idea of bilaterally agreed tax sharing, not on single-channel taxation.[23] In this sense at least, the treaty might indeed be used as a model for other republics, as proposed by President Yeltsin and other Russian authorities.

The treaty has already proved controversial, not least because only the text of the main treaty seems to have been made public, and the more technical issues are covered by additional treaties which at least originally were left secret. As a further looming threat to Russia's integrity, the Tatarstan issue is fiercely criticized in Russia. Nor will Tatar nationalists find it easy to accept the February 1994 treaty.

6 CONCLUSIONS

Three main conclusions emerge from the foregoing discussion. First, the level of global revenue into the Russian budgetary system has, at least until very recently, seemed sufficient to cover not only the needs of a night-watchman state but also to finance the basic expenditure of a modern state. The essence of the Russian financial problem has resided not in tax collecting but in the subsidies and other fundamentally unnecessary expenditure that the Russian state continues to undertake. Second, although there have been attempts at tax reform, Russian taxation remains as non-transparent, complicated and probably inefficient as it ever was. Third, although subnational tax arrears do exist and may be growing, they seem to be a minor problem compared with the ongoing granting of various tax exemptions to the regions. According to the Russian Ministery of Finance, in 1993 'there was hardly a region for the support of which no separate decision had been made' (*Rossiiskie,* 1994, p. 39).

All of these conclusions, however, are marred by serious shortcomings in the available data.

Litvack and Wallich (1993) conclude that 'the next step for Russia is to undertake a careful, concrete empirical study of expenditure assignments, revenue options, and transfers'. There is no evidence of such study being conducted, however, and the picture that emerges of Russian fiscal federalism remains a highly partial, unclear and even chaotic one. The system was never planned; it emerged and continues to evolve owing to the pressures of bargaining, inside dealing and political compromise. Therefore, it would be highly surprising if the system were found to fulfil any of the normal criteria of simplicity, transparency, equity and efficiency. There is a very great deal that we simply do not know.

Matters are exacerbated by the chaotic nature of federal relations, which seriously worsens the governability of the country and significantly contributes to rendering orderly transition policies impossible. Although sufficient empirical information regarding the impact of Russian fiscal federalism on the failure of stabilization is not available, a thorough overhaul of intergovernmental financial relations is clearly imperative from this point of view. Unfortunately, although this is generally acknowledged, there seem to be few grounds for optimism.

Having said this, however, perhaps one should not hastily conclude that power in Russia already rests at the local level.[24] The central government still has many resources – the ethnic homogeneity of the country being just one of them – which it could use to maintain the integrity of the country, if the political will to do so existed. This has been recently emphasized by Gustafson and Yergin (1993).

Finally, one relatively neglected issue in discussion on Russian fiscal federalism concerns the dual implications of the past and present spatial organization of productive activities. On the one hand, there is the cohesive impact – emphasized by Kopits and Mihaljek (1993) – of the traditional Soviet organization pattern which created Russian multiregionalist and indeed multinationalist enterprises. On the other hand – and here our knowledge is seriously deficient – both the emergence of post-Soviet states intent on nation-building and the regionally-based Russian privatization pattern have created severe centrifugal tendencies. The balance of these trends will surely prove critical for the economic cohesion of Russia.

NOTES

1. Conceived narrowly in terms of fiscal federalism, the existence of the centre's own tax base is a crucial difference between federalism and confederation. Its importance was strongly argued by Hamilton in Federalist Paper No. 30 in Madison, Hamilton and Jay (1982, pp. 143–47).
2. It should be pointed out that, in this relative sense, decentralization in Russia might have helped to preserve the USSR.
3. See for instance IMF (1991).
4. Sergey Alexashenko, Deputy Minister of Finance of Russian Federation, personal communication; for Tatarstan, President Shaymiev in *Nezavisimaya gazeta*, 12 February 1994, who also underlines that Tatarstan 'is fulfilling' the obligation undertaken.

5. The Supreme Soviet strongly disapproved of both single channel agreements and unilaterally determined sharing rates and threatened to apply sanctions against *oblasts* involved. The threats included halting all central expenditure on the territory, withholding export and import licenses, denying central bank credit, halting the flow of material from the central supply system and withholding cash or currency.

6. See also see Litvack and Wallich (1993) and The World Bank (1992).

7. See for instance Wallich (1992).

8. These subsidies should be separated from such formal extra-budgetary funds as the Employment Fund, Pension Fund and Social Insurance Fund, which all recorded surpluses. In the case of the Pension Fund, the surplus rose to 2.3 per cent of GDP. See IMF, 1993, Table 14.

9. After the first quarter, when the local government surplus was only 0.9 per cent of GDP. See IMF, 1993, Table 13.

10. Behind these exercises lies an attempt to reduce the budget deficit to a figure as close to the 10 per cent level fixed in the May 1993 economic policy agreement as possible, thus improving Russia's prospects in negotiations with the Bretton Woods institutions. Such cosmetics are unlikely to work. At the same time, however, highly problematic effects are exercised on the 1994 budget.

11. *Finansovye izvestiya*, 24 December 1993, gives a grand total of only SUR 300 billion for the same period.

12. This figure is surprisingly low. Recently, Aleksandr Pochinok, the Deputy Chairman of the Duma Committee on the Budget and Finance, has added another cause for concern: the total number of tax subjects is declining because of poverty and the closure of plants. *Delovoi mir*, 9 February 1994.

13. I am grateful to my colleague Juhani Laurila for information on the Karelian situation. See Laurila (1994).

14. Nikolai Medvedev of the President's Administration in *Rossiiskaya gazeta*, 8 February 1994.

15. Another novel aspect of the proposal is the numerous tax concessions to small enterprises, enterprises producing consumer goods and investment. There will also be a new 3 per cent additional levy similar to value added tax designed to support priority sectors of the economy, and a transport tax of 1 per cent of the wage fund earmarked for improvements to the rural transportation infrastructure.

16. See, for instance, *Kommersant-Daily*, 3 February and, especially, 5 February 1994.

17. This proposal is actually a longstanding hobby horse of Dmitry Lvov, Deputy Director of the Central Mathematical–Economic Institute, and it has been long debated in Russian discussion.

18. As an example see the resolution of the Supreme Soviet-minded All-Russian Economic Conference in *Rossiiskaya Gazeta*, 7 September 1993.

19. Perhaps this is what acting Finance Minister Dubinin had in mind when he characterized the 1994 tax proposals (Reuters, 11 February 1994) as not ideal but unavoidable.

20. 'There shall be no national state entities on the territory of Russia ... only a central power, and only with active and concerted help from the regions, can put in motion the production flywheels of such an immense country as Russia.' *Programme*, 1993.

21. In a recent interview Aleksandr Shokhin stated: 'I have for many months now spoken, amongst other things, about the fact that there is a need for more tax rights and financial resources to be transferred not only to the subjects of the federation but also to the level of local self-government, to the level of towns and villages, for as few resources as possible to be driven into the centre. ... Therefore I would resolve at some moment, while maintaining the same tax rates, to embark on some broad concessions understandable to all, connected with stimulating investment and particular types of activity ... increasing production and services and so on.' *BBC Summary of World Broadcasts*, SU/1913 C/1–3, 4 February 1994.

22. *Segodnya*, 16 February 1994; *Financial Times*, 17 February 1994; for background information see Anulova, 1993. The text of the main agreement is contained in *Rossiiskaya gazeta*, 18 February 1994, and in an English translation in *BBC Summary of World Broadcasts*, SU/1934 B/7-10, 1 March 1994.

23. But President Shaymiev of Tatarstan also emphasises that the republic's revenue must cover 'necessary' expenditure. 'That's why we do and will not sit in Minfin's corridors. That is also a strongly-held position' (*Nezavisimaya gazeta*, 16 February 1994). Presumably Tatarstan thus reserves the right to implement unilateral decisions if some revenue is deemed 'necessary'.

24. To take just one example, Andreas Gummich, deputy director of Deutsche Bank Research, claimed as early as November 1992 that Yeltsin's decrees were only obeyed within a fifty-kilometre radius of Moscow (*Kauppalehti*, 11 November 1992). Surely this is a partial misrepresentation of the situation both inside and outside the radius.

REFERENCES

Anulova, G. (1993), *The Scope for Regional Autonomy in Russia,*. Österreichiches Nationalbank, Auslandsanalyseabteilung Working Paper 12, June 17.

Baranov, A. and C. Pirozhkov (1993), 'Upravlenie regionalnymi finansami v usloviyakh rynka', *Eko*, **12**, pp. 54–62.

Berkowitz, D. and B. Mitchneck (1992), 'Fiscal Decentralization in the Soviet Economy', *Comparative Economic Studies*, **2**, pp. 1–18.

'Byudzhetnaya reforma v Rossii'(1993), *Finansy*, **8**, pp. 49–53.

Easterly, W. and P. Vieira da Cunha (1994a), 'Financing the Storm: Macroeconomic Crisis in Russia', *Economic of Transition 1994*, **4**, pp. 443–465.

Easterly, W. and P. Vieira da Cunha (1994b), 'Financing the Storm: Macroeconomic Crisis in Russia, 1992–93', Policy Research Working Paper 1240, The World Bank, January.

Feldman, A. (1993), 'O nalovogoi systeme Rossiiskoi federatsii', *Ekonomist*, **10**, pp. 55–61.

Gustafson, T. and D. Yergin (1993), *Russia in 2010*, New York.

Hewitt, D. and D. Mihaljek (1992), 'Fiscal Federalism', in V. Tanzi (ed.), *Fiscal Policies in Economies in Transition*, Washington D.C. pp. 330–49.

Igudin, A. (1993), 'Novyi etap mezhbyutzhetnykh otnoshenii v Rossiiskoi federatsii', *Finansy*, **7**, pp. 11–17.

IMF, The World Bank, OECD and EBRD (1991), *A Study of the Soviet Economy*, Paris, **1**, pp. 237–58.

IMF (1993), *Economic Review of Russian Federation*, Washington D.C.

Kopits, G. and D. Milhaljek (1993), 'Fiscal Federalism and the Newly Independent States', in V. Tanzi (ed.), *Transition to Market: Studies in Fiscal Reform*, Washington D.C., pp. 155–76.

Lainela, S. (1993) 'Venäjän federatiivisen rakenteen muotoutuminen ja taloudellinen päätöksenteko; Pietarin asema', The Bank of Finland, *Review of Economies in Transition*, **10**, pp. 5–18.

Laurila, J. (1994), 'The Economy and Financing of Karelia', The Bank of Finland, *Review of Economies in Transition*, forthcoming.

Litvack, J.I. and C.I. Wallich (1993), 'Intergovernmental Finance: Critical to Russia's Transformation?', *Finance & Development*, **2**, pp. 6–9.

Madison, J., A. Hamilton and J. Jay (1982), *The Federalist Papers*, New York.

Musgrave, R. (1959), *The Theory of Public Finance*, New York.

Oates, W. (1972), *Fiscal Federalism*, New York.

'Programme of the Liberal Democratic Party of Russia'(1994), *BBC Summary of World Broadcasts*, SU/1889 B/1–5, 7 January.

Riker, W. (1964), *Federalism: Origin, Operation and Significance*, Boston.

Tolz, V. (1993), *Thorny Road toward Federalism in Russia*, RFE/RL Research Report, 3 December.

Wallich, C. (1992), *Fiscal Decentralization: Intergovernmental Relations in Russia*, Studies of Economies in Transition, **6**, The World Bank, Washington D.C.

Whitlock, E. (1993), *The Russian State Budget*, RFE/RL Research Report, 23 April.

The World Bank (1992), *Russian Economic Reform: Crossing the Threshold of Structural Change*, Washington D.C.

8. Privatization, Decentralization, Competition. Some Lessons from a Concentration Analysis of Hungarian Industries[1]

Zoltán Bara

1 EFFECTS OF PRIVATIZATION ON COMPETITION

The effects of the privatization process currently taking place in the post-communist economies can be considered at three levels:

–   macroeconomic results: these can be measured *inter alia* by the extent of the private sector in the economy;
–   microeconomic effects: at the enterprise level one may expect increased efficiency of production, a reduction in excess capacity, improved quality of product and service, etc.;
–   mesoeconomic effects: this third level is apparently rarely examined in studies of privatization effects. The meso level is that of an industry within the context of a given market as a whole.

At the macroeconomic level, I shall examine the economic environment of privatization, taking Hungary as an example. Privatization in Hungary has been accompanied by a persistent fall in GDP (8 per cent in 1991, 5 per cent in 1992, and 3 per cent in 1993). The balance of international payments has not improved, and the country's total foreign debt has reached $23 billion, the highest level ever recorded. In 1993, Hungary's international trade deficit amounted to around $3 billion. Investments are now decreasing not only in proportion but in absolute value as well. The dynamic increase in the number of small entrepreneurs, which had been the only positive sign in the economy in 1992 has been halted by a huge wave of bankruptcies and the overall deterioration of debt repayment discipline.

The replacement of the markets lost in the East with new solvent markets continued in 1992, but, again, the process was impeded by the lack of necessary financial and other assets needed to modernize and reorganize the state-owned companies. Economic performance therefore was much worse than it might have been with sufficient capital injections. Many state companies lost their last chance to survive and this led to further decreases in the market value of firms to be privatized. At the company level, privatization efforts have been hindered by the huge burden of debt payment obligations, most of which were created in different circumstances, in a different system and under different control.

In the microeconomic context one of the outstanding features of any kind of privatization, either in a developed Western region or an East European country undergoing systemic change, is that of expectations for increased efficiency. There are numerous examples of governments trying to get rid of large state-owned companies only when they can no longer afford to subsidize loss-making economic entities (Kikeri, Nellis, Shirley, 1992). Yet loss-making status itself should not constitute a compelling reason for privatization. A government could easily continue with subsidization, and for a considerable length of time, if there were strong political motives for doing so. But it is difficult to cite a case of the privatization of a successful, profitable state-controlled firm in the Western hemisphere. In the East, however, privatization is not only a solution for the inefficiency problem of a state firm, but also the economic form taken by a fundamental systemic change which affects the whole country. This, of course, gives rise to numerous differences between privatization processes in the two regions. The attention here is focused on the competitive aspects. Table 8.1 summarizes the major differences between the two systems as regards competition.

A typical Western economic system is based on solid market forces, while an Eastern system is undergoing several changes. Although the aim of the changes is – without exception – to establish a market economy, market forces are still weak, which means, amongst other things, that establishing new businesses is relatively much easier in the Western hemisphere than it is in the East. The number of competitors in a given Eastern industry rarely matches technological and economic conditions. In most of the Western economies the regulation of competition can effectively deal with unfair conduct. With respect to competition and privatization, the second major difference between the two regions is the stability of foreign capital participation in the national economies. The third feature is that expectations concerning privatization are mostly economic rather than political in the

developed countries, while they are one of the major political issues
concerning systemic changes taking place in the Eastern countries.[2]

Table 8.1 Privatization and economic systems

West	East
1. The economic systems is based on solid market forces.	1. The system is changing, the market forces are still weak.
1a. Establishing a new business is easy in terms of legal and other administrative requirements.	1a. Establishing a new business is still subject to many contradictory and confused state and local regulations.
1b. The number of competitors tends to correspond to the technological and economic conditions of a given industry.	1b. The number of competitors does not correspond to the technological and economic conditions of a given industry.
1c. The competition regulation effectively attacks unfair practices.	1c. The competition regulation does not have enough power to take effective steps against unfair practices.
2. The relationship between national and foreign capital is well-balanced.	2. The relationship between national and foreign capital is unsteady.
2a. The national capital is strong.	2a. The national capital is weak.
2b. The national capital is well protected where necessary.	2b. There is no clear concept of the national interests regarding strategic industries, important sectors, and such.
2c. Foreign participation in the privatisization seldom generates politically sensitive issues.	2c. Foreign participation in the privatization often generates politically sensitive issues.
3. The expectations concerning privatization are primarily (micro) economic ones mixed with political objectives.	3. The expectations concerning privatization are primarily political ones mixed with (macro) economic objectives.

This paper focuses on the mesoeconomic approach. It is not easy to conduct
analysis of competition regulation in Hungary as yet. The market environment
is only now being built as a result of political and economic systemic
transformation. The transitional period has two characteristics in particular

which make it difficult to evaluate the effects of the privatization on competition in different industries:

a) Compared to developed countries, certain important institutions are lacking or underdeveloped in the Hungarian economy. First, the country lacks several legal regulations and laws, such as the clear and overall regulation of natural monopolies and adequate legal protection for consumers. The environmental and safety regulations are not clear and too bureaucratic in most cases. The capital market is still in its infancy. The monetary system is just developing. There are too many complications surrounding the regulation of land ownership. Last but not least, it is extremely difficult to acquire relevant and reliable data because of the change in the data collecting and data processing system.

b) Compared to other cases of privatization around the world, foreign direct investments have played a much more significant role in privatization during systemic transition in the East European countries. The value of a company is not simply a matter of bargaining; it involves purchasing power as well. As long as national savings are not sufficiently concentrated in private hands, privatization is an extraordinary chance to enter a new market or to take over an entire network of companies, without the usual competition with local forces. The consequences of this lack of competition are twofold. First, a foreign company investing in an East European economy does not necessarily possess the expertise, licences and management skills needed to be competitive. Second, acquiring a dominant position in the local market may have been the primary motivation of a foreign investor when buying out a company to be privatized, since it may help the investor's home firms to reduce excess capacity (Arva, 1994).

Different sources estimate that the share of the private sector in GDP had risen to as much as 45 per cent by the end of 1993. One of the sectors in which privatization may be considered to be complete is the retail sector, where more than 90 per cent of total output is accounted for by privately controlled companies and small private shops. Among the manufacturing industries, the following sectors have certainly reached the 75 per cent level and have therefore been surveyed here (among others): paper-making industry, construction and building materials, cement and gravel, light bulb industry, vegetable oil and margarine, sugar refining, tobacco processing, confectionery.

There is a need to conduct theoretical discussion of what the major role of mass privatization during a transition period would be and what the minor ones are. A possible approach to the problem is comparison between privatizing a large state-owned company in a country with a developed market economy (such as France or the UK) and doing the same in a country in transition (like Hungary or Poland). It would be natural to say that in a developed country the most important expectation of privatizing a state-owned company is that it will increase pressure on the management to make the company more efficient. This pressure derives from two sources: (i) the effect of private ownership, and (ii) the competitive pressure of rivals (Matsunaga et al, 1993); both are indispensable. Without competition a privately owned company is just another form of the exercise of monopoly power, and without private ownership competition could just be an artificial, sophisticated method of controlling the economy from a state centre. It seems fair to say that in Eastern Europe the two sides of efficiency are not equally valued, because creating private ownership has been given much more importance than enhancing competition. This paper aims to present a few examples from Hungarian privatization which, although they may not be incontestable evidence, certainly indicate how competitive aspects have suffered from neglect during the last three years.

2 SOME METHODOLOGICAL ASPECTS

The initial questions addressed by our survey were the following: (i) What are the major privatized or to-be-privatized non-competitive industries and/or sectors in Hungary? (ii) How has the concentration level changed in these industries or sectors? (iii) Has there been any perceptible change in the intensity of competition as a result of privatization? (iv) How are industry-specific competitive aspects involved in privatization activities?

All of the possible market structures can be found in the Hungarian economy today. The classification of the market structures used in this study is based on a combination of different concentration measures:

a) the Herfindhal–Hirschman index[3]
b) the four-firm ratio
c) the largest firm's market share
d) the market share of the second largest firm.

On the basis of these characteristics, six types of market structure can be distinguished: see Table 8.2. The six forms of market structure have been divided into two groups – competitive market structures and non-competitive market structures – according to whether there is a significant possibility of any kind of unfair activity in a given industry. As far as unfair practices are concerned, only monopoly, the dominant firm situation and the oligopoly situations count; these are considered to be endangered markets by Hungarian policy regulating competition. In a (natural) monopoly situation the precondition for effective economic operation is that overall regulation should prevent abuse of monopoly power. In the case of a dominant position, regulation policy must reduce (if not eliminate) the likelihood of that power being abused to the detriment of smaller competitors, and to deter oligopoly firms from collusion. Regulation policy takes the three forms of competitive market structure – oligopolistic competition, monopolistic competition and pure competition – to be operational as regards competitive forces.

Table 8.2 Competitive and noncompetitive market structures

Competitive market structures	Non-competitive market structures
Oligopolistic competition	Monopoly
Monopolistic competition	Dominant firm
Pure competition	Oligopoly

Table 8.3 Classification of industries regarding noncompetitive market structures

Characteristics	Market structures		
	monopoly	dominant firm	oligopoly
H-index	10,000	above 3,600	above 1000
4-firm ratio	100%		
the largest firm's ratio	100%	at least 50%	
the second largest		not higher than	higher
firm's ratio	0%	10%	than 10%

Classification of industries regarding competitive market structures

| Characteristics | Market structures | | |
	Oligopolistic competition	Monopolistic competition[1]	Pure competition
H-index	under 1000	under 3600	under 1000
4-firm ratio	between 20 and 40%	between20 and 60%	under 20%
the largest firm's ratio	at least 5%	at least 30%	
the second largest firm's ratio	at least 5%	not higher than 5%	not higher than5%

Notes:

1. Note that we use the category of *monopolistic competition* differently from most textbooks. In this kind of industry there is one significantly larger firm than the rest but the concentration measures are not high enough for it to qualify as a dominant firm.

Four characteristics have been used here to specify the six market structures, as follows. Aside from pure monopoly, there are two qualified levels of the H-index: 3600 and 1000.

Above 3600 an industry may be an oligopolist or dominant firm depending on the relative sizes of the two largest firms in the market. If there is a firm that controls at least half of the market, and if the second largest has a market share no higher than 10 per cent, the market form predominates, otherwise an oligopoly exists.

Between 3600 and 1000, an industry may be an oligopoly or in monopolistic competition, depending again on the relative sizes of the two largest firms.

If one firm controls at least 30 per cent of the market, and if the second largest has no more than 5 per cent, then the market form is monopolistic competition, otherwise it is an oligopoly.

Markets with an H-index no higher than 1000 may even be in monopolistic competition, if the relative size requirements are met, otherwise they are in oligopolist or pure competition, depending on the four-firm ratios. If the four-firm ratio is no higher than 20 per cent, the market would be purely competitive, otherwise it is characterized by oligopolistic competition. The classification method used is summarized in Table 8.3.

3 NON-COMPETITIVE SECTORS IN HUNGARY

Monopoly means a market in which the consumer has no choice but to purchase from a single seller. In this sense, there is not a particularly large number of monopolies in the Hungarian economy.

As can be seen from Table 8.4, there were only 11 true monopoly industries in 1992 in Hungary.

Table 8.4 The significance of the noncompetitive industries in the Hungarian economy, 1992

	Number of industries	Combined net output in 1992 (billion Forints)	Proportion in the 1992's Gross Output
Monopolies	11	600	9.7%
Dominant firm	15	386	6.2%
Oligopoly	13	195	3.1%
Together	39	1181	19.0%

Our concept of a monopoly does not apply to exclusive rights, special licences, and the like, of which quite a few examples could be cited. The eleven industries of monopolies must be natural monopolies, in which the sources of the monopoly are mostly technological. Table 5 shows these natural monopolies in the Hungarian economy.

As can be seen from Table 5, the regulation of natural monopolies involves a concession in most cases, and price regulation in a few others. A form of state ownership has been preserved for the remaining industries. Another important indicator of these industries is the amount of foreign direct investments (FDI).

There are only three markets in which FDI plays a significant role: conventional and radio-telephone services, railway transport, and legal gambling.

The picture will soon change, however, because new regulations are expected in the very near future.

Table 8.5 Natural monopolies in the Hungarian economy

Industries	Type of government regulation	The amount of FDI[3] (billion Forints)
Electricity	State ownership[1]	
Conventional telephone services	Concessions in local services, price regulation	87.5
Radiotelephone services	Concessions[2]	5.3
Water	State ownership[1]	
Sewerage services	State ownership and concessions[1]	
Natural gas	State ownership[1]	
TV and radio broadcasting	Concessions	
Postal services	State ownership	
Railway transport	State ownership and concessions	1.0
Gambling	Concessions	5.0
Crude oil pipelines	State ownership	

Notes:

1. New regulations are expected shortly
2. Two competitors
3. Foreign direct investments

4 EVALUATING CHANGES IN THE CONCENTRATION LEVEL OF NON-COMPETITIVE INDUSTRIES IN HUNGARY

One cannot expect changes in the level of concentration in the case of a natural monopoly. However, we can certainly expect a significant drop in concentration after privatization in cases of industries dominated by artificially created socialist giant factories, trusts, and so on. A comparative study has been conducted in an attempt to measure the changes of concentration in Hungarian oligopolistic non-competitive industries. The project has been in progress for some time and has examined changes in various concentration measures between 1990 and 1993. The major difficulty of collecting relevant data, however, has not yet been successfully overcome, and increasing problems in obtaining reliable data have been encountered.[4] Consequently, it has been necessary to adopt other methods to measure changing concentration in Hungarian industries.[5]

Table 8.6 H-indexes and numbers of organizations in some selected Hungarian industries in 1990 and 1993

Industries	1990		1993	
	H-index	Number of rganiz.	H-index	Number of organiz.
Building materials				
Lime and cement	1733	14	1247	18
Fine ceramics and				
grinding wheels	1155	42	1402	14
Light industries				
Paper-making	5711	7	6200	7
Printing	421	109	401	103
Food industries				
Meat	400	87	450	87
Poultry	1151	34	810	29
Baking	344	127	250	92
Sugar refining	990	12	1034	11
Chocolates and				
candies	2949	45	4348	22
Vegetable oils	10000	1	9409	2
Distillary and spirits	1785	15	2927	9
Wines	1166	35	3312	23
Tobacco	2462	7	2941	5

The industries listed in Table 8.6 have been studied. Not all of them were dominated by giant factories before 1989, but they were the industries for which sufficient data could be obtained at the company level. The findings are not surprising. In five of the thirteen selected industries we found a decrease in the H-indexes, while eight industries displayed increasing concentration. One possible cause of a clear change in concentration is a change in the number of organizations in the industry, but in the opposite direction. This means that if there has been an increase in concentration, there has been a decrease in the number of organizations, and vice versa. This is true for nine of the selected industries, while the remaining four require some other explanation. Two paper-making and meat industries can be easily accounted for, since in these industries the number of organizations did not change. In the paper-making industry, the rise of the H-index has been due to the growing market share of the largest firm in the market, namely Dunapack Rt. There are so many firms in the meat market that a small change in relative market shares may cause this 'unusual' behaviour by the H-index. The same factor accounts for the parallel trend in the printing industry and in the baking industry.

Table 8.7 Characteristics of market structures in some selected Hungarian industries in 1990 and 1993

Industry number	H-index	4-firm ratio (%)	1990 largest firm ratio (%)	second largest firm ratio
1.	1733	72	33	19
2.	10000	100	100	–
3.	1785	71	37	21
4.	2462	91	32	24
5.	990	51.1	18.7	13.4
6.	5711	81	51	9.2
7.	1155	49	22.2	11.0

Industry number	H-index	4-firm ratio (%)	1993 largest firm ratio (%)	second largest firm ratio
1.	1247	65	25.5	13.7
2.	5013	100	52.56	47.4
3.	2926	96.2	41.7	26.9
4.	2540	92.9	35.7	25.6
5.	1035	54.09	16.1	14.3
6.	6200	84	61.2	21
7.	1402	61	31	15.4

Industries:

1. Lime and cement   5. Sugar-refining
2. Vegetable oil   6. Paper-making
3. Distilling and spirits 7. Fine ceramics
4. Tobacco

Table 8.8 Changes in market forms and concentration in some selected Hungarian industries

Industry number	Market form		Changes in concentration level	
	1990	1993	H-index	4-firm ratio
1.	Oligopoly	Oligopoly	− 486	− 13%
2.	Monopoly	Oligopoly	− 4987	− 47.4%
3.	Oligopoly	Oligopoly	+ 1141	+ 25.2%
4.	Oligopoly	Oligopoly	+ 78	+ 2%
5.	Oligopolistic competition	Oligopoly	+ 45	+ 3%
6.	Dominant firm	Oligopoly	+ 489	+ 3%
7.	Oligopoly	Oligopoly	+ 247	+ 12%

Notes:
As table 8.7

The H-index analysis is one way to approach the problem of measuring changes in concentration, but not the only one. Let us refer to the market form classification suggested earlier (see Table 8.3). Four characteristics were used to identify a market form, including H-indexes. On the basis of that method seven industries were selected, each presently in an oligopoly situation, and an attempt was made to examine changes in concentration levels and in market forms between 1990 and 1993. The results are set out in Table 8.7 and Table 8.8.

5 SPECIAL CAUSES IN THE CASE OF THE SEVEN SELECTED INDUSTRIES

Each of the seven selected industries is considered a sensitive market in the sense of competition regulation. We therefore conclude that the result of our analysis, although not comprehensive, justifies a number of definitive statements concerning the manner in which privatization has affected concentration levels, and through them market forms. The initial question was how privatization could increase competition, or whether there is any necessary relationship between privatization and competition. How can one explain the effect of privatization on changes in market forms or in the concentration measures?

5.1   Lime and cement

Prior to 1990 there was only one state-owned firm in monopoly, which was broken up into five companies even before the establishment of the ASP. Each of these companies had a foreign owner, but foreign participants only received a minority share in a given Hungarian company although all foreign parties obtained interests in more than one Hungarian company.[6] Until 1993, foreign participation did not exceed the 50 per cent mark in each company. But in 1993, the ASP sold its share in the Beremendi Cement to two German companies, whose share is therefore now 77 per cent.

The former state monopoly in the cement industry has been broken, but an interconnected complex foreign ownership structure has formed in the newly established companies. The industry has suffered from deep recession since the late 1980s, and at present firms are operating at less than half capacity. Putting this and the Beremendi case together, there is a significant danger that some kind of a cartel may arise on the basis of these interlocking foreign interests. Furthermore, as in most countries, the cement industry is considered to be a nationally sensitive, strategic sector, one which should have been kept under domestic control.

Another feature of this sector is that the three foreign companies has invested a total of 3.5 billion forint in it during the last few years. Other than this, there has been no other stimulus to development. Although a significant proportion of the invested capital has gone to establishing up-to-date environmental equipment and technologies, there are still several unresolved problems of pollution.[7] Since the early nineties, a few smaller lime manufacturing factories has been separated off from the larger cement companies. This accounts for the large number of organizations and the relatively low concentration level.

5.2   Vegetable oil

The privatization of this industry is a 'textbook case'. Originally, there was only one national state-owned firm (NÖMOV) in a monopoly position. It was subsequently divided into two specialized companies: vegetable oil and other activities (like margarine).[8] Privatization reduced the concentration level insofar as two companies were operating instead of the former NÖMOV, but they do so in tight specialization. Cereol does not effectively compete against Unilever, because the former produces all Hungary's vegetable oil while the latter controls Hungarian margarine production. Imports of both vegetable oil and margarine are subject to quotas.

As far as the other components of competition are concerned, product quality has been improved, supply has been steady and in a sufficient variety. In 1993, the new owners invested more than one billion forint in new refining plants and equipment. Cereol has undertaken to buy up the local growers' oil seed crop at higher prices combined with quality premiums. To date, there have been no worker lay-offs in these companies.

5.3   Distilling and spirits

Three of the six major Hungarian distillery companies have already been privatized and entered three joint ventures with foreign majorities.[9] These three joint ventures control 60 per cent of the industry's capacity. The significant increase in the concentration level in this industry has been due to two causes. Output dropped by at least 35 per cent in two years, while two large producers were able to increase their sales, thereby significantly expanding their market shares.

5.4   Tobacco

The four major companies in the tobacco processing industry have been sold to different tobacco multinationals.[10] In the tobacco-leaf fermenting industry there are two larger companies,[11] and five smaller, so-called conversion plants. Competition in the cigarettes and other tobacco products market was very intense among the major companies even before privatization. Each of the foreign participants was formerly a licence-giver to a Hungarian firm, so that one of their motives for privatization must have been to protect the quality of their products. In fact, in most cases, the differences in the quality and reliability of products produced in Hungary and abroad have been reduced or even eliminated. Consequently, no significant change has taken place in the tobacco industry, which is indicative of the close control exerted by the multinational companies.

5.5   Sugar-refining

There were eleven sugar-refining firms to be privatized in Hungary. The privatization of seven of has been accomplished, in six cases with foreign participation with minority shareholding. These latter six firms account for 75 per cent of the industry's total capacity.[12] The privatization of the sugar industry has been severely criticized because of excessive foreign participation; a criticism which is unjustified, for the minority of shares is in foreign hands. However, there has been another and much more serious threat raised by the concerted action of a group of firms under the same foreign control.

This danger was indicated by allegations of price fixing activity in 1992.[13] As a result of the increased market shares of the three biggest companies, the industry has merely changed market form from oligopolist competition to oligopoly.

5.6 Paper-making

Concentration was extremely high in this industry in 1990, and it increased even further in 1992. Before 1990, there was one national enterprise[14] with twenty-one plants and factories. Because of the special strategic tendencies of the international paper-making business (such as increasing capital accumulations and integrating standards), it was decided that the Hungarian paper-making industry should be privatized *en bloc* and sold to a single buyer.

After a few turns in privatization preferences, the Austrian Thomas Prinzhorn was able to acquire three of the major Hungarian paper-making companies.[15]

The Prinzhorn concern controlled some 60 per cent of the market in 1992. That is the main cause of the increasing concentration.

5.7 Fine ceramics

There has been a significant decrease in the number of business organizations in this industry. Both the largest company[16] and the second largest one[17] were able to increase their markets share while the industry as a whole shrank by 10 per cent, which would explain the 250 increase in the H-index.

6 SOME MORE RESULTS FROM ANOTHER STUDY

The industries discussed above are 'sensitive' in terms of competitive regulation, and this means that the Office of Competition Regulation must monitor developments in their markets. However, they are obviously not the only sensitive industries. Accordingly, another study carried out by the Office of Competition Regulation examined as many as 45 sectors.[18] The method employed was a mixture of the usual concentration analysis complemented by extensive direct inquiries and the use of indirect sources of information like publications and interviews with distinguished representatives of the industry in question. The survey did not compare the same two years (as ours did), but examined the situation during and after the moment when the industry underwent complete privatization. This means that if privatization began in

1991 and was completed in 1992, the comparison was between 1990 and 1993. If privatization only began in 1992, then the initial year was 1991, and so on.

Table 8.9 Changes in market forms as a result of the privatization

Market form	Number of industries before privatization	Number of industries after privatization
Monopoly	13	5
Dominant position	4	11
Oligopoly	8	9
Competition	20	20

Market form before privatization	Market form after privatization				Together
	Monopoly	Dominant position	Oligopoly	Competition	
Monopoly	5	7	1	–	13
Dominant position	–	3	–	1	4
Oligopoly	–	1	4	3	8
Competition	–	–	4	16	20
Togheter	5	11	9	20	45

The study showed no significant change in 20 industries, increases in 15, and decreases in 10 out of the 45 selected. The results are given in Table 8.9. Evaluation of these results shows that privatization decisions by the State Property Agency concerning highly concentrated industries brought significant changes to some industries, but in most cases the privatization process itself had no impact on concentration. The direction of change was almost evenly divided between increases and decreases. There was therefore no typical result of privatization from the viewpoint of concentration at the mesoeconomic level – as one indicator of the intensity of competition. Having said that, however, there are signs of significant restructuring in most of the industries examined. Although these signs may not show up in changes in the concentration level, they may be no less important at microeconomic level.

7 CONCLUSIONS

Having analysed the newly-created situations in the Hungarian non-competitive industries with respect to the level of competition, the findings are mostly as expected: the overall result is not a single characteristic but a complex picture. Competitive pressure can be shown in some cases, but there was no sign of it in others. The Hungarian economy had an extremely concentrated manufacturing industry structure in the early 1980s. The last communist governments, especially that headed by Németh, initiated several decentralization programmes, as a result of which the concentration situation in the economy improved significantly. In 1990, according to our estimations and concentration measures, roughly 20 per cent of gross output was produced in highly concentrated industries. This 20 per cent was again the proportion in 1992. The dominant firm and oligopolist market forms accounted for about 10 per cent, which was not particularly high compared with neighbouring countries. Major progress in decentralization had been achieved even before the second wave of privatization got under way at the beginning of 1991. Most of the privatization activities in 1991 and 1992 failed to bring about significant changes in concentration in the highly concentrated industry sectors.

The concentration analysis is one – and by no means the only – way to measure industrial changes as regards competition. One extremely important aspect of the issue is certainly the international competitiveness of industries.[19] Another is qualitative analysis of the effects exerted by changes on the ownership structure, like prices, product quality, accompanying services, etc. These other aspects must necessarily be taken into account if one is to reach definite conclusions concerning matters related to competition in Hungarian industries.

NOTES

1. A revised version of a paper presented at the Fourth Trento Workshop, 1994.
2. Foster provides strong support for the view that the marked acceleration of privatization in the early 1980s in Britain occurred not so much for political or microeconomic reasons as 'principally because of the power of certain more or less questionable macroeconomic arguments'. However, as regards the success of any privatization, Foster adopts the mainstream view: 'the future of privatization will depend most of all on the extension of competition and the success of regulation' (Foster 1992, ch. 4).
3. The Herfindhal–Hirschman index is calculated as the sum of the squares of the market shares of all firms in a given industry. For example, the H-index for an industry with a

large firm enjoying a 50 per cent market share, and five firms each with a 10 per cent market share, would have an H-index of $(50^2 + 5\cdot102) = 3000$, or an industry with 10 firms of equal sizes, $(10\cdot102) = 1000$. In the United States, an industry with an index below 1000 is considered competitive; above 1800 it would be highly concentrated; between 1000 and 1800, it is considered to be a moderately concentrated industry.

4. Hungary has a Data Protection Act which protects legal and natural persons from illegal inquiry into their personal affairs. This is a very important feature of a democracy, but at the same time it may help companies to conceal their unsatisfactory performance from the public. The only way to force them to publish their reports is through the stock exchange. Companies listed on the stock exchange have been obliged to make their annual performance reports public, but there are relatively few companies listed on the Hungarian stock exchange at the present time. The great majority of companies operating in Hungary are not compelled to provide reliable data, except to the APEH, the Hungarian taxation office.

5. See Dénes and Szombathelyi (1992), Bertáné and Forgács (1990), Kovács and Pogácsás (1994).

6. Beremendi Cement went to the German Heidelberg Zement AG and also to German Schenk KG; Váci Cement és Mészmü to Heidelberg Zement AG, Schwenk KG; Hejöcsabai Cement to the Swiss Holderbank; Lábatlani Cement to Holderbank; Bélaapátfalvai Cement to Heidelberg Zement AG, Schwenk KG, Holderbank.

7. Lábatlani Cement has just appealed against a first-degree resolution on environmental issues.

8. The former went to an Italian multinational (Feruzzi-Cereol), the latter to another multinational, Dutch Unilever. A Hungarian company made a bid (the Mentor Cooperative), but its offer did not even come close to those of the multinationals.

9. Szabadegyházai Szeszip. Rt went to the Austrian–Belgian consortium Agrama, Amylum; Buszesz Rt. to the Austrian consortium Mautner Narkhof; and Buliv Kft to the German Underberg Zwack.

10. SD Tabak Rt was sold to Reynolds; Egri Dohánygyár Kft to the American–Austrian consortium Philip Morris and Austrian Tabak; Pécsi Dohánygyár Kft to British–American Tobacco; Debreceni Dohánygyár Kft to Reemsta.

11. Nyidofer and Budapesti Dohányfermentáló V.

12. The French multinational company Beghin Say acquired three of them, the Austrian Agrana took two, and one went to a French-British consortium (Eastern Sugar).

13. The investigation was initiated by the Hungarian Office of Competition Regulation and it was completed in 1993. The Council of Competition imposed heavy fines on six sugar refining companies.

14. Papiripari V.

15. Dunapack Rt, Szolnoki Papír Rt and Halaspack Rt.

16. Herendi Porcelán Rt.

17. Alföldi Porcelángyár Rt.

18. See Kovács and Pogácsás (1994).

19. Hughes and Hare (1994) have set out a method for assessing the competitiveness of industries in Eastern Europe which takes account of the world market environment in which these countries operate. The use of world market prices, and alternative assumptions about the shadow pricing of capital and labour, have enabled them to calculate measures for profits.

REFERENCES

Arva, L. (1994), 'A müködö töke. Külföldi beruházások Kelet-Europában' (FDI in East Europe), *Figyelö*, July 7.

Bertáné Forgács, A. (1990), 'Between Monopoly and Competition on the Market: Market Pattern of the Manufacturing Industry 1980–1988', *Acta Oeconomica*, (1–2).

Capek, A. (1992), 'Alliances, Bargaining and Privatization in Czechoslovak Economy', Working Papers of the Institute of Economics, Czechoslovak Academy of Sciences.

Dénes, G. and A. Szombathelyi (1992), 'A monopolhelyzetü vállalatok privatizációs stratégiája' (Privatization Strategy of Firms in Monopoly Position), *Prodinform*, November.

Ettlie, J.E. (1993), 'The Emergence of Manufacturing in Hungary. Production', *PRD Studies on East Europe*, August.

Foster, C.D. (1992), *Privatization, Public Ownership and Regulation of Natural Monopoly*, Oxford, Blackwell.

Hanson, R. (1992), 'The Legal Framework for Privatization in Hungary', *Law & Policy in International Business*, spring.

Hughes, G. and P. Hare (1994), 'The International Competitiveness of Industries in Bulgaria, Czechoslovakia, Hungary, and Poland', *Oxford Economic Papers*, **46**, April.

Kikeri, S., J. Nellis and M. Shirley (1992), *Privatization: The Lessons of Experience,* World Bank Publications.

Kováks, C. and P. Pogácsás (1994), 'A privatizáció mezzo szintü hatásai' (Mesoeconomic effects of privatization) unpublished study for Budapest University of Economic Sciences, April.

Matsunaga, N. et al. (1993), *Research Into Economic Assistance and Policy Proposals for Eastern Europe*, Japan Institute of International Affairs, March.

OTHER SOURCES

Privatizációs Monitor (1994), 'Allami Vagyonügynökség. Szervezési, Informatikai és Vagyonnyilvántartási Igazgatóság', számai.

'A külföldi töke szerepe a privatizációban', *Kihvások*, MTA Világgazdasági Kutató Intézet, **33**, szám, 1994, május.

9. Labour Market and Employment Policy in Central and Eastern Europe in the Context of Systemic Change[1]

Jenö Koltay

1 INTRODUCTION

The emergence of a particular labour market in Central and Eastern Europe began well before the change of regime. This market was deformed by the lack of a capital market and it was characterized by a labour shortage and a tendency towards full employment – the results of chronic over-demand and the absorption of all labour reserves.

Constraints on open unemployment disappeared with the change of regime, followed by a substantial fall in employment. In a couple of years unemployment rates of around zero jumped to between ten or fifteen per cent, or even higher in some countries. Unemployment became persistent and the decline in employment is continuing even in cases where unemployment is no longer on the rise.

A change of paradigm can be observed in the labour market and in labour relations. Bargaining and negotiations are taking over the role of central regulation. Economic transformation and the emergence of capital markets is proceeding more slowly than was foreseen, or it is lagging behind, and employment policies have few instruments and resources at their disposal. The functioning of the labour market is still deformed. The state continues to play a dominant role while private sector employers and trade unions are still weak. A long learning process is required if a compromise between economic rationality and social equity is to be found. For the time being, the threat of unemployment and deprivation is highly selective. Long-term unemployment is spreading, together with strong disparities in unemployment rates, especially at the regional level.

2 THE FALL IN PRODUCTION, EMPLOYMENT AND LABOUR FORCE PARTICIPATION

2.1 General trends

In the years during and immediately after the change of regime, declining employment was a general and marked trend in every country which more or less matched a drastic fall in production. At that time, the downturn resulted largely from voluntary separations and from a recruitment ban, or from such soft measures as curtailing the employment of retired people, introducing early retirement schemes, or lay-offs. Then, gradually or suddenly, came the loss of jobs and the consequent unemployment as the major cause of employment decline.

Table 9.1   *Production and employment changes in the period of 1992 (1989=100), 1993 (1982=100), 1994 (1993=100)*

	Czech Rep.	Slovakia	Hungary	Poland	Romania
1992 (1989=100)					
GDP	78.9	80.5	81.8	82.4	71.0
E	91.1	86.4	84.0	87.4	98.8
UE(1993 1stg)	4.3	12.3	12.6	14.3	9.6
1993 (1992=100)					
GDP	91.1	95.9	91.1	103.8	101.5
E	97.5	97.4	93.1	97.5	95.9
1994 (1993=100)					
GDP	102.6	104.6	102.9	104.8	103.9
E	101.3	–	97.8	102.9	98.9
UE (1995 2ndq)	3.5	13.4	8.9	13.9	9.1

Notes:

E = employment, UE = unemployment according to ILO definition, except Romania, where the figure is for registered unemployment

Source:

Employment Observatory, Brusselles, no. 5, 1993; no. 7, 1995; no. 8, 1995

Labour force participation also went into decline, mainly in the age groups close to retirement age or above, in some countries also women, or young people reaching working age, or those living in villages.

The significant drop in the rate of labour force participation (i.e. the ratio between the number of those in employment and waiting for employment on the one hand and those of working age on the other) in Czechoslovakia, in Slovenia, and in Hungary is in part only apparent. Numerous subjects working in small private-sector companies or in the informal economy are omitted from the statistics.

2.2   Structural changes

As regards changes in the branch and ownership structure of employment, the decline of employment in industry, construction and agriculture, in the state and the cooperative sector, and the strengthening of the services and the private sector is a general phenomenon. Employment has increased most rapidly in the private sector, while private enterprises have proliferated more in the services and trade.

In Hungary, Poland and Slovenia the decline of employment in the state-owned sector has been more strongly felt, but these same countries have seen dynamic growth of employment in the private sector.

In the Czech Republic, with some delay and so far to a limited extent, state-sector employment has also started to shrink, and, even if it was initially practically non-existent, private-sector employment has begun to rise rapidly in that country too.

In Slovakia, a more intense reduction of state-sector employment, combined with a weaker private sector, has brought about a less favourable employment situation.

In Romania, laggardly economic transformation, despite a drastic setback in production, has delayed reduction in state-sector employment, although both the economy and individual employees have had to pay a high price, because high inflation and very low consumption are today compounded by high unemployment as well.

The fall-off in state-sector employment has so far been very loosely related to the sectoral shift of employees of state-owned companies consequent on privatization. Moreover, the increased share of private-sector employment is due mainly to the proliferation of brand-new private enterprises. These latter are typically small or medium in size, and not infrequently they offer employment in uncertain, low-standard and low-paid jobs. Not surprisingly, not only does the private sector increase employment but it equally fuels unemployment as well. The majority of its workforce has moved directly from the state to the private sector without becoming unemployed in between. Where it is possible to trace the process with the help of household panels, one finds that the private sector actually employs less unemployed workers than it 'produces' (Köllő, 1993).

Table 9.2 Labour force participation rates (in percentage of the working age population)

Year	Czechoslovakia Czech Rep.	Czechoslovakia Slovakia	Hungary	Poland	Romania
1989		84.8	82.5	76.1	–
males		87.0	85.9	83.6	87.3
females		82.3	78.8	68.6	80.6
1992		78.8	78.4	74.5	–
males		85.7	78.8	80.7	88.2
females		71.4	78.0	68.2	89.9
1992 S	65.4	67.8	73.2	69.0	–
males	72.4	77.9	77.0	76.1	85.8
females	58.5	57.5	69.5	62.1	85.3

Notes:

according to country by country definitions of working age for males and females

S= according to Labour Force Surveys

Source:

Country Studies

Employment Observatory

OECD-CCET Labour Market Database

The reduction in the state sector is as certain and as reliably documented as estimates on private-sector employment are unreliable. In Hungary, in mid-1993, the private sector's share of employment was 38 per cent if only fully private ownership is taken into account, and 49 per cent if partial private ownership is added (Kolosi, 1993). Between late 1991 and late 1992 the proportion of private-sector employment, alongside falling overall employment, rose from 15.7 per cent to 17.2 per cent in Slovenia, from 17.6 per cent to 27.8 per cent in the Czech Republic, and from 47.2 per cent to 58.4 per cent in Poland. In Slovakia 20 per cent of the labour force worked in the private sector at the end of 1992 (Schmögnerová, 1993).

Other studies have offered different figures, but these are equally inadequate for reliable comparison. It is interesting, instead, to consider employment structure data derived from another paper (Blanchard et al., 1993).

2.3   Labour hoarding, over-employment

Analysis of the employment trend has revived, in every country, the concept of company-internal labour reserves, well-known from the old regime, but the background and extent of which, however, are rather difficult to define. It is nevertheless obvious that transition economies should take this phenomenon into account as they struggle with problems of employment decline, mass unemployment, recession, the redistribution of property rights, the threat of bankruptcy, and in spite of the fact that its exact definition and statistical interpretation are still lacking.

In Romania, or more precisely in the case study devoted to it, this phenomenon is present only at the level of macro-economic evidence and its company-level manifestation is termed 'technical unemployment' (Miron, 1993). By late 1992, industrial production had shrunk to half its 1989 level, GDP to 70 per cent; unemployment had increased to 9.2 per cent, and productivity had declined quite dramatically in the same period. The disintegration of the economy, shortages of raw materials and energy, and the breakdown of traffic and transportation systems turned masses of employees into 'technically unemployed'.

In the case of the Czech Republic, analysis of industrial productivity trends (Janacek, 1993) indicates over-employment in the state sector. Disaggregation of productivity changes by company size suggests that productivity has increased very rapidly in the small-company sector (companies with a maximum of 25 employees) and that its weight and productivity have grown in dynamic manner. At the same time, the productivity of large companies with more than 2500 employees – still state-owned in the traditional sense at the time of the research (1992) – has declined sharply.

Rather than such rough estimates, a comparative picture based on more thorough methodology is provided by a Slovenian survey which analyses all the countries under scrutiny here (Drobnic, 1992) in terms of the relationship between trends in industrial production on the one hand, and employment and unemployment on the other. The survey's findings – in an absolute sense as well as compared with developed market economies – point to a very loose relationship: only in Slovenia does unemployment react markedly to changes in production. The opposite case is that of Romania, where the relationship is exceptionally weak. Consequently, the accumulation of company-internal labour reserves is much less of a problem in the Slovenian economy than it is elsewhere – in Romania in particular.

For some time, despite the setback in production, the state-run (mammoth) companies of each country in the region sought to postpone and possibly to avoid redundancies, which still presented themselves in the form of labour reserves, even if – by various means – they managed to minimize net working hours and partly costs as well. This was made possible by eliminating overtime, cutting down on the number of shifts, introducing shorter working hours, unpaid holidays and the like. In reality, the shrinkage of employment lagged far behind the decline in production. And one must also consider the fact that this delay and the continued existence of the reserves may have prolonged the downward trend in employment after production had managed to stabilize and then to revive. This is the conclusion that can be drawn from production and employment statistics in Poland last year.

Table 9.3   The share and evolution of state and private sector employment (percentages)

Year	Czech lands	Slovakia	Hungary	Poland	Romania
1990					
State	91.9	95.1	–	66.4	–
Private	8.1	4.9	–	33.6	–
1991					
State	80.1	87.2	66.0	59.7	93.1
Private	19.9	12.8	34.0	40.3	6.9
1992					
State	70.0	83.0	64.2	55.6	88.0
Private	30.0	17.0	35.8	44.4	12.0
1992/1990					
State	84.0[a]	77.6	66.0	79.7[b]	90.2[c]
Private	111.3[a]	109.6	121.0	107.7[b]	104.4
Total	92.5	87.6	87.7	87.4[b]	96.1

Notes:

a = 1991/1990

b = 1992/1989

c = 1992/1991

Source:

Employment Observatory 1992, 1993

Blanchard et al. 1993

Country Studies

No satisfactory explanation has been provided to date – by any statistics or studies – for the stubborn survival of company-internal labour reserves, although some factors can be cited: survival of the hierarchical, paternalistic relationship between companies and the state and the disintegration of the production system (in Romania); institutional and economic policy constraints in several countries (the banning or limiting of dismissals, the lack of a bankruptcy law or the inadequate implementation thereof).

3   THE EMERGENCE OF UNEMPLOYMENT

3.1   Unemployment patterns

In Poland, Hungary and Slovenia, countries in which transformation was most advanced and partial reforms had already been carried out, the growth of unemployment began with the collapse of the old regime. Unemployment rates of around 13 per cent were registered by the end of 1992: 13.8 per cent in Poland, 13.2 per cent in Slovenia and 12.3 per cent in Hungary. These rates, high even by European standards, continued to rise in all three countries, reaching 15 per cent in Poland, approaching the same level in Slovenia, and rising to just above 13 per cent in Hungary, and then slipping downwards from March 1993 (to 10.9 per cent at the end of 1994).

In Czechoslovakia, where transformation began without any antecedent reform, unemployment grew rapidly in 1991, reaching 6.6 per cent by the end of the year (4.1 per cent in the Czech part and 11.8 per cent in Slovakia), although available data suggest that by the end of 1992 the rate had fallen to 5.5 per cent – less than the year before (the increase culminated in January 1992 and reached its peak in November). This general indicator, however, conceals significant differences. Had Slovakia been independent at the time, its 10.8 per cent unemployment rate would have secured it a place in the top group. With an unemployment rate still below or around 4 per cent, the Czech Republic is the area in the region least affected by unemployment. In Slovakia since the separation, unemployment has risen to over 13 per cent.

In Romania, which has lagged behind in economic transformation, and not only because of the lack of antecedents, unemployment (which was officially recognized only at the end of 1990) began to rise as late as 1991, but as a result of continous acceleration reached 9.2 per cent in 1992 and is approaching the generalized high unemployment rate of the region.

In countries like Romania and the former Czechoslovakia, to a certain extent, unemployment could only be examined through data provided by registration.

Table 9.4 Registered unemployment in percentages of the labour force (active population), unemployment rates at the end of the period

Year	Czecho-slovakia	Czech lands	Slovakia	Hungary	Poland	Romania	Slovenia
1989	–	–	–	0.5	..	–	3.2
1990	1.0	..	..	1.0	3.0	..	5.9
1991	6.6	4.1	11.8	8.5	11.8	3.0	10.1
1992	5.5	2.6	10.8	12.3	13.8	9.2	13.2
				10.4^S	13.5^S		8.3^S
1993							
1st quarter		2.9	12.0	12.9	14.2	9.3	13.5
2nd quarter		2.8	13.5	12.7	15.2	9.4	14.5
		3.9^S	12.4^S	12.0^S	13.8^S		
3rd quarter		3.2	13.7	13.4	15.4	9.1	
		3.8^S	12.5^S	11.9^S	13.1^S		
4th quarter		3.5	14.0	12.8	16.4	10.4	
		3.7^S	13.0^S	11.5^S	14.9^S		
1994							
1st quarter		3.5	14.5	12.2	16.7	11.5	14.0
		4.0^S	13.7^S	11.5^S	16.0^S	8.2^S	
4th quarter		3.2	14.6	10.4	16.0	10.9	
1995							
2nd quarter		2.8	13.3	10.1	15.2	9.9	
3rd quarter		3.7^S	12.5^S	10.1^S	12.9^S	8.2^S	

Note:
S = Data according to Labour Force Survey

Source:
Employment Observatory 1992, 1993, 1995
Country Studies
Labour Force Surveys

Labour Force Surveys were introduced first in Slovenia (1989), then in

Hungary and Poland (1991) and only much later in the other countries. Since 1989, survey-derived data in Slovenia have conformed to international standards and eliminate the difficulty of cross-country comparisons due to substantial discrepancies between the registration systems of different countries, and the difficulty of comparisons over time due to frequent changes in the eligibility criteria for unemployment benefit.

As in market economies, the survey data tend to be slightly lower, except for Czechoslovakia (later the Czech Republic), where unemployment according to preliminary survey data – becoming regular only in late 1992 – is higher than the official data calculated from the register. In extreme cases the two figures may diverge considerably: official statistics in Russia showed 1.5 per cent unemployment early in 1993, while a survey claimed that the rate was between 4 per cent and 5 per cent (Ginsburg and Student, 1993).

Of course, surveys do not cover the unemployed who have some kind of work, do not actively seek a job, or who – for some other reason – are not available for work but satisfy the more loosely worded requirements of registration. However, the registered unemployed do not include those who are really out of work but are no longer entitled to benefit and for this or some other reason do not find it essential to have themselves registered. The difference in the contents of the two indicators may amount to as much as one-third in the countries of the region, although they are close to each other.

3.2   The unemployment pool: inflow and outflow

In European market economies, the growth of unemployment has correlated significantly with the decline and slow-down of outflow (those leaving the unemployment register) and the longer period of unemployment (extending the unemployment benefit period).

In the United States, besides changes on the outflow side, the alteration of inflow (entering the register) has also played an essential part. In Western Europe, unemployment, which was high once before, seems to have been longer lasting and to fall much more slowly than in the USA, even after the releasing factors disappeared.[2]

In the Central-Eastern European region, unemployment started to rise with the sudden growth of inflow and remained at a higher level than the initially marked low outflow for some time in nearly every country of the region. Later, in 1992, unemployment continued to grow, so that the difference between the two rates diminished partly as a result of a reduction in inflow and of some growth of outflow.

Table 9.5 Unemployment and inflow and outflow data (per month, by 1992 average)

	Unemploy-ment rate	Inflow rate	Outflow rate		Outflow rate into emp.	Share of long-term unemp.
		a	a	b	b	b
Czech Rep.	3.1	0.6	0.8	25.8	18.0	28.4
Slovakia	11.4	1.0	1.2	9.8	4.8	25.5
Hungary(c)	11.7	0.5	0.5	7.0	3.0	37.3
Poland	14.9	0.7	0.6	4.0	2.3	43.4
Romania	8.3	..	..	1.2	0.9	..
exGDR Germany	15.6	1.5	..	10.8	3.9	..
Fed.Rep.	5.8	0.9.	16.3	6.9	..	
France	9.5	0.9	..	11.4	4.8	..
Austria	3.7	1.0	..	25.8	16.3	..

Notes:

a in percentages of the economically active population

b in percentages of the registered unemployed

c inflow and outflow in percentages of unemployed receiving compensation

Source:

Employment Observatory 1992, 1.2; 1993, 3,4; Blanchard et al., 1993.

The situation now taking shape in Central-Eastern Europe resembles that of most Western European countries, i.e. a relatively high level of unemployment, coupled with slow turnover, with a large number of long-term unemployed and a rapidly lengthening period spent on the register. The apparent difference is that turnover is slower and inflow indicators are definitely lower than in Western Europe, while the case of outflow indicators is very similar. At the beginning of 1994 the proportion of the unemployed who had been on the register for more than a year rose above 45 per cent in Romania, 40 per cent in Poland, reached 40 per cent in Hungary and 33 per cent in Slovakia. There is a danger that unemployment preserving hysteresis-phenomena will be stronger than in Western European countries. This could be related, among other things, to cost-raising and labour-demand-reducing factors (such as contributions financing unemployment compensation, the

raising of the average wage or minimum wage, or the high level of severance pay, etc.).

Initially, there were fewer people who became unemployed after leaving their jobs (giving up mostly state employment, partly voluntarily). Also, many left the labour market and many others were re-employed without being unemployed in between. However, very few of those who ended up unemployed managed to find a new job. Later, a growing proportion of those who left their jobs became unemployed. In Poland, taking every sort of termination into account – from dismissal to resignation – the number of those entering the register exceeds 30 per cent, and only in the Czech Republic is the corresponding figure below 20 per cent. In the overwhelming majority of cases, those forced to seek employment pass through a longer and longer period of unemployment. The chances of finding new employment are fairly low. A substantial proportion of those leaving unemployment end up outside the labour market.

The new unemployed are increasingly those forced to give up their jobs, i.e. they are dismissed, even if mass lay-offs seem to be relatively rare. In Poland 56.4 per cent of the unemployed in late 1992 had been dismissed, while 16.9 per cent entered the labour market for the first time, 19.9 per cent re-entered and 6.8 per cent gave up their jobs (Witkowski, 1993). According to other sources, 56.5 per cent of the terminations in 1992 were ascribable to lay-offs, 26 per cent of the cases to unforced resignation, 18 per cent to the relinquishing of an economically active position. In Romania, dismissals have been increasingly frequent only since 1992.

In Slovenia, where overt unemployment has a longer history than in any of the other countries (the figures date back to 1964), the rapid increase in unemployment during the early 1990s was attributed to the growth of inflow, accompanied, moreover, by a substantial growth of outflow. Although the number of those cancelled from the register for unknown reasons also increased, the dynamism of the Slovenian labour market can be inferred from the fact that a larger number of the unemployed found work. Even in the Czech Republic, significantly more people change their employment status from unemployed to employed, and the outflow rate is altogether higher than in either Hungary or Poland, not to mention Romania. This is at least partly due to a more dynamic growth of jobs in the private sector, starting from scratch.

3.3   Some characteristics of the unemployed

In the Central Eastern European transformation economies unemployment threatens certain well-defined groups, with a selectivity even more ruthless than that experienced in market economies over a longer period.

Table 9.6 Long-term unemployment (the share and rate of those unemployed for at least 1 year at the end of the period)

Year	Czech Rep.	Slovakia	Hungary	Poland	Romania
Share (in percentage of all unemployed)					
1991	3.9	6.1	13.2	–	
1992	17.1	36.3	24.5	30.2	
1993 2nd quarter	18.1	32.8	32.3	42.9	
1994 1st quarter	19.0	33.3	40.0	42.2	45.0
1995 2nd quarter	31.1	53.8	39.4	41.0	48.1
Rate (in percentages of the economically active population)					
1991	0.2	0.7	1.0	–	
1992	0.4	3.7	3.4	4.8	
1993 2nd quarter	0.4	4.1	3.5	6.7	

Source:

Country Studies Employment Observatory Labour Force Surveys (1993, 1994)

The unskilled and underqualified are considerably over-represented among the unemployed. Unemployment among those with the highest qualifications, on the other hand, is well below the average.

In the Czech Republic, at the end of 1992, people with elementary educations constituted 20.6 per cent of the total active population and as much as 37.8 per cent of the unemployed, while the corresponding figures for those with higher qualifications were 10.8 and 2.6 per cent, respectively.

In Poland, those with primary educations represented 23.5 per cent of the unemployed, and their unemployment rate was 12.7 per cent. Skilled workers made up 40.6 per cent of the unemployed contingent and their unemployment rate was 16.9 per cent, whereas the share of those with university degrees was 3.6 per cent at a 5.3 per cent unemployment rate.

In Romania 2 per cent of the unemployed have received higher educations, while 88 per cent consist of workers with vocational training, which was very easy to obtain under socialism.

As far as age is concerned, young people run a higher-than-average risk of unemployment in Poland, Czechoslovakia and Romania, while the unemployment rate of those over 45–50 is usually below the average.

By the end of 1992, 30 per cent of the age group below 25 was unemployed in Poland; in Romania more than the half of registered unemployed were aged under 30. In general the situation of women is worse than the average. Their unemployment rate is, for the most part, much higher than that of the male population.

In Poland, for example, the unemployment rate of the latter was 12.7 per cent, that of the former 15.9 per cent, at the end of 1992. In Slovenia, women are less threatened by unemployment, and Hungarian figures similarly indicate that the risk of unemployment is much lower for women than for men.

As regards minorities, gypsies are the most vulnerable: large numbers of them have been crowded out of the labour market because of their low level of education and lack of vocational training.

High unemployment in their case – the rate of unemployment among gypsies is around 50 per cent in Hungary according to the survey data of Nagy and Sík (1993) – is obviously due to the accumulation of the factors mentioned above.

3.4   Regional disparities

Unemployment statistics show striking, often extreme, territorial disparities within all the countries of the region, from the smallest to the largest.

These differences increased in the period 1989–1993 and are definitely larger than in market economies, while at the same time the constraints on geographical mobility – housing conditions and deeply rooted traditions instilled by the planned economy – are much stronger compared with the United States and even with Western Europe.

At the county level (the figures are for 1993), in Poland the unemployment rate was higher than 25 per cent in 6 voivodeships while in Hungary it exceeded 20 per cent in four counties. Differences – at the level of larger territorial units – in Czechoslovakia were smaller: in the same year, in Slovakia, the highest rate was about 12.5 per cent in Eastern Slovakia, while in the Czech Republic it was 4 per cent in Northern Moravia.

In Romania the highest rates are to be found in Moldova: in mid-1993 in one county the unemployment rate was above 28 per cent, in two counties around 20 per cent (Vincze, 1993). If we consider smaller units, much bigger differences can be discerned. At the end of 1992, in 10 out of the 176 Hungarian placement districts the registered unemployment rate amounted to more than 33 per cent.

Table 9.7 The evolution of regional disparities in unemployment rates (a)

	Number of regions	UE rate national (%)	Coef. of variation e	UE rate of top quartile (%)f	UE rate of bottom quartile (%)	Top/ Bottom
Czech Rep.b	76					
1991		2.9	0.36	4.6	1.4	3.2
1992		3.0	0.44	3.5	0.9	3.8
1993		3.2	0.46	4.6	1.0	4.6
Slovakiad	38					
1991		7.0	0.25	9.9	4.5	2.2
1992		11.3	0.27	16.1	6.7	2.4
1993		14.4	0.29	21.7	7.5	2.9
Hungary	20					
1991		4.8	0.40	8.3	1.5	3.1
1992		10.3	0.29	16.0	5.0	3.2
1993		12.9	0.29	19.2	6.9	2.8
Poland	49					
1991		11.4	0.28	16.6	5.9	2.8
1992		13.6	0.29	18.4	7.7	2.4
1993		15.6	0.31	21.5	8.5	2.5
Romaniac	41					
1991		2.0	0.68	3.4	0.7	4.9
1992		5.3	0.41	8.3	3.0	2.8
1993		9.4	0.41	14.6	5.7	2.6
France	22					
1991		10.2	0.19	12.9	7.9	1.62
Sweden	24					
1991		3.3	0.23	4.4	2.5	1.76
U.K.	11					
1991		9.0	0.13	10.5	8.0	1.31

a   National unemployment rates and vacancy rates are weighted by the size of the regional labour force, annual average of monthy data.

b   Annual averages except for missing data in February and August 1991.

c   Romanian unemployment rates were calculated using the same 1993 labour force data.

d   Annual average in 1991 and 1992, December in 1993.

e   Coefficient of variation is the standard deviation divided by the mean of regional unemployment rates.

f   Unemployment rates for the top quarter of the labour force by regions were calculated by ordering regions in terms of descending unemployment rates; taking regions until the cumulative labour force exceeded one quarter of the total and similarly for the bottom quarter.

Source:
Scarpetta, 1994; OECD Employment Outlook, 1993.

In Slovakia, in 38 districts, unemployment was around 20 per cent in two districts, five districts proved to have between 17 per cent and 19 per cent unemployment, and seven districts saw their levels exceed 20 per cent in 1993 (Employment Services Department, 1993). In units similar in size to Hungarian units, even higher rates of unemployment can be discerned. In the Czech Republic, at the level of public administration units, unemployment rates were around 9 per cent in the Pribram district and in some Northern Moravian districts. In 1993–94, the highest figures exceeded 25 per cent in Slovakia, but remained around 10 per cent in the Czech Republic. In Hungary, from March 1993 onwards, in parallel with the downward shift of unemployment, also its regional disparities have shrunk in terms of stock indicators, although inflow and outflow differences persist.

The regions most threatened by unemployment in all countries are those with a unilateral economic structure based on some declining branch of heavy industry, textiles or sometimes the electricity industry (which plays a major role in the deterioration of employment in both parts of Czechoslovakia) or engineering (especially military industries in Slovakia). The same applies to mining areas and disadvantaged regions, especially agricultural ones. Serious problems are caused by those 'citadels' of socialist industrialization where one or another large state company plays a decisive role in employment. In industrial areas, unemployment is more stagnant, while vacancies and job creation remain at a very low level.

Differences are related to a shared past (nationalization, socialist industrialization, agricultural collectivization) and a shared present (the decline of state-owned industry, the fall in employment). For further explanation of the discrepancies observed, we can only refer to Hungarian surveys, which highlight regional differences in the role of family wealth, private savings and investments, the number of small enterprises (Köllő, 1993), entrepreneurial capacity, the quality of arable land and income levels (Fazakas, 1993).

Large territorial differences, the uneven distribution of the risk of unemployment, discriminatory dismissal and recruitment practices, the marginalization or squeezing out of significant groups of employees from the labour market, the institutionalization of fragile, less protected forms of employment, the transformation of economic governance and organization, the temporary disorganization of the economy – all these factors will fragment the evolving labour markets. This process can be made to parallel the experiences of market economies described (see Piore, 1983; Becker, 1971) in terms of growing labour market segmentation and discrimination in periods of increased unemployment. Of course, it would be premature to say whether these so far poorly-defined processes in Central and Eastern Europe are similar to their more sharply delineated Western counterparts.

4   LABOUR MARKET POLICIES AND INSTITUTIONS

The measures and institutions combatting the economic and social consequences of unemployment have been established in haste. Yet they were introduced with some delay in every country of the region by adapting structures commissioned over decades in market economies (except Slovenia, where measures have been operational for several years). This is why it has been frequently necessary to alter the passive and active measures introduced.

In Slovenia, institution building began much earlier than in the other countries of the region, and it had already taken shape under the previous regime. In Hungary, the 'preventive' measures and employment services of the late 1980s were drastically reorganized by the legislation of 1991 and modified several times thereafter. The new institutions are responsible for unemployment compensation and employment services (the Solidarity Fund, which is financed by employers' and employees' contributions). Active labour market policies are financed out of the budget, and related expenditures are disbursed by the Employment Fund co-managed by the social partners. Institutions follow more or less the German model at national and county level, assisted by some two hundred territorial units. Solutions adopted region-wide are similar in that they follow Western models with country-specific differences.

4.1   Expenditures

The related expenditures grow proportionately to the increase in unemployment. The ratio between total expenditure on all active and passive employment measures – ranging from benefit payment to job creation – and GDP in Hungary had more or less reached the average level of the OECD countries in 1992, followed by the other countries of the region, with Poland in the lead. In Hungary, the reverse tendency can be observed moving in parallel with the decrease in unemployment and, especially, in the number of unemployed receiving compensation (expenditure figures in percentage of GDP are: 1.7 per cent for 1991, 3 per cent for 1992, 2.9 per cent for 1993 and 2.5 per cent for 1994).

In several OECD countries, expenditures also show a tendency to shrink: from 3 per cent in 1985 to 2.6 per cent in 1990 in Sweden, from 2.9 per cent to 1.6 per cent in the United Kingdom, from 2.3 per cent to 2.2 per cent in Germany, from 3.7 per cent to 2.9 per cent in Belgium, from 0.9 per cent to 0.8 per cent in the United States. In some others the situation has stagnated: at 3.2 per cent in Spain; at 1.2 per cent in Austria; or an increase from 3.5 per cent to 4.1 per cent in Denmark, from 1.8 per cent to 2.1 per cent in France (OECD, 1993).

The expenditure level attained within a short period of time in the countries of Central and Eastern Europe relates to an unemployment level exceeding the average of the developed market economies and which is still on the rise. In the respective countries, this expenditure is flanked by declining GDP and growing budget deficits. Thus the fight against unemployment in order to prevent intolerable tensions and the threat of social explosion may itself lead to an unacceptable level of budget deficit and over-taxation. This, in turn, may negatively influence labour demand, and may contribute to the formation of hysteresis phenomena which extend the duration of high unemployment. The threat inherent in such a situation has been recognized not only in Hungary – where unemployment benefit has been the most generous, and where (besides the central budget) direct contributions by employers and employees are highest – but in other countries of the region as well.

Table 9.8   Expenditures on employment policy over time (in percentages of GDP)

Year	Bulgaria	Czechoslovakia	Hungary	Poland	Romania	Slovenia
1990	–	–	0.4	0.6	–	
1991	0.6	0.6	1.2	1.6	0.3	
1992	0.9	0.9	3.0	2.0	0.8	
1993	–	0.2cz	1.7slk	3.0	2.8	

Note:
GDP data do not fully compare to each other in several countries not directly comparable to OECD country data.

4.2   Unemployment compensation and its adjustment

Not coincidentally, since 1991 the newly introduced system of unemployment benefit has been altered at least once in Poland, Czechoslovakia and Hungary, and it has become more severe. The reason for this is that unemployment benefit payments are usually the largest single item of expenditure, constituting, in Poland, 51 per cent of all expenditures in 1990, 82 per cent in 1991 and over 87 per cent in 1992 (Witkowski, 1993), which is even higher than the 61 per cent of Hungary in 1991, 79 per cent in 1992 and 1993, and 75 per cent in 1994. Czechoslovakia was the only country in which the share of unemployment compensation in the total was smaller (39 per cent in 1992) than a large number of market economies (for example 30 per cent in Portugal, 38 per cent in Germany, 45 per cent in Sweden, 51 per cent in France, 69 per cent in the United States and 74 per cent in the United Kingdom in the same year) (OECD, 1993).

Czechoslovakia saw the most spectacular cutback. The 1989 system offered a benefit corresponding to 95 per cent (or 60 per cent) of net income for six months and 60 per cent for a further six months, while everyone else received 60 per cent. In 1991 eligibility was restricted to those who worked, studied, were doing military service or had been on sick or maternity leave for at least six months during the two previous years, the amount being 60 per cent in the first six months and 50 per cent for another six months. In 1992, eligibility was limited to those who worked, who were on military service or who had taken part in school education or vocational training for at least twelve months in the previous three years. The time span of the benefit was limited to six months, with payment of 60 per cent in the first half and 50 per cent in the second (70 per cent throughout the whole period for those undergoing re-training). The benefit must not exceed Kc3000; there is no compulsory minimum. Severe sanctions are applied to those who do not cooperate adequately with the employment office.

Elsewhere – even after modifications – the possible maximum period of unemployment benefit is still longer: 9 months in Romania, 12 months in Poland, while in Hungary it sank from 18 months to 12 months in 1993. In Poland, however, in crisis areas, benefit may be payable for up to 18 months since 1993. There is usually a set minimum to the benefit: 40 per cent of the minimum wage in Romania, 80 per cent in Slovenia, 90 per cent in Bulgaria, 96 per cent in Hungary (not anchored to the minimum wage), and in Poland the benefit and the minimum wage have been virtually equal since 1992. The maximum amount of compensation has been adjusted downwards in other countries as well, and eligibility has also been restricted, so that the excessive generosity of the benefit system by European standards is about to disappear.

The majority of those on benefit receive the minimum, and the average benefit is close to the minimum wage, or has sunk below it (in Hungary it was 42 per cent of the average wage at the end of 1992).

Those no longer entitled to unemployment benefit may apply for a lower social benefit, which in Hungary is set at 80 per cent of the minimum pension (this amounts to about 50 per cent of the minimum wage, while the average paid was 20 per cent of the average wage at the end of 1992) with, for the moment, no limit on duration. In Romania it is 40 per cent of the minimum pension, and it is payable for 18 months. In Slovenia, for up to three years after the beginning of unemployment compensation a social benefit equal to 80 per cent of the minimum wage is available. Similar assistance is available in the other countries, also on a more or less substantial means-tested basis. In Romania, all the owners of land (minimum two acres or four acres in mountain areas) and those with an income (half of the minimum wage or more) are excluded from unemployment benefit.

The unemployed may receive benefits on the basis of various criteria which come into force when their spell of unemployment begins. On the other hand, only some of them are paid according to the general rules: 25 per cent in Hungary at the end of 1992 (Nagy and Sík, 1993). Others, the majority, get the minimum. Limiting the conditions of eligibility, shortening the period of benefit payment, reducing the amount payable, and the expiry of entitlement for the long-term unemployed, has reduced the number of those receiving unemployment benefit. In Poland, this ratio was 75 per cent in 1992 and had fallen to below 50 per cent by 1993. In December 1992, it was over 60 per cent in Romania, but in mid-1993 only 48 per cent; and in Czechoslovakia a mere 38 per cent of all registered unemployed were receiving benefit at the end of 1992. In mid-1993 this ratio was even lower, standing at 33 per cent, in Slovakia, while the same indicator stood at 45 per cent in the Czech Republic.

4.3   Active employment policy measures

These measures aimed at attenuating labour market tensions and mismatches include all the instruments used in market economies, but to a rather different extent and with different degrees of effectiveness. Their impact remains difficult to evaluate, their 'unit cost' often seems to be high.

At the beginning of transformation, in 1990, the share of active measures in expenditures was relatively high in Poland (about 30 per cent) and in Hungary (about 60 per cent). Later, as the number of unemployment compensation applicants grew, the share of active spending in sharply rising total expenditure dropped. In 1991, Hungary still had the highest ratio (30 per cent, as opposed to 20–25 per cent in Poland and Czechoslovakia). In Romania – where at that time unemployment and total spending was low – the ratio was around 35 per cent. There was a turn-around in 1992, when the share of active expenditures, still growing in absolute terms, dropped to 20 per cent in Hungary, while it suddenly plummeted in Czechoslovakia, a country with a much lower unemployment and expenditure level and which cut back on unemployment benefits.

These figures show that, in 1992, the share of spending on active measures increased to 65 per cent in Czechoslovakia. A great deal more was spent on creating what are called 'socially purposeful' jobs than on passive measures. Part of the very dynamic increase in 1992 was due to the fact that assistance – ranging from job creation by companies to the self-employment of the unemployed – was increased to Kc50.000 per employed. (In Slovakia, for instance, the number of jobs created in this way rose from 24,436 to 115,976 from one year to the next.)

By comparison, the success of the public work programme was rather modest; the main result of re-training (which involved about 2 per cent of the active population in 1992) was the development of a regional network, though it should be pointed out that much less was spent on these measures, and also on wage subsidies for those with shortened working hours, and handicapped workers.

The other country in which the bulk of the money does not go on unemployment benefits and active employment measures is Slovenia. The relatively wide range of active employment policies (almost 60 per cent of all expenditures) in that country is at least partly explained by its long past. 28,000 people took part in various training and re-training programmes at their workplaces and elsewhere (which corresponds to nearly one-third of the total number of the unemployed). The second largest item after benefit is the wage subsidy allocated to help enterprises staggering under the burdens of transformation, but offering competitive programmes and productive employment, to preserve their existing jobs. In 1990–91, income allowances associated with early retirement played a rather significant role, which, in turn, led to an unprecedented rise in the number of pensioners. Interestingly enough, instead of mobilizing the underqualified manual workforce, Slovenian public work programmes mostly involve people with secondary or higher education, in groups of 20 at most, providing them with social, administrative, cultural and similar tasks appropriate to their qualifications, and a salary ranging from 80 per cent of the minimum wage to 70 per cent of the usual wage for the given activity.

In comparison to market economies, the role of re-training and training is, at present, less prominent in every country of the Central Eastern European region. Only 0.3 per cent of the labour force took part in training programmes for unemployed adults in the Czech Republic, 1 per cent in Slovakia, 1.3 per cent in Hungary, 0.4 per cent in Poland, 0.3 per cent in Romania, as against 2.9 per cent in Germany, 3.2 per cent in Sweden – but only 0.2 per cent in Portugal (figures for 1992: OECD, 1993). This is both because of the financial constraint and the lack of experience, and because of the difficulty of anticipating the vocational structure requirements of economies in transition and structural change. In some countries, Hungary for example, especially at first, these training programmes mostly involved people in employment, rather then the unemployed. Only in Poland were most of what otherwise were very low active expenditures allocated to training programmes; the money was primarily used to avoid or reduce the likelihood of unemployment among young people completing their regular educations.

Table 9.9   Breakdown of expenditure on active employment measures (percentages)

	Czecho-slovakia	Hungary	Poland	Romania	Slovenia
(Re)training					
1991	6.9	17.8	58.7	5.2	25.0
1992	7.0	22.3	69.2	3.8	21.5
Job creation					
1991	61.6	24.9	20.4		3.5
1992	76.2	33.5	22.5		13.5
of this:					
public work					
1991	14.4	8.2	–		
1992	11.3	12.8	6.1		
communal, social					
1991	47.2	–	20.4		
1992	64.9	12.8	16.4		
Employment subsidy					
1991	–	2.2	–	87.1	35.0
1992	–	6.8	–	81.7	50.0
Assist. to new enterprises					
1991	17.1	41.2	18.2	0.5	4.0
1992	4.5	18.5	8.3	1.1	
Employment of young people					
1991	4.8	–	–	2.3	

Table 9.9 continued

	Czecho-slovakia	Hungary	Poland	Romania	Slovenia
1992	7.7	0.1	–	3.2	
Assistance to long-term unemployed persons					
1991	–	0.3	–	–	
1992	–	2.5	–	–	
Employment of persons with changed working abilities					
1991	0.5	–	2.7	1.8	
1992	1.4	–	–	3.3	
Regional programmes					
1991	–	4.3	–	–	
1992	–	8.1	–	–	
Early retirement					
1991	–	5.4	–	–	25.0
1992	–	5.8	–	–	12.0
Reduced working time					
1991	7.3	–	–	–	
1992	2.9	–	–	–	
Other					
1991	1.8	4.2	–	3.0	7.5
1992	0.3	2.7	–	1.9	3.0
Total					
1991	100.0	100.0	100.0	100.0	100.0
1992	100.0	100.0	100.0	100.0	100.0

Note:

Due to differences in contents the above data are not fully comparable

Source:

Employment Observatory (1993), n4; Country Studies.

As well as Czechoslovakia, also Hungary has set job-creation as a major target expenditure, initially with the principal purpose of easing local tensions. Then in 1992 the emphasis shifted to promoting the employment of disadvantaged groups of employees, and to providing temporary employment for the under-educated and the long-term unemployed. The limited use of public work programmes is probably due less to scant financial resources than to the limited organizational skills of local governments and their inability to raise additional funding.

Early retirement is also under-used compared with Western Europe and the Eastern *Länder* of Germany. Slovenia and Hungary are the two countries in which notable programmes are under way to safeguard existing jobs. In the meantime, in Romania, the bulk of the already very low expenditure on active measures is allocated for precisely this purpose. By comparison, a great deal was spent in Hungary on helping the unemployed to start businesses, expenditure which took the form of interest subsidy for a launch credit. However, the scheme worked with doubtful efficiency and has been abandoned.

The still limited impact of active labour market policies is certainly due to the fact – amongst others – that 'imported' programmes, implemented in several cases with Western help, do not fit the specific conditions of these countries and their employment problems. Measures able to combat frictional and structural unemployment lose their efficacy in a dual context of transition and crisis.

5   EMPLOYMENT POLICY AND ECONOMIC POLICY

The chances of re-establishing a balanced labour market and the success of the fight against unemployment in the Central and Eastern European region obviously do not depend exclusively on employment policies, on the right choice of active and passive employment measures, or on the proper definition of objectives and of target groups. They also depend on the general shape of the economy, and on the broader context of economic policy.

Even if employment policies were entirely appropriate to the situation, and even if there were no hysteresis phenomena to hamper change, a short-term reduction in unemployment could only be expected in those countries of the region which have advanced furthest along the road of economic transition; and also in these countries this depends on the take-off of economic growth. On this basis, Poland – which plunged first and deepest into turmoil and yet showed palpable economic growth as early as 1993 – should be the first country to see its tensions reconciled. Nonetheless, its statistics reflect further growth in unemployment, which also contradicts the argument frequently advanced in the case of Poland that the abandonment of restrictive economic policy (shock therapy) – blamed for the sudden plunge of demand for labour – will bring about nearly automatic recovery in the labour market. This has proved not to be the case, and for this the demographically induced over-supply of manpower should also be held responsible. Nor has the growth of unemployment halted in Slovenia, despite the fact that the gradual slowing of the downward trend in production, the moratorium on bankruptcies due to insolvency, the tighter administrative wage control which replaced collective agreements in 1993, as well as other economic policy measures, raised hopes that the surge in unemployment following plant closures in 1990–91 would subside. At the same time, in Hungary, whose production figures are somewhat more favourable than those of Slovenia but not as good Poland's, unemployment began slowly to decline in the spring of 1993.

In the Czech Republic – which has reached the critical phase of economic transformation – the consequences of economic policy measures (bankruptcy legislation, full-fledged privatization), shrinking export demand, and a number of other factors, foreshadow a potential worsening of the presently encouraging unemployment statistics. However, these seem to be counterbalanced by other economic policy measures, such as restricted and shortened unemployment benefit payment compounded by a wide range of active employment measures. Registered unemployment is still quite low, but the higher rate derived from recently introduced Labour Force Surveys is a tentative indication of growing tension. And this also applies to Slovakia, despite an employment policy similar to that of the Czech Republic, while under less promising economic conditions, the unemployment rate, a great deal higher so far, has risen further, thus justifying pessimistic forecasts and bearing out those studies which predict further rises.

In cases in which no deeper insight into the situation is available, when seeking an explanation for the irresistible advance of unemployment we may only refer to an unprecedented drop in production figures and a reduction of demand triggered by recession. On this basis, in Romania, where production fell dramatically and has probably not yet reached the bottom of the trough – and where essential economic changes still await implementation – one may anticipate a further and considerable growth of unemployment. The current high levels of unemployment in every country of the region are undoubtedly related to the shrinking of overall demand, and to falling demand in the commodity and labour markets. Tensions in the labour market will only increase if demand-restricting policies and the low level of overall demand are complemented by a significant restructuring of the production system.

It is less obvious that improvement would take place in the reverse case: i.e. if the demand constraints were reduced or if they disappeared altogether. In reality, the elimination or the relaxation of the restriction would have a contradictory effect on employment and on unemployment even if economic growth were to take off. It may, on the one hand, trigger an expansion in employment by allowing demand to grow, and, on the other, it may ease and accelerate the restructuring necessary to overcome the crisis and bring about the modernization of the economy. Yet by so doing it might again contribute to the growth of unemployment. It is very difficult to foresee the balance of job destruction and job creation in a vigorous restructuring process even with sustained economic growth. In a longer perspective, steady growth could halt the decline and induce employment to grow. In a shorter perspective the issue is evidently a great deal more complex than this dilemma of economic policy.

NOTES

1. This paper is based on my contribution to the conference, and relies on the data and information of country studies (see references) prepared in the frameworks of an ACE funded international research program (Institute of Economics, Hungarian Academy of Sciences, Budapest and LICOS, Katholieke Universiteit, Leuven) and of a research project (Institute of Economics, Hungarian Academy of Sciences, Budapest) funded by OTKA (National Scientific Research Fund). Most of the country studies and a regional overview of the author appeared in Jackson, Koltay, Biesbrouck (1995). Data and arguments in this version are prolonged in time and rearranged in order to take account of recent developments and to fit in the context of the present volume. Responsibility for any remaining errors is born by the author.
2. On this labour market hysteresis see Blanchard and Summers (1986).

REFERENCES

Burda, M. (1993), 'Unemployment, Labour Market and Structural Change in Eastern Europe', *Economic Policy*, **16**.

Becker, G. (1971), *The Economics of Discrimination*, Chicago: University of Chicago Press.

Blanchard, O. and L. Summers (1986) 'Hysteresis and the European Unemployment Problem', *NBER Annual Report*, **1**, Cambridge Mass.: MIT Press.

Blanchard, O., S. Commander and F. Coricelli (1993), 'Unemployment and Restructuring in Eastern Europe', paper presented at World Bank Conference on Unemployment in Eastern Europe, Washington, October 1993.

Commission of the European Communities (1992, 1993), *Employment Observatory Central & Eastern Europe*, nos. 1, 2, 3, 4, 5.

Drobnic, S. (1992), 'Rigidities in the Labour Markets of Transition Economies and New Organizational Forms', Working Paper no. 7, Leuven, LICOS.

Drobnic, S. and V. Rus (1993), 'Unemployment in Transition Economies: The Case of Slovenia', paper prepared for the second workshop of the ACE research network on unemployment, Erdőtarcsa.

Employment Services Department (1993), *Unemployment Statistical Data in the Slovak Republic*, Ministry of Labour, Social Affairs and Family, Bratislava, September.

Fazekas, K. (1994), paper prepared for the regional network.

Ginsburg, H.J. and D. Student (1993), 'Swacher Trost', *Wirtschaftswoche*, **48** (26), November.

Janacek, K. (1993), 'Unemployment and Labour Market in Czechoslovakia (Czech Republic, 1990–1992)', paper prepared for the second workshop of the ACE research network on unemployment, Erdótarcsa.

Kolosi, T. (1993), *The Poor and the Rich in Hungary*, Transit Club Series 7, Budapest: Institute of Economics.

Köllő, J. (1993), 'Unemployment and the Prospects for Employment Policy in Hungary', paper prepared for the second workshop of the ACE research network on unemployment, Erdótarcsa.

Miron, M. (1993), 'Romania: The Challenge of Unemployment', paper prepared for the second workshop of the ACE research network on unemployment, Erdótarcsa.

Nagy, G. and E. Sík (1993), 'Munkanélküliség és munkanélküliek. Jelentés a Magyar Háztartási Panel I. hullámának eredményeiríl' (Report on the first wave results of the Hungarian Household Panel Survey), Budapest.

Nesporova, A. (1993), 'Recent Labour Market Development in Czechoslovakia', paper prepared for the second workshop of the ACE research network on unemployment, Erdótarcsa.

OECD (1993), *Employment Outlook*, Paris.

Piore, M. (1983), 'Labor Market Segmentation: To what Paradigm does it Belong?', *American Economic Review*, **2**.

Scarpetta, S. (1994), 'Spatial Variations in Unemployment in Central and Eastern Europe', Technical Workshop Paper, Vienna, IAS, OECD.

Schmögnerová, B. (1993), *Munkaerïpiac a Szlovák Köztársaság-ban* (Labour Market in the Slovak Republic), Institute of Economics, Slovakian Academy of Sciences.

Witkowski, J. (1993), 'Employment in Poland in the Period of Transition', paper prepared for the second workshop of the ACE research network on unemployment, Erdótarcsa.

Vincze, M. (1992), *Munkanélküliség, segélyezés és munkaerï-politika. Intézmények és tapasztalatok Romániában* (Unemployment, benefits and employment policy in Romania), KTI/IE Institute of Economics, Hungarian Academy of Sciences, Budapest.

Vincze, M. (1993), 'A munkanélküliség alakulása Romániában' (The rise of unemployment in Romania), Kolozsvár (manuscript).

PART THREE

Creation and Development of Markets in
Eastern Europe

10. Behavioural Constraints and the Creation of Markets in Post-Socialist Economies[1]

Wim Swaan

1 INTRODUCTION

The first years of the transition to a market economy in Eastern Europe have shown a sharp decline in output in all the countries concerned, even if the initial conditions and the policy pursued have differed considerably. This transformational recession is related to a complex of macro- and microeconomic factors (Kornai, 1993). Particularly disquieting is the fact that liberalization and removal of barriers to entry have not led to a growth of economic activity: for the first two years at least, the transformation has been characterized by an L-curve, rather than the expected J-curve (Nuti and Portes, 1993, pp. 8–9).

The present study is concerned with behavioural aspects of the recession, in particular with the constraints on behavioural change deriving from bounded rationality (Simon, 1945) and from the tacit character of skills and knowledge (Polanyi, 1958). Its argument relies closely on the synthesis provided by Nelson and Winter (1982). Bounded rationality implies a huge potential for behavioural change, but it also entails that the actualization of potential change may be a complicated and slow process. The tacit character of a large part of human knowledge limits the transfer of knowledge and the speed of learning, especially in large organizations. By taking the theoretical behavioural literature as a frame of reference, one can evidence to what extent special aspects of behaviour in post-socialist transition are rooted in general characteristics of human economic behaviour.

Given the complex character of transformational recession, it would be misleading to consider behavioural constraints as constituting a single cause of it (cf. Kornai, 1993). Yet the literature on economic history suggests that they play a major role in economic development. On the one hand, macroeconomic stability, institutional change and the creation of effective governance structures are indispensable in bringing about behavioural change. On the other hand, the effectiveness of policy measures in these fields also depends upon the prevailing level of entrepreneurial and managerial competence. Low capabilities throughout the economy imply a higher chance of policy failure (cf. Fishlow, 1991, p. 1736 on developing countries). The behaviour of firms is not merely determined by the market environment and by the state of technology; rather, markets and technology are themselves created by individual firms and their organizational capabilities.[2] Similarly, under dispersed knowledge, performance is not just a result of appropriate incentives, but also of individual competence and of the degree to which individuals with different skills succeed in coordinating their activities (Foss, 1993; Minkler, 1993).

The argument of this study focuses on two aspects of behavioural constraints in post-socialist economies: the difficulties faced by already-existing firms in reorganization, and the difficulties faced by both already-existing and new firms in undertaking transactions. Section 2 provides a framework for the argument by maintaining that, in the short run, behaviour is not primarily determined by the degree of economic liberalization, but rather by the sudden disintegration of the party-state hierarchy. Sections 3 and 4 consider the response by existing firms: the initial reaction by state enterprises, and the costs of reorganizing firms. In section 5 the argument is extended to the process of entry and exit, and a tentative comparison is carried out between developed market economies and post-socialist ones. The problem of undertaking transactions is considered in section 6, and the impact of the low level of economic competence on coordination in section 7. Section 8 draws together the various strands of the thesis developed in the preceding sections, arguing that differences in reorganization costs and the costs of establishing transactions will generate differences in the speed of market creation throughout the economy, and that this may have an impact on the effectiveness of governance structures. Section 9 draws some conclusions.

2 THE DISINTEGRATION OF THE PARTY-STATE HIERARCHY AND TRANSACTION COSTS

The literature on post-socialist transformation might give the impression that behaviour is mainly influenced by economic liberalization and stabilization policy. In the short run, however, behaviour is much more closely influenced by the collapse of the institutional structures in which individuals and organizations used to operate. Whereas liberalization and stabilization policies can be seen as (partly) intentional processes, the collapse of the socialist system was largely an unintentional one. Stabilization policies, if implemented at all, have in fact been harshest in countries where the process of disintegration was most chaotic, such as Poland and Russia. Apart from a number of very desirable changes, the sudden disintegration of the party-state hierarchy also had negative consequences. Here I will focus on the impact on economic transactions.

Given the central role of the party-state hierarchy in coordinating economic activities, it is evident that its disappearance caused major disruption in transactions. Kornai (1993) and Ábel and Bonin (1993) have pointed to the problem of 'state desertion' as being responsible for the ineffective regulation of state enterprises. However, if the role of organs of the party-state hierarchy had been restricted to regulating enterprises, its disintegration would have caused much less disruption.

In the U-shaped hierarchy of Soviet-type economies (Qian and Xu, 1993), all transactions were arranged through the channels of the hierarchy. This not only led to extremely high coordination costs, now that the hierarchy has disintegrated it also implies that enterprises entirely lack the experience and skills with which to initiate and effect transactions on their own.

The problem is particularly serious in trade and distribution, since this mostly requires multi-stage transactions. Producers in centrally planned economies operated in almost total isolation from retail and wholesale activity, both in domestic and foreign trade. Distribution depended entirely on intervention by countless party and state organs, since neither producers, nor wholesale companies, nor retailers had any interest in active marketing. Most producers were not even allowed to engage in direct relations. The disintegration of the party-state hierarchy has accordingly dealt a serious blow to very feeble distribution networks.

The lack of appropriate supporting institutions entails high transactions costs for firms, in addition to their lack of transaction skills. One example widely discussed in the literature is the absence of a well-functioning banking system, which has given rise to misallocation and to the underallocation of credits (Calvo and Corricelli, 1993; Kornai, 1993). I shall here discuss another example: namely the absence of satisfactory mechanisms for contract enforcement.

In discussing contract enforcement in market economies, Williamson (1985, pp. 70–1) stresses the major role of third party assistance in resolving disputes. Third party assistance may take many forms: from *ad hoc* arbitration by professionals to the institutionalized boards of branch organizations. In the context of centrally planned economies, the term 'third party enforcement' is to be understood almost literally: it was the party – in particular its local organs – that was continuously involved in resolving the disputes that arose in the execution of transactions planned by state organs (Hough, 1969; Grossman, 1983; Csanádi, 1990). As a consequence, the disintegration of the party-state hierarchy does not only mean that enterprises have suddenly to conclude transactions on their own; they also lack the institutions to settle their conflicts. In the former Soviet Union, Gorbachev's measures designed to remove the party from the economy had a disastrous impact on output (Ellman and Kontorovich, 1992, pp. 22, 26). Since a court order is just one form of third party assistance, legal change in itself is not sufficient to solve these problems of contract enforcement. Indeed, most forms of third party enforcement arise not by design but organically.

3   THE INITIAL RESPONSE OF STATE ENTERPRISES

The lack of transaction skills and the lack of appropriate institutions supporting transactions clearly has a major impact on enterprise behaviour. This section discusses the initial response of state enterprises to the disintegration of the party-state hierarchy. Later sections will discuss the problem of restructuring and the process of entry and exit.

In order to focus on the problem of transaction costs and behavioural constraints, let us assume that prices and output are liberalized and that the authorities are able to maintain or impose a certain minimum degree of financial stability. In its response to the simultaneous occurrence of liberalization and the disintegration of the party-state hierarchy, a firm faces two problems: how to set its prices, and how to establish transactions with actors potentially interested in its products. Let us consider each in turn.

The chief problem faced by enterprises in setting prices is that they have not the slightest knowledge of the shape of the demand curve for their products. Following Estrin and Hare (1992, pp. 12–17) one might say that pre-transition firms do not face a demand curve, but merely a demand point. Accordingly, in setting their prices following liberalization, firms are forced to make wild estimates of demand elasticity. Unfortunately, however, they are likely to underestimate demand elasticity because they rely on their experiences of the shortage economy. Unsatisfied demand in a shortage economy arises for all firms in a particular branch, and through forced substitution also in other branches. As a result, firms structurally overestimate the residual demand that they face, underestimate the elasticity of demand, and set their prices too high once they have been liberalized, whatever decision criterion they follow. Consequently, the level of inflation following price liberalization depends, among other things, on the extent to which firms underestimate the elasticity of demand for their products.

Even if enterprises accidentally set their prices 'right' – that is, even if they estimate the demand elasticity for their products correctly – they will face serious problems in capturing all the potential demand at this price level. The more relative prices change, the more output is negatively affected by the costs of (re-)establishing transactions.

Firstly, firms are unlikely to know exactly which purchasers are willing to pay the new price. They may fail to contact potential purchasers willing to pay higher prices, and superfluously offer the product to purchasers not willing to pay the current price. Secondly, their lack of marketing skills will shift all search costs to purchasers, whose utility (and demand) will decline correspondingly. Thirdly, firms need to redefine their product mix from a uniform low quality/high quantity supply to a more heterogeneous mix. Even if technology and capacity allow this change to be made, firms must discover which consumers want which products.

In the above discussion of the firm's output and price decision it was implicitly assumed that firms search for the best feasible solution. Although firms faced close constraints on their knowledge, they would adjust instantaneously to all the new information available. Unfortunately, there are strong grounds for doubting whether this is indeed the case. Research on firms' response to adversity in market economies suggests that they are able to handle limited amounts of adversity, but strong adversity actually decreases the ability of organizations to change. If undertaken at all, the endeavour to change more often than not proceeds in the wrong direction when adversity is strong.

Typically, however, firms choose not to respond at all. They carry on as before, but at a lower level of activity, and may eventually disappear altogether (Nelson, 1981; Nelson and Winter, 1982, pp. 121–3; Murrell 1992c, pp. 40–43).

A theoretical explanation for these phenomena is provided by Heiner (1983). The decision to change a given repertoire of actions depends not only on the potential gains from new types of action, but also on the degree of stability in the actor's environment. High instability in the environment leads to a low likelihood of selecting the right action at the right time and accordingly encourages actors to stick to a previously developed repertoire of actions. Heiner (1983, p. 562) speaks in this regard of a C–D gap between the agent's competence and the difficulty of the decision problem which is manifest in exacerbated form in post-socialist economies.

4   THE COSTS OF REORGANIZING FIRMS

Having discussed the initial response of state enterprises to economic disintegration, let us now turn to the prospects of behavioural change in the economy. As was already indicated when describing the initial response of state enterprises to the disintegration of the party-state hierarchy, the abilities of firms to adapt to changing circumstances are limited. Although this does not at all preclude change, it incurs costs in terms of the effort and time to be spent on reorganization.

The extent of reorganization costs may be clarified by discussing some of the problems that arise when a firm is taken over by an active owner who has shown competence in managing firms elsewhere, for instance abroad. This would indeed provide the best conditions for reorganization and behavioural change. I will discuss reorganization costs in general terms; obviously they will differ across branches and firms, depending, for instance, on the degree of technological complexity and the relative importance of firm-specific knowledge.

Consider first the organizational boundaries of the firm. Firstly, under state socialism, the boundaries of the firm were not primarily influenced by transaction costs considerations at the level of the firm, but rather by transaction costs in hierarchical relations between central organs and firms (Schweitzer, 1981; Ben-Ner and Neuberger, 1988). The costs of redrawing the boundaries of the firm accordingly depend upon the extent to which the two considerations may give rise to a different organization of firms. Particularly important is the degree to which technology was affected by centralization. The costs of reorganizing megafactories in, for instance, the textile industry, the shoe industry or meat processing are likely to be prohibitive. In industries where centralization was merely an administrative matter, and did not affect plant size and technology, reorganization is less costly.

Secondly, a considerable part of reorganization consists of organizational learning and the absorption of new knowledge. As Nelson and Winter (1982) have argued at length, the knowledge of a firm cannot be reduced to a book of blueprints, or to the knowledge of its engineers and scientists. Instead, the firm's knowledge can be considered to be embodied in the routines that develop as a response to bounded rationality. By implementing activities according to certain regularities, and by adapting these only marginally, employees need not be instructed or consult with each other on every detail of their work. The costs of coordination in an organization in constant flux would be prohibitive. Like individual knowledge, organizational knowledge is partly tacit or personal: it is difficult to articulate, and neither the management nor other participants in the organization may be completely aware of its content (Nelson and Winter, 1982, pp. 99–124, following Polanyi, 1958).

The tacit character of organizational knowledge restricts both to the ability of a new owner to transfer knowledge and the ability of the existing firm to absorb new knowledge. The former aspect is not typical of post-socialist economies. Replication of successful business routines is fraught with difficulties, which are only reinforced by cultural barriers in schemes for the international transfer of knowledge (see for instance Black and Mendenhall, 1990; Hamel, 1991). Since routines are the expression of an 'organizational truce', as Nelson and Winter (1982, pp. 107–12) term it, attempts to change routines are likely to be costly. All this does not in itself raise a barrier against knowledge transfer; rather, it represents a costs in terms of delayed adjustment. Indeed, the limits to the possibilities of transferring firm-specific skills constitute the rationale itself for the existence of multinational firms, since these skills cannot be transferred through arm's length market contracts (Caves, 1982).

As to the ability of existing firms to absorb new knowledge, the existing stock of individual and organizational capabilities in post-socialist economies poses special problems. Since tacit knowledge develops through experience, it is closely related to the institutional structure in which it developed (Murrell, 1992a, 1992b). Those capabilities that are most lacking are precisely the ones that in market economies have evolved as part of tacit knowledge. The basis for acquiring marketing and organizational capabilities can be imparted by means of standard education, but a thorough command of these skills can only be acquired through practice, for instance by following the example of others.

On the other hand, tacit knowledge on how to operate as a *Homo Sovieticus* (Dembinski, 1991, pp. 47–9) has lost most of its value. In other words, whereas the new owner of a firm in developed market economies only faces the problem of transferring its specific knowledge, the new owner of a post-socialist firm is confronted with an organization which lacks the basic capabilities to respond to endeavours at transferring knowledge. According to Nelson and Winter (1982, pp. 130–4), the success of organizational change depends on the degree to which new routines are built upon reliable subroutines with which the organization is already familiar. Post-socialist firms will be weak in this respect: insofar as they operated according to reliable routines, these latter have largely lost their value after the disintegration of the socialist system. What amounts to a reversal of routines is required: the priority regime within the organization must shift from the supply department to the sales department, and the focus of attention must shift from quantity to quality (Keren, 1992).

In the more developed post-socialist economies, the low level of appropriate tacit skills is partly offset by a relatively high level of technical and easily transferable skills, as is reflected in high levels of education. This combination is indeed rare in economic history, since the social stock of tacit and technical skills has largely developed through mutual interaction. Unfortunately, the different levels of tacit skills, and of more easily transferable skills, is not always perceived by programmes aimed at the international transfer of knowledge. Foreign trainers frequently identify the low level of skills with a lack of technical skills and end up by teaching things that have long been familiar. The recipients, on the other hand, may be unaware of the importance of tacit aspects of skills. Accordingly, they may either expect success from a further increase in their technical skills, or they may simply deny the importance of learning new skills and see the role of foreign partners mainly as providing capital and equipment (see Dander, 1993; and Vecsenyi, 1992, on Hungary).

In addition to the high level of technical, transferable, skills there is another relative advantage that might derive from economic reforms under state socialism, like those underway in Hungary or Poland. Although socialist reforms did not achieve a breakthrough towards market-oriented business organization, managerial perception has at least been moulded in the direction of market concepts, which may facilitate the absorption of organizational and marketing skills (see for instance Swaan and Lissowska, 1992a, 1992b; Hooley, 1993).

The extent of reorganization costs is illustrated by the findings of empirical research on enterprise behaviour in Hungary and Poland. Karsai (1992) and Laki (1992) discern an increasing endeavour to implement organizational change in Hungary, yet at the same time note that these attempts are mostly not part of deliberate planning, but instead arise *ad hoc*. While in Hungary behavioural change is a rather gradual process, which had already started in the 1980s before the disintegration of the system (Swaan and Lissowska, 1992a), more rapid change can be noted in Poland which did not immediately follow the stabilization and liberalization programme of 1990 but occurred with a delay of around two years (Pinto, Belka, and Krajewski, 1993; Lissowska, 1993). Pinto, Belka, and Krajewski (1993, pp. 217–22) identify managers as the driving force behind change and point to firm-specific capabilities in behavioural change. Interestingly, behavioural change is not a direct result of changes in ownership and governance structures: the main incentive for successful managers is their anticipation of future rewards once privatization has progressed.

5   CREATIVE DESTRUCTION?

In developed market economies, a much larger amount of change derives from the development of new organizations than from the adaptation and reorganization of existing firms. This was emphasised long ago by Schumpeter (1934, 1939, 1942). Innovation or 'doing things differently in the realm of economic life' implies mostly the creation of a new plant and a new firm by new men (Schumpeter 1939, pp. 84–96), and this gives rise to creative destruction, 'the essential fact of capitalism' (Schumpeter 1942, pp. 83).

The destruction of institutional structures in post-socialist countries and the collapse of output has frequently been compared to this Schumpeterian-type creative destruction. Such comparisons might suggest, intentionally or not, that the decline in output due to the destruction of inefficient state enterprises will be more or less automatically offset by the creation of new enterprises, albeit with a certain time lag. As will be argued, however, the process of recovery more closely resembles the initial development of market economies, and this was much less smooth than the type of creative destruction taking place in developed market economies in the second half of the twentieth century (see Schumpeter 1939, in particular pp. 220–448). In a sense, post-socialist economies must repeat part of a development process that they have already passed through, both during state socialism and before.

Consider first, for the purpose of comparison, the process of creative destruction in developed market economies. Given the importance generally attributed to creative destruction, surprisingly little empirical research has been conducted on it. Dunne, Roberts and Samuelson (1988) present revealing data on entry and exit in manufacturing industry in the United States in the period 1963–82. They distinguish three types of entrants: entirely new firms, existing firms which construct new plants, and existing firms which alter the product mix of existing plants. Of these, the second group – existing firms which construct new plants – is the most successful. Although the entry rate of this group is the lowest of the three, it achieves both a lower rate of failure and a much higher average size. The failure rate of the first group (entirely new firms) is slightly lower than that of the third group (existing firms which alter the product mix of existing plants), but the latter attains a considerably larger size. Dunne, Roberts and Samuelson's study also reveals a high level of turnover of firms: of all firms entering in a particular year, 55–65 per cent disappear within five years.

The vulnerability of new firms has been characterized as a 'liability of newness': the failure rate of firms decreases with age (Stinchcombe, 1965, pp. 148–50; Hannan and Freeman, 1984, 1989). New firms have not yet built up levels of reliability and accountability sufficient to ensure an uninterrupted flow of resources and sales. They do not yet operate according to established routines: although this gives them considerable flexibility, it also renders them much more vulnerable to unforeseen developments.

The process of entry and exit in post-socialist economies shows marked differences from what one notes in developed market economies. The destruction of existing firms is only partly related to the entry of new ones, and much more closely related to the disintegration of the institutional structure in which they used to operate. As a consequence, destruction is not necessarily related to efficiency (Nuti and Portes, 1993, p. 9).

Schumpeter (1942, p. 83) described creative destruction as a 'process ... that incessantly revolutionizes ...' the economic structure from within, incessantly destroying the old one, incessantly creating a new one'. In post-socialist economies, destruction is neither from within nor incessant. Rather, it is characterized by an abrupt shock to existing firms, while recovery through the successful entry of new firms is likely to be a relatively slow process. There is, *a priori*, no reason to assume that newness is less of a liability to entrants in post-socialist economies. Existing state firms, on the other hand, are very vulnerable. They lack the support of the institutional environment of the party-state hierarchy, and their endeavour to reorganize may well end in failure.

Moreover, entry by existing firms through the building of new plants – the most successful type of entry in the United States, according to Dunne, Roberts and Samuelson (1988) – will initially be restricted mainly to foreign firms. Although entry of this kind is taking place, its effectiveness is constrained by cultural and knowledge barriers similar to the costs of reorganizing existing firms, as discussed above.

6   THE COSTS OF ESTABLISHING TRANSACTIONS

In discussing the impact of the disintegration of the party-state hierarchy on enterprise behaviour, mention was made of the fact that firms face high transaction costs owing to the absence of supporting institutions. Here the transactions costs argument will be developed further by focusing on the costs of establishing transactions; costs which accrue both to existing state firms and to new ones.

Following Coase (1937), much of the transaction costs literature has focused on comparative static aspects of transactions, in particular the question of whether or not transactions will come about, and what form they will eventually take.[3] In this literature, emphasis is on the costs of *ex-ante* contract negotiation and *ex-post* control and enforcement. However, before contract negotiation can begin, a contact has to be established. In other words, transactions are determined by the triad of contact, contract and control, and not just by the latter two (see Nooteboom, 1992a, p. 7).

Establishing transactions with new partners has a cost of its own. Agents should first of all be aware of each other's existence and of the value of potential transactions. Producers and traders should have a broad perception of the composition of demand. Consumers, on the other hand, should be aware of their preferences for a particular product, and of the existence of particular retail outlets. Search processes are restricted to products and trade partners which are known to exist.

The costs of establishing contact prior to negotiating and effectuating gives transaction cost economics a dynamic aspect. Even if the costs of contract negotiation and enforcement in themselves were not prohibitive, the set-up costs may prevent transactions from taking place, at least temporarily. As has been pointed out by Beije and Groenewegen (1992), transactions in market economies develop in network patterns. The structuring of transactions has important information and knowledge advantages, facilitating decision-making under bounded rationality. Accordingly, the restructuring of a post-socialist economy is not merely a matter of creating a new industrial structure, both in terms of the distribution of firm size and distribution over sectors. It also requires the creation of a new network of transactions and the development of the knowledge related thereto. As long as prospective buyers and sellers are unaware of potential transactions, these latter will not come about.

The costs of establishing transactions were a major concern of Schumpeter in his works (1934, 1939) on economic development. Firms do not face a given demand curve, they have to create demand themselves. Each innovation involves a chain of minor events. This chain of events cannot be reduced to one particular moment but takes historical time. Resistance from the environment must be overcome, technical and organizational problems must be tackled, distribution must be solved, consumers must be induced to forget about unfavourable experiences at the initial stage of product development, and so on.[4]

7 ECONOMIC COMPETENCE AND COORDINATION

The problems of establishing transactions are reinforced by the low level of economic competence in post-socialist economies. As was already pointed out when discussing the costs of reorganizing existing firms, marketing and organizational capabilities are, for the most part, tacit skills which are developed through experience and by imitation of the example of others. The relatively high level of technical skills in the more developed post-socialist economies gives them a high potential for growth: the problem is not that development is ruled out; rather, that it takes time to take effect.

Underdeveloped skills not only limit the actual scope of actions that an actor can undertake itself but also, and at least as much, the possibilities of establishing transactions. If potential partners possess only a limited ability to communicate the type of transactions that they might potentially be willing to demand or supply, actual transactions will be limited accordingly. Foss (1993, p. 138) refers in this respect to a potential lack of receiver competence and sender competence. Let me for the moment restrict the discussion to sender competence – in other words, the ability to delegate tasks to others.

The planning and implementation of skills – that is, knowing how to get a particular task done by another person or another firm – requires a certain minimum amount of knowledge of the task (see Nelson and Winter, 1982, pp. 85–91). First, one should be able to communicate the skill one is looking for. This requires awareness of the skill and awareness of whether the task related to it can be contracted out. Second, one should be able to select among the firms offering the task or skill. Third, one should be able to control performance and to communicate about inadequate performance. Shortcomings at any of these levels may prevent transactions from coming about. This can be partly dealt with by the standardization of services, certification arrangements and interpersonal trust. However, if a certain minimum amount of competence does not exist in the economy, such arrangements are unlikely to be effective initially, thereby requiring a higher level of individual skills in effecting transactions.

An example is in order. In a country with high bicycle density and longstanding certification arrangements and interpersonal trust, technical illiterates or persons with high opportunity costs of leisure will not encounter serious problems in having their bicycles repaired at local shops. In countries where these conditions are absent, the contracting-out of bicycle repairs may require serious technical preparation; repeated detailed supervision and discussion during the repair process; and substantial corrective work afterwards in order to deal with new (minor) failures arising as a side-effect of the repair process. The repair fee may well be proportionally lower, but willingness to pay more will not make the repair process proceed more smoothly.

The problem of planning and implementing skills is especially important in markets for intermediate goods and services. Faced with the costs of selecting and controlling outside contractors or even subordinates, producers may in the end decide to perform the task entirely by themselves, even if they are aware that their own skills are not entirely adequate to the task. The resulting underspecialization will reduce the quantity and quality of output and also the number of transactions in the economy. The phenomenon of successful entrepreneurs who do not contract out work may not only stem from their attempts to maintain secrecy; it may also derive from their inability to transfer knowledge to potential suppliers. Reliance on tacit knowledge is particularly marked in small innovative firms (Nooteboom, 1992b, pp. 289–90). In order to grow, entrepreneurs should be able to articulate part of their tacit knowledge and to transfer it to new personnel.

In post-socialist economies, small entrepreneurs engage in a wide variety of tasks, exploring the opportunities that they find along their way. Local, independent retailers typically sell wide (and weird) product assortments which vary greatly over time. At least at the initial stage of development, small entrepreneurs are more concerned with striking quick bargains than with offering a stable assortment. This is in part related to the origin of firms in the second or informal economy, where their behaviour (and that of their consumers) was principally determined by prevailing shortages (Gábor, 1991).

8 THE CREATION OF MARKETS

The discussion so far has not distinguished between firms and branches. To the extent that reorganization costs and the costs of establishing transactions differ among firms and branches, however, market creation will proceed at a different pace throughout the economy. Some tentative conjectures in this regard are presented below, although both empirically and theoretically they are a matter for further enquiry.

The first proposition is that investors will invest more in firms and branches in which they expect reorganization costs and transactions costs to be lower. Consider two examples: franchising agreements between international franchisors and domestic franchisees, and the heavily advertised consumer products of firms with international marketing experience.

For domestic entrepreneurs, investment in the franchise outlets of international firms is a much safer investment than setting up a business of their own. They need not bother with all the aspects of searching for potential consumers and of creating markets for their products. They can instead rely partly on the experience of the franchisor which has proved successful elsewhere. Moreover, operating in the framework of franchising agreements makes it much easier to secure supplies, ranging from material inputs to bank loans. Accordingly, the relative advantage of franchising agreements as compared to other governance structures is much greater in post-socialist economies than it is in developed market ones. McDonalds, for instance, to its surprise received hundreds of replies to an advertisement for the setting-up of a number of franchised outlets in Budapest (*The Economist*, April 6th, 1991; Nicholls, 1992, pp. 57–8).

Similarly, the producers of heavily advertised consumer products in possession of international marketing experience may more easily create markets for their products. By contrast, local producers with little marketing experience, or foreign firms whose products are less suitable for intensive advertising, will lag behind in market growth because they face greater difficulties in establishing transactions with new customers. In Hungary, for instance, only 8 out of 62 branches of manufacturing industry did not register a decline in domestic sales in the period 1988–91. Among these were the soft drinks industry (1), the manufacture of organic and inorganic chemical products (2), the beer industry (4), the manufacture of households chemicals and cosmetics (5), the manufacture of pharmaceutical products (7) and the tobacco industry (8) (see OECD, 1993, pp. 187–94). All of these were branches in which the producers of heavily advertised products and internationally well-established brand names expanded their activities on the domestic market or entered as newcomers. Another example is provided by Coca-Cola, which doubled its sales in Central and Eastern Europe in 1992, although the company is no longer entirely a newcomer on these markets (*Central European Economic Review*, Summer 1993, p. 36).

The second proposition is that it will be easier to establish effective governance structures within firms and branches in which the costs of reorganization and establishing transactions are lower, since these firms and branches will more easily attract investments. Likewise, it will be difficult to impose an effective governance structure on state firms unable to attract sufficient investors. Moreover, given the low level of economic competence prevailing in the economy, it will be difficult to find actors able to handle high organization and transaction costs. It might be argued that voucher privatization through financial intermediaries could compensate for this outcome (see Frydman and Rapaczynski, 1992), but in these cases, too, the effectiveness of governance will be greater in enterprises that can easily be sold off; that is, enterprises in which investors expect the costs of reorganization and of establishing transactions to be lower. Furthermore, the effectiveness of privatization through voucher schemes may differ among countries. In the Czech Republic, for instance, the costs of reorganizing firms and establishing transactions can be expected to be lower than in, for instance, Russia; while at the same time the economic competence of prospective fund managers is likely to be higher in the Czech Republic.

In countries where privatization does not proceed through vouchers, but through individual sales of firms or plants, like Hungary and Poland, hybrid governance structures are likely to arise around firms that find it difficult to attract investment funds. Stark (1993) refers to this phenomenon as 'recombinant property' and gives the example, amongst others, of the transformation of state ownership into inter-enterprise ownership in Hungary (see also Voszka, 1991). On the one hand, inter-enterprise ownership can be seen as a continuation of the interest structures of the party-state networks and as an absence of effective governance structures, since former state firms are not likely to exercise strict and effective control over each other. From this point of view it would be merely an objectionable development.

On the other hand, as Stark (1993, pp. 13–14) points out, the diversity of property forms, including inter-enterprise ownership, can also be seen as springing from hedging strategies. In terms of the argument put forward in the present study, this means that firms finding it difficult to attract investment and new owners – for instance because of high reorganization costs and the costs of establishing new transactions – try to reduce transaction costs by formalizing and re-establishing links with their suppliers and purchasers from the party-state network. For successful firms, this may be a stepping stone to the establishment of new transactions. For the firms which fail to establish new types of transaction, however, inter-enterprise ownership is likely to be the prelude for a process of 'withering away'.

Another example of transitional governance structures is labour ownership. While, in itself, this arrangement may have several disadvantages, it could well prove to be the only viable structure for a substantial number of firms when other alternatives fail to materialize. In market economies, labour ownership is frequently the only option for firms in crisis (Ben-Ner, 1988). At any rate, labour ownership is preferable to the absence of any governance structure. In countries with a strong commitment to self-management, labour ownership as an initial transformation stage for some firms may prove more effective than attempts to establish other governance structures with much higher reorganization costs (see Murrell, 1992b, pp. 12–16).

Neither inter-enterprise ownership nor labour ownership are necessarily definitive property arrangements. In some cases they may appear viable over a longer period of time, but in many others they may develop into other types of governance structures: this, indeed, is what used to happen to labour ownership in market economies (Ben-Ner, 1988). The transformation of ownership and governance structures in post-socialist economies is a dynamic process; and from this perspective, the initial transformation from party-state ownership to new forms of governance structures is perhaps less important than the dynamics of the process. Consequently, bringing about a variety of organizational forms may be more important than striving for one optimal form (see Stark, 1993).

9   CONCLUSIONS: BEHAVIOURAL CONSTRAINTS AND TRANSFORMATIONAL RECESSION

This study has argued that after the disintegration of the party-state hierarchy, economic actors face barriers to behavioural change. Broadly speaking, these barriers can be divided between the costs of reorganizing existing firms and the costs of establishing transactions. A common denominator is the limits on the transfer of knowledge, which increases reorganization costs in terms of both time and effort. Apart from investments in plants and equipment, reorganization requires the considerable investment of effort in organizational learning and the transfer of knowledge, even under optimal governance structures (section 4). Similarly, barriers to the transfer and delegation of tacit knowledge limits the effectiveness of economic coordination and places a constraint on the growth of newly-founded small firms (section 7). Independently of knowledge constraints, actors face high costs in establishing transactions (section 6).

Most of the phenomena evident in post-socialist economies can also be discerned in developed market ones: new firms, for instance, suffer from a 'liability of newness' (section 5); firms are largely unable to respond to strong adversity (section 3); any firm engaged in taking over another one faces the problem of transferring its firm-specific knowledge, particularly in cross-cultural takeovers (section 4). Although these phenomena are in themselves not specific to post-socialist economies, the extreme scale on which they occur and their particular combination are typical of the post-socialist transformation process. In addition to all this, the initial response of state firms contributes to a decline in output because of their structural underestimation of demand elasticity and because of their inability to capture potential demand (section 3). In the short run, behaviour is much more closely influenced by the collapse of the institutional structures in which individuals and organizations previously operated than it is by the effectiveness of economic liberalization and stabilization policy (section 2). This may explain why macro-economic performance in the first years of the transformation process has shown marked similarities among various countries, despite their considerable differences in initial conditions and the policy pursued.

The contribution of behavioural constraints to transformational recession does not in the least preclude behavioural change at the level of the firm. Yet the success of one firm is offset by the failure of another, and a precociously successful firm may suddenly face bankruptcy at a later stage. As was argued in section 8, differences in the costs of (re)organization and of establishing transactions may give rise to different paces of growth of firms and markets. This may also have repercussions on the effectiveness of governance structures. These conjectures require further study at the level of firms and markets.

NOTES

1. The research on which this study is based was financed by the Research Fund of the Institute of Economics of the Hungarian Academy of Sciences.
2. Schumpeter (1934, 1939) and recently Teece (1993), who draws on Chandler's (1990) study of the United States, Britain and Germany .
3. See Williamson (1985, pp. 23–29) for an overview of the various branches of transaction cost economics.
4. See Schumpeter (1939), for instance pp. 84–6, 226–27, 243–45 .

REFERENCES

Ábel, I. and J. Bonin (1993), 'State Desertion and Convertibility: The Case of Hungary', in I. Székely and D. Newbery (eds), *Hungary: An Economy in Transition*, Cambridge: Cambridge University Press, pp. 329–41.

Beije, P. and J. Groenewegen (1992), 'A Network Analysis of Markets', *Journal of Economic Issues*, **26** (1), pp. 87–114.

Ben-Ner, A. (1988), 'The Life Cycle of Worker-Owned Firms in Market Economies', *Journal of Economic Behaviour and Organization*, **10** (3), pp. 287–313.

Ben-Ner, A. and E. Neuberger (1988), 'Towards an Economic Theory of the Firm in the Centrally Planned Economy; Transaction Costs: Internalization and Externalization', *Journal of Institutional and Theoretical Economics*, **144** (5), pp. 839–48.

Black, J. and M. Mendenhall (1990), 'Cross-Cultural Training Effectiveness: A Review and a Theoretical Framework for Future Research', *Academy of Management Review*, **15** (1), pp. 113–36.

Calvo, G. and F. Coricelli (1993), *Output Collapse in Eastern Europe*, IMF Staff Papers, **40** (1), pp. 32–52.

Caves, R. (1982), *Multinational Enterprise and Economic Analysis*, Cambridge: Cambridge University Press.

Chandler, Alfred D. Jr. (1990), *Scale and Scope: The Dynamics of Industrial Capitalism*, Cambridge, Mass.: The Belknap Press of Harvard University.

Coase, R. H. (1937), 'The Nature of the Firm', *Economica*, 4, pp. 386–405.

Csanádi, M. (1990), 'Beyond the Image: The case of Hungary', *Social Research*, 57 (2), pp. 321–46.

Dander, T. (1993), 'Practical Aspects of Technical Assistance to Hungary', Budapest: Institute of Economics, Hungarian Academy of Sciences, Discussion Paper no. 12, February.

Dembinski, P. (1991), *The Logic of the Planned Economy: The Seeds of the Collapse*, Oxford: Oxford University Press.

Dunne, T, M. Roberts and L. Samuelson (1988), 'Patterns of Firm Entry and Exit in U.S. Manufacturing Industries', *RAND Journal of Economics*, 19 (4), pp. 495–515.

Ellman, M. and V. Kontorovich (1992), 'Overview', in M. Ellman and V. Kontorovich (eds), *The Disintegration of the Soviet Economic System*, London: Routledge, pp. 1–39.

Estrin, S. and P. Hare (1992), 'Firms in Transition: Modelling Enterprise Adjustment', London: Centre for Economic Performance, London School of Economics, Discussion Paper no. 89, July.

Fishlow, A. (1991), 'Review of *Handbook of Development Economics*', *Journal of Economic Literature*, 29 (4), pp. 1728–37.

Foss, N. (1993), 'Theories of the Firm: Contractual and Competence Perspectives', *Journal of Evolutionary Economics,* 3 (2), pp. 127–44.

Frydman, R. and A. Rapaczynski (1992), 'Privatization and Corporate Governance in Eastern Europe: Can a Market Economy Be Designed?', in G. Winckler (ed.), *Central and Eastern Europe: Roads to Growth*, Internationally Monetary Fund/Austrian National Bank, pp. 255–85.

Gábor, I. (1991), 'Második gazdaság – modernitás – dualitás: tegnapi jövőképeink mai szemmel' (Second economy – modernity – duality: yesterday's pictures of the future as seen today), *Közgazdasági Szemle*, 38 (11), pp. 1041–57.

Grossman, G. (1983), 'The Party as Manager and Entrepreneur', in G. Guroff and F.V. Carstensen (eds), *Entrepreneurship in Imperial Russia and the Soviet Union*, Princeton: Princeton University Press, pp. 284–305.

Hamel, G. (1991), 'Competition for Competence and Inter-Partner Learning within International Strategic Alliances', *Strategic Management Journal*, 12, Special Issue, summer, pp. 83–103.

Hannan, M. and J. Freeman (1984), 'Structural Inertia and Organizational Change', *American Sociological Review*, 49, pp. 149–164.

Hannan, M. and J. Freeman (1989), *Organizational Ecology*, Cambridge, Mass.: Harvard University Press.

Heiner, R. (1983), 'The Origin of Predictable Behaviour', *American Economic Review*, 73 (4), pp. 560–95.

Hooley, G. (1993), 'Raising the Iron Curtain: Marketing in a Period of Transition', *European Journal of Marketing*, 27 (11–12), pp. 6–20.

Hough, J. (1969), *The Soviet Prefects: The Local Party Organs in Industrial Decision-Making*, Cambridge, Mass.: Harvard University Press.

Karsai, J. (1992), 'Is There Plenty of Time? – Internal Enterprise Cutbacks', *Eastern European Economics*, **30** (2), pp. 44–75.

Keren, M. (1992), 'The Planned Enterprise Syndrome: Covert Properties, Bureaucratic Allocation and the Agonies of Transition', Jerusalem: The Hebrew University of Jerusalem, Department of Economics, Working Paper 263.

Kornai, J. (1993), 'Transformational Recession: A General Phenomenon Examined through the Example of Hungary's Development', *Economie Appliqué*, **46** (2), pp. 181–227.

Laki, M. (1992), 'A vállalati magatartás változása és a gazdasági válság' (Changes in enterprise behaviour and the economic crisis), *Közgazdasági Szemle*, **39** (6), pp. 565–78.

Lissowska, M. (1993), 'La politique économique en Pologne et le comportement des entreprises', *Reflets et Perspectives de la vie économique*, **32** (3/4), pp. 209–22.

Minkler, A. (1993), 'The Problem with Dispersed Knowledge: Firms in Theory and Practice', *Kyklos*, **46** (4), pp. 569–87.

Murrell, P. (1992a), 'Evolutionary and Radical Approaches to Economic Reform', *Economics of Planning*, **25** (1), pp. 79–95.

Murrell, P. (1992b), 'Conservative Political Philosophy and the Strategy of Economic Transition', *East European Politics and Societies*, **6** (1), pp. 3–16.

Murrell, P. (1992c), 'Evolution in Economics and in the Economic Reform of the Centrally Planned Economies', in C. Clague and G. Rausser (eds), *The Emergence of Market Economies in Eastern Europe*, Oxford: Blackwell, pp. 35–53.

Nelson, P. (1981), *Corporations in Crisis: Behavioural Observations for Bankruptcy Policy*, New York: Praeger.

Nelson, R. and S. Winter (1982), *An Evolutionary Theory of Economic Change*, Cambridge, Massachusetts: The Belknap Press of Harvard University.

Nicholls, R. (1992), 'The Neglected Service Industries of Eastern Europe: Some Quantitative and Qualitative Aspects', *International Journal of Service Industry Management*, **3** (3), pp. 46–61.

Nooteboom, B. (1992a), 'Small Business, Institutions and Economic Systems', Paper presented to the 2nd EACES conference, Groningen, September.

Nooteboom, B. (1992b), 'Towards a Dynamic Theory of Transactions', *Journal of Evolutionary Economics*, **2** (4), pp. 281–99.

Nuti, D. and R. Portes (1993), 'Central Europe: The Way Forward', in R. Portes (ed.), *Economic Transformation in Central Europe: A Progress Report*, Luxembourg: European Communities.

OECD (1993), *OECD Economic Surveys: Hungary*, Paris: Organisation for Economic Co-operation and Development.

Pinto, B., M. Belka and S. Krajewski (1993), 'Transforming State Enterprises in Poland: Evidence on Adjustment by Manufacturing Firms', *Brookings Papers on Economic Activity*, 1, pp. 213–70.

Polanyi, M. (1958), *Personal Knowledge: Towards a Post-Critical Philosophy*, London: Routledge & Kegan Paul.

Qian, Y. and C. Xu (1993), 'Why China's Economic Reforms Differ: The M-form Hierarchy and Entry/Expansion of the Non-State Sector', London: Centre for Economic Performance, London School of Economics, Discussion Paper no. 154, June.

Schumpeter, J. (1934), *The Theory of Economic Development*, Oxford: Oxford University Press.

Schumpeter, J. (1939), *Business Cycles*, New York: McGraw-Hill.

Schumpeter, J. (1942), *Capitalism, Socialism and Democracy*, New York: Harper & Row.

Schweitzer, I. (1981), 'Some Interrelations between Enterprise Organization and the Economic Mechanism in Hungary', *Acta Oeconomica*, **27** (3–4), pp. 289–300.

Simon, H. (1945), *Administrative Behavior*, 3rd edition, 1976, New York: The Free Press.

Stark, D. (1993), 'Recombinant Property in East European Capitalism', Wissenschaftszentrum Berlin, Discussion Papers Labour Market and Employment 1993, No.3.

Stinchcombe, A. (1965), 'Social Structure and Organizations', in J. March (ed.), *Handbook of Organizations*, Chicago: Rand McNally, pp. 142–93.

Swaan, W. and M. Lissowska (1992a), 'Economic Reforms and the Evolution of Enterprise Behaviour in Hungary and Poland during the 1980s', Working Paper 4, Leuven: Leuven Institute for Central and East European Studies.

Swaan, W. and M. Lissowska (1992b), 'Enterprise Behaviour in Hungary and Poland in the Transition to a Market Economy: Individual and Organizational Routines as a Barrier to Change', in W. Blaas and J. Foster (eds.), *Mixed Economies in Europe: An Evolutionary Perspective on their Emergence, Transition and Regulation*, Aldershot: Edward Elgar, pp. 69–102.

Teece, D. (1993), 'The Dynamics of Industrial Capitalism: Perspectives on Alfred Chandler's "Scale and Scope"', *Journal of Economic Literature*, **31** (1), pp. 199–225.

Vecsenyi, J. (1992), Management Education for the Hungarian Transition, *Journal of Management Development*, **11** (3), pp. 39–47.

Voszka, É. (1991), 'From Twilight to Twilight: Transformation of the Ownership Structure in the Big Industries', *Acta Oeconomica*, **43** (3–4), pp. 281–96.

Williamson, O. (1985), *The Economic Institutions of Capitalism: Firms, Markets, Relational Contracting*, New York, Free Press.

11. Decentralization and Centralization in the Enterprise Sphere of the Czech Republic

Jana Sereghyová

1   INTRODUCTORY REMARKS

The measure of centralization of economic power which developed in the four Central-Eastern European countries (i.e. in Hungary, Poland, the Czech and the Slovak Republics) under communist rule – when state ownership became supreme – is well known.[1] This centralization was most conspicuous in heavy industry, where in the former Czechoslovakia enterprises with fewer than 10000 employees were rare, while even in Hungary and in Poland staff usually exceeded 5000 persons. But also in other industrial branches the incidence of huge economic units (with several thousand employees) was high. And as the supply of subdeliveries was erratic in times of the command economy, most industrial enterprises also produced a wide range of semiproducts for their own use, even if this prevented them from achieing appropriate innovativeness and economies of scale in their production.

They also performed numerous services which were entirely unrelated to their main activities, from transport to catering. Thus they represented not only horizontal but also vertical monopolies of considerable scope. Taking into account that in these countries also an all-encompassing state-owned wholesale and retail trade network had also been established, competition was almost completely eliminated.

Economic reforms introduced in the late 1960s, and then in the early 1980s, brought only small improvements in this respect, though in Hungary and in Poland efforts to decentralize production were much more pronounced than in the former ÇSFR.

Thus in 1990 – when these countries embarked on their transformation to market economies – the structure of their enterprise sphere was still totally unsuited to developing a competitive climate which would engender economic rationality and efficiency.

Since then the process of decentralization has proceeded in the enterprise sphere of all these countries at a rapid pace. This process implies not only the break-up of huge economic units which mirror the past structures of the economic power that shaped them (see above), but also the emergence of a grass-roots economy and the founding of numerous small new private enterprises, incorporated as well as unincorporated.

This process has brought fundamental changes in the size-structure of the enterprise sphere of these countries, as well as the formation of new patterns of economic power, not only in their production but also in their financial sectors.

As the following paper will show, these two tendencies do not necessarily lead in the same direction.

It should be stressed that not only the pace and the manner in which this process is proceeding, but also the 'mix' of the various policy-measures which have been applied in order to get it started, differ in each of the Central-Eastern European countries.

In Poland the relatively high measure of decentralization of production which can be observed at present was only due to a small extent to the disintegration of some of the big state-owned enterprises. It stemmed mainly from the dramatic growth of the grass-roots economy, as well as from the fact that small private farms had existed even in past decades. All this is illustrated by the fact that the private sector – mostly constituted of small and medium-sized enterprises – accounted in 1993 for more then half of Poland's GDP, i.e. at a time when it was still the only transformation country that had achieved a remarkably high growth-rate.

In Hungary this process of decentralization proceeded at first mainly under the influence of 'spontaneous privatization'. Subsequently it was driven by rapid growth in the number of small and big private enterprises established in small crafts, in the service sector and in industry, the increased incidence of the latter being helped by the emergence of numerous enterprises with foreign capital participation. These developments in the enterprise sphere of Hungary and Poland have already been the subject of numerous publications.

The aim of this paper is only to depict the specific manner in which this decentralization of production, as well as a tendency towards the centralization of economic power, is developing in the enterprise sphere of the Czech Republic.

2   DECENTRALIZATION IN THE INDUSTRY OF THE CZECH REPUBLIC.

In the former CSFR as well as in the Czech Republic the decentralization of production was influenced by the growth of the 'grass-roots economy'. But although the number of small and medium-sized enterprises[2] was relatively high already by the end of 1993 (the number of unincorporated small enterprises was assessed at more than a million at the end of 1993 – after a sharp decrease in their numbers at the beginning of that year – while the number of incorporated firms on the business register reached about 20000),[3] the share of small and medium-sized enterprises in the formation of the Czech GDP still remained very low. Thus in the Czech Republic the main vehicle of decentralization was and still is the privatization of formerly state-owned enterprises, a process which is proceeding extremely rapidly.

In the so-called 'first wave' of voucher privatization[4] about 35 per cent of the total number of state-owned industrial enterprises were privatized, and the majority of the remaining ones are to be privatized in the 'second wave' of privatization to be concluded by the middle of 1995. Moreover, speedy privatization of some of the public utilities – from transport to health care – is envisaged.

Though the intention to break up the huge economic units established in the Czech economy in the past was not declared as one of the aims of this privatization, it was implicitly regarded as such. Therefore it was assumed that those privatization projects which envisaged such a break-up would have a better chance of approval by the authorities (by the founding ministry and the ministry of privatization). Thus, as well as cases in which this break-up was economically rational and necessary, numerous break-ups were proposed and realized which were in fact to the detriment of the competitiveness of the enterprises involved.[5] Nevertheless even these break-ups may have helped to improve the competitive climate of the country.

The amount of decentralization achieved in the course of the 'first wave' of voucher privatization is not yet clearly defined, since most statistics date back only to the middle of 1993 – to the time when the distribution of the shares which had been acquired for the vouchers had only begun. But if we use data representing the situation at the end of 1992, we see that although the composition and/or the rating of the biggest industrial enterprises has changed considerably since 1989 their share in the overall industrial output remained nearly the same until that time.

The data for 1993 confirm this picture, showing only a very slight decrease in the share of the five biggest industrial enterprises in overall industrial output. (While in 1989 their share was 52.3 per cent, in 1993 it was assessed at 51.7 per cent). But in the remaining half of industrial capacities decentralization obviously proceeded rapidly. This can be concluded from the fact that the number of industrial enterprises with more than 5000 employees decreased between 1989 and 1992 from 65 to 20, and those with a number of employees between 2000 to and 5000 decreased from 220 to 98. The incidence of enterprises with a number of employees between 1000 and 2000 remained approximately the same in this period, while the number of enterprises with a lower number of employees increased dramatically. (Those with between 500 and 1000 employees increased approximately twofold; those with 200 to 500 employees approximately tenfold, those with 100 to 200 employees more than twentyfold. The number of industrial enterprises with 51 to 100 employees increased from 4 to 250, those with fewer than 25 employees from 5 to 2770).[7]

Table 11.1   The composition of the ten industrial enterprises with the largest output in 1989 and 1992 (output in billions of Kçs)[6]

Firm in 1989		Firm in 1992	
NHKG (production of iron)	15,5	EZ (energy production)	51,6
Zaluzí (oil refining)	13,7	Škoda-VW (cars)	26,1
VZKG (Steel manufacturing)	12,3	Zaluzí (oil refining)	24,3
Trinec (steel production)	10,5	NHKG (production of iron)	20,4
CKD.(heavy machinery)	9,2	OKD (coal mining)	19,2
AZNP (cars)	8,7	Spolana (chemicals)	14,9
Kaucuk (rubber production)	8,0	VZKG (steel, iron)	14,8
Poldi (steel)	7,3	Trinec (steel, iron)	14,3
Škoda Plzen(machinery)	7,2	Kaucuk (rubber production)	7,3
JM (meat processing)	6,8	NESTLE-Cokol.	
		(confectionery)	7,0

Source:
Zemplínerová, A.. and J. Stíbal (1993), 'Transition and the Problem of Monopoly', Discussion Paper No. 17, Economics Institute of the AVČR, Prague.

It may be assumed that these changes in the size–structure of industrial enterprises will accelerate in the next few years, not only because of the increasing number of newly established medium-sized industrial enterprises but also because the 'second wave' of voucher privatization is proceeding along similar lines as the 'first wave', leading to the disintegration of many of the huge enterprises established in the past. But whether this will lead simultaneously to a disintegration of economic power and ownership, still remains to be seen. The following developments indicate that reality may be moving in the other direction.

3 SIGNS OF A NEW CENTRALIZATION OF ECONOMIC POWER

If we look back at the 'first wave' of voucher privatization, we see that at that time more than 70 per cent of vouchers were either entrusted to one or the other of the 434 privatization investment funds established after 1992 or they were invested in these funds (the *dikes* buying up their shares).[8] Thus 20 of the biggest investment funds became the rightful owners (or were proxies for the *dikes*) of more than half of the equity of the state-owned enterprises privatized in this wave.

Table 11.2   Connections[12] *of the 13 biggest investment funds and the size of their portfolio.*

	Points acquired	Shares held (a)	% in total points (b)
IF of the Czech Savings Bank	950,432,200	21,375,611	11.10
IF of the Investment Bank	724,123,600	13,594,068	8.45
Harvard Investment Fund	638,548,000	15,225,108	7.45
IF of the General Bank Blva	500,587,700	11,985,444	5.84
IF of the Commerce Bank	465,530,400	11,931,808	5.43
IF of the Czech Insurance Company	334,040,900	7,707,865	3.90
IF of the Slovak Investment Bank	333,045,400	10,986,751	3.89
IF of the Slovak Savings Bank	168,864,400	7,707,865	1.97
IF of the Creditanstalt	166,256,000	3,610,773	1.94
First privatization fund	117,541,500	4,920,213	1.37
IF of the Crafts Bank	117,541,500	1,885,287	1.37
IF of Slovak Insurance Company	116,682,500	4,362,299	1.36
IF of the Agrobank	111,087,900	3,941,916	1.30

Notes:

(a) In the 'first wave' of voucher privatization a total of 8,565,642,000 investment points were 'for sale'.

(b) A total of 277,711,577 shares were sold in voucher privatization, 175,975,880 of these being acquired by all the investment funds, while 101,731,697 shares were acquired by individual investors.

Source:

Mejstřík, M. et al. (1993), 'Privatization and Opening the Capital Market in the Czech and Slovak Republics', Discussion Paper No. 21, Economics Institute of the AVČR, Prague.

Though regulations forbid investment funds from aquiring more then 20 per cent of the equity of any single enterprise (and even several investment funds cannot acquire more then 40 per cent of its equity, if they were founded by the same parent company), these 20 investment funds control far more than half of the industrial enterprises privatized in the first wave of voucher privatization. This is due to the fact that in order to achieve this control often much less than a 20 per cent share in the equity is sufficient (especially if the remaining stocks and shares of the respective enterprise are dispersed among a larger number of new owners, which is usually the case in voucher privatization). In this manner an enormous centralization of economic power developed,[9] in spite of the decentralization of production which was and still is going on – showing up in the changes of the size–structure of the enterprise sphere described above.[10]

Moreover, there are only four investment funds among the strongest twenty which are not directly connected with big banks, whereas most of the other huge investment funds have been established by banks. (Those seemingly 'unconnected' are the Harvard Investment Fund,[11] the First Privatization Fund and the investment funds of the Czech and the Slovak Insurance companies.)

4   SOME IMPLICATIONS OF THE NEW CENTRALIZATION OF ECONOMIC POWER.

The above-mentioned parentage of many of the investment funds helps us to clarify the unusually low incidence of bankruptcies in the Czech Republic to be observed even after the bankruptcy law came into full force in April 1993. This is strongly influenced by the fact that the debts of the huge recently-privatized industrial enterprises which might be considered as 'ripe' for bankruptcy[13] constitute part of the 'bad loans'[14] on the balance-sheets of the big banks which are the parent companies of one or the other of the investment funds to whose portfolio the equity of the respective enterprise belongs. Naturally these banks do not insist on bankruptcy proceedings against such an enterprise, for, by doing so, they would not only cause their own debt-assets to diminish (it can hardly be expected that the enterprise will pay its debts in full) but simultaneously reduce also the volume of the portfolio of their daughter companies, the 'investment funds' established by them.

Obviously not only could the strongest banks postpone indefinitely the introduction of bankruptcy proceedings against their main debtors among the newly-privatized enterprises, but the above-mentioned links of ownership could create conditions for a respite being granted to them, during which their financial situation could be improved. In some cases the investment privatization fund which has become a shareholder of such an enterprise may help it to acquire urgently needed investment capital (in spite of the fact that it is still carrying 'old debts'). In other cases such an investment fund might initiate changes in its management which would strengthen the competitiveness of the respective enterprise on domestic or foreign markets. It might also give the enterprise time to link into distribution networks abroad which would enable it to utilize more fully the imminent uptake on the conjunctural situation in partner countries or help it in some other manner to escape the predicament in which the respective enterprise has found itself. But this will probably depend also on the 'financial engineering' which is applied in conjunction by the creditor banks and the debtor companies, mainly on the incidence of debt-equity swaps which might be applied by them.

While in Hungary such swaps already have a long history, in the Czech Republic they are a relatively new phenomenon whose use will probably develop rapidly. This will occur first because these swaps represent a solution to the otherwise unresolvable situation of some of the local industrial enterprises described above, second because company law in the Czech Republic (as well as other related laws) does not prohibit them (on the contrary, it permits them to occur in a legal manner). It may be assumed that, especially in such cases where enterprises threatened by bankruptcy are in the portfolio of investment funds which were founded by their main creditor banks, these debt equity swaps will be frequent.

It might be argued that this should be regarded as a positive development, as it could help many of the deeply indebted recently privatized enterprises to survive. Thus it might also prevent a increase of the unemployment rate in the Czech Republic such as was observed in Hungary following the 'wave of bankruptcies' which occurred in 1992. But at the same time these debt-equity swaps may bring about a further concentration of economic power into the hands of a few banks,[15] which may have serious consequences in terms of the slow uptake of adaptibility and efficiency of the enterprises owned by them.

But it should be taken into account that the share of imports will probably reach half the total domestic consumption of goods (not services) in the Czech Republic before long; that because of the rapid dismantling of trade barriers on imports since 1990, and which will accelerate in the next three years (mainly in the course of implementation of the Association Agreement with the EC[16]), its economy will be one of the most 'open', world-wide. Obviously under these conditions the consequences of such centralization might be far less serious than in countries whose markets are much more closed to foreign competition.

5   CONCLUDING REMARKS

It is obviously much too early to draw conclusions as to the effects of the present changes on the measure of centralization in the enterprise sphere of the Czech Republic (mainly its industry). At present we can only acknowledge that, besides the tendency towards decentralization in the industrial production proper, a strong tendency towards the centralization of economic power can be observed. This is obviously a new – hitherto unusual in these countries – type of centralization which differs even from that which can be observed in market economies of long standing. It is a type of centralization which is strongly influenced by the overall situation that has developed during the transformation of these countries, mainly by specific changes in property rights ongoing in Central-Eastern European countries at present.

NOTES

1. This centralization in the state sector was weakest in Poland, where not only a vast number of small businesses (mostly in the small crafts sector and in the service sector) survived, but numerous farms remained in private hands (being mostly only a few hectares in size). Although in Hungary the collectivization of agricultural property was applied more strictly, some family farms were able to survive, and also small crafts and services remained relatively numerous under the command economy. But in the Czech Republic practically all private enterprises operating in small crafts were closed down, while agricultural production was increased to more than 84 per cent in huge state-owned or cooperative farms. Differences in the extent of centralization in industry – especially if mining is included – were less conspicuous. In the former Czechoslovakia the highest centralization of production was in industry, whereas in Poland it was in mining. In Hungary the incidence of huge enterprises with more than 10000 employees was somewhat lower in both these spheres. See Sereghyová et al. (1993)

2. The identification of enterprises to be regarded as small or medium-sized is still under discussion in most of the transformation countries. As yet it is possible to differentiate statistically only between incorporated and unincorporated firms, the former of which belong among mediumsized ones, the latter being assumed as small (if they were bigger, regulations would require them to become incorporated). In the Czech Republic only enterprises with more than 25 employees are included in the statistics on output by individual branches and/or on the performance of enterprises belonging to them. Smaller ones – especially unincorporated enterprises – are statistically monitored only according to their number and to the type of activities reported when registering, which in reality must not have become their main orientation.

3. See Hospodárské noviny, 16 March 1994.

4. So-called 'voucher privatization' is a unique type of privatizing state-owned enterprises applied as yet only in the former CSFR and in the Czech Republic. The privatization of enterprises included in the two 'waves' of this process (the first wave was concluded in the middle of 1993, the second one is still in progress) comprises a privatization project elaborated by any legal or physical person interested in the privatization of the respective economic unit; a project which has to be approved by the 'founder ministry' and by the Ministry of Privatization. These projects can envisage any of the following types of privatization: the sale of shares of a still state-owned joint-stock company; direct sale to an individual buyer (mostly foreign firms); sales by public tender or auction; handing over of part of the property to the municipalities for free. In the 'first wave' of voucher privatization more than half of the assets were 'sold' for voucher coupons, for which more than eight million Czechoslovak citizens had applied, i.e. nearly all the persons entitled to become recipients of these coupons.

5. The splitting-up of groups of economic units which had been producing complementary products (usually sold as part of the same assortment by one supplier) often led to a decrease in the prices that the newly-established 'independent' enterprises could achieve on domestic and foreign markets (not only in comparison with the price levels they were able to achieve previously, but also with those achieved by other firms still able to supply a full assortment of their products). Still more detrimental in certain cases has been the break-up of groups of engineering enterprises which had been supplying whole plants 'on key'. The expectation that sub-deliveries formerly provided by their 'own' enterprises would continue on a commercial basis among the newly-established independent firms proved often to be wrong – sometimes because the subdelivery plants had adopted another more profitable production programme, or because some of the 'loss-making' ones were unable to survive their 'independence' and had to close down. Thus the 'finalist' had often to import those parts and aggregates which it purchased formerly from its 'own' sub-delivery plants, which usually led to a steep increase in its costs. Or it had to revert to supplying only those machines that it produced itself, which usually resulted not only in a steep decrease in its profits (in comparison with those it was able to achieve while supplying plants 'on key') but also in a narrowing of its sales possibilities at home and abroad. Thus a split-up of a group of engineering enterprises which had acted for decades in mutual symbiosis as sub-deliverers and finalists had often serious consequences, not only for the former but also for the latter. The benefits achieved by 'getting rid' of a loss-making sub-delivery plant were often largely exceeded by the above-mentioned 'costs' of such a split.

6. Taking into account that in the former CSFR the inflation rate reached about 10 per cent in 1990, 58 per cent in 1991 and about 11 per cent in 1992, the above-mentioned data concerning the value of output of the ten biggest enterprises indicate that though their composition had changed, their size remained in fact approximately the same as before. However, their economic power was obviously stronger in 1992 than in 1989, for in this period total industrial output had decreased in the country by more than 30 per cent.

7. The above-mentioned decrease in the number of industrial enterprises with more than 5000 and with between 2000 and 5000 employees was not caused by closures or bankruptcies but

mainly by the split-ups of huge state-owned enterprises during their privatization. These split-ups are also the main cause of the increase in the number of enterprises with between 500 and 2000 employees. Even among enterprises with 100 to 200 employees there are some which were established on the basis of such split-ups or as a consequence of the restitution of property to its former owners, but the majority of them were newly-founded private enterprises.

8.   The owners of the voucher-booklets, the so-called dikes, could use these vouchers either to acquire shares in individual state-owned enterprises put up for sale in the first 'wave' of voucher privatization, or they could invest them in investment privatization funds, thereby becoming their shareholders. The inexperience of the dikes, as well as a lack of information about the prospects of individual enterprises included in this 'wave', induced nearly three-quarters of the dikes to choose the second alternative.

9.   This concentration of power is proceeding at a rapid pace, but its use is still rather feeble. Although many of the investment privatization funds have strong positions on the boards of directors of numerous enterprises – in industry as well as in some of the service-sectors – as yet they very seldom interfere with decision-making processes, even less so in the formation of their development concepts.

10.   The decentralization of production has proceeded mainly on a legal basis, by the dividing up of huge, formerly state-owned enterprises into numerous smaller private ones. The physical decentralization of production – leading to a dislocation of parts of enterprises and to the reduction of the size and of the output of individual plants – is much less frequent.

11.   By becoming one of the major shareholders in the Komercní banka, also the Harvard Investment Fund became closely connected with the banking sector.

12.   Relations between the founder banks and the investment funds established by them are usually those of parent and daughter companies, with arms-length relations to be preserved between them. In one case – that of the Harvard Investment Fund and the Komercní banka – the situation is reversed, the former being a major shareholder in the latter. Financial interconnections among investment privatization funds are still very rare, but their emergence cannot be ruled out since their shares will soon be traded on the stock exchange.

13.   As recent Hungarian experience has shown, the 'purging' of the enterprise sphere of the transformation countries by initiating a 'wave' of bankruptcies can have very serious economic as well as political consequences. Moreover, also in market economies bankruptcies often lead to the loss of 'human capital', of technological know-how, and possibly also of the goodwill bound up in a certain trademark. It can be assumed that the sum of these experiences was taken into account when the bankruptcy law of the Czech Republic was formulated and the manner of its implementation stipulated. This is revealed in the introduction to the regulations, which give the debtor one more chance to settle its debts out of court, which is meant to encourage creditors to participate in the elaboration of a new more viable business plan for the debtor and to help it in its implementation, thus increasing its solvency and also its ability to repay loans.

14.   As long as an enterprise is a 'going concern' credits granted to it are only seldom qualified as

'bad loans' even if its financial situation is precarious. Banks are usually very discreet, even about those loans whose inferior quality cannot be doubted, since by publishing their share in their debt assets would make increased demands on their reserve funds and in extreme cases might reduce their own credit-worthiness.

15. Thus the question whether a 'bank-led capitalism' is in the offing in the Czech economy might be raised. This question obviously cannot be answered only on the basis of the developments described in this paper. They might be regarded either as the first steps in this direction, or as a sign of the 'normalization' of the situation in the Czech banking sector, bringing it nearer to Western standards. Whether these developments will bring it nearer to the 'German model' or to different models applied in other market economies remains to be seen. In any case it can be assumed that not only the benefits but also the disadvantages of each alternative will be different from those achieved in market economies when applied in a transformation country.

16. The Interim Agreement on Trade and Trade-Related Matters, which is part of the Association Agreements concluded between the four Central-Eastern European countries and the EU, envisages that all trade barriers between these countries and EU countries will be dismantled by 1997 at the latest. The implementation of this agreement is being discussed by economists and policy-makers in East and West Europe. See Sereghyová (1993) or Sereghyová (1994).

REFERENCES

Kubišta, V. (1993), 'Profits and Behaviour of Czechoslovak Industrial Enterprises in the Changing Economic Climate', Discussion Paper No. 2, Economics Institute of the AVČR, Prague.

Matesová, J. and R. Šedá (1993), 'Financial Markets in the Czech Republic as Means of Corporate Governance in Voucher Privatised Companies', Discussion Paper No. 14, Economics Institute of the AVČR, Prague.

Mejstrík, M. et al. (1992), 'Privatization and Opening the Capital Market in the Czech and Slovak Republics', Discussion Paper No. 21, Economics Institute of the AVČR, Prague.

Sereghyová, J. et al. (1993), *Entrepreneurship in Central-Eastern Europe,* Heidelberg: Physica Publishers.

Sereghyová, J. (1993),'External Determinants of Enterpreneurial Activities in the Czech Republic – Trade-Political Issues', Discussion Paper, Institute of Economics of the AVČR, December.

Sereghyová, J. (1994), *Regionale Aspekte und Weltmarktintegration Zentral-Osteuropaischer Staaten,* Berlin: Freie Universitat.

Zemplínerová, A. and J. Stíbal (1993), 'Transition and the Problem of Monopoly', Discussion Paper No. 17, Economics Institute of the AVČR, Prague.

12. The Collapse of the Russian Economy: an Institutional Explanation

Ruud Knaack

1 INTRODUCTION

The year 1989 brought the most profound political and economic changes to Eastern Europe since the end of World War II. In these countries it was generally felt that the economy had been greatly distorted by the system of central economic planning, and that it was in need of a 'shock therapy' that would transform the command economy into a genuine market economy as rapidly as possible. The Anglo-Saxon model, in which the economy is deregulated to the utmost, became the dominant model for the market economy.

In Russia, on 2 January 1992, the Gaidar government initiated a transition process based on such a 'shock therapy'. At a stroke, most prices were decontrolled, and within a short period of time a programme had been launched for the rapid privatization of the entire economy. The major aims of these measures were monetary stabilization, the destruction of the Soviet system and transition to an economy based on private enterprises.

As we now know, these were measures that produced the adverse result of driving the Russian economy into deep crisis. During the period 1990–92 the national income decreased by 40–50 per cent. In the same period, both the real sphere and the monetary sphere grew increasingly unbalanced. In the year 1992 alone, inflation was 2500 per cent, and retail sales at state shops decreased by 40 per cent.

As a result, heated debate concerning whether or not the shock therapy should be discontinued broke out in both political and academic circles. From a political point of view, the Chernomyrdin government answered in the affirmative: the shock therapy policy was abolished officially in the late summer of 1993, and the decision was confirmed by personnel changes in January 1994.

This paper approaches the issue from an academic point of view. It argues that shock therapy is based on a simplistic theory of the functioning of a market economy. By destroying old routines and institutions, Russian shock therapy created an institutional vacuum that was used by criminals and speculators for purposes that were not productive but redistributive. It can be argued that, by behaving in this manner, the Yeltsin regime actually continued a policy that had unconsciously been initiated by Gorbachev.

2   THE FUNCTIONING OF A MARKET ECONOMY

2.1   Statics

The abovementioned misconception regarding the functioning of a market economy stems from the neoclassical formalization of Adam Smith's argument of the 'invisible hand' which induces self-interested agents to serve the common good. Neoclassical theories investigate the conditions (taste, endowment, technology and market structure) necessary for the existence of competitive equilibria that are Pareto-optimal. These conditions are summarized in the First Fundamental Theorem of welfare economics, which in plain words runs as follows: if there are enough markets, if all consumers and producers behave competitively, and if an equilibrium exists, then the allocation of resources in that equilibrium will be Pareto-optimal (Leyard, 1991, p. 407). Moreover, by assuming that contract disputes are settled in court in an informed, sophisticated and low-cost way, the models have implicitly a 'legal centralist' point of view (Williamson, 1985, p. 20).

The possible existence of an optimal, Pareto-efficient solution in a market economy cannot be cited in evidence against the functioning of a real planned economy. From a methodological point of view, it is only legitimate to compare the properties of ideal systems, or the properties of real systems. We cannot condemn a real existing economy by comparing it with the ideal properties of the alternative to it. In practice, however, this 'nirvana approach' is often adopted (Demetz, 1969). When the properties of an optimally functioning market economy are compared with the properties of an optimally functioning planned economy, both based on utility maximizing individuals, it can be shown that under appropriate assumptions both regimes will lead to the identical allocation of resources (Pareto, 1966, p. 364). Following a different line of argument, Samuelson came to the same conclusion: 'under perfect competition workers can rent capital goods or capitalists can rent workers' (1972, p. 237).

These general equilibrium models have various flaws. First, the optimal conditions are often not met. Second, these models are only interested in the possible *existence* and properties of an equilibrium. The difficulties of what would happen if prices were not at the equilibrium level are often glossed over.

The possibility of 'market failure' is recognized by the neoclassical economists. The seminal works of the 1940s and 1950s gave rise to an extensive literature on the conditions for a Pareto-efficient allocation of public goods, externalities, and economies of scale. The prevailing idea of that period was that when these conditions are not met, political intervention in the market place is justified to create the optimal conditions through the exercise of authority. Later, mainstream economists devoted a great deal of time to avoiding this conclusion and to finding instead market-conform solutions for so-called market failures. For example, problems with public goods and external effects can be easily overcome by completing new markets. However, in both cases the theoretical solution fails when the number of individuals involved is large. With respect to public goods, this failure is due to 'free riding'; with respect to externalities, it is due to transaction and bargaining costs (Mueller, 1989, p. 35). In these cases, a Pareto-optimal allocation of resources can only be achieved with the help of a government able to economize on transaction and bargaining costs, and able to protect 'free riders' against themselves by forcing them to cooperate. Within this market failure framework, the state is viewed as merely a second-best 'artificial' substitute, one which only acts when the 'natural' order of the market fails to produce the promised outcome.

The competitive balance between market and planning shifts in favour of the market if we take the Austrian view that life is permeated by fundamental uncertainties. Von Hayek concluded from the notion of the existence of pervasive uncertainty that only a market economy is able to cope with these uncertainties, and that a planned economy is doomed to fail. Planning would require the formulation of millions of equations on the basis of millions of individual computations. By the time the equations had been solved, the information on which they were based would have become obsolete, and they would therefore have to be calculated once again.

The experience of the centrally planned economies shows that there is some truth in this statement; and yet the same statement can also be used against the Austrians themselves. How can they explain, for example, the existence of hierarchically organized firms within market capitalism (Wagener, 1992, p. 29)? And how do they conceive a human mind which can fully and rationally process all the information relating to individual human action at the highest level of deliberation (Hodgson, 1988, p. 114)? Hence, in a decentralized economy too, uncertainty creates problems for which solutions must be found; problems which in a static world ultimately arise from the existence of bounded rationality, asset-specificity and incomplete markets (Williamson, 1985, Stiglitz 1994).

The problems created by uncertainty can be found at all the levels of the economy. At the micro level, for example, Heiner (1983) has discussed the problem resulting from the gap between the competence of an individual and the complexity of the decisions problem to be solved. He develops a Reliability Condition which states that individuals must ignore actions which are appropriate only for rare or unusual situations. This Reliability Condition resembles Simon's satisficing behaviour. With regard to firms, Alchian and Demsetz (1972) have advocated the monitoring of the workforce in order to minimize opportunistic behaviour ('shirking'). Because the employer buys only the use-value of labour, it is difficult to gauge and reward individual contributions to collective effort under conditions of team production. The problem of 'disciplining the labour force' can be solved using a different strategy. Modern organization theory stresses the importance of trust and loyalty for the efficiency of the firm. Many authors suggest that the relative efficiency of Japanese firms stems in part from the long-established relations of give-and-take and trust (Imai, 1986).

At the meso level – that is, at the level of relations between firms and consumers – many problems are solved by creating uncertainty-reducing institutions. Some of these institutions deal with the problem of asset-specificity. Consumers will be protected by goods inspectors, consumer agencies and quality marks. Firms are brought into contact by Chambers of Commerce, auctions and fairs. Other institutions address the problem of the lack of information. Prices are published in newspapers, on radio and on television. Many firms work together on joint research projects. Again, trust and personal relations are uncertainty-reducing devices.

At the macro level, too, there is a need for uncertainty-reducing institutions. In general, the need for coordination at the macro level stems from the problem of the 'fallacy of composition' (Hodgson, 1988, p. 233). In macroeconomics, relationships may be the reverse of the corresponding relationships at the microeconomic level. For example, wage reduction may increase a country's competitiveness on the world market. But if every country follows this policy the overall demand for products will fall; this will lead to reduced business expectations, and a general decline in economic activity will ensue.

Hence, an efficiently functioning market economy requires the stability and support of an overall institutional framework. Order and stability at the macro level are mainly brought about by stable political rules and by the norms set forth by tradition and culture. Order and stability at the meso level are realized by the stability of organizational forms. Stability at the micro level is created if economic agents behave in an orderly way; orderly behaviour which is brought about by the permanent durability of the structure of human perception and behavioural routines (Nelson and Winter, 1982).

Institutions are required for other reasons as well. Neoclassical models do not analyse the problem of what would happen if the economy were not in equilibrium. They define away the problem by assuming that individuals have full knowledge of the entire economy in which they operate. Obviously, this assumption is too strong: if it were correct, there would be no need at all for an economic science. Individuals have at best some knowledge about prices and their own wishes and possibilities. When they are price-takers and do not know whether or not prices are equilibrium prices, a stable equilibrium can only be achieved with the help of a Walrasian auctioneer who administers potential demand and supply, or with the help of merchants willing to act as shock-absorbers by carrying stocks (Kaldor, 1972, p. 1248).

2.2   Dynamics

The foregoing analysis has shown that a stationary market economy, characterized by the pervasive presence of bounded rationality, opportunism and asset-specificity, must be a regulated market economy if it is to function efficiently. However, we can enquire as to how important the problem of allocative efficiency actually is. According to Leibenstein (1963) the problem is a trivial one. Empirical studies of the 'social welfare costs' of some market imperfections show that the welfare losses calculated as a percentage of gross or net national product attributed to misallocations of resources are negligible: they range between 0.07 and 1 per cent of national income. For example, the gains to be achieved by increasing only allocative efficiency are likely to be made up by growth in matter of months. Hence in many instances, other types of efficiencies, for example dynamic efficiency, are much more significant.

This was a conclusion previously shared by many Soviet authors. For example, Ellman (1989, p. 302) quotes Kudrov in noting that the USSR was less efficient than the USA in its use of many raw materials and intermediate products; however, as far as growth was concerned, the socialist countries were markedly superior. In the period 1950–75 the growth rate of the Soviet economy significantly exceeded that of the US economy, and this substantially reduced the gap between the two countries.

The picture changed in the second half of the 1970s. At that time the sources of extensive growth became exhausted and the economy had to reorient towards an intensive growth path. From that moment onwards, competition between the two systems ultimately depended on the dynamic efficiency and productivity levels of the economy. Hence, to prove the superiority of the Soviet economic system, it was essential for the USSR to achieve an internationally superior rate of innovation over a period of time. To this end, the USSR placed extraordinary emphasis on technical education, research and development. It is estimated that 1.5 million scientists and engineers were engaged in R&D in the USSR in 1984, which was roughly equal to the number in all the OECD countries combined (Fusfeld, 1986, p. 11). Nevertheless, there was no great concern over competition from Soviet-made high-technology products, nor was the Soviet Union considered to be the leader in a substantial number of technical fields. The focus of American concern over international competitiveness obviously concentrated more closely on Japan, with half the number of professional R&D personnel, than on the USSR with twice as many. In the 1970s, the member countries of the CMEA imported ten times more licences than they exported in terms of dollars paid (Gomulka, 1985, p. 13).

This brings us back to the issue of the sources of dynamic efficiency in a market economy. Strangely enough, the existence of uncertainty, resulting from bounded rationality, opportunism and asset-specificity, creates an impetus not only for the creation of uncertainty-reducing institutions, but also for economic growth and technological development. Without these 'imperfections', entrepreneurs have no incentive to take risks. The incentive to invest, for example, depends in part on knowledge of a limited competitive supply from other firms, or on establishing the belief that others do not possess information regarding the opportunity open to the investor. A profit opportunity which is known to everybody is available to nobody in particular. Hence markets have a double function. They are instruments for the allocation of resources and for the transmission of impulses to change (Kaldor, 1972, p. 1240). At the heart of Schumpeter's analysis was its emphasis on the dichotomous role of markets and its investigation of the relationship among allocative processes, economic behaviour, innovation and economic change (Rosenberg, 1986).

Entrepreneurs change their environment. They produce non-static conditions in the environment. A market with fragmented product and process innovations creates new uncertainties for both consumers and producers, not only over the content of the present state but also over the content of future states. Uncertainty about future status can have several aspects (Littlehood, 1986). In neoclassical models, the form that the future can take, the set of possible states of the world, is known in advance. We only do not know which state of the world will eventually materialize. This is the world of Knightian risk. Entrepreneurs are uncertain about the future price of honey, but they know that honey will be traded. In the Austrian model, the set of possible states of the world is partially known. The problem is not uncertainty of risk, but ignorance. The entrepreneur knows that there will be other states of the world, but he does not know what they will be. Finally, in evolutionary models, the set of states of the world is undetermined at the time when the decision is taken. The task of entrepreneurs is not to discover the set of states, but to create the future. Entrepreneurs must use their imagination. They are aware of the flimsiness of their conjectures about the future and of the vulnerability of their plans to the independent imagination of other agents. These three models reveal that uncertainty about the future can have both quantitative and qualitative aspects.

How can one cope with these types of uncertainty? Of course, different schools give different answers. Neoclassical models have developed the concept of *search*: the costs of acquiring information have to be set against the possibility of lower prices. The Austrian models focus on *alertness*: the entrepreneur must actively look for positions where profitable opportunities can be expected. In evolutionary models, uncertainty stems from the still undetermined actions of other agents. It is then necessary either to become privy to the decisions of others, e.g. by agreements or by collusion, or to reduce one's dependence on others, e.g. by securing supplies.

More in general, there are two kinds of response to change and uncertainty (Hodgson, 1988, p. 263). First, structural flexibility can be created to match the uncertainties of the environment. For example, a firm can diversify so that, as the market for each product fluctuates, the firm as a whole is more resilient. Second, an attempt can be made to reduce external variety by creating uncertainty-reducing institutions, e.g. by increasing the range of control. It is important to realize that that these two kinds of response may contradict each another. Too much control may lead to gigantic principal–agent problems; too much flexibility may create a lack of coordination between the various parts.

This dialectical relation between the need for both flexibility and rigidity can be found at all levels of the economy. At the micro level the individual, facing an uncertain world, relies on behavioural rules from the past and on the sentiments of the present. 'Knowing that his individual judgement is worthless, we endeavor to fall back on the judgement of the rest of the world which is perhaps better informed' (Keynes, 1973, p. 114). On the other hand, in periods of uncertainty the individual creates flexibility by building stocks and by learning new techniques. At the firms' level, enterprises may respond to environmental uncertainties by creating internal structural variety by undertaking organizational subdivision, by improving the internal labour market, and by introducing more flexible payment schemes. On the other hand, however, the firm has an interest in stable labour relations. These relations can be harmonized by enhancing group feeling (the 'Philips family', the 'Sony spirit'), and by creating possibilities for worker-participation. At the meso level, the firm can create flexibility by diversification and product innovation, and stability by means of vertical integration and the forming of long-standing and quality-responsive relations with customers and other firms. At the macro level, the government can create flexibility by stimulating schemes for *éducation permanente*, by improving the infrastructure and by deregulating. On the other hand, it can create stability by resolving uncertainties over the investment process. 'When the capital development of a country becomes a by-product of the activities of a casino, the job is likely to be ill-done' (Keynes, 1971, p. 159). Keynes' policy conclusions are well known: government intervention to regulate the overall level of effective demand and the 'socialization of investment'.

The foregoing analysis leads to the conclusion that a dynamic and innovative economic system will require a structured combination of variety and rigidity, of statics and change, of centralized guidance and decentralized autonomy. Neither the liberal ideology of the free market nor the state power of Marxism–Leninism lend themselves to this type of conclusion (Hodgson, 1988, p. 269).

2.3   Coordination and transformation

When the economy is analysed from a dynamic point of view, the question is not how to achieve a static equilibrium, but rather how to explain the relatively orderly patterns of growth which have characterized industrialized capitalist economies for substantial periods of time. We can speak of order in a dynamic sense when an economy generates messages which do not induce agents to change the theories they hold or the policies they pursue (Dosi and Orsenigo, 1988).

In analogous fashion to the Walrasian auctioneer required to create static order, institutional rigidities (including the state) are needed to create dynamic order. Order is also created by technological rigidities. Technology does not progress randomly but follows trajectories. The relatively stable combination of the available technology, the organization structure and the dominant type of management is frequently referred to as the 'techno-economic paradigm' (Dosi, 1982).

In order to obtain a dynamic model of institutional change it is advisable to draw a distinction between *regime* and *structure* (Pelikan, 1988, p. 375). A structure can be defined by three groups of parameters: a collection of economic agents, their competences, and the organizational arrangements that link them together (the coordination mechanism). A regime can be defined as the rules of the game that constrain the behaviour of the economic agents involved. There is a hierarchical relation between the regime and the structure. Whereas agents can enter, exit or change their arrangements in the various ways permitted by the rules, the rules themselves are fixed. The regime of a national economy is a rather complex matter. Basically, it involves all the institutional rigidities at the macro level: labour law, patent law, and also various customary and ethical norms deriving from the underlying culture. An important component of the regime consists of the rules that specify the economic role of the government. It is important to note that every regime typically allows for the formation of several alternative arrangements, and that identical arrangements may display different performance abilities. An arrangement has only a certain potential to perform; but its actual performance depends closely on the competence of the participating agents.

There is a widely-held view in social science that for an economy to function well, all the parts of the economic system must be integrated. The parts must correspond to each other, they must support each other's functioning. 'The economy is not a supermarket in which we can make our choices as we like. Every real system constitutes an organic whole' (Kornai, 1980). The Regulationists assert that the economic regime, the structure and the technological paradigm must be fine-tuned to each other in order to obtain the harmonious development of society. They explain the 'golden age' of capitalism, the period 1950–1973, as resulting from a 'functional fit' in the already-mentioned aspects of the economic system. According to the Regulationists, this period was characterized by a social compromise between capital and labour: the capitalists took the main decisions about the organization of the labour process; the entrepreneurs produced standardized mass-products with the aid of Taylorist organization principles; and the workers, for their part, obtained their fair share of total production by linking their wages to labour productivity. In this way there was an automatic connection between mass-production and mass-consumption. In addition, it was illegal to dismiss workers for purely individual, non-financial reasons. The government also had an important role to play, since its task was to expose the realization of sales through fiscal policy and welfare arrangements. The Regulationists call this type of society 'Fordism'. In the literature other names are also used: welfare state, Rhineland model and social partnership (Kornay, 1980; Boyer, 1988).

As a consequence of changes in a particular subsystem, functional misfits may arise in the system as a whole. These changes may stem from different sources (Lin, 1989; Knaack, 1994): changes in the institutional choice set (e.g. permission for private agriculture in Eastern Europe), changes in technology, long-run changes in relative factor and product prices (e.g. the rise in oil prices of 1973 and 1979), demographic changes (e.g. the increasing share of elderly people), changes in the ideology and value systems (e.g. the weakening of the revolutionary spirit). These changes may be the outcome of 'accidents', of economic laws, or of deliberate actions. However, whatever their source may be, the question is whether or not they will force adjustments in the other subsystems.

There are two ways in which a system can adapt to a functional misfit (Lin, 1989). An *induced* institutional change is a modification or replacement of an existing institutional arrangement which is voluntarily initiated, organized and executed by an individual or a group of individuals in response to a perceived opportunity for profit. In a dynamic context an entrepreneur must possess not only allocative competences, but also associative competences (the competence to change structures) and technological competences (the competence to innovate). Associative competence is the main source of self-organization: the way in which the structure of an economy is organized and reorganized as a result of the decentralized actions of independent agents.

As a result of the process of self-organization, the institutional arrangement of the society will change slowly. The process of self-organization is basically an evolutionary process (Alchian, 1950; Nelson and Winter, 1982). This is not to say that the sum total of marginal alterations cannot have significant consequences. The fundamental properties of a structure will alter when the accumulation of changes in individual arrangements reaches a certain critical point. This will give rise to a Hegelian switch from a quantity to a quality paradigm. As long as the time-path is not specified, the distinction between evolution and revolution remains an open question (Wagener, 1992, p. 45).

It is important to note that the process of self-organization is not limited to capitalist economies. It also took place in the former USSR, where enterprises were caught in a decision trap by being obliged to fulfil non-fulfillable plans (Knaack, 1983, p. 116). As a result, they had to develop alternative strategies in order to meet the demands made on them. These strategies could be legal (e.g. risk-averting behaviour by asking for slack plans and more investments), or semi-legal, by creating unofficial market channels (the 'second economy'). This 'second economy' functioned as a corrective mechanism which protected the first economy against extreme and disastrous results.

An institutional change can also be *imposed* on an economy by the state. A persistent institutional misfit can be remedied by state intervention. This may be a government measure designed to facilitate a new institutional arrangement resulting from the process of self-organization. But a government may also pursue its own goals. An institutional change can be imposed purely for the purpose of redistributing income among different groups of individuals. An interesting question is whether the state has the competence to design a suitable institutional arrangement, as well as the executive competence to implement the decision. In any society, there may be a contradiction between the overload of rules and the ability to implement these rules. Whether or not this contradiction exists depends also on the competences and the goals of the bureaucratic apparatus. As we shall see, this is an urgent problem in present-day Russia.

So far, I have postulated in abstract that a change in a particular subsystem tends to force adjustment in the other subsystems, thereby transforming the entire social system 'into the image' of the original change. However, this transformation process may develop less smoothly than planned. First, the reactions of the other subsystems may lag behind (Gregory and Stuart, 1980, p. 33). This delay may be very long or even infinite because of the inertia and stability of the other subsystems. For example, Swaan (1993, ch. 7) describes the evolution of behaviour and institutions during the Hungarian reform process. In absolute terms, the reform produced only minor changes when compared to the orthodox system of directive planning. Moreover, those improvements that did occur were achieved only gradually, as a result of a slow process of behavioural learning by state officials and enterprise managers. The slow pace of change was partly due to the cognitive constraints normal to human beings, but it was considerably delayed by the inertia of the system itself. Individual behaviour, the institutional arrangements among individuals, and the regime as technology, may be 'locked' into formal and informal networks of social interaction from the past. The prolonged functional misfit among the subsystems, which results in unexpected falls in production, is one of the major explanations for so many frustrated reform movements and defeated revolutions.

Second, the efficiency of the adaptation process depends on the system's environment. As said earlier, a subsystem (e.g. a firm), may adapt by creating static or flexibility. A firm in a rapidly changing environment may be far better able to survive by means of a flexible organizational structure compared to a less flexible firm, which may have excellent abilities for minimizing transaction costs in a more stable environment (Langlois, 1986, p. 20). This creates path-dependency problems. The process by which a more efficient institution will supplant less efficient ones in the short run may not be the same in the long run. Hence a structure which was efficient during its evolutionary process may be a misfit in the long run. It is therefore possible that subsystems which function smoothly in a stably functioning capitalist regime will function differently when they are imitated in a socialist economy in transition. As an example we may hypothesize that, in a transition period, there may be a contradiction between the goals of democratization and those of liberalization, whereas in the long run this contradiction may not exist.

The fact that each subsystem has a different adaptation time may lead to the hypothesis that an economic reform that seeks to minimize transformation costs in terms of loss of production must minimize the possibility of institutional misfits. Such a reform process can only be an evolutionary process, one of learning-by-doing, of trial and error. What is needed is 'piecemeal social engineering', incremental improvements which can be continually improved upon.

This is especially true of the transformation process from a planned economy towards a market economy. As explained earlier, imitation of the regime and structure properties of a capitalist economy in a different environment, where individuals have different competences and where a different technology is used, will create such misfits that it may end in catastrophe. These misfits will arise because, in a market economy, the institutional arrangements between individuals and firms, given individual competence, cannot be known beforehand. There is no single blueprint for an efficiently functioning market structure. The optimal market structure can only be found through a long process of self-organization which allows for the specific characteristics of individuals and the constraining regime. As such, it develops as part of the competitive process (Langlois, 1986, p. 15). This account applies less to the transformation process from a market economy towards a planned economy, and especially when the environment is not complex and individual behaviour is almost completely constrained by the planning routine and technology used. Therefore, in some respects, a Bolshevik transformation process is less difficult than a reverse-Bolshevik transformation process.

3   DE-INSTITUTIONALIZATION IN THE USSR

3.1   The old system

Lack of variety is often seen as the basic problem of the former USSR, although it was an argument of little validity during the first five-year plans. After the October Revolution, the Bolsheviks found themselves in possession of political power in an internationally isolated and underdeveloped country.

Therefore, their main task was to industrialize the country at full speed, using internally raised investment funds. It was for this purpose that the Soviet planning system was created. This system must be judged not from an allocative efficiency point of view or from a Marxist perspective, but in terms of dynamic growth. The Soviet planning system, as it was shaped during the 1920s and 1930s, was not the successor of capitalism, but a substitute for capitalism. It was a non-capitalist method for organizing a rapid industrialization process (Knaack, 1983, ch. 2).

Also the Soviet Union experienced a 'golden age'. In the 1950s the Soviet economy grew rapidly, propelled by increases in capital and labour and in the efficiency of their use. Economic growth directly benefitted consumers as their diets and housing improved apace (Schroeder, 1992). At the same time, there was no price inflation. Space flights and Nobel prizes symbolized the achievements of Soviet science. Life expectancy reached the level of most developed countries in the late 1950s. Among the newly emerging independent countries of Asia and Africa, the Soviet system was widely considered to be a model for emulation.

From the 'golden age' of the 1950s onwards, the Soviet economy settled on a slower growth path. A continuous decline set in which culminated in the absolute slump in output at the end of the 1980s. According to Ellman and Kontorovich (1992), the slow-down of economic growth can be explained by several factors.

First, by the loss of control. When an economy becomes more complex, co-ordination becomes increasingly difficult. If decision-making is concentrated at the top of the pyramid, it becomes remote from the actual task performed. Information transmitted through longer channels is more likely to become distorted along the way, and the quality of decisions based on this information deteriorates.

Second, by changes in the growth rates of the factors of production (labour, capital and land) and of their productivity. In the 1960s and 1970s the labour force grew as a result of increasing participation by women. In the 1970s this growth factor was exhausted. Moreover, natural resources were running out: in the antiquated mines, for example, the conditions for extraction grew increasingly difficult.

Third, by the weakening of the 'entrepreneurial spirit'. In a command economy, the counterpart of the pressure to innovate exerted by competition is the authoritative pressure to innovate. Pressure 'from above' provides the chief source of dynamism in an economy. The history of the USSR from the 1950s onwards is one of an almost constant slackening of pressure 'from above'. Brezhnev's policy of 'stability of cadres' represents more or less the final codification of this process.

Declining growth figures alone cannot explain the collapse of the Soviet economy at the end of the 1980s. According to Kornai (1992, p. 378), the system was still able to guarantee the population a decent way of life. Although the system showed great inconsistencies, it was not unstable enough to collapse immediately. What caused the crisis was its weak economic performance relative to that of the USA and the other OECD countries. As said earlier, the dynamic efficiency argument was the *raison d'être* of the USSR. Consequently, the poor growth figures in comparison with the West in the 1980s threatened the political legitimacy of the whole system (Dirksen and Klopper, 1986).

Economic reform in the USSR under Gorbachev must be understood as part of his effort to revive and modernize the Soviet economy. In order to improve the economic situation, Gorbachev changed both economic policy and the economic system. Changes to the former involved alterations to investment policy, the 'non-labour incomes' campaign, the anti-alcohol campaign. The system-related changes comprised changes both within the traditional economic model, like a variety of administrative reorganizations, and changes to the traditional economic model. The most important changes in the early *perestroika* period concerned individual economic activity, state enterprises, producer cooperatives, family contracts and leases in agriculture, joint ventures and the expansion of the rights of enterprises in foreign trade (Ellman, 1989a).

The results of all these changes were disappointing. This cannot be entirely blamed on Gorbachev, since the disappointing results stemmed partly from unfavourable environmental circumstances. For example, after 1986 the terms of trade with both the non-socialist and the socialist countries deteriorated. But with hindsight we now know that the collapse of the economy at the end of the 1980s was the unintended result of Gorbachev's own well-intentioned policies. The following factors seem to have been important.

First, from the beginning, his economic policy was not feasible (Hewett, Roberts and Vanous, 1987, p. 32). The rapid shift of resources to the machine-building industry entailed that other sectors had to forgo substantial resources, for example the energy sector, agriculture and the nonproductive sectors. This explicitly contradicted the social goals of the 12th Five-Year Plan: an increase of 50 per cent in the production and sale of consumer goods over the five-year period, and the promise that nearly every family would have an apartment or other form of self contained dwelling by the year 2000.

Second, participants in the economy behaved differently from what was anticipated. This was most noticeable with respect to the anti-alcohol campaign. The idea was to reduce alcohol abuse and thus increase labour productivity. The result was that in 1985–1987 sales of alcohol in the state shop system dropped by 37 billion roubles, or to almost a quarter of 1985 food sales, with devastating effects on the state budget. On the other hand, it was not clear whether alcohol abuse in fact diminished; the drop in the sales of vodka, for example, was partially offset by an increase in the sales of illegally brewed *samogon*. A further unexpected outcome was that the high targets set for investments led to an excessive growth of money wages.

Third, the government policies themselves were often harmful. The combination of disappointing incomes and unplanned expenses resulted in a budget deficit of 183 billion roubles in 1988. A significant proportion of the budget deficit was financed through monetary expansion. This in turn led to excess money supply, which allowed excess purchasing power to be created.

Fourth, in spite of all these changes, the ministerial system as such continued. The old power relation between the enterprises and the ministries did not fundamentally change. In this respect Gorbachev's *perestroika* could have learned some lessons from Kosygin's abortive 1965 reform and from the Hungarian reform process. As long as each enterprise was dominated by a branch ministry responsible for the overall performance of 'its' industry, enterprises could not freely exercise their rights. The reason for this was that the meetings of the Central Committee continued to instruct the branch ministries to put this or that problem in this or that industry to rights. This ministry could only intervene in the operations of its enterprises if it was held responsible for the sum total of their activities.

As a result of the disappointing results of his first measures, in 1987–1988 Gorbachev started to experiment with economic reforms. Once again, his measures did not appear to be very successful. In agriculture, for example, farms failed to take advantage of opportunities to sell their above-plan production on the free market, because under conditions of shortages of supply it was safer to 'please' the local leadership by fulfilling their non-obligatory demands (Aven and Shironin, 1988, p. 36). Another area where quick results could be achieved were the individual, family and small group business. In May of 1988, a Law on Cooperatives was enacted which gave cooperatives a great deal of room for manoeuvre. It was hoped that, through ownership and incentives, cooperatives would contribute to the economic revitalization of the Soviet economy. This hope was not entirely fulfilled. Many of the new cooperatives were not in fact new, but former state enterprises which had been transformed. These cooperatives often took advantage of shortages by asking for higher prices than they could have charged as an official state enterprise (Knaack, 1992).

The negative results of the economic reforms were not interpreted by Gorbachev as resulting from his own policies, but more as a consequence of the behaviour adopted by non-cooperative bureaucrats. His *glasnost* policy was intended to unmask the bureaucrats sabotaging the reform process. In contrast to Brezhnev's policy of maintaining the stability of the cadres, Gorbachev removed many officials and arrested several corrupt officials (Ellman, 1989, p. 17). Again, these policies had an adverse result. Latent nationalism was fuelled by new publications about the Chernobyl catastrophe and the contents of the Molotov–Ribbentrop pact. And Gorbachev also had to pay the price for his struggle against officialdom. By eliminating the Party, he also eliminated its coordinating role in the economic process. By weakening the party ideology he created an ideological vacuum that became rapidly filled by new ideologies, like nationalism and religion (Knaack, 1993).

After the abortive *coup d'état* of August 1991, the USSR disintegrated and Yeltsin became president of the new Republic of Russia. On 2 January 1992, the Gaidar government introduced a number of measures which shook the Russian economy (van der Lijn, 1993, ch. 7). The greatest shock was the liberalization of most prices, but the government also introduced a value added tax of 28 per cent, an enterprise tax of 32 per cent and a progressive income tax ranging from 12 to 60 per cent. (Foreign) exchange dealings became liberalized and nearly all private trade was legalized. The official policy was to reduce the budget deficit, to make the rouble internally convertible, and to privatize the majority of the state enterprises. The overall goal of these measures was to restore monetary stability and to create a stimulating environment for the transition to a market economy.

As mentioned in the introduction, the results were disastrous. Production declined sharply and prices rocketed at a nearly hyperinflationary speed. The principal reason for this was the bad sequencing of the reform measures. The privatization process ruined the incomes of the state, because the best officials started their own businesses in the private sector and the weakened state apparatus was unable to collect the taxes due. Moreover, a number of autonomous regions refused to pay their share to the central government. On the other side, a populist parliament managed to increase expenditure. As a result of all these factors, real wages decreased sharply and the distribution of incomes grew increasingly uneven. Also, the crime rate soared.

3.2   The present situation

How can we perceive the present situation? Schmieling (1993) discusses some standard explanations for the crisis, one of which is that the command economy was grossly inefficient. The structure of production was distorted and the capital stock outdated. After internal liberalization and exposure to the world market, these inefficiencies and shortcomings were laid bare, leading to a fall in GDP. This argument is wrong, for it mistakes a low level of GDP for a decline in GDP. It might be true that, with a different allocation and use of the factors of production, the socialist countries could have attained a higher level of GDP. But without a drastic decline in the quality and quantity of the production factors and the production technologies, the former socialist countries could still produce the same goods at the same low level of GDP.

Many authors argue that a change in relative prices may lead to a short-run decline in GDP, because these changes warrant structural adjustment. This argument holds true when it is assumed that internal prices adjust to the world market prices and that firms adjust to the new situation. However, if firms stick to their old routines, which is the case in Russia, the total value in unchanged world market prices will not change.

In line with the above argument, neither can wage rigidities explain the fall in GDP. The wage rigidity argument states that wage rigidity results in a situation where the marginal productivity of labour is lower than real wages, and that this leads to unemployment and a decline in GDP. However, there is no major unemployment at the moment; consequently the basic problem is finding an explanation for the present combination of a decline in GDP, real-wage flexibility and the absence of massive unemployment.

Wage flexibility also invalidates the claim that the macroeconomic stabilization programme has caused a short-run fall in economic activity, given a wage lag which resulted in an overshooting of real wages. However, since real wages have decreased in Russia, this argument would instead provide a rationale for an immediate output gain.

Decreased real wages might provide support for standard Keynesian arguments. Brada and King (1992) identify a reduction in autonomous consumer demand as the major culprit. They also mention the real wealth effect on the monetary balances of households in domestic currency. Other authors stress that redistribution of revenue from wages to profits, which leads to changes in savings. Although it is true that real wages have fallen, the demand effect has been compensated by the expenditures of the government. On their own, these arguments cannot explain the persistent inflation.

This paper has offered an alternative explanation which states, in essence, that the systematic transformation in Russia is an institutional revolution. The old institutions have vanished, while the necessary institutions of capitalism are either absent or do not fit with the institutional remnants of the old system or with the inherited competences of individuals and firms.

At the level of the regime, Gorbachev changed both the legal structure and the ideology. However, these legislative acts were never implemented in practice: partly because of the disintegration of the USSR and Russia whereby the various parts are now going their own separate ways; and partly because of a breakdown in the rule of law. Also, the Marxist–Leninist orthodoxy has dissolved to clear the way for an upsurge in nationalism. At the level of the structure, the Law of State Enterprise enacted in 1988 increased the scope for independent decision-making by the state enterprises. It was hoped that this would improve the efficiency of such enterprises, but under conditions of macroeconomic imbalances they have behaved differently. In practice, this has led to sharp price increases, a decreasing level of production, increases in wages and a fall in state income. More importantly, however, Gorbachev ruined the traditional supply system. By attacking the bureaucracy, he eliminated the economic role of the party. Informally, the party committees functioned as a coordination mechanism by using their contacts if something went wrong. After their elimination the enterprises lapsed into a void which was not filled by the creation of markets and the establishment of new formal and informal relations with suppliers and consumers. At the process level, the traditional organizational separation between most R&D and design work and production had dramatic consequences in a market environment characterized by monopolistic structures. Enterprises no longer bought the products of the R&D departments, which – in order to survive – sold many of their patents to Western companies. Moreover, there was a massive brain-drain to the West. As was mentioned earlier, this destabilization process was exacerbated by Yeltsin's shock therapy.

As a result, individuals and firms must operate in an *institutional vacuum* which explains many of the present features of the Russian economy. First, current management has little or no incentive to think in terms of long-term projects. This is reflected in the catastrophic fall in investments, which have more than halved over the past two years. People are pursuing short-term goals which can be better achieved by redistributive activities than by productive activities. Lower-grade personnel take home from their workplaces anything that might prove to be of value: most second homes around the large cities are furnished with equipment pilfered from the factories. Almost everything that can be easily removed and sold on the market is indeed being removed and sold. For management, the situation is still that of a one-shot game. Double bookkeeping now takes the 'legal' form of establishing 'small enterprises' parallel to existing ones and selling most of the output through the former. The revenues are deposited in (foreign) banks instead of being paid to the mother enterprise. By the decision of top management, plots of land, buildings, equipment and whole factories are being diverted to dubious business practices. This is nothing but the 'mafiazation' of the economy (Yavlinksi and Braguinsky, 1994).

If this is indeed the situation, how can we explain the fact that the economy is still functioning, albeit at a lower level? By citing the behavioural rigidities and habits of the old management structures. Those who operate in an institutional vacuum are forced to rely on old networks and behavioural routines. Enterprises still deliver their products to each other. Payment problems are solved by mutually extending credits. From this perspective, the resistance of the old *apparatchiks* against the economic reform process under Gorbachev can be perceived differently: bureaucratic resistance to reform is not necessarily one reason for the failure of the reform, but rather the logical behaviour of bureaucrats seeking to restore order.

4   EVALUATION

In general, the negative outcomes of *perestroika* have been caused by too much reform rather than too little. Gorbachev destroyed the old system without creating a new system at the same time. According to Popper (1991), the fact that he was unable to create a new system is not surprising. Any economic system constitutes an organic whole. The behaviour of economic actors is learned behaviour. It takes time for both the system and the actors to adapt to new circumstances. Seventy years of communism is a difficult heritage to rid oneself of, even if one is absolutely determined to do so; and to imagine that it can be done in five hundred days is an ideological fallacy. Accordingly, social institutions should be designed, not in accordance with some 'grand design' but on a cautious basis of trial-and-error. Those who try to remodel society in accordance with 'a definite plan or blueprint' run the risk of building a deformed social structure whose flaws can be corrected only with the greatest delay and difficulty. Those in the East and in the West who still believe that it can be done have an attitude similar to that of the early generations of communists who were anxious to 'build communism', regardless of the short-run consequences (Ellman, 1993). They tend to ignore the system-specific features of these countries and are surprised when the outcome of the policies that they support is quite different from what they anticipated.

   The fact that the socio-political economic transformation of the former Soviet Union will be a long and difficult process has important consequences for the sequence of the measures to be taken in reform and transition. A reform process is fundamentally a social process, one of learning-by-doing, of trial and error. What is needed is 'piecemeal social engineering', incremental advances which can be constantly improved upon. Hence the one thing the leadership in the former Soviet Union must not do is dismantle their industrial system abruptly. On the contrary, before other measures are taken, the post-

Soviet economies must be stabilized. Only when this policy of stabilization has succeeded can one move further along the road of institutional change.

Only when the economy is stable, therefore, can institutional reforms be resumed. Here too, however, a certain amount of 'fine-tuning' is required. The experiences of China and Hungary have shown very clearly that it is much easier to stimulate the small-scale private sector than to reform the state sector in industry. Only when the state enterprises are embedded in a sea of small-scale enterprises will the time be right to liberalize the state enterprises completely (Kornai, 1990, p. 101).

REFERENCES

Alchian, A.A. (1950), 'Uncertainty, Evolution and Economic Theory', *Journal of Political Economy*, **58**, pp. 211–22.

Alchian, A.A. and H. Demsetz (1972), 'Production, Information Costs, and Economic Organization', *American Economic Review*, **62**, pp. 777–95.

Aven, P.O. and V.M. Shironin, (1988), 'The Reform of the Economic Mechanism', *Problems of Economics*, June.

Boyer, R. (1988), 'Technical Change and the Theory of "Regulation"', in G. Dosi, C. Freeman, R. Nelson, G. Silverberg and L. Soete (eds), *Technical Change and Economic Theory*, London and New York: Pinter Publishers.

Brada, J. and A. King (1992), 'Is There a J-Curve for the Economic Transition from Socialism to Capitalism?', *Economics of Planning*, **25**, pp. 37–53.

Demetz, H. (1969), 'Information and Efficiency: Another Viewpoint', *Journal of Law and Economics*.

Dirksen, E. and M. Klopper (1986), 'Is There an Economic Crisis in the USSR?', *Comparative Economic Studies*, **XXVIII** (1).

Dosi, G. (1982), 'Technological Paradigms and Technological Trajectories: A Suggested Interpretation of the Determinants and Directions of Technical Change', *Research Policy*, **2** (3), pp. 147–62.

Dosi, G. and L. Orsenigo (1988), 'Coordination and Transformation: An Overview of Structures, Behaviours and Change in Evolutionary Environments', in G. Dosi, C. Freeman, R. Nelson, G. Silverberg and L. Soete (eds), *Technical Change and Economic Theory*, London and New York: Pinter Publishers.

Ellman, M. (1989a), *Socialist Planning*, Cambridge: Cambridge University Press.

Ellman, M. (1989), 'Intellectual and Ideological Barriers to Economic Reform in the USSR', Mimeo, University of Amsterdam.

Ellman, M. (1993), 'General Aspects of Transition', in M. Ellman, E. Gaidar and G. Kolodko (eds), *Economic Transition in Eastern Europe*, Oxford: Basil Blackwell.

Ellman, M. and V. Kontorovich (1992), 'Overview', in M. Ellman and V. Kontorovich (eds.), *The Disintegration of the Soviet Economic System*, London and New York: Routledge.

Fusfeld, I. (1986), *The Technical Enterprise*, Cambridge (Mass.).

Gomulka, S. (1985), 'The Incompability of Socialism and Rapid Innovation', in M.E. Schaffer (ed.), *Technology Transfer and East-West Relations*, London: Croom Helm.

Gregory, P. and R. Stuart (1980), *Comparative Economic Systems*, Boston.

Heiner, R.A. (1983), 'The Origin of Predictable Behavior', *American Economic Review*, **73** (4), pp. 590–95.

Hewett, E.A., B. Roberts and J. Vanous (1987), 'On the Feasibility of Key Targets in the Soviet Twelfth Five Year Plan (1986–90)', in Joint Economic Committee, *Gorbachev's Economic Plans*, Washington.

Hodgson, G.M. (1988), *Economics and Institutions*, Cambridge: Polity Press.

Imai, M. (1986), *Kaizen*, New York: Random House Business Division.

Kaldor, N. (1972), 'The Irrelevance of Equilibrium Economics', *Economic Journal*, **82**, pp. 1237–55.

Keynes, J.M. (1971), *The Collected Writings of John Maynard Keynes*, Vol. VII, London: Macmillan.

Keynes, J.M. (1973), *The Collected Writings of John Maynard Keynes*, Vol. XIV, London: Macmillan.

Knaack, R. (1983), *Contradicties in socialistische planing*, Enschede.

Knaack, R. (1984), 'Dynamic Comparative Economics: Lessons from Socialist Planning', in A. Zimbalist (ed.), *Comparative Economic Systems: Present Views*, Boston/The Hague/Dordrecht/Lancaster: Kluwer Nijhof.

Knaack, R. (1992), 'On the Efficiency of Soviet Cooperatives: A Critical Appraisal', in B. Dallago, G. Ajani and B. Grancelli (eds), *Privatization and Entrepreneurship in Post-Socialist Countries*, Basingstoke: The Macmillan Press.

Knaack, R. (1993), 'The Ten Commandments of Economic Reform', in C. Frateschi and G. Salvini (eds), *The Socialist Enterprise Between Autonomy and Constraints*, Dartmouth: Aldershot.

Knaack, R. (1994), 'Social Partnership, Western Experiences', *Voprosi Ekonomiski*, **5**, May.

Kornai, J. (1980), 'The Dilemmas of a Socialist Economy: The Hungarian Experience', *Cambridge Journal of Economics*, **4** (2).

Kornai, J. (1990), *The Road to a Free Economy*, New York: Norton.

Kornai, J. (1992), *The Socialist System*, Oxford: Clarendon Press.

Langlois, R.N. (1986), 'The New Institutional Economics: An Introductory Essay', in R.N. Langlois (ed.), *Economics as a Process*, Cambridge: Cambridge University Press.

Ledyard, J.O. (1991), 'Market Failure', in J. Eatwell, M. Milgate and P. Newman (eds), *The New Palgrave: the World of Economics*, London and Basingstoke: The Macmillan Press.

Leibenstein, H. (1963), 'Allocative Efficiency vs. "X-Efficiency"', *American Economic Review*.

Lin, J.Y. (1989), 'An Economic Theory of Institutional Change: Induced and Imposed Change', *Cato Journal*, **1**, pp. 1–33.

Littlehood, S.C. (1986), 'Three Types of Market Prices', in R.N. Langlois (ed.), *Economics as a Process*, Cambridge: Cambridge University Press.

Lijn, N. van der (1993), 'Stabilisatiebeleid in Rusland: Schok of Therapie?', in N. van der Lijn (ed.), *De overgang naar een markteconomie in Oost-Europa*, Culemborg: Stenfert-Kroeze.

Mueller, D.C. (1989), *Public Choice II*, Cambridge: Cambridge University Press.

Nelson, R.R. and S. Winter (1982), *An Evolutionary Theory of Economic Change*, Cambridge (Mass.): Harvard University Press.

Popper, K. (1991), 'The Best World We Have Yet Had', *Report on the USSR*, **3** (22).

Pareto, V. (1966), *Manuel d'Economie Politique*, Geneva.

Pelikan, P. (1988), 'Can the Innovation System of Capitalism be Outperformed?' in G. Dosi, C. Freeman, R. Nelson, G. Silverberg and L. Soete (eds), *Technical Change and Economic Theory*, London and New York: Pinter Publishers.

Rosenberg, N. (1986), 'Schumpeter and Marx, How Common a Vision', in R. MacLeod (ed.), *Technology and the Human Prospect*, London.

Samuelson, P. (1972), 'A Summing Up', in R.C. Merton (ed.), *The Collected Papers of Paul A. Samuelson*, Cambridge (Mass.).

Schmieling, H. (1993), 'From Plan to Market: On the Nature of the Transformation Crisis', *Weltwirstschaftliches Archiv*, Band 129, Heft 2, pp. 216–53.

Schroeder, W. (1992), 'Soviet Consumption in the 1980s. A Tale of Woe', in M. Ellman and V. Kontorovich (eds), *The Disintegration of the Soviet Economic System*, London and New York: Routledge.

Stiglitz, J.E. (1994), *Whither Socialism?*, Cambridge (Mass): Mit Press.

Swaan W. (1993), *Behavior and Institutions under Economic Reform*, Amsterdam: Thesis Publishers.

Wagener, H.-J. (1992), 'System, Order and Change – On Evolution and Transformation of Economic Systems', in J. van den Broeck and D. van den Bulcke (eds), *Changing Economic Order*, Groningen: Wolters-Noordhoff.

Williamson, O.E. (1985), *The Economic Institutions of Capitalism*, New York: The Free Press.

Yavlinksi, G. and S. Braguinsky (1994), 'The Inefficiency of Laissez-Faire in Russia: Hysteresis Effects and the Need for Policy-Led Transformation', *Journal of Comparative Economics*, **19** (1).

13. The Revival of Redistribution in Hungary

Éva Voszka

1 INTRODUCTION

Politicians and analysts, businessmen and citizens, generally agree that economic transformation should amount to market economy creation. Paradoxically enough, the gradual establishment of the basic institutions of the market, including private ownership, is contrasted by the signs of the reactivation of another integration mechanism, namely redistribution. Following temporary withdrawal in the late 1980s and early 1990s, the direct redistributive function of the state seems to have gained new vigour.

Redistribution[1] in the 1990s began with the recentralization of state ownership rights. As one of the main features of previous economic reforms, these ownership functions had been delegated to enterprise managements. The last stage of decentralization came in the mid-1980s, when enterprise councils set up by representatives of management and employees were authorized to exercise most ownership rights, including the appointment of enterprise managers, decision-making on mergers and acquisitions, and the establishment of companies with state assets. After 1990, several dozen enterprises were brought under direct administrative control; a process followed by the enactment of mandatory corporatization in 1992. Direct state control and corporatization mean the removal of enterprise councils and the assignment of all ownership rights to the central privatization and asset management organizations: the State Property Agency (SPA) and the State Holding Company (SHC), both controlled by and reporting to the government.[2]

Thus corporatization, which was for the most part complete by the end of 1993, can be identified as 'renationalization'.[3] According to Polanyi's definition, this in itself amounts to redistribution, i.e. the collecting of controlling rights. The question is this, however: to what extent will central authorities be able or willing to utilize their new position? In other words: will formal centralization be followed by the redistribution of company positions and incomes, or will it not?

This is not an easy question to answer. The new redistribution process is less transparent and more difficult to quantify than it was under the planned economy. This is due to the fact that it is in its initial stages and because of the new methods that it employs (which typically do not result in direct budgetary expenditure). Therefore the extent of redistribution cannot be captured by macroeconomic data alone. Instead of defining the share of redistribution and drawing final conclusions, this paper instead outlines some typical phenomena and formulates hypotheses for future empirical study.

2 OLD AND NEW METHODS

Analysis of these methods will focus on redistributive effects that are often not evident. I shall try to outline their range of application, their financial consequences and their underlying reasons and motivations, and I shall seek to show that most of the new features of the 1990s that come under the headings of reorganization, debt consolidation and market protection belong to the category of redistribution.

2.1 Special policies

The traditional forms of redistribution of enterprise positions, like the replacement of management and change in the organizational framework, have also been used in the state-owned enterprise (SOE) sector in recent years. The preconditions for these measures were created by the corporatization of SOEs, which enabled SPA and SHC, instead of enterprise councils, to take decisions on mergers or the splitting-up of a firm, or on the appointment of new managers.

2.1.1 Changing the guard
The position and opportunities not only of the persons concerned but also of enterprises may be directly affected by the replacement of managements and by the appointment of board and supervisory board members in corporatized firms. New managers who enjoy the confidence of the state owner can help stabilize the firm's position through their good political or business contacts, thereby acquiring additional resources or preferential treatment. Nevertheless, employees often perceive the new unknown managers as threatening their

vital interests; a reaction which has been overt on several occasions and which has also included strikes.

Statistical data are not available on the overall range of management replacements, except for the data published by SPA for the year 1992. According to these figures, 72 chief executives were fired from 126 enterprises brought under administrative control. Twelve cases were recorded in companies after corporatization and before privatization. Replacements were made in several big firms like the national oil company, the Hungarian airline and several pharmaceutical enterprise. In sectors like the printing industry or state farms, the majority of firms were affected by the wave of management change. In 1992, SPA appointed some 5000 people as board members or supervisory committee members of state companies (Government of the Republic of Hungary, 1993a). SHC had appointed 1300 managers and board members by the spring of 1994, and ten per cent of these were replaced over one and a half years (State Holding Company, 1994).

In justification of these replacements, the central organizations cited their intention to accelerate the privatization process or to prevent the loss of state assets. Both of these are soft categories. Without clear-cut criteria for evaluation made transparent for all those concerned, managers are constantly threatened and have good reason to feel that 'anything may happen'. In a climate of general and incalculable threat, managers are preoccupied with showing loyalty and a 'positive attitude' towards government organizations and discovering the values and intentions of the bureaucracies. In these circumstances it is difficult to dispel the general belief that the appointment of managers and board members is subject to direct political influence.

2.1.2 Changing the organizational framework

The merging and splitting of firms has always meant the redistribution of enterprise positions and future opportunities. In the last few years, however, some of these actions have also entailed direct income redistribution in the form of the compulsory purchase of another company's assets or else they have served as substitutive or complementary subsidies.

The crisis management of SOEs through the merger of autonomous firms was a method frequently resorted to in planned economies. Such measures in Hungary were rare in the 1980s but reappeared in the early 1990s.

The 'integration' of coal mines and electrical power plants provides one of the best-known examples. The merger was motivated by the losses and imminent bankruptcy of the mines. The government sought to overcome the financial and market problems by vertical integration which merged the strong supplier/customer relations into one organization. The aim was to establish a system of direct control and transfer prices. As a result, the acquired firms were given a chance to survive, even though they now complain about the loss of their independence. Budgetary subsidies were replaced by draining the resources of the acquiring units (in this case the power plants), while in compensation they were assigned the role of controlling shareholder.

The splitting-up of big SOEs into smaller units became more widespread after organizational decentralization was given priority by the revised privatization policy of 1992 (see Privatization Strategy Task Team, 1992). According to this new strategy, the main goal of privatization is to create a strong property-owning middle class in Hungary. This requires modification of both the demand and the supply side. The instruments proposed to increase domestic demand for state assets include preferential loans, ESOP and privatization leasing constructions, as well as so-called credit notes. An adequate supply structure is to be created through organizational restructuring: that is, by splitting up large units.

From the company point of view, the traditional form of organizational decentralization instituted by the centre is perceived as a hostile administrative decision. It is seen as restricting the company's capacities, market share and negotiating power against business partners or government bodies, without any compensation. This type of splitting-up has so far mainly concerned the food industry and retail trade: well-known examples include numerous cases of small privatization, the grocery networks in Budapest and in Northern and Southern Hungary, and the baking industry.

In the 1990s a new type of organizational decentralization has appeared in Hungary. This splitting-up in order to rescue the SOEs typically involves the sale of property, factories or plants on the initiative (or at least with the approval) of the large SOEs but also with the consent of SPA. The income from these sales is recycled to remaining units in order to consolidate their financial position – mainly to repay their debts. According to experts, the majority of recent decentralizations belong to this category.

The result of this process is similar to the 'asset depletion' that used to be blamed on spontaneous privatization. There is an important difference, however, given that in this case the final decision is taken by government bodies. Permission to sell units and the granting of the income to the SOEs can be regarded as an individual preference for these enterprises, while the state's direct income from privatization is significantly reduced by such measures.[4]

2.1.3 Income redistribution
Direct income redistribution among SOEs began in industry. The dramatic reduction of budgetary subsidies at the turn of the 1980s and 1990s coincided

with a shrinking of the market brought about by the loss of most COMECON contracts and the sudden sharpening of import competition. According to the Ministry of Industry and Trade (1991), 40 per cent of industrial firms became loss-makers. Because of the general depression, growing pressure by regions particularly affected by the crisis, and in an attempt to stabilize its own position, the Ministry of Industry and Trade (MINIT) declared a new policy of 'getting closer to the enterprises', claiming that 'the state must not withdraw from its own property and the ministry has to deal with operative matters' (Kovács, 1991).

As a first step taken late in 1991, the industrial administration sought to address the regional crises. A comprehensive industrial policy was drafted which included such measures as state guarantees, preferential credit rates, cancelling of debts, debt-to-equity swaps and other subventions. On this occasion the ministry also published a plan to investigate the situations of forty big SOEs.

Direct governmental management of enterprise crisis began in 1991 with a number of exceptional, individual decisions taken with regard to coal mining and metallurgy in Northern Hungary and provoked by mass demonstrations, strikes or other trade union action. The measures, however, amounted to nothing more than 'fire fighting': the several billion forints spent as a result brought only temporary and marginal relief for the firms concerned.

These examples, however, showed other firms that it was not impossible to obtain subsidies. The institutionalization of redistribution was intended to create a framework for enterprise bargaining.

2.2   Attempts at creating a formal system of redistribution

2.2.1 The 'Big Thirteen'

The creation of a formal system (i.e. institutionalization) of financial redistribution began with the special treatment afforded to thirteen firms. According to a government resolution,[5] these enterprises were shortlisted on the basis of the following criteria. Their operation 'on competitive basis is a national economic interest and the prevention of their liquidation is supported by industrial policy considerations', such as significant weight in exports and in regional employment or in the safeguarding of certain professional cultures. Regarding this larger group, central assistance was provided for firms producing competitive products or able to change their markets, at least in the longer run. A further argument was that the state would not in fact suffer any real loss: the repayment of debts was in any case unlikely.

MINIT initially studied the special treatment of forty organizations. This list was reduced, not according to competitive potential but according to the nature of indebtedness: the government could help firms which were indebted directly to the state (and not to suppliers or commercial banks).

The total asset value of the thirteen firms selected was assessed at almost HUF 150 billion and their total debts at HUF 56 billion. (These figures do not include supplier credits amounting to a further 25 or 30 billion.) The SOEs involved employed more than 80 thousand people. Their turnover plan for 1992 was 230 billion.

According to MINIT (1993), the debts of seven companies were cancelled, rescheduled or swapped for shares to a total amount of HUF 12.4 billion. For some members of the group, new credit of HUF 3.3 billion was underwritten by the state. HUF 5.1 billion were allocated out of privatization incomes to reorganization, and custom duties and tax debts amounting to HUF 3.5 billion were cancelled. Nearly half of the total outlay of more than HUF 24 billion was received by one firm.

Typically, these methods have not directly increased current budgetary expenditure, although they do imply lost revenue and deferred burdens. From the point of view of the companies concerned, special treatment has meant individual preferences, and an opportunity to solve acute liquidity problems. Nevertheless, also according to the MINIT evaluation (1993), the programme achieved only partial success measured by the number of rescued companies, by the amount of the assets or people concerned,[6] and by the stability of results. 'It is true ... for each firm that the long-term improvement of their position depends largely on the successful debt consolidation and the accompanying reorganization process, implemented in due time.' In other words, crisis management, again, was no more than 'fire fighting' even in the most successful cases: it brought some temporary financial relief, without any structural adjustment.

Even in this restricted sense, crisis management proved unsuccessful when debts did not directly concern the state. Commercial banks could be subjected to informal and prolonged pressure by either the government or companies. The leading state-owned commercial banks rarely undertook liquidation,[7] while they continued to dispense loans to key debtors. (Therefore, for example, the credits of the Big Thirteen were not recorded as 'non-performing'.) Partly due to this 'permissive' banking attitude, partly to the poor portfolios allocated to the banks at the time of their creation in 1987, and partly to uncertainty and recession, which equally hindered credit rating and repayment, the capital structure and the liquidity position of leading banks were steadily eroded.[8] It was for this reason that the process of debt consolidation was launched.

2.2.2 Debt consolidation

The first round of consolidation, in 1992, sought to improve the yearly balance sheets of banks by 'cleaning' their portfolios and by swapping bad debts for government bonds. This first round included a package of HUF 102 billion at face value and HUF 80 billion at swap. It was already clear when the decision was taken that, if nothing else changed, a further substantial proportion of debt would slide into the non-performing category by 1993.[9] It was also predictable that even the benefits of the banks would be devalued by the consolidation fees that they were obliged to pay and by the low interest rate on government bonds. By international auditing standards, no appreciable improvement was achieved in capital adequacy ratios.

For the above reasons, each participant assumed that consolidation would not remain a once-and-for-all cleaning-up operation. The 1993 plans focused on capital raising.[10] The banks' position was improved by the swapping of bonds for higher coupon rate bonds and by the abolition of debt consolidation fees, although these measures worsened the position of the state budget. The achievement of a zero capital adequacy ratio required a capital injection of HUF 116 billion. An additional package of government bonds of HUF 22.4 billion was issued in May 1994 in order to achieve a 4 per cent capital adequacy ratio at seven banks.

The bank consolidation of 1992–94 required an investment by the state amounting to HUF 300 billion. This in itself constituted redistribution, since the interest on government bonds was to be paid out of the state budget.[11] Redistribution occurred not only in favour of the bank sector but also went on among banks. Their relative positions were adjusted by eliminating differences in their earlier performances. The highest gains were achieved by those banks which had accumulated more bad debts without building adequate reserves, since consolidation enabled them to offload their non-performing loans cheaply.

Consolidation also modified the ownership structure by reducing the weight of the actual shareholders (mainly companies) and by considerably increasing the state's direct share. Thus the intricate financial manoeuvres resulted in renationalization, and this time literally, not virtually, as in the case of compulsory corporatization.[12]

In return, the balance sheets of the banks involved in consolidation improved, but only temporarily since more and more investments are required to keep the state-owned bank alive. Although, in the second round, the banks concerned had to sign debt agreements with the Ministry of Finance, experts agree that without privatization there is no real guarantee that the bank's performance can be improved and the consolidation process brought to an end.[13]

Besides ownership structure, the other main reason why the same problems have arisen in the banking sector is the financial situation of the debtor firms. In 1993 'consolidation' was split between the two branches of narrower 'bank consolidation' and the new arrangement of 'debtor consolidation'.

All firms with bad loans in the consolidated banks may apply to participate in debtor consolidation.[14] According to the agreement among the bank, the state owner (SPA or SHC) and the branch ministry, loans can be cancelled, rescheduled or swapped for shares. If the bank does not consider the reorganization plan for the firm to be viable, it must sell its debts to the state owners.

The initial estimate was of around 30000 loan agreements mostly involving (small) private companies and not state-owned ones. By mid-1994, however, no more than 2000 firms had applied for consolidation. The decision-making process, however, is rather slow and operates mainly in cases in which the state budget or the state owners buy out bad loans.

Following a government resolution, the debts of 22 firms were bought out for HUF 57 billion in 1993. By Spring 1994, SPA had taken decisions on the consolidation of twelve companies, investing HUF 3 billion (State Property Agency, 1994). SHC proved to be more active: it bought and then cancelled the debts of seven firms to a value of HUF 21 billion (State Holding Company, 1994), five of them belonging to the 'Big Thirteen' group. Thus in these cases debtor consolidation was a direct continuation of the special treatment provided earlier.

By removing the disinterest of banks in cancelling or rescheduling the debts, the government eliminated the obstacles hindering the financial restructuring of the 'Big Thirteen'. Through debtor consolidation, which concerned several hundreds of firms, the bank consolidation process may gradually turn into a comprehensive programme of reorganization involving a large part of the economy.

2.2.3 State guarantees
Bank consolidation has the backwash effect of mitigating the risks resulting from bad debts. There are accepted forms of risk mitigation in market economies whereby guarantees to share the expected burdens operate in parallel with a loan contract. Increasingly greater use of underwriting has been made in Hungary, too.

According to the Ministry of Finance (1993), a total of HUF 4.3 billion, including HUF 3.6 billion enterprise credit, was guaranteed in 1992 by the state budget. By May 1993, state guarantees had amounted to a sum almost as high as the total application in 1992. The guarantees made by other government authorities should be added to these amounts. According to the report of the State Audit Office (1993), HUF 24 billion had been underwritten by SPA by the end of 1992, and the amount had nearly doubled by mid-1993. The guarantees underwritten by the State Holding Company exceeded HUF 9 billion in 1993 and 20 billion in Summer 1994 (State Holding Company, 1994), by which time the total sum of state guarantees was HUF 197 billion (Financial Research Ltd., 1994).

Initially individual cases (i.e. guarantees given to the loans or bonds of various firms in the form of case-by-case decisions) were gradually followed by institutionalized arrangements. Underwriting Co., an organization whose majority owner is the state, began its activities in early 1993. Its objective is to support the credit rating of private businesses able to promise high returns but which cannot meet the collateral requirements of commercial banks. The company guarantees up to 80 per cent or HUF 100 million of commercial bank loans. Underwriting Co. is backed by the Small Business Guarantee Fund, which is financed out of the central budget. This financial facility offers guarantees up to 70 per cent of the amount guaranteed by Underwriting Co., which means that the greater part of the risk is directly hedged by the state.

Until December 1993, Underwriting Co. guaranteed HUF 3.7 billion for HUF 6.6 billion credit. More than half of this debt was raised under the highly preferential Existence Loan scheme provided for the privatization of state assets. About one-third of the proposals were turned down, mainly because of unacceptable business plans (Veres, 1993).

If the borrower fails (a likelihood officially estimated by experts at 30 per cent but informally at a high 60 per cent), the assets offered as collateral are transferred to the shared ownership of the commercial banks and Underwriting Co. In the short run this means renationalization, just like many other forms of state support.

The second important component in the formal system of underwriting by the state is Export Guarantee Co., set up in 1991 and whose range of operation initial capital has recently been significantly increased. Unlike the case of Underwriting Co., loans linked to export should be available mainly for major transactions. Bearing in mind the market problems of large enterprises, this method may tend to finance sales where the buyer is more or less clearly insolvent.[15] Thus export guarantees may become a market-building tool of the state with consequences similar to those of COMECON trade as far as the production pattern and payment processes are concerned.

A state guarantee may be crucial for enterprises, especially if they need to borrow funds to purchase the raw materials or components required for production. Thus the position of a company is directly influenced by guarantees obtained via a process of case-by-case state decision-making. If borrowers fail to pay, the central budget meets their liabilities, which is tantamount to income redistribution. Consequently, state guarantee may become a new and increasingly popular method of redistribution, because it matches those redistribution instruments whereby budgetary expenditure is postponed and deficit financing is transferred to future governments. The crucial factor here, of course, is the amount of underwriting claims.

According to a summary report based on data from the Ministry of Finance (Financial Research Ltd., 1994), this type of budgetary expenditure amounted to HUF 7.3 billion in 1993, and it is expected to rise to 49 billion in 1994. By autumn 1993, SPA as an underwriter had paid HUF 8.7 billion, and estimates for 1994 are 15 billion (Asset Policy Guidelines, 1993). The SHC calculated an expenditure of HUF 5 billion for this purpose in 1994 (State Holding Company, 1994). If the amount of guarantees continues to climb, and if more and more organizations fail to meet their liabilities in a lingering recession, then the burdens on the state budget will steadily grow.

Formalized systems are double-edged swords in general, and also in the particular case of state guarantees. A formal system can establish standard processes and thereby control the scope of bargaining. On the other hand, however, institutionalization establishes a forum for bargaining and suggests to all market actors that there is a chance for them to obtain preferences. Thus the effect of institutionalization may be escalation of these processes rather than their control.

3   ESCALATION OF REDISTRIBUTION

The escalation of redistribution over time has already been mentioned. Indeed, the realization grew that the methods used for consolidation in 1992 and 1993 were unable to achieve any long-term 'final' solution. Partial portfolio cleaning was insufficient for bank consolidation, while the mitigation of direct indebtedness to the state was not enough to reorganize the major SOEs.[16] The government insists that 1993 was the last year of consolidation; although the parties concerned, and with good reason, consider this statement to be more wishful thinking than realism.

Analysts agree that this proliferation stems from the nature itself of the problem: namely that it is not a group of banks or firms which is in crisis but the entire economy. Successful treatment entails the creation of a healthy economy, but a problem as huge and dynamic as this cannot be addressed by partial and static tools.

Besides its expansion over time, the extension of redistribution to an increasingly larger group of companies is also striking. The initial exceptions have been followed by institutionalization. The special treatment of the 'Big

Thirteen' resulted in proposals for the rescue of 40 large companies as originally suggested by the Ministry of Industry and Trade. If such measures are taken in industry, why should food processing or the agricultural sector as a whole be excluded? Accordingly, the Ministry of Agriculture came up with a comprehensive programme for restructuring based on the premise that if help was to be given to sectors then it should also be given to depressed regions. In 1993 the government approved a detailed project for crisis management in two counties of northern Hungary.

Also private firms may expect to receive state support. The agricultural sector was the first to suggest publicly that private farmers should be allowed to bid for the consolidation of their debts if their debt-to-equity ratio was higher than 25 per cent. The ministry was aware that it was creating a precedent for the conversion of private debts into state ones. Nevertheless, in late 1993 the proposal to extend the debtor consolidation process to private businesses, irrespective of their field of operations, was accepted.

The private sector cannot be discriminated against: this is the principle on which this approach is based. Paradoxically, it is an argument which, having promoted private business in the period of the planned economy, is now used in favour of extending state subsidies in favour of renationalization. From the point of view of the entrepreneurs concerned, acceptance of this principle means nothing less than 'enterprising without risk' by courtesy of the taxpayers. Bank experts already claim that, on hearing that debts can be cancelled or rescheduled, even those debtors who could pay avoid doing so.

Private firms – mainly well-known international investors – are the pioneers of extension protectionism. In addition to privileged competitive positions, the preferences can also mean that capital is raised by the state or access is granted to preferential funds.

According to an expert from the Ministry of International Economic Relations (MIER), multinationals are just as keen to obtain privileges as Hungarian companies, and they also expect the state to play a major role in economic decisions. This opinion is corroborated by the comments of companies. A manager of a big joint venture states: 'We are much more concerned about the matters of the ministry than our customers'. The importance of this approach is illustrated by the finding that many joint ventures with foreign participation have hired Hungarian managers with professional backgrounds in large SOEs or in the former administration; managers who thus have widespread personal contacts and well-developed skills in informal bargaining.

The volume of investment, employment or export are key arguments in the pressure applied by the (foreign) private firms, too. This reasoning is often accompanied by threats such as substitution of domestic suppliers by imports and a closedown of production either temporarily or for good.

The Association of International Companies in Hungary was established in 1992 by fourteen multinationals which initiated an offensive strategy which took the form of 'dialogue' with the government. During negotiations over taxation, employment or industrial policy they too claimed that they had invested more than HUF 100 billion in Hungary and employed around 25000 people. Suzuki, for instance, asked for capital to be raised by the state for its suppliers rather than for itself, claiming that when it came on full stream in 1995 its production would reach 5 to 6 per cent of GDP. The plan to curb or to halt production was first mooted in General Electric–Tungsram and in the paper industry.

Most preferences for the control of international trade envisage the central redistribution of enterprise positions, irrespectively of any claims by major international investors concerning the overall economic benefits of their successful negotiations with the government.

Conflicts among organizations operating in the same business and at different points of the vertical system are direct manifestations of the redistributing effect. Higher customs duties and the restriction of import volumes are obvious benefits for domestic producers, while they punish the importers. The selective reduction of customs duty works to the disadvantage of competitors interested in imports. Conflicts are further escalated by relationships with international organizations. This became clear recently when the two-year term of payment of the customs duty on television sets was terminated. According to a MIER expert, customs duty cannot be increased unless compensation is offered to key partners in the GATT negotiations; that is, if customs on other items are reduced according to their preferences. Likewise, the limit of 15 per cent set on EC imports means that, say, the entire steel producing sector can be protected but that no other industry can. In other words, any preference for a sector or a product may be given at the costs of the others.

To sum up, most of the international investors with strong negotiating positions, and which have seen the increasingly helpful attitude of the government, tend to apply for preferences and to receive individual or group subsidies in precisely the same way as the 'big socialist enterprises'. Although the products of these joint ventures with foreign participation are not inherently unmarketable, and although the companies are not hopeless cases, the income earned on the markets available is obviously not enough for a profitable operation. Thus foreign entrepreneurs do not always inject a market-style business culture into the Hungarian economy. Instead, for quite understandable reasons, they take the line of least resistance by adapting themselves to the prevailing business culture of 'milking' the state budget.

This form of redistribution, too, tends to escalate privileges in space and time. While the extent of such an escalation is limited by international contracts, especially in foreign trade, the preference for joint ventures provokes due criticism from domestic firms and provides them with a bargaining counter in demanding privileges for themselves as well. Escalation in time is indicated, among other things, by the argument advanced by foreign investors that the business environment has changed since they planned or made their investments. However, if changing conditions are considered to be sufficient grounds for obtaining preferences, it will be hard to stop the cascade effect that ensues.

4   TRADITIONAL REDISTRIBUTION OR A NEW MODEL?

Recent redistribution has many features comparable with the decades of the planned economy, as well as several new ones. First, the specific microlevel decisions that define company positions are taken by the central authorities (parliament, government or inter-ministerial committees) just as before. Sub-centres of redistribution also continue to exist. In this group, the role of the branch ministries is being taken over by organizations representing the state as owner (like SPA and SHC). These organizations have adopted the old ministry attitude in the representation of company interests.

Second, as far as the methods and criteria of decision-making are concerned, the old approach of central selection and negotiation by individual companies or groups of companies persists. Decision-makers make closer consideration of the competitive potential of a business or a product. Although this evaluation can now be more securely based on the judgement of the global market, the key criteria continue to include the size of the company (volume of production, sales or employment) and its monopolistic position.

Third, the tools of central restructuring include the traditional methods of changing the organizational structure and the financial position of firms. Direct budgetary subsidies have been superseded, however, by new forms characterized more by loss of income, postponed expenses and increased state debts than by current budgetary expenditure.

Fourth, in the early 1990s, preferences were given to state-owned enterprises (and commercial banks). Several large SOEs, however, were left to their own devices, while their rescued group was swollen by foreign investors and domestic private entrepreneurs. This obviously reflects the shift in bargaining potential and negotiating positions within the company sector.

Redistribution thus operates at several levels. The first of these comprises the rescuing of SOEs whereby the government acts simultaneously as an owner and as a regulator of the market. At the second level the government only appears in the role of regulator, granting preferences to fully or largely privately-owned firms. The third level (not covered by this paper) includes the allocation of state-owned assets where the state does not perform a direct regulatory function but distributes its assets to preferred strata or institutions free of charge.

If the central redistribution of company positions and incomes is not limited to state ownership, this implies that privatization in itself does not put an end to state redistribution. It should be added, however, that there are a number of interfaces between the methods of privatization and the potential spread of redistribution.

One of these connections is the tendency towards renationalization, in both the senses of the term used in this paper (the expansion of state ownership and the centralization of ownership rights in state-controlled areas). Any form of renationalization paves the way for the distribution of assets; that is, for the use of privatization methods other than sell-offs. On the other hand, if distribution means the streamlining of privatization, then companies must first be restructured. An ailing company with a heavy debt burden is unacceptable even as a free gift. In the case of sale with substantial preferences, granted to foreign investors or lately to domestic ones, dependence on state support is likely to be revived in the operation of these private firms.

It is clear that pressure by firms plays a crucial role in the expansion of state redistribution. This pressure stems from the loss of markets, the strengthening of competition, inherited or newly amassed debts and growing costs, including high interest rates and taxes. The government's attitude is also understandable. Ideological commitments or direct political election objectives are not the only point, their doubtless implications notwithstanding. Besides these factors, state intervention is prompted by the domino effect of the bankruptcy law, the continuous dwindling of production and exports, the upsetting of the external financial equilibrium and the regional concentration of unemployment.

For these reasons, the key question is not the advantages of redistribution for the state or for the firms. Paradoxically, five years after the collapse of planned economy, we must return to the old question posed by reform economists: what are the disadvantages of central redistribution?

The costs of realizing benefits must be paid in strict economic terms, including the preservation of a non-competitive production structure, the surge of budgetary deficit and foreign debts as well as growing inflation. Since the unfavourable effects on equilibrium can be delayed but not eliminated, a redistribution spiral may be triggered. Costs will be financed, *inter alia*, out of growing taxes which further hamper entrepreneurship, while simultaneously increasing the need for subsidies and reducing the funds available for distribution.

A still higher price has to be paid for the short-term relief of redistribution in terms of a distorted orientation of firms and of the economic mechanism as a whole. Companies, including private firms, try to obtain governmental preferences in order to overcome their market problems. This leads to laziness, the reproduction of disequilibria and the restoration, with all its implications, of the soft budget constraint characteristic of the planned economy (Kornai, 1980). This approach is anti-competition because the entry of new actors is hindered by the advantages of others and by non-transparent rules and regulations. It is also anti-consumer because it limits choices by keeping prices and taxes high in order to cover the costs of redistribution.

The undesirable implications of redistribution and the mechanisms supporting its proliferation must be taken into account, even if the redistribution of company positions and incomes cannot be considered the sole, or even a decisive, feature of the economy. There is no homogeneous integration mechanism at work in the recent Hungarian economy. The lack of such a unified system, however, does not disguise the simple formula whereby state ownership and private ownership are entirely separate and operate according to quite different models. There is no standard integration mechanism even within the different ownership groups. Undoubtedly, there is a competitive market which operates in several segments of the economy; nevertheless, private firms (especially big foreign investors) demand privileges from the state. As regards the future, the degree of difference between the old and new model of redistribution in terms of motivations and effects is a crucial question.

The trends of recent years suggest that there is no clear-cut demarcation line between the planned economy and the emerging market economy. Moreover, the hypothesis can be formulated that the transformation process does not necessarily lead to an 'ideal' competitive market system; an alternative to which is a mixed economy grounded on the economic and sociological traditions of redistribution. This may be a mixed system not only from the point of view of ownership, i.e. the coexistence of state and private firms. Its mixed character may indicate mixed ownership, that is, the presence of state and private owners in one firm, and also the mixed (market-oriented and redistribution-oriented) values and behavioural patterns of any firm, regardless of its proprietary structure. It is worth investigating the possibility, as has already been suggested by Stark (1993), that a new economic model may emerge in Hungary and Eastern Europe as a result of transformation. Empirical verification of this hypothesis is one of the most interesting tasks to be addressed in the years to come.

NOTES

1. Following the definition proposed by Polányi (1976) and generally used in evaluation of the planned economy, the term 'redistribution', as the opposite of market and reciprocity, means the central pooling and redistribution of rights and goods. This definition is restricted here to the redistribution of enterprise incomes.

2. SPA was set up in 1990 to control privatization, while SHC was founded in 1992 with the task to manage state assets not to be privatized in the short run. Between 1990 and 1994 roughly 1850 firms belonged to the SPA with an asset value of HUF 1670 billion. SHC included 160 firms with an asset value of HUF 1000 billion.

3. For details see Sárközy (1993) and Voszka (1993). 'Renationalization' is used here in quotation marks because the form studied below involves the reallocation of controlling rights within the framework of state ownership. The term renationalization appears in its original meaning.

4. There is no registration of the incomes recycled to the SOEs. In 1993, however, an SPA director estimated the amount of this 'reorganization fund' as equal to official privatization proceeds (about HUF 130 billion between 1990 and July 1993). According to a government report (Government of the Hungarian Republic, 1993b), the SHC made about four hundred decisions of this type, concerning mainly state farms and research institutes.

5. Government Resolution No. 3298/1992. For a detailed history of the 'Big Thirteen' see Karsai (1993).

6. According to MINIT (1993), 'Crisis management was successful in the case of six companies and the position of one firm was improved as a result of earlier measures'. The number of SOEs seems to conceal even worse rates. According to calculations based on MINIT data, less than half of the assets and employees of the 'Thirteen' were rescued.

7. In 1992, the year of the great wave of bankruptcy and liquidation, only about eighty proceedings were initiated by banks, representing less than 1 per cent of all cases.

8. Moreover, the new laws on banking and accounting, enacted in 1992, introduced much more rigorous international standards. This worsened the positions of banks, or, more precisely, brought hidden problems to the surface.

9. As a result of consolidation in 1992, the amount of bad debts decreased by 100 billion and then increased by 30 billion in the first half of 1993, while total qualified debts were more than twice this sum.

10. The first round of consolidation concerned fourteen banks, while eight banks were involved in the second one.

11. Bank consolidation will increase budget expenditures by HUF 60 billion in 1995.
12. The extended ownership rights of the state are exercised not only by the present shareholder of the banks, i.e. the State Holding Company, but also by the Ministry of Finance, because of budgetary investments. The Ministry controls more than 75 percent of voting shares in consolidated banks.
13. A new package of capital injection is under discussion at the time of writing (Autumn 1994) in order to raise the 8 per cent capital adequacy ratio. For more details of the consolidation process and its evaluation see Financial Research Ltd. (1994).
14. That is, 'bad' debtors of 'good' banks are excluded from consolidation.
15. Russian wheat exports in 1992 may be quoted here as an admonitory example. A 100 million dollar guarantee has already been called in by the lending bank.
16. It is not hard to predict that passive treatment which concentrates on existing credit burdens will soon prove inadequate. Like the banking sector, also firms will need fresh capital to cover their losses and to modernize their production systems.

REFERENCES

Asset Policy Guidelines (1993), 'Az 1994. évi Vagyonpolitikai Irányelvek' (Draft Resolution tabled in Parliament), October.

Financial Research Ltd. (1994), 'Gazdasági helyzetkép a kormányváltáskor' (Economic situation at the time of changing the Government, manuscript), September.

Government of the Hungarian Republic (1993a), 'Beszámoló az Országyülésnek az Állami Vagyonügynökség 1992. évi tevékenységéröl' (Report to Parliament on the 1992 activities of SPA), September.

Government of the Hungarian Republic (1993b), 'Beszámoló az Országyülésnek az Állami Vagyonkezelö Részvénytársaság 1992. évi és 1993. I. félévi tevékenységéröl' (Report to Parliament on the activities of SHC in the year 1992 and the first half of 1993), November.

Karsai, J. (1993), 'Fedöneve: reorganizáció (Pseudonim: Reorganization)', Körgazdasagi Szemle, September.

Kornai, J. (1980), *The Economics of Shortage*, Amsterdam: North Holland.

Kovács, A. (1991), 'A müszaki fejlesztés több pénzt igényelne, interjú László Jenö közigazgatási államtitkárral' (More funds needed for technical development, an interview with Administrative State Secretary Jenö László), *Magyar Hírlap*, October 11.

Ministry of Finance (1993), Kimutatás az állami garanciákról' (Data on state guarantees), July.

Ministry of Industry and Trade (1991), 'Jelentes az ipar teljesítményének alakulásárál' (Report from the result of the industry), February.

Ministry of Industry and Trade (1993), 'Beszámoló az ipari válságkezelési program keretében elvégzett válságmenedzselés tapasztalatairól' (Report on the experience of crisis management performed under the industrial crisis management programme), August.

Nagy, I. (1993), 'Romló vagyon, növekvö garanciák' (Eroding assets, growing guarantees), *Magyar Hírlap*, October 9.

Privatization Strategy Task Team (1992), 'A magyar privatizáció áttörési koncepciója és kormányzati munkaprogramja' (The breakthrough plan and government working programme of Hungarian privatization), September.

Polányi, K. (1976), *Az archaikus társadalom és a gazdasági szemlélet* (The archaic society and the economic attitude), Gondolat Publisher.

Sárközy, T. (1993): 'A privatizációval kapcsolatos kormányzati teendö – jogászi megközelítés' (Government responsibilities in privatization – a lawyer's view), manuscript.

Stark, D. (1993), 'Recombinant Property in East European Capitalism', manuscript.

State Audit Office (1993), 'Jelentés az Állami Vagyonügynökség 1992. évi tevékenységének ellenörzéséröl' (Audit Report on the 1992 Activity of the State Property Agency), July.

State Holding Company (1994), 'Beszámoló az Állami Vagyonkezelö Részévénytársaság 1993. évi tevékenységéröl' (Report on the activities of State Holding Company), May.

State Property Agency (1994), 'A privatizáció helyzete' (The state of privatization), June.

Veres, I. (1993): 'A bírálati elvek nem szigorodnak' (No more rigorous criteria), *Magyar Hírlap*, December 23.

Voszka, É. (1993), From Renationalization to Redistribution? (The Effect of Renationalization on Privatization)', International Workshop on Privatization Experiences in Eastern Europe, manuscript, May.

14. Inter-Enterprise Arrears in Economies in Transition: Analytical, Empirical and Policy Issues

Fabrizio Coricelli

1 INTRODUCTION

Inter-enterprise arrears have played an important role in the early stages of transition. In fact, in some countries, like Romania and Russia, they have been a major stumbling block to the reform process (Ickes and Ryterman, 1993; Calvo and Coricelli, 1993; Clifton and Kahn, 1992). Potentially good and bad firms were intertwined in a chain of arrears which threatened the financial collapse of the economy. However, attempts by governments to 'clean' the chain of arrears by injecting bank credit coincided with a fundamental loss of credibility by the stabilization programmes. Moreover, after these clean-ups, arrears grew again, both in Romania and Russia. Interestingly, in other reforming economies (Hungary, Poland and former Czechoslovakia) arrears, although present, did not grow into a systemic problem.

Several interpretations of the explosion of arrears and of the heterogeneity of country experiences have been put forward.

To simplify, three groups of explanations may be identified. First, there is the view that arrears reflect a sort of continuation of soft budget constraints, with inefficient, even non-viable, firms absorbing liquidity from more efficient ones. A corollary to this interpretation is that at the root of the phenomenon there lies a credit policy which is too soft. A credible policy of tight credit would have prevented the explosion of arrears (Rostowski, 1993). Second, a more optimistic explanation considers the phenomenon of arrears as a natural tendency towards a market for trade credit, which plays an important role in market economies (Begg and Portes 1992). Third, there is the view, which I favour, according to which the explosion of arrears reflects a systemic phenomenon which, in response to a liquidity squeeze, yields an equilibrium characterized by a generalized default on inter-enterprise payments. This equilibrium is likely to be inefficient, since arrears are a form of involuntary lending which involve costs similar to those associated with shirking and stealing in market economies (Calvo and Coricelli, 1993). This approach emphasizes the interaction between macroeconomic policies and the microeconomic features of the phenomenon of inter-enterprise arrears. In particular, it underlines the fact that an excessive credit tightening may have persistent negative effects on the economy, and may even weaken the credibility of the stabilization programmes. However, this approach does not suggest a loose monetary policy as the solution; rather, it stresses the complex trade-off between financial discipline and liquidity needs for economies with underdeveloped financial markets.

Each of the above views implies different features of arrears and different remedies. Whichever interpretation is chosen, there is no doubt that the phenomenon of arrears offers an important perspective on the reform process in previously centrally planned economies (PCPEs), on the effects of policies and on the interaction between macroeconomic policies and structural and institutional aspects of economies in transition. In particular, the study of arrears may shed light on the process of the creation of a market, with its attendant set of incentives, penalties and enforcement rules. Moreover, the paper argues that in this process of market creation, dysfunctional institutions and modes of behaviour may emerge. Inter-enterprise arrears may in fact be an example of a such dysfunctional market.

The paper is organized as follows. Section 2 briefly reviews the main stylized facts on arrears. Section 3 reviews the literature. Section 4 discusses more detailed, enterprise level, empirical evidence, focusing on the experiences of Romania and Poland as two polar cases. Section 5 discusses policy options, reviewing the policies followed by the various countries. Section 6 concludes the paper and discusses directions for future research.

2   ARREARS: MAIN DEVELOPMENTS

Following the implementation of stabilization programmes in the PCPEs, inter-enterprise arrears invariably increased in relation to bank credit (Table 14.1). This could be interpreted as a signal of the tightening of the supply of bank credit. Indeed, if the drop in real bank credit simply reflected the drop in output – caused by exogenous forces – one would have expected inter-enterprise credit to fall proportionally with respect to bank credit.

Table 14.1   *Inter-enterprise arrears (ratio of inter-enterprise arrears to bank credit)*

	Poland[1]	Romania	Hungary	Former CSFR	Russia
1989.iv	1.6	n.a.	0.2	0.0	n.a.
1990.i	1.7	n.a.	0.1	0.0	n.a.
1990.ii	1.2	n.a.	0.2	0.0	n.a.
1990.iii	0.9	n.a.	0.2	0.1	n.a.
1990.iv	1.0	0.1	0.2	0.1	n.a.
1991.i	0.9	0.5	0.2	0.1	n.a.
1991.ii	0.9	0.7	0.2	0.2	n.a.
1991.iii	0.8	1.1	0.2	0.2	n.a.
1991.iv	1.0	1.9	0.2	0.2	0.0
1992.i	0.9	0.0^2	n.a.	n.a.	0.9
1992.ii	0.9	1.1	n.a.	n.a.	2.3
1992.iii	n.a.	0.9	n.a.	n.a.	0.8^3
1992.iv	1.2^4	n.a.	n.a.	n.a.	n.a.

Notes:

1. For Poland, the figures refer to inter-enterprise credit, while for the other countries the figures refer only to arrears, i.e. overdue credit.
2. At the beginning of the year arrears were cleared through the Global Compensation Scheme.
3. The figure is only for July. In July bank credit was injected into the system to clear the arrears.
4. At the end of 1992 the ratio of arrears to total payables was 0.3.

However, the correlation between the tightening of bank credit and the growth of arrears is far from simple. Indeed, there is no indication that the magnitude of the increase in arrears closely reflects the magnitude of the initial contraction in bank credit.

In particular, after the launching of stabilization programmes, inter-enterprise arrears exploded in some countries like Romania and Russia, but not in others, for instance Poland and Hungary.

Countries that experienced an explosion of arrears also experienced high and persistent inflation and a continuous increase in the velocity of money circulation (Figures 14.1 and 14.2). The experience of the former Czechoslovakia is a sort of outlier, since arrears grew rapidly despite a stable macroeconomic environment.

Figure 14.1   Inflation after reform, monthly inflation rates

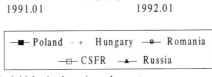

Notes: The figure excludes the initial price jump in each country

Figure 14.2   Money velocities, 1988–1992

Notes:

1. Velocity is measured as GDP/average broad money (M2)
2. 1992 data for Russia is up to June

In addition, in high-arrears countries (like Russia) producer prices have increased much faster than consumer prices.[1] Figure 14.3 shows the behaviour of producer relative to consumer prices for several PCPEs. In most of them, producer prices increased more than consumer prices at the beginning of price liberalization. However, only in a few countries did this gap persist or even widen over time. Interestingly, in countries in which arrears did not explode there was a convergence between the two price indices (Poland, the former Czechoslovakia and Hungary). The case of Romania is not readily comparable because producer prices have continued to be affected by central authorities even after reforms. Thus, the erratic movement of the ratio of producer and consumer price changes reflects the fact that producer price changes took place in 1992 at discrete intervals through negotiations with the government. In fact, this form of control on producer prices was singled out in interviews with firms as a major reason for the accumulation of arrears, as firms' cash-flow was squeezed by rising costs (of labour and imported inputs) and stable producer prices.

Figure 14.3   Ratio of producer to consumer price changes

Russia: inflation (ratio of PPI to CPI changes)

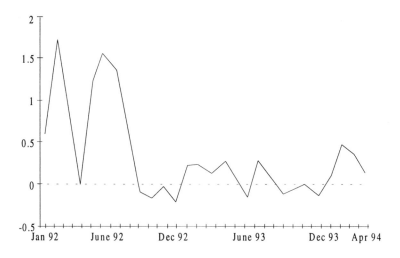

Poland: inflation (ratio of PPI to CPI changes)

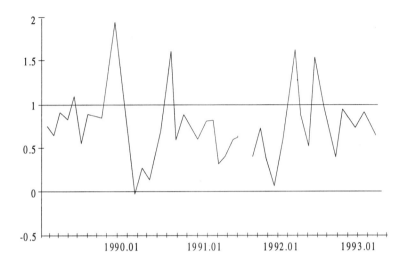

Former Czechoslovakia (ratio of PPI to CPI changes)

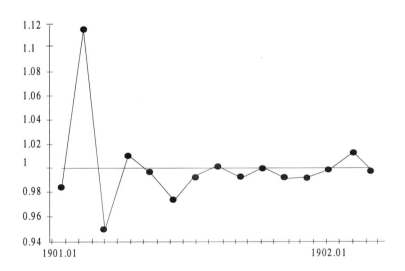

Romania (ratio of PPI to CPI changes)

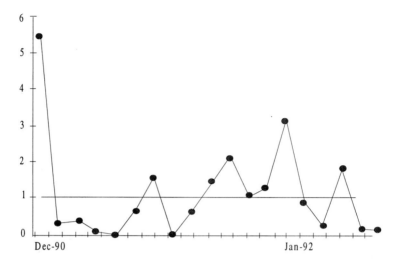

Hungary (ratio of PPI to CPI changes)

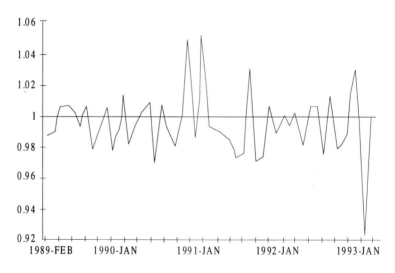

The fact that producer prices in Russia increased much more than consumer prices could be linked to the arrears. As discussed below, the presence of arrears modifies the effective money price of goods. Indeed, rational firms are likely to factor into the price the unpaid proportion of their sales. The higher the unpaid proportion of bills, the higher the price. Notice that this phenomenon applies to inter-enterprise transactions and thus affects producer prices. Consumption of final goods tends to be dominated by cash payments. Thus a scissor effect to producer and consumer prices may arise. In the extreme case, if firms do not pay at all for their inputs, the price of inputs becomes indeterminate (see Calvo and Coricelli, 1993).

Important differences across countries relate not only to the magnitude of arrears but also to their characteristics. In Hungary, Poland and the former Yugoslavia, there was a system of trade credit in the pre-reform period. Arrears were just a proportion of this trade credit: amounting to about thirty per cent. Thus arrears represented the non-performing component of a largely voluntary trade credit system.[2]

By contrast, in Romania and Russia, there was no developed system of trade credit. Arrears were the main, albeit special, form of involuntary trade credit. This difference points to the importance of institutional aspects in the development of private credit markets.[3]

There is another feature of inter-enterprise arrears which is worth emphasizing: a large proportion of arrears was associated with firms which had roughly similar payable and receivable arrears.

This brief overview raises three main sets of issues which any explanation of inter-enterprise credit in PCPEs should address. First, experience shows a high degree of heterogeneity across countries. There are consequently different possible outcomes to an initial credit squeeze, given that arrears exploded only in Romania and Russia but not in other countries. Second, explanation should be provided as to why a network of arrears can persist in a context of decentralized decisions by firms. Finally, account should be given for the fact that the network of arrears is highly 'circular', so that firms have similar amounts of arrears on both sides of their balance sheet. The next section addresses these issues, sketching a simple framework for analysis of arrears.

3 EXPLANATIONS

Five main explanations can be put forward.

3.1 Arrears and soft budget constraints

In centrally planned economies, firms' decisions are not constrained by financial variables. It is conceivable that in the initial stages of transition, when bankruptcy procedures are still lacking or are not implemented, firms will not be subject to financial discipline. If their income/production targets conflict with their financial resources, they are likely to fall into payment arrears rather than reduce their scale of activity. If the government validates such financial indiscipline by injecting credit in order to clear the inter-enterprise arrears, an inflationary process may be ignited. High inflation would in turn reduce the use of money by enterprises, and thus increase arrears further. If the government can credibly commit itself to a non-accommodating monetary policy, arrears will not increase because creditor firms will realize that they will lose out, to the advantage of debtor firms (Rostowski, 1993).

3.2   Arrears as a natural movement towards a trade credit market

It has been suggested that the increase in inter-enterprise arrears (IEAs) is a natural movement towards the trade credit markets typical of market economies. From a pure quantitative point of view, in most transition economies the amount of arrears is similar to that of market economies, both in terms of sales or bank credit. Studies of episodes of significant increases in inter-enterprise credit (IEC) in market economies tend to conclude that IEC expands during periods of contraction of bank credit, because firms which are rationed by banks receive credit from liquidity rich firms (Meltzer, 1960; Brechling and Lipsey, 1963). Thus the net transfer of liquidity from one set of firms to another seems to represent a salient feature of the increase in IEC in market economies. Briechling and Lipsey, for instance, report that, during the contractionary monetary policy of the second half of the 1950s in the United Kingdom, more than 60 per cent of the increase in gross credit involved an increase in net credit.

3.3   Arrears and loss-making firms

Another widespread view is that reforms have left non-viable firms to their own devices, without state subsidies (either direct or through the banking system). As a result, these firms have been unable to pay their suppliers, thus replacing state subsidies with implicit subsidies from other firms. Of course, this view cannot explain the persistent increase in arrears; that is, the fact that suppliers continue to sell to delinquent firms. Usually appended to this view, therefore, is the hypothesis that creditors expect the government to bail out debtors, as in the first explanation. In sum, this view emphasizes (i) the lack of an effective bankruptcy procedure able to select non-viable firms out of the economy, and (ii) the lack of credibility of a no-bail-out stance by the government. This view predicts that arrears should be concentrated in loss-making firms. Of course, it is conceivable that while the source of arrears is loss-making firms, a chain involving viable firms may ensue (Ickes and Ryterman, 1993). However, it is still unclear why such a phenomenon of arrears would be sustained over time. The hypothesis of the expectation of a bail-out is attractive, although it may require an unrealistic degree of coordination among firms.

Differently from the second explanation, this view argues that the phenomenon of arrears involves social costs, because resources are transferred from more efficient firms to non-viable ones. The negative effect is thus distributive, while in terms of aggregate output the effect may be positive, at least in the short run.

3.4 Monopolistic structure of industry

A fourth view, which shares some of the implications of the third one, is based on the monopolistic behaviour of firms belonging to a rigid structure of vertically integrated production lines. With price liberalization, large monopolies producing intermediate inputs raised their output prices. Firms using these inputs could not pay for them. The lack of alternative sources of input supply forced these firms to maintain their relation with their traditional suppliers, despite the sharp increase in prices. Arrears in payments did therefore arise. Suppliers continued to sell their inputs in the expectation of a government intervention to monetize the arrears. This monetization would in the end validate monopolistic pricing, thereby generating inflation.[4] In addition to the behaviour of producer prices indicated above, some empirical support for this view derives from the fact that in Russia in the first half of 1992 bank credit was channelled to firms with receivables (Ickes and Ryterman, 1993). An implication of this view is that the root cause of arrears lies in the monopolistic structure and rigid integration of industry. Thus simple changes of payment rules, such as the imposition of pre-payment, would not improve the situation.

3.5 Equilibrium chain: A model of contagion

Finally, a fifth view – one which is not necessarily incompatible with the previous four – emphasizes the equilibrium nature of the phenomenon of arrears. To present this interpretation in its most straightforward form, Calvo and Coricelli (1992, 1993) illustrate how a phenomenon of high and generalized arrears may arise within a context of viable and rational firms. Firms are assumed to be controlled by workers, who maximize the discounted value of the stream of income produced by the firm (sales net of non-labour input costs). Firms face a liquidity-in-advance constraint on their purchases of

inputs. Indeed, in order to buy inputs a firm needs a stock of money. However, this constraint can be slackened by accumulating arrears. As a result, a firm can acquire an amount of inputs which is larger than its stock of money. Furthermore, it is assumed that arrears involve a cost for the firm. This cost is proportional to the size of arrears, which makes the social cost proportional to the size of total arrears in the economy. The model implies that, in response to a liquidity squeeze, firms' output falls. Following this initial shock, firms may respond in different ways. One possible adjustment, which can be called 'hard-budget-constraint', takes place through the accumulation of internal liquidity by firms which cut their wage costs and recover over time their previous level of output. An alternative adjustment occurs when firms reach the maximum level of default on their payments. This equilibrium implies a level of output lower than the previous one. The key determinant of arrears is the relation between marginal returns and marginal costs of arrears. The marginal return is equal to the marginal return of one unit of money saved in the payment of inputs, which can thus be used by workers. This return is equal to the interest rate workers can earn on that unit of money, while the marginal cost of arrears is assumed to be an exogenous constant. Note that if the marginal cost of falling into arrears is lower than its marginal return, firms will tend to accumulate arrears. These arrears will spread through the system as firms which have not been paid for their sales default on the payments for their inputs. The phenomenon grows as a contagious disease.

The important implications of this model are that arrears may develop even with viable and rational (optimizing) firms. Although the key parameters affecting arrears are exogenous, Calvo and Coricelli indicate several economic variables which may affect the incentive to move towards the high-arrears equilibrium. High inflation and a short time-horizon of workers will tend to push the economy towards the high-arrears equilibrium by increasing the marginal return to arrears. By contrast, an appropriate wage tax rule would reduce the incentive to fall into arrears.

As regards the cost of arrears, several institutional factors are likely to be important. First, the presence of alternative customers and suppliers. In most PCPEs this might have been equivalent to the degree of openness of the economy. Access to foreign markets, which are supposedly characterized by more discipline in payments, would allow firms to escape the chain of arrears. Private ownership could provide incentives to build a good reputation as a customer, and thus induce firms to pay their bills. In addition, the cost of arrears could be related to the size of aggregate arrears in the economy, giving rise to self-sustaining chains of arrears.[5] Finally, there is the moral hazard associated with government bail-out. Once the government has intervened to clear arrears by, for instance, injecting credit into the system, firms may act under the assumption that the government will step in again if arrears grow to their former levels.

The next section analyses microeconomic data to evaluate the explanatory power of these various views. However, a robust test of different theories is not feasible. With the exception of Calvo and Coricelli, the above explanations have not been framed in a consistent analytical model and therefore cannot be properly tested. In the case of Calvo and Coricelli's model, a test would require specification of parameters, such as the marginal cost of arrears, which – at least at this stage – cannot be identified empirically. Thus the evidence should be considered as suggesting the empirical relevance of the different views.

4   ANALYSIS OF MICROECONOMIC DATA: POLAND AND ROMANIA

Analysis of aggregate data has shown that the phenomenon of arrears has been a fundamental by-product of stabilization programmes. Moreover, the phenomenon has been markedly heterogenous across countries, both in terms of the magnitude of the arrears and – even more importantly – of the characteristics of arrears.

The present author has carried out microeconomic analysis for Romania and Poland, countries with different macroeconomic performances and different characteristics of arrears. The idea of the chain of arrears as a bad equilibrium induced by the interplay between a liquidity squeeze and unfavourable microeconomic incentives can also be explored in a comparative perspective. Indeed, it is interesting to contrast the Romanian experience with that of another economy in transition, Poland, which apparently did not suffer from the 'disease' of a widespread chain of arrears.

4. 1   Romania

The evidence on Romania shows that arrears followed an explosive path during the first year of stabilization (Clifton and Khan, 1992; Calvo and Coricelli, 1992,1993; Daianu, 1993). To avert an impending financial crisis, the government intervened at the end of 1991 with a generalized clean-up operation which substituted net inter-enterprise debts with bank credit. Soon after this operation, arrears grew rapidly again. Two features of arrears in Romania are worth stressing. First, the phenomenon is generalized and affects almost all industrial firms: in 1992, around 85 per cent of industrial firms showed payment arrears. Second, most firms displayed arrears in payables and receivables of similar magnitude. Thus most firms had roughly zero net debt positions. Indeed, 80 per cent of net debts were concentrated in one hundred firms, which accounted only for 30 per cent of gross arrears. The two features just described indicate that arrears developed as a long chain formed by firms with similar debt and credit positions.

Table 14.2   Romania: inter-enterprise arrears, 1992

		payable (arrears) /sales	Receivable (arrears) /sales	Export sales	Profits sales	Material/ total costs
Paysa = 0	267 firms	0.00	0.06	0.12	0.11	0.48
Paysa > 0	1338 firms	0.23	0.26	0.11	0.07	0.52
Paysa > 0.23	514 firms	0.24	0.44	0.08	0.05	0.54
Paysa > 0.44	157 firms	0.70	0.65	0.06	0.04	0.57

Table 14.2 groups firms in terms of the size of arrears (in relation to sales) and clearly shows the close association between arrears in payables and arrears in receivables.[6] The table also highlights the relation between the ratio of payables to sales and several enterprise characteristics. Firms with higher arrears tend to be: (i) less exposed to foreign markets, with a ratio of exports to total sales which is half that of firms with no arrears; (ii) less profitable, and thus less able to generate an internal cash-flow to pay for their inputs, and (iii) more intensive in the use of material inputs.

These features are further confirmed by regression analysis, which reveals a close association between arrears in payables and receivables (see Table 14.3). Note that the variable 'arrears' has the characteristics of a limited dependent variable, since there are several firms with no arrears: about 15 per cent of the sample. In this case OLS estimates would be inconsistent; consequently I also present the results from a Tobit model (Table 14.3(b)), which broadly confirm the results of the OLS estimation.[7] In fact, the chain element seems to be dominant (using t-statistics to rank them), even though several other structural variables, encompassing enterprise- and sector-specific factors, are included in the regressions.

The roles of export orientation, profitability (or change in enterprise deposits) and the share of material inputs in total costs appear statistically significant. Note, incidentally, that the negative (and statistically significant) relation between enterprise liquidity (as proxied by profits or by the change in deposits) and arrears on payables is, by and large, consistent with the model in Calvo and Coricelli (1993).

The negative coefficient on exports has a less obvious interpretation, although it is again largely consistent with the predictions of the model. Indeed, assuming that foreign markets are not affected by the problem of arrears, it follows that firms integrated into foreign markets tend to escape the chain of arrears.

Table 14.3   Romania: regression on inter-enterprise arrears September 1992. Sample: 1655 firms

(a)   Ols regression

Variable	Coefficient	t-Statist.	Coefficient	t-Statist.
Constant	0.08	4.68	0.10	4.97
Material/total costs	0.11	4.65	0.11	4.41
Profits/sales	−0.45	−8.32		
Exports/sales	−0.07	−2.62	−0.17	−5.77
Receivables/sales	0.28	20.84		
Change in deposits/sales			−0.02	−1.63
Sd1	−0.04	−1.18	−0.00	−0.06
Sd2	−0.06	−2.86	−0.07	−3.14
Sd3	−0.04	−1.07	−0.05	−1.36
Sd4	0.19	6.81	0.29	9.44
Sd5	0.07	3.33	0.11	4.90
Sd6	0.01	−0.35	0.02	0.79
Sd7	0.01	0.62	0.03	1.02
Sd8	0.07	3.72	0.09	4.20
Sd9	0.01	0.35	0.03	1.12
Sd10	0.05	2.24	0.07	2.96
Sd11	0.18	1.91	0.15	1.35
Sd12	0.16	2.72	0.15	2.26
Fd11	−0.02	−0.57	0.10	2.15
Fd13	−0.10	−1.80	−0.10	−1.60
Fd21	0.19	2.42	0.13	1.44
Fd22	0.12	3.11	0.04	0.96
Adjusted R-squared	0.34		0.12	

Notes:

Sd$_i$ denote sectoral dummies

Fd$_i$ denote firm-type dummies

(b)   Tobit model

Variable	Coefficient	*t*-Statist.	Coefficient	*t*-Statist.
Constant	0.28	1.77	−0.09	−0.60
Material/total costs	0.18	6.98	0.18	7.02
Profits/sales	−0.51	−7.90		
Exports/sales	0.00	0.02	−0.04	−1.50
Receivables/sales	0.35	21.61	0.36	21.68
Change in deposits/sales			−0.02	−2.05

The view of arrears as an equilibrium chain is also supported by a small-scale survey of industrial firms in Romania, the results of which are summarized in Tables 14.4 and 14.5[8]. Table 14.4 shows that the main cause of arrears is considered to be the accumulation of overdue receivables, and also that overdue payments to other firms are perceived as being much less costly than overdue payments to non-enterprise creditors, like workers and government; a fact which is consistent with the finding that there is no correlation between inter-enterprise arrears and arrears to government.[9]

Table 14.4   Romania: main causes of arrears

Accumulation of overdue receivables	2.65
High interest rates	3.52
Increase in input over output prices	3.66
High profit tax	4.69
Loss of markets	5.38
Inventory accumulation	5.66
High turnover tax	5.66
Insufficent bank credit	5.76
High wage bill	7.86

Note:

Lower rating, on a scale from 1 to 10 to the more important cause

Source:

World Bank, 'Fiscal Study on Romania' (1993)

Table 14.5   Romania: priorities of payments

Payments	Average rating
Employees	1.45
Foreign suppliers	2.41
Banks	2.59
Budget	2.69
Domestic suppliers	3.28

Note:
Lower rating, on a scale from 1 to 10 to the more important priority

Source:
World Bank, 'Fiscal Study on Romania' (1993)

4. 2 Poland

As noted above, the Polish experience appears to be very different.[10] If the focus is on industry for the purpose of comparison with Romania, three main aspects stand out. First, the phenomenon of arrears is highly concentrated (Table 14.6).

The vast majority of Polish industrial firms have negligible arrears, and 85 per cent of arrears are accounted for by a hundred branches, representing 39 per cent of sales. The data on the ten branches with higher arrears reveal an even more striking degree of concentration of the phenomenon (Table 14.6).

Second, the concentration of gross arrears coincides with a concentration of net arrears in the same set of firms. The hundred branches indicated above absorb 88 per cent of net arrears. Thus the phenomenon of default on obligations with respect to other firms implies an involuntary net transfer of liquidity among firms. Notice, however, that the ratio of net to gross arrears for this group of firms is about 35 per cent, which is similar to the ratio observed in Romania. In Poland too, therefore, the phenomenon of arrears is highly circular. Nevertheless, the fact that both gross and net arrears are concentrated in the same group of firms implies that the group of large debtors receive a net transfer of close to 5 per cent of their sales. Furthermore, in the Polish case the concentration of the phenomenon indicates that there are no systemic risks of chain reactions associated with arrears. By the same token, such generalized solutions as netting-out operations would not be necessary. Third, the group of firms with the largest share of arrears – both gross and net – can be identified with loss-making state-owned firms. Indeed, the same group of one hundred branches accounts for almost 80 per cent of the total losses in industry. Furthermore, the private sector is only marginally represented among these branches, with 1.5 per cent of total arrears.

Table 14.6   Poland: concentration of arrears

	Largest 100 debitors (in terms of gross areas)
Gross arrears (payables)	85%
Net arrears	88%
Sales	39%
Losses	77%
Payables	62%
Tax arrears	69%
Bank credit	47%
	Largest 10 debitors (in terms of gross areas)
Gross arrears (payables)	58%
Net arrears	64%
Sales	21%
Losses	56%
Payables	41%
Bank credit	22%

For the industrial sector as a whole, the private sector displays a share of total arrears much lower than its size in terms of sales (Table 14.7). However, the private sector share of trade credit is similar to its share of total sales, indicating that private firms differ in the degree of default and not in the propensity to use trade credit.

Table 14.7   Poland: arrears in the private sector (share total industry)

Gross arrears (payables)	8.3%
Gross arrears (receivables)	11.2%
Sales	31.0%
Losses	15.3%
Payables	24.6%
Receivables	22.9%
Bank credit	35.0%
	Share in largest 100 debitors (areas)
Gross arrears (payables)	1.5%
Sales	4.7%
Losses	5.9%

In sum, the experience of Poland differs significantly from that of Romania in terms of both the magnitude of the phenomenon of arrears and their characteristics. As noted above, if one considers the sum of voluntary and involuntary trade credit, Poland displays levels of inter-enterprise credit even higher than those of Romania.

What sharply distinguishes the two cases is the systemic nature of the phenomenon in Romania, with most firms falling into payment arrears. By contrast, the phenomenon is restricted to a small number of firms in Poland. The two countries may reflect the high and the low arrears equilibria.

Regression analysis confirms that the main variables affecting arrears are the liquidity conditions of firms, including the failure of customers to pay the receivables of the firms.

The findings are summarized in Tables 14.8, 14.9 and 14.10.

*Table 14.8   Poland: regressions on inter-enterprise arrears December 1992
Observations: 2119 (industry), tobit estimation*

Dependent variable: arrears (payables)/sales

Variable	Coefficient	*t*-Statistics
Constant	−0.01	−11.70
Profits/sales	−0.81	−5.72
Losses/sales	0.05	4.45
Bank credit/sales	−0.04	−2.45
Arrears receivables/sales	1.78	22.23

Dependent variable: arrears payables/sales

Variable	Coefficient	*t*-Statistics
Constant	0.03	3.47
Profits/sales	−0.58	−1.54
Losses/sales	0.16	4.45
Bank credit/sales	−0.06	−2.01
Receivables/sales	0.16	9.52

Table 14.9 *Poland: regressions on inter-enterprise arrears December 1992 Observations: 2119 (Industry)*

Dependent variable: arrears (payables)/sales

Variable	Coefficient	*t*-Statistics
Constant	−0.09	−6.55
Profits/sales	−1.31	−6.16
Losses/sales	0.03	1.65
Bank credit/sales	−0.02	−0.96
Arrears receivables/ receivables	0.92	31.21

Table 14.10 *Poland: regressions on state and private manifacturing firms (t-statistics in parenthesis)*

Dependent variable: payables/sales

	Private	State
Constant	0.16 (5.2)	−0.01 (−0.9)
Receivables/sales	0.37 (3.1)	1.2 (38.2)
Bank credit/sales	−0.08 (−1.6)	0.02 (1.8)
Profits/sales	−0.82 (−1.8)	−1.0 (−3.7)
Losses/sales	0.19 (4.2)	0.17 (7.0)
Adj. R^2	0.02	0.79

Dependent variable: arrears (overdue payables)

	Private	State
Constant	0.02 (3.2)	−0.00 (−1.1)
Receivables/sales	1.00 (13.6)	1.3 (18.0)
Bank credit/sales	−0.00 (−0.5)	0.00 (0.8)
Profits/sales	−0.23 (−2.7)	−0.2 (−1.2)
Losses/sales	0.03 (3.9)	0.09 (6.4)
Adj. R^2	0.12	0.46

The results on arrears (Table 14.8) are similar to those obtained for Romania. In particular, arrears on receivables appear to be a significant factor in the determination of arrears on payables. Also significant are liquidity constraints as proxied by bank credit and profit/losses. These results suggest the existence of 'local' chains of arrears. Unfortunately, the available information does not allow verification of this conjecture.

In addition, as in Poland arrears and trade credit are two distinct concepts, as there is also voluntary trade credit (payables and receivables). Table 14.8(b) reports results on regressions on payables. The fact that receivables appear to have a crucial impact on payables suggests that the 'transaction motive' dominates trade credit, rather than a 'financial motive' based on a significant transfer of liquidity among firms (in contrast with some experiences in market economies: see Meltzer (1960), Brechling and Lipsey (1963)).

Having information on both trade credit and overdue trade credit, we ran a regression on the 'degree of default', the ratio of overdue to regular payables. Results are similar to those obtained in the regressions with the ratio of arrears to sales as a dependent variable (Table 14.9).

Finally, distinct regressions were run for the subset of private and state firms in order to detect whether these firms behaved differently from state-owned ones. Interestingly, the results are analogous (Table 10), which suggests a similar behaviour despite the fact that private firms account for a marginal share of total arrears. This implies that once other variables, such as liquidity, are taken into account, ownership *per se* does not play a significant role in the phenomenon of arrears. Although further analysis would be necessary before drawing strong conclusions, these findings give support to the conjecture that what mostly matters are the 'rules of the game' in the credit market, and much less whether the firm is in private or public hands. However, one interesting difference emerges in the regression on payables. While bank credit enters with a negative sign in the regression for private firms, it is of positive sign in the regression for state firms. Although the effects are not very significant, we can conjecture that the different sign indicates that banks have different attitudes towards private and state firms. In particular, since firms with higher payable-to-sale ratios tend to be those in a worse financial condition, the positive coefficient for state firms may be indicative of the inertial behaviour of banks – the so-called credit passivity discussed by Begg and Portes (1992) – which continue to lend to these firms despite their weak financial conditions. By contrast, the negative coefficient for private firms may signal a different attitude towards firms which are new customers. In fact, it is likely that their recourse to trade credit is partly due to their lack of access to bank financing.[11]

Since the phenomenon of arrears may manifest itself in different forms, it follows that policies to deal with them should also differ across countries.

Accordingly, the next section reviews the policies adopted in several countries.

5   POLICIES

There have been two major clean-up operations in Romania and Russia. In the former Czechoslovakia, operations have taken place on a more limited scale, some of them involving the simple netting-out of mutual debts. No significant attempts have been made in Poland and Hungary to come up with a generalized solution to the problem. The policies adopted in the former Czechoslovakia, Romania and Russia illustrate a number of different considerations determining government decision-making.

5.1   Former Czechoslovakia

The approach to inter-enterprise arrears in the former Czechoslovakia has been similar to that adopted for bank bad loans. It is recognized that enterprises have inherited many of their financial problems from the previous system, and that policy intervention is therefore justified as a measure to create a level playing field for enterprises. In 1991, IEAs were cleared through the Czechoslovak commercial bank, the holder of unpaid bills. The result of this clearing operation was a 20 per cent reduction in the stock of gross debts (Rostowski, 1993).

However, arrears continued to increase. Three years after the introduction of reforms, it seems that a major source of arrears is constituted by firms which have accumulated large non-performing credits with former COMECON countries (Hrncir, 1993; Hrncir and Klacek, 1994). The financial difficulties of large exporters are transmitted to other firms, thereby creating a chain of arrears. It was this latter phenomenon that the government tried to solve in 1993 by instituting a privately-run system for the netting-out of arrears. This system was based on voluntary participation, but proved to be a failure because only a limited number of firms participated. The failure of a voluntary process of netting-out may suggest that firms with net positions do not look favourably on a change in the ultimate debt holder. Indeed, in the presence of an intermediate chain, netting-out leads to the transfer of claims from, say, firm B (the firm's original customer) to firm n. It is conceivable that the creditworthiness of firm n could be worse than that of firm B. Certainly, firm A has less information about firm n than about its direct partner. This phenomenon, in fact, illustrates a basic feature of inter-enterprise credit, namely its inefficiency from the point of view of risk diversification. Indeed, through the chain of arrears, firm *B* is exposed to the risk of default by its customer because of default by firm *n* further down the chain. The assessment of the credit risk of customers would require information on the whole chain of mutual debts which is extremely costly to acquire.

5.2 Romania

At the end of 1991 Romania implemented its so-called Global Compensation Scheme (henceforth GC). This scheme consisted of a multilateral netting-out operation effected through the issue of bank credit at market interest rates. Firm *a* received 'compensation' credit (short-term) upon submission of the invoice for its purchase of inputs. At the end of the process, creditor firms would have increased their cash position, and thus their bank deposits, while net debtors would have swapped inter-enterprise debt for bank debt. Apparently, most of the increase in enterprise deposits went to pay for arrears in bank repayments. The operation was 'technically' successful, and most arrears were cleared very quickly. Interestingly enough, compensation credit was usually repaid before the expiration date of the loan. Furthermore, the increase in broad money necessary to cover net positions was less than 20 per cent.

On policy grounds, however, the results were more debatable. Indeed, arrears grew rather quickly after GC and by September 1992 had reached 90 per cent of bank credit (compared with 190 per cent at the end of 1991). This recurrence of arrears can be rationalized in terms of: (i) the moral hazard problems associated with the GC, which might have signalled the 'soft' character of the government and thus its propensity to bail out enterprises also in the future; and (ii) the tight liquidity conditions faced by enterprises after the GC. Of course, these two explanations may be complementary. Interestingly, the government has resisted pressures for the implementation of a new GC. Thus, if expectations of a generalized bail-out were the driving force behind the recurrence of IEA in 1992, then these expectations were disappointed ex post. Liquidity tightening is indicated by the increase in interest rates, which, for the first time since the beginning of the stabilization programme, became positive in real terms in the first half of 1992.[12]

Fear of the inflationary implications of the GC scheme prompted the authorities to adopt a tight monetary policy, which resulted in a contraction in non-compensation credit which more than offset the expansion of compensation credit. Together with the contraction in bank credit, limits on the growth of arrears were agreed with international institutions. It was thus assumed that the enterprise sector could operate with a much lower level of liquidity to finance working capital. Not surprisingly, arrears grew again. This points to the fact that, in the context of underdeveloped financial markets, production tends to be constrained by enterprise liquidity.

In order to deal with this liquidity problem the Romanian authorities, in agreement with the IMF, designed a monetary programme which took into account the behaviour of inter-enterprise arrears. Specifically, the programme recognized the substitutability between bank and inter-enterprise credit. Thus, credit ceilings were adjusted to accommodate – partly – the reduction of arrears. Banks could lend above the ceilings if arrears had declined. The rationale for this measure was the preference, within a given total stock of credit, for bank versus inter-enterprise credit. Before discussing this rationale, however, it is useful to address the issue of the relevant measure of arrears to be included in the programme. The Romanian authorities included a measure of net arrears, associating the latter with money. This was a highly debatable choice. Indeed, as pointed out earlier, in a world with liquidity-constrained firms, gross and not net arrears matter. Inter-enterprise transactions can be effected with inter-enterprise credit even though net credit is zero. If gross arrears (or credit) decline, if they are to be effected, these transactions require the use of cash or bank credit. Only in the presence of a continuous clearing system will net arrears indicate the liquidity needs for financing inter-enterprise transactions.

Despite this technical – although important – aspect, it is worth noting that the role of arrears in designing credit programmes has been belatedly recognized. One important conclusion to be be drawn is that these types of credit programmes could have been implemented at the outset in stabilization programmes. The second observation is that, at the beginning of transition, when the banking system is still highly concentrated, countries are in a favourable position to use banks in order to net out arrears, isolating net positions. In this way the authorities can monitor firms in net debt position and, if necessary, impose penalties on them, through wage policies for instance. The risk of a chain of arrears would thus be averted. The GC operation in Romania highlights two other important aspects, both of which relate to the issue of the quasi-fiscal nature of the inter-enterprise arrears. First, GC exerted a significant effect on budget revenues, increasing tax revenues by an estimated 2 per cent of GDP. This was because inter-enterprise arrears had two negative effects on tax revenues.

The first of these effects was associated with the fact that profit taxes were computed on the basis of cash transactions. Thus, as long as sales were not paid, firms were not compelled to pay profit taxes on those transactions. Indeed, this tax rule might have been an incentive for the enterprise sector as a whole to build up arrears. Delaying tax payments, in a context of high inflation, meant a sharp reduction of the real tax burden.[13] Second, firms with unpaid receivables tended to fall into arrears on their sales tax payments. These arrears were extinguished once firms received compensation credit.

Thus, in the short run, the GC scheme produced a significant improvement in the budget. However, one could interpret the GC scheme as a shift of liabilities within state firms to liabilities with respect to the banking system. Net arrears could thus be considered as bad loans with respect to banks, and insofar as they were insured, implicitly or explicitly, by the government, as a form of quasi-fiscal expenditure, or a contingent liability. If this interpretation is correct, one could argue that a sound fiscal policy should have earmarked the tax revenue accrued as a result of the GC scheme for the purpose of covering these contingent liabilities.

The above discussion illustrates how a netting-out operation can help make explicit the magnitude of the underlying fiscal problem associated with the phenomenon of arrears. However, if the phenomenon of arrears does not acquire the systemic nature that it manifested in Romania and Russia in 1991–92, such netting-out operations are not warranted. Indeed, the market values of different debt positions depend on the conditions of the debtor-firms, and hence their market value differs from the nominal values. Netting-out entails the attribution of the same value to all debt positions (as noted by Rostowski, 1993). Thus, in economies with more stable conditions and more developed financial markets, a secondary market for corporate debt can develop and be part of the solution to the inter-enterprise debt problem. Indeed, in Poland (and in Hungary) a market of this kind has developed.

5.3   Russia

The scheme adopted in Russia in the summer of 1992 differed from the Romanian one in that it did not involve a direct increase in bank credit. The Russian scheme was meant to be a multilateral clearing process. At the end of the process, net debtors should have repaid net creditors by disposing of their assets, if necessary. A debt management institution was created to organize the liquidation of the assets of net debtor firms. However, on closer scrutiny, the differences between the Russian and the Romanian schemes are not significant (Rostowski, 1993). Indeed, special accounts were created, and net creditor firms could draw on these accounts to pay other liabilities, such as tax arrears and arrears in payments to banks. Therefore, also in the Russian case, the result of the netting-out was a swap from inter-enterprise liabilities to state and bank liabilities. In the clearing process, which took place in October and in November 1992, about 2.3 trillion arrears were cleared, while around 0.4 trillion remained as unsettled net arrears. Thus the latter amounted to about 16 per cent of total gross arrears (0.4 out of 2.7 (2.3 plus 0.4)).

As in the case of Romania, the schemes adopted in Russia highlight the *de facto* fiscal nature of inter-enterprise arrears in economies in transition. After an initial decline, arrears began to grow again at the end of 1993 and in 1994 (Figure 14.4). The problem of arrears has returned to the centre of economic and political debate, and, in the summer of 1994, the government created an institution to monitor arrears and if necessary to design policies to tackle the problem (see *The Economist*, 20–26 August 1994).

Figure 14.4   Russia: inter-enterprise arrears (ratio to monhly industrial production)

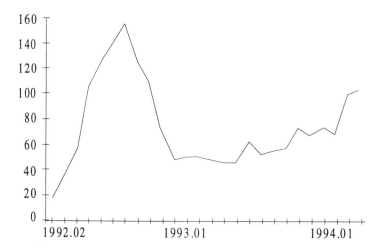

5.4   Hungary and Poland

No significant policies have been adopted in Poland and Hungary to tackle the problem of inter-enterprise arrears. In both countries, forms of secondary markets – albeit rudimentary – have developed.

5. 5   Some general observations on policies

Although precise evaluation may be premature, one may conclude that the policies adopted have not been particularly effective; indeed, they may sometimes have been even counterproductive.

A first observation is that, once arrears have developed into a widespread chain, the system may get locked into a 'bad' equilibrium. Attempts to push the system out of this equilibrium may in fact worsen the situation by signalling the government's attitude towards a generalized bail-out of firms.

Another important policy issue to have emerged in the above discussion relates to the usefulness of the netting-out operation, irrespective of the measures adopted to deal with the remaining net debt positions. It seems that this policy is advisable in countries with very underdeveloped financial structures and, in general, little experience of market behaviour (i.e. the countries of the former Soviet Union, Romania, perhaps Bulgaria). In the more advanced countries of Central and Eastern Europe, policies should aim to link the problem of inter-enterprise arrears with the overall strategy of debt restructuring. In this regard, efforts to foster a securitization of the inter-enterprise debt market by providing incentives and even insurance for financial institutions operating in that market, should be welcomed.

Finally, in the case of Romania, the problem of the relation between arrears and the design of credit programmes has emerged very clearly. One possible conclusion is that gross arrears, and not net arrears, should be included in the credit programme. Net arrears may indeed be a more relevant proxy for the subsidies needed to support loss-making firms, rather than being a proxy for the liquidity needs to finance inter-enterprise transactions.

6　CONCLUDING REMARKS

The phenomenon of arrears has played an important role in the early stages of transformation of PCPEs. In some instances, arrears have crucially affected the overall course of reforms. The importance of arrears goes beyond their effects on monetary policy. Indeed, in economies in transition arrears offer insights on the evolution of budget constraints, and on the evolution of market institutions. In particular, the study of arrears may shed light on the question of how rapidly private markets can be introduced, and the factors that enable them to work efficiently or else develop in a dysfunctional manner.[14] However, integration of these aspects into simple theoretical models, ones capable of producing policy implications, still lies a long way in the future.

The analysis conducted in this paper suggests a number of directions for future research. First, as firm-level data for several countries become available it will be necessary to pool country data in order to verify the presence of statistically significant country effects. This should lend support for the view of multiple equilibria. Second, more detailed analysis of the time development of the phenomenon for each country would be highly informative. Also important in this respect is study of the relation between arrears and the behaviour of banks, and analysis of the evolution of bank lending to firms in arrears. A pooled time-series/cross-section analysis would help to isolate macroeconomic effects, such as credit policy, interest rates, overall level of economic activity, and the microeconomic effects related to enterprise characteristics. Third, the peculiarities of the experience of PCPEs could be analysed by comparing the econometric results on these countries with those obtained from estimation of the same relations for a market economy. Finally, the role of ownership should be explored more thoroughly by controlling for size and sectoral effects.

NOTES

1. The case of Romania is hard to evaluate because of the presence of controls on producer prices. Until 1992 increases in producer prices were negotiated between firms and the government. Note, however, that when producer prices were free to adjust they grew well above consumer prices (Figure 14.3).
2. Of course, even in Hungary and Poland, the system may be still rudimentary. Nevertheless, there is a secondary market, a few banks are involved in factoring operations, bills of exchange are used, and, finally, information on firms' creditworthiness is published in specialized journals.
3. In this respect, although a failure in most aspects, the partial reforms carried out in Hungary and Poland before 1990 were important because they laid down the basic structure of market institutions.
4. This view has not been developed rigorously in the literature. To my knowledge it has been advanced in different forms in McKinnon (1991) and, orally, by Leijonhufvud.
5. The idea behind this channel is simple. The more firms are involved, the less likely is punishment for the individual firm.
6. The groups are formed with each successive group containing firms with a payables/sales ratio larger than the average of the preceding group.
7. The Shazam package was used or the Tobit model.
8. The survey was conducted by the World Bank and focused on inter-enterprise arrears. The sample comprised twenty-nine state-owned firms covering all the main industrial sectors.
9. It appears that firms with overdue receivables delay tax payments. However, there is a small correlation between overdue payables and delayed tax payments.
10. Unfortunately, I do not have data that fully correspond to those utilized for Romania. Since enterprise data were not available, I had to make do with a 1992 sample of firms with more than five workers, aggregated by branches at the three-digit level. The sample includes all the sectors of the economy and is disaggregated by region, size, and ownership. It consists of 4765 firm groups, which is an adequate size for statistical analysis, given that the total number of firms with more than five workers is estimated at around 70000.
11. As data on 1993 become available, it will be interesting to check whether the same behaviour emerges, or whether, with the passage of time, banks have adjusted their behaviour.

12. The role of high interest rates is also stressed by interviews with firms (World Bank, 1993).

13. A similar effect has been detected for Russia by Ickes and Ryterman (1993).

14. Unfortunately, economists (and, more in general, social scientists) are not well equipped to address these topics. Work by economic historians and the (neo) 'institutional' approach has dealt with these problems, providing interesting insights. The work of Douglass North and Oliver Williamson is certainly relevant.

REFERENCES

Begg, D. and R. Portes (1992), 'Enterprise Debt and Economic Transformation: Financial Restructuring of the State Sector in Central and Eastern Europe', Centre for Economic Policy Research, Discussion Paper no. 695.

Brechling, F.P.R. and R.G. Lipsey, (1963), 'Trade Credit and Monetary Policy', *Economic Journal*, **LXXIII**, December, pp. 618–41.

Calvo G. and F. Coricelli (1992), 'Stabilizing a Previously Centrally Planned Economy: Poland 1990', *Economic Policy*, **14**.

Calvo G. and F. Coricelli (1993), 'Credit Market Imperfections and Output Response in Previously Centrally Planned Economies', mimeo, May.

Calvo, G. and J. Frenkel (1991), 'From Centrally Planned to Market Economies: The Road from CPE to PCPE', International Monetary Fund Staff Papers, **38** (2), pp. 268–99.

Clifton, E. and M. Khan (1992), 'Inter-Enterprise Arrears in Transforming Economies: The Case of Romania', IMF Paper on Policy Analysis and Assessment.

Daianu, D. (1993), 'Arrears in Post-Command Economies: Thoughts from a Romanian Perspective', mimeo.

Ferris, S. (1981), 'A Transactions Theory of Trade Credit Use', *The Quarterly Journal of Economics*, May.

Hrncir, M. (1993), 'Financial Intermediation in the Czech Republic: Lessons and Progress Evaluation', Discussion Paper on Economic Transition 9302, Department of Applied Economics, Cambridge University.

Hrncir, M. and J. Klacek (1994), 'Inter-Enterprise Indebtedness and Performance of Banking System: The Czech Case', mimeo.

Ickes, B. and R. Ryterman (1993), 'The Inter-Enterprise Arrears Crisis in Russia', mimeo.

McKinnon, R. (1991), *The Order of Economic Liberalization*, The Johns Hopkins Press.

Meltzer, A.H. (1960), 'Mercantile Credit, Monetary Policy and the Size of the Firm', *Review of Economics and Statistics*, **XLII** (2), pp. 429–97.

Nadiri, M.I. (1969), 'The Determinants of Trade Credit in the U.S. Total Manufacturing Sector', *Econometrica*, **37** (2), pp. 408–23.
Rostowski, J. (1993), 'The Inter-Enterprise Debt Explosion in the Former Soviet Union: Causes, Consequences, Cures', mimeo.
World Bank (1993), *Fiscal Study on Romania*, Washington, D.C.

PART FOUR

The Quasi-Market Formula

15. The Privatization of Welfare Services and the Role of Non-Profit Organizations

Carlo Borzaga

1 INTRODUCTION

In all the developed countries, and in the European ones in particular, a process of privatization of welfare systems is in progress. However, with rare exceptions (Snower, 1993, 1994; Bartlett and Le Grand, 1993) European economists have paid little attention to identification of the nature of this process and to analysis of its consequences on individual and collective welfare and on the structure of supply and demand for welfare services. In particular, European economists, unlike their American colleagues, have largely neglected the role that non-profit organizations (henceforth NPOs) can play in a welfare system which is at least partly privatized.

There is a widespread conviction that the explanation for the attitude of European economists lies in the acceptance of the division of tasks between coercive action by the state and the organizational independence of private organizations that predominates in Europe. Whereas in the European countries until recently the state has committed itself to supplying the majority of welfare services, financing itself out of the overall tax system, in the USA the state provides only some of these services, leaving it to private enterprise to satisfy most needs. It is within this specific context that private supply, both profit and non-profit, has developed in the USA and, hence, the interest of social scientists (including economists) in the phenomenon.

This explanation, however, is not completely satisfactory. Also in the European countries, in fact, a proportion of welfare services has always been produced by private organizations, chiefly non-profit. In some European countries, most notably Holland and Germany, the majority of social services are produced by private organizations mostly financed by the state. In recent years, moreover, the proportion of private production has increased in all countries, mainly as a consequence of processes, more or less overt, of privatization. Most European countries have also devised or are currently implementing programmes for the reform of welfare systems which envisage a reduction of public supply and the increasing involvement of private supply units.

Given these premises, this paper argues that more systematic economic analysis is required of the privatization of welfare systems and, internally to it, of the possible role of NPOs. This interest is motivated by at least four considerations:

1. Actual and potential privatization processes of the welfare services are wider and more pervasive than those which have been examined and implemented to date; at least in theory, the privatization of these services can yield benefits in terms of efficiency, effectiveness and equity.
2. Demand for welfare services is growing and will grow even more in the future; the adjustment of supply, especially in the presence of tendencies towards privatization, requires analysis of which private supply facilities are best suited to the production of these goods.
3. In the private production of welfare services the role of NPOs is currently extremely important and their weight has grown in all the market economy countries since the mid-1970s; moreover, following privatization, NPOs have undergone major qualitative changes.
4. Services in general, and among them welfare services, constitute one of the sectors on whose growth will depend a good part of the increase in employment and therefore reduction of the high unemployment rates currently characterizing the European economies.

These observations combine to confirm the importance of the non-profit sector in ensuring an adequate supply of services and in increasing employment as privatization of the welfare system proceeds. This importance justifies more systematic economic analysis of these organizations in order to identify their specific features and potential (especially compared with firms for profit) and in order to adopt the measures necessary for their regulation and support.

The aim of this paper is to provide a descriptive outline which demonstrates the importance of the non profit sector in a largely privatized welfare system and to underline some conditions for the consolidation of the sector. To this end, the paper analyses the significance assumed by the concept of privatization when it is applied to welfare services (section 2) and the evolution of demand for such services (section 3). The paper then presents a synthesis of the quantitative dimensions of the non-profit sector in a number of countries and of its evolution (section 4), and of the economic theories that seek to explain its existence and role (section 5).The conclusions propose a number of conditions necessary for the development of the non-profit sector in the European countries.

Two specifications are in order before analysis begins:

a. The term 'non-profit organization' normally only denotes an organization subject to the non-distribution-of-profit constraint. Many of the observations contained in this paper, however, also apply to organizations not subject to this constraint but whose organizational surplus accrues to a beneficiary category other than investor (the so-called 'third sector', including NPOs, cooperatives and mutuals) (Gui, 1991); in the European countries these organizations are very important also in the welfare services provision;

b. It is assumed that welfare services are constituted prevalently by collective and trust goods. Collective goods comprise pure public goods, charitable goods, mixed goods with a large and expensive-to-produce non-rival component, and which necessitate voluntary price discrimination when provided by a private (for-profit or otherwise) organization. Trust goods comprise club goods and mixed goods concerning which there is an asymmetric information problem detrimental to stakeholders, as well as 'merit goods' (Ben-Ner and van Hoomissen, 1991).

2   THE PRIVATIZATION OF THE WELFARE SYSTEM

The economic debate on processes of privatization conducted in recent years has centred principally on firms producing private goods and tool goods. It has therefore focused mainly on the various forms of transfer of property rights. In actual fact, however, there are numerous signals which indicate that the privatization process has assumed a much broader dimension, although it has not always been conducted in an explicit and conscious manner. However, this broader process seems to have attracted less attention from economists. This is perhaps because, whereas it is easy to analyse the privatization process when it entails passage from one definite state to another, as happens when property rights are transferred, it is much more difficult to subject a tendency to change to analysis. And this in fact seems to be a definition applicable to current developments in the welfare systems of all the developed countries seeking to transfer functions, productive as well, to date performed by the state or else closely governed by it to the market and households. In this case it is difficult to give univocal definition to the contents and features of the privatization process, because it depends on the mix between public and private and on the functions involved. Since the privatization process is normally accompanied by a decentralization of functions and responsibilities, difficulties arise in determining which of the organizations involved are public and which of them are private.

Moreover, if we take as our reference, for the developed countries, the set of goods and services which, until the mid-1970s, were produced mostly by public supply units (collective and trust goods, in particular health, educational and training services, recreational and cultural services, social services), we can single out at least three patterns of privatization:

1. an increased amount of production assigned to private units with public financing through forms of contracting-out or vouchers;
2. the progressive curtailment of public supply or of supply financed by public funds and the tendency to restrict free access to services only or largely to more disadvantaged social groups.
3. the state's withdrawal from the production of goods and services designed to meet new needs, with the consequent passage of potential consumers either to substitute goods or services or to private supply units. This process is defined a 'demand-driven privatization'(Kamerman and Kahn, 1989); it is not a result of a deliberate government action, but of the choices of individuals or firms that a government is unwilling or unable to satisfy or control.

In many cases, some of the patterns overlap, as in the case of the partial public financing of private supply units.

From an economic point of view, these privatization processes are equally or even more interesting than those under way for firms producing private goods and tool goods, and for at least four reasons.

Firstly, because the economic size of the activities involved is very large. Spending on social security, health and education rose in the OECD countries from and average 14 per cent of GDP after the war to 26 per cent in 1990. In most European countries this per centage is considerably higher (Mundell, 1994). Although more than 50 per cent of this spending consists of transfers and subsidies, there seems to be room to restore efficiency by also privatizing supply units.

Secondly, because the containment of public spending, and therefore of the services paid out of the public purse, has become one of the principal economic policy goals of the developed countries.

Thirdly, because this is a process which will affect the developed economies, especially European, for a relatively long period of time, and it will bring a major shift in the boundaries between public and private and a revision of fiscal and transfer systems (vouchers and selective de-taxing).

Fourthly, this process is driven by a search not only for greater efficiency but also for greater effectiveness, equity and capacity to satisfy new needs. The debate on government failures has in fact given rise to the hypothesis that the privatization of welfare may help to attenuate four shortcomings in the model of predominant public production (Savas, 1987):

1. its poor efficiency due to rigidity, low productivity and scant attention to the cost/efficiency ratio;
2. its poor effectiveness and quality due mainly to the bureaucratization of public supply units, and a lack of attention paid to the customer;
3. the tendency of public welfare systems to give priority to the average consumer, who is able to influence both decisions on services to create or upgrade, and the behaviour of the public supply units, with a consequent worsening of the conditions of the most needy groups in the population;
4. its inability to respond promptly to new needs, especially when these are differentiated or expressed by specific subgroups of citizens. Public production is subject to the bureaucratic constraint, which requires that the services supplied by the public administration should be organized according to universalistic criteria, and in order that it should always be possible to demonstrate managerial correctness, the penalty being loss of public consensus. This produces a categorical constraint which sets an objective limit on public services production for differentiated demand by minority groups (Douglas, 1987).

Although empirical research is not available which shows unequivocally that privatization eliminates these shortcomings, or that it is immune to other problems (for example, the reduced quality of services),[1] the debate on these limits has nevertheless set in motion a process, more or less intense, of privatization.

Exhaustive quantification of the process of privatization of the welfare services is impossible because of the almost total lack of statistical data. However, it is confirmed by the expansion of private supply units, both profit and non-profit, and by the increasing dependence of these on public financing (which signals the spread of forms of contracting-out) and on the proceeds from the sale of goods and services. The tendency is also confirmed by analysis of legislation in European countries, notably that of the United Kingdom.

3   THE EVOLUTION OF DEMAND

One aspect of the privatization of welfare services that should be examined carefully, because of the importance that it has assumed in recent years and may assume even more so in the future, is the effects that derive from an increase in demand for services.

Since the end of the 1980s demand has progressively shifted towards services such as education, health, culture and care, giving rise to an intensification of the tertiarization process. The impact on employment has been greater than that on GDP following increased productivity in the goods producing sectors. Table 15.1 confirms this trend: compared with negative or extremely minor changes in the number of workers employed in industry, employment has grown in services as a whole at an annual rate of between 1.6 and 3 per cent, and at an even higher rate in community, social and personal services (with the exception of the United States and the United Kingdom).

Tab. 15.1 Employment by sector in selected countries

	Industry		Services		Community social and personal services		Total
	% var. 80–90	% of tot. 1990	% var. 80–90	% of tot. 1990	% var. 80–90	% of tot. 1990	% var. 80–90
United States	0.19	26.2	2.94	38.8	2.59	32.2	1.87
France	−1.51	29.9	1.60	33.8	1.96	30.2	0.19
Germany	−0.41	39.8	1.68	30.1	1.79	26.7	0.53
Italy	−1.11	32.4	2.06	31.1	3.62	27.5	0.40
Spain	0.10	33.4	2.79	31.4	4.19	23.4	0.89
United Kingdom	−1.82	29.0	1.24	34.8	1.12	28.1	0.63

Source:

OCDE, *Labour Force Statistics 1970–90*, Paris, 1993

One notes that that rate of growth of community, social and personal services employment in the United States was higher than in many European countries, even though the weight of this sector was already the highest in the USA at the beginning of the 1980s. Only Italy and Spain exhibit rates of employment growth in community, social and personal services higher than those in America.

Tab. 15.2 Employment by major industry division: 1979, 1992 and projected to 2005

	Absolute change		% change	
	1979 1992	1992 2005*	1979 1992	1992 2005
Non-farm wage and salary	18398	25072	1.58	1.79
Goods producing	−3319	575	−0.96	0.19
Service producing	21717	24497	2.65	2.22
Hotels and other lodging places	512	637	3.72	3.12
Personal services	290	721	2.72	4.99
Business services	2903	3057	9.27	4.43
Auto repair, service and garages	303	415	4.05	3.64
Motion pictures	176	95	5.94	1.81
Amusement and recreation services	418	457	4.28	3.01
Health services	3530	4016	5.44	3.62
Legal services	455	440	7.61	3.70
Educational services	610	462	4.30	2.09
Social services	877	1733	6.24	6.81
Museums, zoos, and membership organizations	512	510	2.38	1.81
Engineering, management	1029	1168	5.90	3.79
Transportation, communications, utilities,wholesale trade, retail trade finance, insurance and real estate	7367	7763	1.87	1.59
Federal government	196	−154	0.54	−0.40
State and local government	2509	2525	1.47	1.24
State and local government hospitals	−18	160	0.12	1.13
State government education	419	504	2.34	2.16
Local government education	1115	1790	1.68	2.21

Note:

* = The scenario in the one with moderate growth.

Source:

Plunkert, 1990 and Franklin, 1993

The tendency towards growth in demand for services, and the increase in the employment associated with it, is confirmed by forecasts. These are only available for the United States, but one may plausibly maintain that the behaviour of the other developed economies will not be dissimilar.

As Table 15.2 shows, between 1992 and 2005 a further expansion of employment in services in general (to persons and to businesses) is expected. The highest growth rates are predicted for social services (6.81 per cent), personal services (4.99 per cent) and business services (4.43 per cent). Much lower rates of growth are predicted instead for employment in the public sector in general, and especially in public health and education services (Plunkert, 1990; Franklin, 1993; Godbout, 1993).

Differences among rates of growth of services in general, and in particular of community, social and personal services, help to explain the differing trends of overall employment in Europe and the United States. These differences may in turn be in part attributed to the different organization of welfare systems and to the differing capacity of supply to react to the evolution of demand in the two systems.

In the USA, thanks to more restricted public supply and to the maturity achieved by the non-profit sector, the increase in demand for collective and trust goods has stimulated an increase in private, mainly non-profit supply (and in associated employment) thereby off-setting the slower growth of public supply (and employment).

In the European countries, the increase in demand for these goods has encountered the budget and organizational rigidities of public supply and an underdeveloped private sector, especially non-profit. Public production (and employment) have increased, but probably to a lesser extent than that necessary to satisfy demand completely.

This differing gowth of supply and of employment in community, personal and social services in the United States and in the European countries is probably one of the reasons for the diverse occupational intensity of growth. In the present stage of economic development and given the difficulties of the public institutions, a welfare system less dependent on public decisions and organizational forms and with broader private supply, profit and non-profit, like that of the United States, is better able to transfer the inputs made available from the sector of increasing productivity – industry – to that of stagnant productivity – services and in particular community and social sevices (Baumol, 1967). If this observation is – at least partially – correct, one may conclude that growth in the supply of collective and trust goods and of relative employment will be greater the more a private supply of them is able to develop in Europe.

The experience of both the USA and the European countries during the last decade, however, suggests that the growth of the private supply of these services is conditioned by the diffusion of non-profit organizations. This seems to indicate that, in these specific sectors, NPOs offer advantages compared with for-profit firms, and that they are therefore preferred by both governments and consumers. Identification of these advantages might therefore enable the development of efficient strategies for the privatization of welfare systems.

4 THE EVOLUTION OF THE NON-PROFIT SECTOR

Even if there has recently been an increasing number of studies of the quantitative size of the non-profit sector in European countries, an overall picture based on homogeneous and therefore comparable information is not yet available.

Lacking in many countries is a precise definition of non-profit organizations, although all legislations prescribe organizational forms for activities with objectives other than proft. This obliges the authors of these studies to construct *ad hoc* definitions of the sector, and it makes the gathering of statistical information even more difficult.

Comparison among the most recent studies, however, allows a number of estimates to be made of the size and the recent evolution of the sector, identifying its features and highlighting a number of important changes.

The first finding to emerge from comparative analysis is that, by the end of the 1980s, the NPO sector had grown to significant size in all the developed economies – after particularly sustained growth throughout the decade.

The most complete data refer to the United States, where the sector is the most highly developed and has been subjected to empirical analysis for a number of years.

According to estimates, in 1986 the contribution by the sector to national income amounted to 4 per cent (compared with 3.6 per cent in 1977) and to 7 per cent if one also includes voluntary work. In the same year, 7700 thousand workers were employed by NPOs (compared with 5991 thousand in 1977), 7.14 per cent of overall employment (without considering voluntary workers, estimated at 3629 thousand equivalent workers in 1977 and at 5200 thousand in 1984).

The annual rate of growth of employment in the NP sector was therefore 3.17 per cent compared with an overall rate of employment growth of 2.34 per cent (Hodgkinson and Weitzman, 1988; Barbetta, 1990).

As regards the European countries, Eurostat has recently tried to estimate the size of the social economy sector. The results are given in Table 15.3

(Eurostat, 1993). According to this estimate, 261630 organizations were operating in 1990, with 3775236 workers and a volume of business amounting to 1554 billion 640 million ECUs.

The social economy sector, according to these estimates, therefore accounts for 2.8 per cent of total employment in the Community. Even though less widespread than in the USA, the NP sector has therefore become of considerable importance in Europe as well.

Table 15.3   Social economy: number of organizations, members, employees and volume of business in the EEC, 1990

	Number of member organizations	Number of members	Number of employees	Volume of business (Mio ECU)
Cooperatives	96422	52338221	2657543	1226987
Banking and credit	12134	27762890	1333702	925261
Insurance and pensions	251	6000000	19301	2518
Agriculture, etc.	37211	3828223	363346	149740
Construction, etc.	27108	1005708	214070	22440
Trade (wholesale, retail)	6590	9299503	409493	87432
Others n.e.s.	13128	4441897	317631	39596
Mutuals	13929	96612244	226312	75570
Banking and credit	164	107000	623	1586
Insurance and pensions	12284	96155244	225689	72914
Others n.e.s.	1481	350000	·	1070
Associations	151279	32162593	891381	252083
Banking and credit (house financing)	1029	9867211	83043	218506
Others n.e.s.	150250	22295382	808338	33577
Total social economy sector	261630	Not additive	3775236	1554640

Source:
EUROSTAT, A Statistical Profile of the Cooperative, Mutual and Non Profit Sector and its Organisations in the European Community, Service and Transport, 1993, Supplement 2.

A number of analyses of specific European countries enable further elaboration of these estimates and verification of the sector's evolution during the 1980s.

In Germany, the sector employed 1165655 workers in 1987 (4.3 per cent of total employment, compared with the 0.5 per cent in the agricultural sector and the 3.6 per cent in banks and insurance companies). Between 1970 and 1987 employment in the non-profit sector rose by 99 per cent, compared with the economy's increase of 10 per cent and the public sector's of 45 per cent (Anheier, 1991).

In the United Kingdom, the number of non-profit organizations increased by 27 per cent between 1975 and 1985 (reaching 350 thousand) and their contribution to GDP rose from 3.4 per cent in 1981 to 4 per cent in 1991 (17 billion pounds). The figures on employment are less specific, although the partial sources confirm its growth (Knapp and Kendall, 1991).

At the end of the 1980s, the 200 thousand French non-profit organizations employed 6 per cent of the overall labour force – an increase of 33 per cent since 1979 (Archambault, 1990).

As regards Italy, recent estimates indicate that workers in the NP sector at the beginning of the 1990s amounted to 350000 units (excluding voluntary workers), contributing 1.3 per cent to overall employment, with a growth during the 1980s of 38.9 per cent, compared with an increase in total employment of 7.4 per cent (16.7 per cent in the sector of non-marketable services) (Borzaga, 1991). More detailed research (Barbetta,1994) has shown that the Italian non-profit sector employs 418000 full-time workers, equal to 1.8 per cent of the total labour force, 273000 volunteers, 15000 conscientious objectors and 16000 people seconded by their employers and paid by them.

These findings are corroborated by the results obtained by an international research group coordinated by Salamon (1994) which considered Hungary, Italy, Japan, Germany, the United Kingdom, Canada and the United States. The share of the non-profit sector in total employment, although it ranges from the 0.8 per cent of Hungary to the 6.8 per cent of the USA, is on average 3.4 per cent, while the ratio between the sector's operational costs and GDP is, on average, 3.5 per cent.

As well as this quantitative information, also confirming the increasing economic importance of the non-profit sector, are the changes that have marked its growth:

a. There have been progressive changes in the composition of receipts: almost all countries have seen an increase in payments by both private individuals (clients) and public bodies (central governments and local authorities), while the amount of donations (philanthropic contributions) has diminished (Salamon, 1992 and Salamon and Anheier 1994; Barbetta, 1990; Pasquinelli, 1993). There has been an increasing tendency for public administrations to delegate to private supply units the production of goods and services of collective interest, and for the entrepreneurial side of NPOs – i.e. their ability to adjust to changing private demand – to strengthen. This latter feature is confirmed by the tendency of a number of non-profit organizations to engage in the production of private goods in order to earn resources for the financing of their statutory activities. Both these tendencies bring NPOs closer to for-profit organizations – so that one may now speak of the growth of a 'new entrepreneurial class involved in closely-knit work of experimentation in innovative forms of service delivery' (Pasquinelli, 1993).

b.   The growth of the NP sector stems less from the strengthening of certain large-scale organizations, closely dependent on entrepreneurial groups (USA) or on religious institutions (Italy, Germany, the UK), than from the birth of new initiatives, mostly of small size, with restricted ranges of action and managed directly by their members. In general, a progressive 'secularization' of the sector seems to be in progress, and this has favoured the decentralization of supply and the positioning of many non-profit organizations in well-defined market niches.

c.   The specialization, and especially the professionalization of non-profit organizations has increased. Organizational consolidation and greater recourse to workers with specific skills has accompanied this increasing specialization in the production of specific goods or services; that is, it has helped to curtail the action of advocacy and the political role typical of the large-scale NPOs and has strengthened their productive role and their management according to entrepreneurial criteria. This development has not necessarily been accompanied by a fall-off in voluntary work, although analysis of its role is still not forthcoming.

d.   Despite their quantitative growth, non-profit organizations have preserved a strong sectoral specialization. Comparison among very different national situations reveals that the areas of activity of NPOs are the same everywhere: social services, education, museums and cultural institutions, recreational activities, health services. Growth has occurred almost entirely within these sectors, and has been inversely proportional to the existence of a solid and generalized presence of public facilities. In many of these sectors, non-profit organizations are responsible for the bulk of production.[2]

For all their heterogeneity, the figures nevertheless confirm that the privatization of welfare services has been accompanied by an increasing role of the NP sector, both by indicating that its contribution to income and to employment has grown, and by showing that NPOs have assumed a more productive role in sectors where for-profit firms are few or non-existent and have adjusted their organization, human resources and commercial departments to the new role.

5 THE ADVANTAGES OF NON-PROFIT ORGANIZATIONS

Economic analysis of NPOs conducted mainly during the 1980s showed that the assumption by them of the non-distribution constraint not only differentiates them from for-profit firms but renders them more attractive to consumers. This is particularly the case when information asymmetries arise and when the goods are characterized by non-rivalry in consumption. The information asymmetry arises because consumers have little opportunity to check whether the effective quantity and quality of the good correspond to that agreed when the contract for purchase was signed (Hansmann, 1980; Nelson and Krashinsky, 1973). If the supplier is a profit-maximizing firm, it finds it advantageous to reduce quantity, and especially quality, if the consumer is unable to verify these adequately. The non-profit organization, by contrast, has no such incentive.

More specifically, there are three principal situations in which asymmetric information arises to the disadvantage of consumers:

a. when there is a lag between the time of purchase and the time when the good can be evaluated;
b. when the payer and the consumer of the good are different entities;
c. when the good is complex and its precise characteristics are difficult for stakeholders to evaluate (Ben-Ner and van Hoomissen, 1991).

In these situations the consumer is motivated to resort to organizations which, since profit is not their sole or principal purpose, are less interested in exploiting information asymmetry to their advantage.

These considerations have been subjected to empirical verification, with results that confirm the hypothesis (Lyons, 1989). It has also been shown that when information asymmetry is reduced by the introduction of consumer protection rules (for example, in financial markets), the role and weight of non-profit organizations have diminished (Hansmann, 1990).

The NPO is also favoured by the presence of non-rivalry for consumption. A typical example is 'day care for children', where the quality of the service is a good subject to non-rivalry, even at considerable expense. The consumer in this case is willing to pay a higher price as long as quality is assured, but this means that the organization cannot exploit the information asymmetry (Ben-Ner and van Hoomissen, 1991).

Obviously the majority of collective and trust goods – today produced principally by the state in the European countries but currently subject to privatization – display the features described above.

The problems created for private production by information asymmetries and non-rivalry, moreover, are greater the smaller the size of the markets and therefore the more demand is differentiated and restricted to small catchment areas.

However, these explanations of the comparative advantages of NPOs leave two problems unsolved:

a.   the voluntary adoption of the non-distribution-of profit-constraint by the organization is not sufficient to guarantee the trust of consumers and to protect them adequately;
b.   the existence of demand for non-profit organizations is not enough to explain their existence; one must also identify the incentives, other than profit, which induces individuals to set up these organizations.

The non-distribution-of-profits constraint can be easily eluded. To be effective, it must be clearly defined and subject to systematic controls. This should be the responsibility of both the state and of the stakeholders themselves. In actual fact, stakeholders' control over these organizations is sufficiently widespread to be taken as a specific feature of them (together with the non-proft constraint). The most common form of control by stakeholders, especially in the new NPOs that have arisen in European countries in recent years, is that of their direct participation in the creation and management of organizations. This is confirmed by the fact that the preferred organizational forms are the association and the cooperative, rather than the foundation. However this control is not sufficiently generalized, which renders clear definition of the constraint and relative controls by the state indispensable.

The second problem is identifying the motives that lead to the creation of NPOs. Economic theory has not yet supplied satisfactory answers to this problem. Traditional theory (James, 1987) has singled out three main reasons:

a.   the existence of hidden profit motives;
b.   the pursuit of goals other than profit, but favourable to the organization, such as the diffusion of a certain religious doctrine;
c.   the existence of public incentives to the creation of non-profit activities.

All three of these explanations are unsatisfactory. The first becomes weaker as control by the state and stakeholders increases; the second explains the birth and growth of large-scale NPOs, but not the more recent emergence of small-scale lay and autonomous organizations; the third does not explain the birth of new NPOs in countries where specific incentives were not established.

If analysed from the supply side (that is, in terms of the motives for their constitution), NPOs are not a homogeneous phenomenon. A wide range of reasons for their birth may therefore be identified. With no claim to completeness, one can single out at least three groups of reasons apart from those mentioned above:

a. For organizations created and run directly by the stakeholders, the main motive is that of overcoming information asymmetry by means of direct control over the organization; this makes it possible to chose the quantity and quality of the service and to monitor the correspondence between these and the cost. It is also possible to discriminate the price if the good is non-rival (Ben-Ner and van Hoomissen, 1991).
b. For organizations created and run directly by those who work for them (cooperatives, but also numerous associations), the main motive lies in the employment opportunities that they provide; a factor which becomes more important the higher the unemployment rate, especially among groups of workers with specific skills. The condition for the development of these NPOs is the existence or the prediction of paying public or private demand. The adoption of the non-distribution constraint stems from a desire to give credibility to the organization.
c. More complex is the explanation of the creation of NPOs by people who have no direct interest in the services delivered, and who do not wish to work in these organizations. This is principally the case of charitable goods, in which altruistic behaviour predominates, apparently in conflict with traditional economic theory. However, if we adopt a less restrictive definition of 'self interest' it is possible to give an explanation for this behaviour too (Bordignon, 1994): It may also be the outcome of a demand for 'justice' or 'equality' which increases as public service delivery decreases and which takes concrete form in demand for goods and services for the most disadvantaged sectors of society.

Although this typology is not exhaustive, it accounts for most of the phenomenon, especially if one considers mixed forms (a and b, b and c, a and c) which are extremely widespread, mainly because each of the three types of interest helps to provide the resources needed for the creation and development of these organizations (voluntary work and financial resources provided by stakeholders and subjects with strong demand for equity, systematic work commitment provided by those in search of employment, etc.). Also very common is passage from one organizational form to another (from a to b and especially from c to b) as the organization grows.

Economic theory therefore furnishes sufficient explanation for the existence of NPOs and also enables identification of their advantages compared with for-profit firms and public production units. With respect to the for-profit firm, they are better able to overcome problems created by the presence of information asymmetry, especially when NPOs are characterized besides the profit-distribution constraint by the direct participation of stakeholders and by control exerted by the community in which they are located. With respect to public supply units, they are more flexible, better able to assess demand and its evolution and, especially if of small size, they encounter less constraints in gathering essential resources.

As well as these advantages, however, NPOs also exhibit a number of disadvantages. The most important of these is the fact that non-profit firms are constrained in their access to capital. They cannot raise capital by issuing equity shares; rather, they must rely on debts, donations and retained profit (Hansmann, 1987). These sources do not ensure the prompt adjustment of financial means to needs, especially when the demand for services induced by accelerated privatization or by consumer behaviour increases rapidly.

6   CONCLUSIONS

The foregoing analysis has shown that NPOs have reacted positively to the privatization of welfare services. They have taken the place of public supply units in countries which have privatized production but have continued to finance the welfare services, and they have developed autonomous supply aimed at directly satisfying private demand. This latter tendency seems bound to strengthen in the future, thereby confirming the importance of NPOs for the decentralization of economic systems. Although theoretical analysis is still incomplete, it is sufficient to account for the existence of NPOs and to confirm that they are an important complement to the structure of supply. Reducing the role of the state in the economy and especially in the production of welfare services requires adequate development of NPOs.

Theoretical analysis also demonstrates, however, that the development of the non-profit sector rests on a number of conditions, namely:

a.   a clear definition of the non-distribution constraint and of ways to ensure that it is respected (statements of account, checks by the tax authorities, etc.);

b.   definitions of the organizational forms adoptable by NPOs with the aim of enhancing control by the stakeholders and the consequent reduction of information asymmetry, even when the stakeholders do not control the organization.

For greater involvement of these organizations in privatization processes it is also necessary:

a. to give precise definition to the tax advantages granted to these organizations, perhaps differentiated according to the social value of the services produced;
b. encourage, by means of the defiscalization of both donations and contributions, the economic consolidation of these organizations;
c. make privatization policies, the public resources used for the purchase of services, and bargaining forms, explicit and definite.

The European countries lag behind on all these counts. Many countries, indeed, still have not clearly defined the non-profit constraint. Fiscal regulation is complex, fragmentary and frequently incoherent with ongoing privatization processes (Bises, 1993). This lack of clarity restricts, and will continue to do so in the future, the ordinary development of the privatization of collective and trust goods, with a consequent resistance against the reduction of public intervention, an increase in unsatisfied needs, and limited job creation.

It is likely that the regulations governing the NP sector will be revised in the next few years, and it is important that economic analysis should also be involved in the definition of its new characteristics.

NOTES

1. For an analysis of the problems created by privatization see Dallago (1993).
2. For the United States see Salamon (1992). Ben-Ner and van Hoomissen (1991) conclude that 'the industrial incidence of nonprofit organizations depends in attributes of different goods and services' (p. 545). See also Ben-Ner and van Hoomissen (1992).

REFERENCES

Anheier, H. (1991), 'Employment and Earnings in the West German Nonprofit Sector: Structures and Trends 1970–1987', *Annales de l'Economie Publique, Sociale et Cooperative*, **62**.

Archambault, E. (1990), 'Public Authorities and the Nonprofit Sector in France', in H.K. Anheier and W. Seibel (eds), *The Third Sector. Comparative Studies of Nonprofit Organizations*, Berlin: De Gruyter.

Barbetta, G.P. (1990), 'Il Terzo Settore negli Stati Uniti', in M.C. Bassanini and P.E. Ranci (eds), *Non per profitto. Il settore dei soggetti che erogano servizi di interesse collettivo senza fine di lucro*, Rome: Fondazione A. Olivetti.

Barbetta, G.P. (1994), *Le dimensioni economiche nel settore nonprofit in Italia*, Università Cattolica di Milano, mimeo.

Bartlett, W. and T. Le Grand J. (eds.) (1993), *Quasi Markets and Social Policy*, London: Macmillan.

Baumol, W.J. (1967), 'Macroeconomics of Unbalanced Growth: The Autonomy of Urban Crisis', *American Economic Review*, June, pp. 415–26.

Ben-Ner, A. and T. van Hoomissen (1991), 'Nonprofit Organizations in the Mixed Economy: A Demand and Supply Analysis', *Annales de l'Economie Publique, Sociale et Cooperative*, **62**.

Ben-Ner, A, and T. van Hoomissen (1992), 'An Empirical Investigation of the Joint Determination of the Size of the For-profit, Nonprofit and Government Sectors', *Annales de l'Economie Publique, Sociale et Cooperative*, **63** (3).

Bises, B. (1993), 'Il trattamento tributario delle organizzazioni private senza scopo di lucro aventi finalità sociali', *Economia Pubblica*, **12**.

Bordignon M. (1994), *Beni pubblici e scelte private*, Bologna: Il Mulino.

Borzaga, C. (1991), 'The Italian Nonprofit Sector: An Overview of an Undervalued Reality', *Annales de l'Economie Publique, Sociale et Cooperative*, **62**.

Commissione delle Comunità Europee (1993), *Crescita, competitività, occupazione. Le sfide e le vie da percorrere per entrare nel XXI secolo*, Brussels.

Dallago, B. (1993), *Some Reflections on Privatization as a Means to Transform the Economic System: The Western Experience*, Department of Economics, Trento, mimeo.

Douglas, J. (1987), 'Political Theories of Nonprofit Organizations', in W.W. Powell (ed.), *The Nonprofit Sector: A Research Handbook*, New Haven: Yale University Press.

Eurostat (1993), 'A Statistical Profile of the Cooperative, Mutual and Nonprofit Sector and its Organizations in the European Community', Preliminary Issue, *Services and Transport*, Supplement 2, Luxemburg.

Franklin, J.C. (1993), 'The American Workforce: 1992–2005. Industry Output and Employment', *Monthly Labor Review*, November.

Godbout, T.M. (1993), 'Employment Change and Sectoral Distribution in 10 Countries, 1970–1990', *Monthly Labor Review*, October.

Gui, B. (1991), 'The Economic Rationale for the "Third Sector". Nonprofit and other Noncapitalistic Organizations', *Annales de l'Economie Publique, Sociale et Cooperative*, **62**.

Hansmann, H.B. (1987), 'Economic Theories of Nonprofit Organization', in W.W. Powell (ed.), *The Nonprofit Sector. A Research Handbook*, New Haven: Yale University Press.

Hansmann, H.B. (1980), 'The Role of Nonprofit Enterprise', *The Yale Journal of Law*, **89** (5).

Hansmann, H.B. (1990), 'The Economic Role of Commercial Nonprofits: The Evolution of the Saving Bank Industry', in H.K. Anheier and W. Seibel (eds.) *The Third Sector: Comparative Studies of Nonprofit Organizations*, Berlin: De Gruyter.

Hodgkinson, V.A. and M.S. Weitzman (1988), *Dimension of the Independent Sector: Statistical Profile*, Independent Sector Publications.

James, E. (1987), 'The Nonprofit Sector in Comparative Perspective', in W.W. Powell (ed.), *The Nonprofit Sector. A Research Handbook*, New Haven: Yale Univerity Press.

Kamerman, S.B. and A.J. Kahn (1989), *Privatization and the Welfare State*, Princeton: Princeton University Press.

Knapp, M. and J. Kendall (1991), 'Policy Issues for the UK Voluntary Sector in the 1990s', *Annales de l'Economie Publique, Sociale et Cooperative*, **62**.

Lyons, M. (1989), *Funding Option for Children. A Supplement to the Background Paper*, Melbourne.

Mundell, R. (1994), 'Disoccupazione, competitività e Stato Sociale', *Rivista di Politica Economica*, **11**.

Nelson, R.R. and M. Krashinsky (1973), 'Two Major Issues of Public Policy: Public Subsidy and the Organization of Supply', in R. Nelson and D. Young (eds), *Public Subsidy for Day Care for Young Children*, Lexington, M.A., D.C. Heath.

Pasquinelli, S. (1993), 'Stato sociale e "terzo settore" in Italia', *Stato e Mercato*, **2**.

Plunkert, L.M. (1990), 'The 1980's: A decade of Job Growth and Industry Shifts', *Monthly Labor Review*, September.

Salamon, L.M. (1992), *America's Nonprofit Sector. A Primer*, Baltimore: Johns Hopkins University.

Solamon, L.M. and H.K. Anheier (1994), *The Emerging Sector: The Nonprofit Sector in Comparative Perspective. An Overview*, Baltimore, Johns Hopkins University.

Savas, E.S. (1987), *Privatization. The Key to Better Government*, Chatham: Chatham House Publications.

Snower, D.J. (1993), 'The Future of the Welfare State', *Economic Journal*, **103**.

Snower, D.J. (1994), 'Possiamo permetterci il Welfare State?', *Rivista di Politica Economica*, **13**.

16. Quasi-Markets and Incomplete Information: the Case of Medical Services in the UK and Italy

Luigi Mittone[1]

1 INTRODUCTION: THE CHARACTERISTICS OF QUASI-MARKETS IN BRITAIN

The term 'quasi-markets' came into being simultaneously with the debate on revision of the welfare system in Great Britain (Le Grand, 1990), and it relates to certain features common to policies for the reform of the British public services delivery system as proposed or implemented between 1988 and 1989.[2] More specifically, quasi-markets display two principal features, namely:

1. The state abandons the dual role of financier and producer of public services that it performed in the welfare state, and only engages in the financing and planning of services, the production of which is assigned to a wide range of firms or bodies in direct competition with each other.
2. the resources allocated for the financing of services are not assigned to the producers through a process of bureaucratic intermediation, but directly to users, either through the use of special government vouchers for each specific service or through other non-monetary forms expressing 'approval' of the consumers.[3]

The introduction of quasi-markets was undoubtedly prompted by the search for an automatic mechanism which would improve both the internal efficiency of public services production and allocative efficiency. It is therefore obvious that the basic premise for this search was a very simple one: efficiency is achieved as an effect of supply-side competition, and no form of planned intervention can accomplish levels of efficiency comparable with those of competitive markets. An interesting corollary to this premise is this: the arbiter of competition, or the judge of the productive success of the various bodies involved, is the user–consumer of the service. Thus the role of the state is restricted to macroeconomic decisions of resource allocation (i.e. the choice of the services to finance) or to the monitoring of results, thereby restoring the principle of consumer sovereignty. These 'reduced' functions of the state could also – if one wished to apply the logic of quasi-markets to its fullest extent – be left to the discretion of the citizen, who would receive lump-sum transfers (again in the form of vouchers) only generically tied to the consumption of public services; that is, without their use being specified, so that they could be spent on health treatment, or on transport, or on education, etc.

The originality of the definition of quasi-markets, the assumption that greater efficiency (internal to bodies and allocative efficiency in specific markets) necessarily results from the introduction of competition, as well as the idea that the user can be the judge of the public services provided by the supplier bodies, are all assertions that are susceptible to considerable criticism. The originality of the expression 'quasi-markets' – that is, the legitimacy of introducing another item into the taxonomy of market forms – is not a matter on which one need dwell at length, since it is almost entirely a question of terminology. In this connection I merely point out that, for almost twenty years now, several other countries have had forms of financing for the production of public services which are almost identical[4] with the British quasi-markets.

Much more complex, though not less well-known, is the problem of verifying, both theoretically and empirically, the role of competition and profit-seeking as the engine of efficiency. As is common knowledge, from a generically microeconomic point of view the main argument in favour of privatization is that because the public bodies do not operate under competitive conditions and do not seek profits, they tend to undervalue the efficient use of the resources assigned to them. In this sense the survival within quasi-markets of non-profit bodies already raises questions concerning the actual improvements in efficiency that this organizational model supposedly produces. Apart from this, however, the introduction of quasi-markets in order to enhance efficiency is accompanied by other and more serious difficulties which apply to almost every privatization plan. More specifically, it is argued (Le Grand, 1990) that the introduction of quasi-markets may create a series of costs in addition to those associated with direct public production. These costs mainly regard the necessity to create and maintain a competitive market (creation of a network of commercial and contractual exchanges, introduction of advertising and of market research), and they relate to the changed role of the state from monopoly-holder over the production of labour in certain sectors of the social services to that of monopoly-holder over the financing of service production. This change may in fact be accompanied by an increase in the cost of labour, resulting from a shift in the power relationships between trade unions and producers. The monopolist role often occupied by the state in direct service production, in fact, equips it with much greater bargaining power in its dealings with the unions than that available to the individual firms or organizations which operate in quasi-markets.

The third and last criticism of the quasi-markets formula regards the election of the user as the ultimate judge of the competition among the producers of public services. This decision raises problems as regards both the nature of the services financed by the state, and the relationships between state and producers, between producers and users, and between state and users. In Britain, all the services financed by the state belong to the vague (terminologically as well) category of 'merit goods', which comprises goods and services which the state believes it should encourage by superimposing itself on consumer choices. One of the justifications for this restriction of consumer sovereignty is the phenomenon of the distorted perception of the quality content of goods. The most frequently quoted examples of the inability of consumers to order all possible states of quality are health and education, but other types of social welfare services display the phenomenon as well. This perceptive distortion stems from the complexity of the effects produced by consumption of these services on the well-being of the consumer, and especially from the role that certain of the production factors used to realize these services may have in determining their quality. The former problem is closely connected to the risks involved in the consumption of these services, while the latter emphasizes that production factors should be used, not for signalling purposes but in order effectively to improve the quality of services. A good example of both these phenomena is provided by many of the services in the health sector, which may involve even considerable risks (to life) and for whose production extremely costly inputs (e.g. sophisticated diagnostic apparatus) may be used, although they do not effectively improve the quality of the service but rather the image (the reputation in the eyes of the user) of the organization which possesses them.

The importance of this information problem in services covered by the British quasi-markets programme is well known, both to authors who have examined the topic (e.g. Bartlett, 1991) and especially to the British government, which has in fact made some changes to the model. Certainly the most important of these changes is the care taken over the type of contract drawn up between private producers and the state, so that different kinds of contract are adopted for each sector involved in the quasi-markets project. In certain services, this instrument is flanked by a public intermediary (case manager) who helps users to choose among service producers and to decide how best to spend their vouchers.

All three thematic areas briefly indicated above – comparative analysis between the quasi-market formula and other forms of public service production-delivery, the effective improvement in efficiency offered by quasi-markets compared with direct public supply, and quality control and the risks associated with the consumption of certain public services – could be fruitful areas of inquiry. Analysis of them all, however, is precluded here for reasons of space, and I shall deal with only the third: namely, the possible role of cognitive–computational constraints on consumer decision processes in determining the success or failure of the quasi-markets model. To this end, once I have conducted more detailed examination of the role of weak demand in influencing public policy decisions, I shall examine one of the markets affected by the British reform – the family practitioner service – as providing a case for empirical verification.

2 MERIT GOODS AND INFORMATION

As I have already mentioned, the quasi-markets reform has involved only those services which belong to the heterogeneous and vague category of merit goods. This in turn is a subset of the broader category of publicly produced private goods. Common to both these taxonomic classes is the fact that the services belonging to them are individual demand goods; that is, goods which permit perfect exclusion and which may generate competition for their consumption. Since the reasons for public intervention in the production of these services are well-known, following D. Bös (1986) I shall mention only the principal ones:

1. They are essential goods ; the essential character of these goods derives from the fact that their suppression would lead to the partial or total collapse of an economy. From this point of view, the infrastructural nature of these goods means that they closely resemble pure public goods in that at least some of the benefits that ensue from their production and consumption tend to propagate through society as a whole in the form of diffused externalities. There are numerous examples of such goods with the capacity to generate positive externalities: apart from the services subject to quasi-markets reform, like health and education, they include

transport, energy production, in certain cases insurance, savings banks, and so on.

2. They are goods which permit the implementation of redistributive policies. This is the argument which comes closest to Musgrave's original formulation of merit wants, and it relates most closely to the point made above concerning cognitive perceptions. The delivery of free services, or at any rate at prices lower than both market prices and production costs, is a redistributive policy instrument which implicitly incorporates the assumption of insufficient information-processing capacity among individuals belonging to disadvantaged social groups. As Musgrave himself explains:

While consumer sovereignty is the general rule, situations may arise, within the context of a democratic community, where an informed group is justified in imposing its decision upon others. ... The advantages of education are more evident to the informed than the uninformed, thus justifying compulsion in the allocation of resources to education; interference in the preference patterns of families may be directed at protecting the interest of minors. (Musgrave, 1959, p. 14)

This may also account for the decision to intervene via the supply of merit goods in order to correct possible cognitive–evaluative distortions in consumers. Musgrave notes:

In the modern economy, the consumer is subject to advertising, screaming at him through the media of mass communication and designed to sway his choice rather than to give complete information. Thus, there may arise a distortion in the preference structure that needs to be counteracted. (Ibid.)

Of course, perceptive correction could also be accomplished by the normative regulation of advertising, an instrument which often replaces and sometimes flanks public supply. It should be stressed, however, that Musgrave starts from the hypothesis of a democratic state in which collective choices are made on the basis of a preference measurement mechanism which, although not unanimous, is at least majoritarian. This specification obviously does not resolve the complex problem of the interaction between individual preferences and collective decisions implicit in the assumption of informational–cognitive distortion, as justification for state intervention. Discussion of this problem would be beyond the scope of this article; nonetheless it should not be dismissed too casually because, as we shall see, it will return to our attention during discussion of the limits of the quasi-markets formula.

3. They are goods which permit the implementation of allocative policies. This argument principally concerns those services which involve natural monopolies and which may give rise to predatory behaviour. In the specific case of quasi-markets, it is less likely that this type of situation will arise, even though access to certain services is closely constrained by local factors which may generate outright position monopolies. A good example is provided by the service used here as a case study, namely the family practitioner service. Another example is the school, especially at the secondary level.

    As in the previous case, direct intervention may be replaced by the normative instrument – for example, by introducing a controlled price regime. The most evident of the problems associated with this policy is that price regulation must be accompanied by parallel definition of the qualitative–quantitative content of the good on offer. Of course, the setting of production standards, above all ensuring that they are respected, is a difficult undertaking – and especially as regards services which are typically characterized as 'complex'. Even though it is by no means proven that direct production resolves the problems of quality monitoring and of distributive equity, one may legitimately presume that a private producer will favour production choices that enable it to come as close as possible to its optimal strategy, which may only coincidentally match that which has been decided by the community represented by the state.

In summary of the argument so far, it is evident that as regards both these reasons – redistributive as well as allocative – for public intervention in service production, the role of information is crucial. More specifically, the central role of information stems from the twofold assumption that producers are perfectly informed about the qualitative contents of the goods they produce and that, as a result of market competition and selection, they are also the best informed concerning the efficient use of resources in their productive processes. Competition over access to resources should therefore guarantee, at least in the long run, the survival only of the best producers – that is, those that have implemented the most efficient form of production.

This supposed informational dominance by producers combined with the assumption of consumers' insufficient information-processing capacity generates an interesting paradox: on the one hand it is deemed desirable to protect consumers against possible 'abuses' by producers; on the other, it seems advisable to preserve the advantages in terms of efficiency that private production allegedly yields. As the following case-study will show, the attempt by the quasi-markets model to achieve these two objectives raises numerous problems.

3   THE BRITISH REFORM OF THE FAMILY PRACTITIONER MARKET

The reform of the British National Health Service (BNHS) was set out in 1990 by a government White Paper (HMSO, 1990) drawn up by the Ministry of Health, the contents of which became law in 1991. The White Paper envisaged comprehensive reform of the services produced by the health sector, with especial reference to the organization of hospitals, the family doctor service, and the Scottish, Welsh and Northern Irish health systems. I shall restrict myself here to illustration of the family practitioner market, since in my opinion it represents a good example of the application of the quasi-markets model. The principal innovations made to the family practitioner service are the following:

1.   Family practitioners take on a sort of 'managerial' function whereby they must help patients in their decisions – that is, guide their choices of health service use – and manage the available health resources in the best manner possible.[5]

2.   The per-patient fee paid by the state to the doctor becomes the most important item in his or her income (equal to almost 70%).

3.   Patients are assisted in their choice (or change) of doctor by two innovations: the family practitioner is obliged to provide comprehensive information on the service offered; the procedure that patients must follow to change doctors is streamlined by the abolition of the Family Practitioner Committee (FPC).[6]

4.   A system of permanent auditing is introduced in order to ensure high quality standards in health care.

5.   In order to reduce spending on medicines, and more in general in order to restrict overall expenditure on the hospital and clinical services decided by the family practitioner, each health centre receives a fixed budget, the amount of which is decided on a year-by-year basis and according to the overall resources available for each of the fourteen health regions into which the country is divided. The criteria determining the allocation of resources at the regional level depend on the features of the population served, and they are submitted for approval by consultative bodies elected by the doctors themselves.

6.   The overall number of family practitioners is fixed by the state, and the

number of members sitting on the Family Practitioner Committee is reduced from 30 to 11.

All these changes introduced by the reform are important; but the fixing of doctors' budgets certainly warrants more detailed examination since it is the most innovative aspect of the British quasi-markets model. It should first be pointed out that the reform prescribed a period of transition to the new organizational arrangement, with the budget rules applying initially only to doctors with proven administrative skills. In what follows, my analysis will refer solely to those doctors responsible for managing their own budgets; that is, those actually affected by the innovative aspects of the reform.

The budget of each doctor – which comprises money for medical prescriptions and hospital services – is decided by the Regional Health Authority on the basis of guidelines provided by the Ministry of Health. It consists of three funds:

–   a component relative to hospital services and financed out of the fund for the local hospital and health service which each RHA receives from the government. The amount of money that each doctor receives depends on the number of his/her patients adjusted to take account of socio-demographic features (age, percentage of the elderly in the total number of patients, economic features of the district, etc.);
–   a component for routine and special running costs, as well as for improvements to the surgery, proportional to the resources that the FPC has earmarked for the purpose;
–   a component for medical prescriptions allocated out of the fund for medicines administered by each RHA. In this case too, the criteria determining the budget of each doctor depend on the number of patients and other indicators, such as the average spending on medicine in the region.

The two most important funds – the first and the third – are determined by the number of patients, although they are adjusted according to a number of simple socio-demographic indicators. Thus, general practitioners with more patients on their registers will be those with the more favourable budget constraint in the absolute sense, although, in theory, the relative constraint (i.e. per patient) should be the same for everyone.

This, however, is only true in abstract terms, because the amount of resources – both pharmacological and, more generally, diagnostic and therapeutic – may be influenced, even decisively, by the clinical characteristics of the doctor's patients. Furthermore it is important to stress that among the incentives for the practitioners to reduce their spending on medicines one of the most important is founded on the possibility, recognized by the law, to use the budget surplus to buy diagnostic machinery, and more in general to invest the money saved to improve the surgeries' quality. This opportunity can be obviously seen as an indirect way to increase the practitioners' disposable income, and it may therefore produce perverse effects on the practitioners' recruitment strategies. As has been stressed, it is a matter of fact that a population of elderly patients with chronic health problems requires a higher amount of resources than a population of equal size but consisting of healthy young people. Therefore, in order to obtain a greater budget surplus, practitioners may try to recruit only 'low effort patients'.

Examination of the points illustrated above shows that the reform of the family practitioner system contains all the distinguishing characteristics of the quasi-markets model. It therefore provides an interesting empirical case for appraisal of the advantages and disadvantages of the model. More specifically, if we summarize the innovative features of quasi-markets we find that most of them are present in the reform of the family practitioner service. Distinguishing between quasi-market features and the information and equity considerations mentioned above, we have:

Government objectives:
1a)   promoting competition among producers;
2a)   shifting from a role as the direct producer of services to the position of financier–consultant;
3a)   reducing real costs.

Equity problems and informational features:
1b)   existence of complex information asymmetries;
2b)   the difficulty of assessing the quality of the service;
3b)   the difficulty of ensuring equal levels of qualitative–quantitative use of the service;
4b)   the risk of patient selection by doctors.

The promotion of competition among producers relies mainly on innovations 1, 2 and 3; the government's role as to financier–consultant is to be brought about by 4, 6 and partly 3; the reduction of costs should be made possible by innovations 5 and 6.

The problem of information asymmetries stems mainly from the introduction of innovations 1, 3 and 5; the difficulty of making correct assessment of the qualitative level of the service arises from innovations 1, 5 and rather curiously (as we shall shortly see) from the requirement that doctors must provide information; finally, the problem of equity (points 3b and 4b) is caused principally by the introduction of innovations 1, 2 and 5.

These complex interactions among the various features of the reform of the family practitioner service on the one hand, and the role of information and the goal of respecting the equity principle on the other, require detailed and rather complex analysis. Figures 16.1 and 16.2 should help to clarify matters.

Figure 16.1 The General Practitioners market information flow

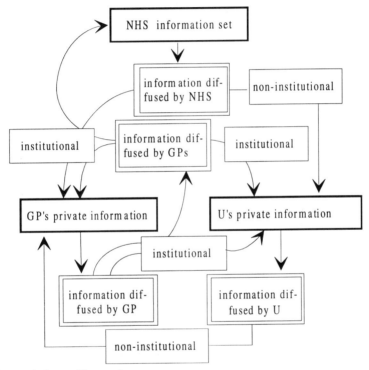

GP = generic doctor; U = generic user

Figure 16.1 provides a simplified diagram of the information flow circulating in the market for the service supplied by the family practitioner. Inspection of the figure reveals immediately the considerable complexity of the information flows which tie the doctors to the users of the service and to the other health structures.

More specifically, the figure plots three 'institutional' and 'non-institutional' circuits, where by 'institutional' is meant flows explicitly envisaged by the government reform.

It should be stressed that the reform does not prescribe the production and diffusion of specific information, only institutional vehicles for the transmission of information.

It is thus possible to distinguish between the information sets possessed by each agent participating in the market and the information sets which each agent, or group of agents, decides to transmit.

The result, therefore, is that the generic GP – given that the government formally encourages him/her to produce information for his/her patients – decides to transmit an information subset taken from his/her private set of information. This will follow two different institutional flows and feed into the information set transmitted by doctors and the private information sets of his/her clients. Likewise, the Family Practitioner Committee, the BNHS, and the family practitioners themselves, as members of the auditing committee, are obliged to supply information which flows into the doctors' private information sets.

Alongside these official information circuits, at least two important non-institutional information flows can be identified. These transmit, respectively, information from the BNHS structures to individual users, and from individual patients to individual doctors. The former of these two flows consists of the information that each user may add to his/her own information set by conducting a personal information search in one of the various health system structures.

The latter flow consists of the information that the patient gives to his/her doctor in order to ensure that the doctor makes an accurate diagnosis and prescribes the appropriate therapy.

The importance of these various information flows is evident when one passes to analysis of the process of resources allocation, thorough understanding of which requires analysis of the role of information in this particular market.

As Figure 16.2 shows, users must make two main choices on the basis of the information made available to them by the health system: first, they must choose a family practitioner; second, they must decide which specialist structure to use if they require specialized treatment (for example, which hospital to go to if they need an operation)

Whereas the first of these choices is only direct, in that it is made by the user in first person, in the case of the second choice the patient can either decide directly or consult his/her doctor. Users thus act on their own in coping with uncertainty concerning the doctor's professional skills (that is, uncertainty over the quality of the service), while they can rely on the doctor's help in subsequent decisions. Obviously, therefore, the first decision – which doctor to choose – is absolutely crucial, since a bad choice at the first decision stage may have a chain effect on all subsequent choices, with results that may even prove traumatic for the patient.

Figure 16.2 Resource allocation process

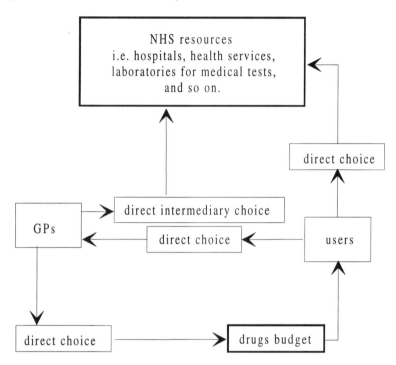

It seems that the British government is aware of this problem, since it has tried to deal with it by using three principal instruments: encouraging family practitioners to produce and distribute information about their services; allowing users to change doctors without going through complicated bureaucratic procedures; and introducing auditing committees to monitor family practitioners. Unfortunately, the effectiveness of the first two measures is mitigated by three factors: (i) the differing capacities of users to handle information; (ii) the degree of effective substitutability among family practitioners; (iii) the rigidity of the market for family practitioners, the number of whom is fixed by the government.

Regarding the first problem, the service furnished by family practitioners clearly belongs to the category of goods whose effects on the consumer are potentially complex, and whose consumption is difficult to predict *ex ante* and difficult to assess *ex post*. Hence it follows that the information made available by the doctors will not be used equally efficiently by all users, and consequently that the problem of the possibly unsatisfactory use of the service persists. It is also worth stressing that the reform implicitly prescribes, following competitive logic, that the information produced by the doctors should also serve to attract customers. Evidently, therefore, the information provided may be distorted by doctors in order to attract the largest possible number of patients. In this case, the decision-making capacity of users may be weakened rather than strengthened, because their perception of the real qualitative level of the service offered is influenced by distorted information signals. This danger is acknowledged by the government, which has stipulated that the information produced by the family practitioners should be 'subject only to safeguards necessary to protect the quality of the professional services available' (The Health Service, 1989). One notes with interest that patients should be protected 'only' as far as the quality of the professional services is concerned – a rather vague concept, given that no indication is given as to which other type of service should be supplied by the family practitioner and therefore not subject to information safeguards. I shall return to this topic in the next section.

The second problem indicated above stems mainly from the density of the geographical distribution of family practitioners. It is obvious, of course, that greater distances entail higher transport costs, so that ease of access to this type of service diminishes as the distance between the doctor's surgery and the patient's home increases. One also notes that the decision to change doctors incurs other costs for the user, who must transfer information (i.e. his/her clinical records) to the new family practitioner and spend time building a confidential relationship and learning how to interact efficiently with him/her. All these costs may decisively influence the patient's decision process and reduce his/her real opportunities for choice. One observes, moreover, that because of the mobility constraint, the family practitioner market has a structure that is more oligopolistic than anything akin to perfect competition.

Mention should once again be made of the constraint imposed by the decision to plan the number of doctors; a decision which reduces the impact of the competitive mechanism, which should promote the spontaneous appearance of microeconomic efficiency but which instead artificially reinforces the oligopolistic nature of the market.

The principal aim of the third measure to safeguard patients – the introduction of doctor auditing committees – is to fix standardized protocols of clinical treatment; that is, to establish the qualitative–quantitative contents of the service provided by the doctor. Although the application of this principle should resolve at least some of the patients' decision-making problems, and although uncertainty about the characteristics of the service offered by a specific doctor should be eliminated by standardization, once again the goal of enhancing efficiency by means of competition is not achieved. It is clear, in fact, that if the most important components of the service are standardized, there should be a consequent levelling of production choices, at least as far as the search for quality improvements is concerned. One may therefore legitimately expect competition on the supply side to shift towards relatively 'marginal' service components – like, for example, the amount of time spent in the waiting room, or the helpfulness of the doctor, or the quality of furniture in the waiting room, etc. Without wishing to underrate the importance of these aspects for the well-being of the patient, it nevertheless seems unreasonable to assume that they are the principal object of the drive for improvements in the medical service.

Returning to Figure 16.1, a number of points can be made concerning the decision process of doctors, the structure of which is only partially illustrated by the figure. The decisions taken by doctors, in fact, are not restricted solely to choice among the services available within the national health system (choices at once direct and intermediate insofar as doctors decide on behalf of their patients) or to the allocation of the medicines budget. They also and principally concern the characteristics of the service that they intend to provide. Each of these three decision contexts warrants brief analysis.

As far as choice among the services offered by the various health structures is concerned, doctors may find themselves in a state of uncertainty similar to that experienced by their patients when choosing their family practitioner. This analogy only holds in a static context, however. If we admit the existence of some kind of learning process, then the differences between doctor and patient become substantial. Whether one posits learning based only on the gathering and interpretation of information signals, or whether one assumes that subjects acquire knowledge through a process of learning by doing, the doctor enjoys an advantage over the patient. In fact, the doctor is a specialist in the analysis and interpretation of the information signals concerning a health structure. The 'average' patient, by contrast, is usually a non-specialist agent unequipped with specific tools for the decodification of information signals concerning the resources made available by the health service. Moreover, the learning by doing process available to the patient is wholly based on personal experience, whereas the doctor is able to monitor the results of the experiences recounted by all of his or her patients. Thus the nature of the two learning processes is structurally different: the doctor learns from the actions undertaken by his/her patients, while the patient learns from direct experience.

The second and third decision contexts described above – the decisions involved in the allocation of the medicines budget, and the production choices that the doctor must make – are closely connected. There are two main resources directly allocated by the doctor: the time spent visiting patients, and the budget. Both of these, however, are fixed (that is, constrained) within maximum limits by the government. Consequently, the doctor's main task is to reconcile limited resources with the needs of the individual patient. A distinctive feature of this production process is the fact that the environmental factors which may condition its outcome are at least in part internal to the actors using the service; that is, they coincide with the clinical features of those who benefit from the service. As I have already mentioned in discussion of the criteria applied in drawing up the budget, the type of patient concerned influences the complexity and difficulty of resources allocation. A further point is that the advantage gained by the doctor from the optimization of this process is wholly negligible.[7] Whether or not the doctor has prescribed the right medicine, whether or not s/he has provided the correct treatment to patients effectively in need of it, is entirely irrelevant to the determination of his/her level of income – unless the market, i.e. the users, 'punishes' the inept doctor by changing to a more efficient one. Even more important is the fact that no bonus is offered to doctors who take on difficult patients rather than look for an optimal clientele composed only of healthy individuals with minimal therapeutic and pharmacological needs.[8]

This latter problem partly links with the analysis conducted earlier, and it is of crucial importance for the entire analysis of the quasi-markets formula – which is carried out in the next section together with a brief summary of the argument so far.

4   THE ADVANTAGES AND DISADVANTAGES OF THE QUASI-MARKETS FORMULA: AN ANALYSIS AND COMPARISON WITH THE FAMILY PRACTITIONER SERVICE

In the previous section I briefly illustrated the salient features of the British reform of the family practitioner service and its main weaknesses, which can summarized as follows:

1.   The introduction of increased competition among doctors – in order to encourage the efficiency and the effectiveness of the service – is vitiated by the persistence of oligopolistic features in the market which may give rise to collusive behaviour among doctors practising in the same health district.

2. The creation of auditing committees may provoke rigidities in supply and further restrict competition in the market.
3. The imperfect competition nature of the market, combined with severe information asymmetries between doctor and patient, as well as the complex[9] nature of the service supplied, may induce doctors to alter their productive choices in favour of aspects of the service characterized by relatively low production costs, low or zero therapeutic value, with powerful promotional impact[10] (an elaborately furnished surgery, a glamorous secretarial service, etc.).
4. The absence of correctives to purely market rewards (doctors who are able to recruit more patients with fewer medical needs are more advantaged than those who accept more medically demanding patients) may induce doctors to resort to patient selection. This may therefore give rise to discrimination (even severe) against users, thereby generating grave inequalities in the qualitative–quantitative distribution of the service and also creating the paradox of rewards for opportunistic behaviour.

As well as these disadvantages, one should also stress the advantages that the quasi-markets formula offers when compared with its possible alternatives. However, it must be pointed out that, in actual fact, there are no forms of public intervention which are radically different from the model illustrated above (I am still referring, of course, to the example of the family practitioner service). Whether one looks at the organization of this service in Great Britain before its reform, or whether one analyses the equivalent service in other countries, no substantial differences emerge except in specific aspects.

For the purpose of international comparison, I refer only to the Italian case and distinguish between shared features and substantial differences between the British and Italian health care systems.

1. *Substantial differences:*
(α) measures to restrict spending on medicine;
(β) measures to restrict spending on specialist examinations, laboratory tests, etc.;
(χ) measures to enhance the quality of the service.

2. *Shared features*:
(α) criteria determining doctors' pay;
(β) supply-side planning criteria;
(χ) tasks formally assigned to the doctor;
(δ) procedures for the choice of a doctor by the patient;

(ε) criteria for the acceptance of patients by doctors (the formation and attribution of catchment areas).

I begin with examination of the novelties, principal among which are the devices introduced into the two health systems in order to curb the uncontrolled growth of spending on drugs. In Great Britain in the two-year period 1987–88, spending on drugs accounted for more than two-thirds of total expenditure by the family practitioner service. Moreover, in the years immediately prior to the reform, the growth trend of spending on medicines was on average 4 per cent higher than the rate of inflation. The situation in Italy was even worse, given that between 1980 and 1987, and calculated in terms of percentages of total health expenditure, spending on medicines rose from 12.1 to 16 per cent, while in Great Britain it rose from 9 to 10.1 per cent. Even bearing in mind that health spending in Great Britain represents a greater proportion of GDP (5.17 per cent of GDP in 1980, 5.14 per cent in 1986) than it does in Italy (4.24 per cent in 1980, 4.64 per cent in 1986), the gap between the relative weights of spending on medicines and the trends in the two countries is substantial, although at the same time it signals their shared need to curb the amount and growth of spending. To this end, Italy has decided to restrict eligibility for free prescriptions by introducing the system of a financial contribution by the patient to the cost of medicines (the so-called 'ticket').

Therefore, in the Italian case too, one may speak of some sort of market corrective adopted in order to introduce a proxy for the medical costs sustained by the community into the consumer's utility function. Apart from the fact that in Italy the prices of medicines are decided by the government and that the device of a quasi-price on the demand side has therefore been superimposed on outright planning logic on the production–supply side, with all the incoherences and distortions that this creates,[11] the basic difference is that in Britain the patient has replaced the doctor as arbiter of consumption choices regarding medicines. In other words, Great Britain has attempted to make doctors perceive medicines as a scarce resource, while Italy has preferred to transmit this constraint directly to patients.

This difference reveals diverse normative attitudes to the role of the doctor. At the same time it has important economic repercussions, at both the aggregate and micro levels. The reform of the British health sector entirely endorses the assumption that users are unable to process information about the effects of medicines – an assumption which I previously examined in discussion of Musgrave's view of merit goods, and which gives the doctor sole responsibility in deciding the level of medical consumption by the patient. In Italy, however, this assumption seems weaker, since patients are required to take cognizance of a budget constraint on the consumption of medicines. In actual fact, this consequence of the introduction of the ticket is an almost wholly theoretical one, because in practice patients are in any case constrained in their choice by the prescriptions issued by doctors, who may decide to reduce their patients' consumption of medicines regardless of their wishes. The Italian measure is therefore a typical compromise and seems principally intended to prevent the onset of a perverse cycle of fictitious consumption of medicines prescribed and collected at the chemist's but not actually used, rather than restrict the level of effective consumption by means of a market mechanism.

The principal macroeconomic advantage that the British instrument of the pharmacological budget should yield, at least compared with the Italian 'ticket', is the possibility of planning the annual amount of spending on medicines with a good degree of accuracy. Of course, the other side of the coin is that this amount will remain largely invariant over time, at least as long as it is determined by 'historical' mechanisms – criteria whose downward adjustment entails high political costs and which therefore tend to be kept constant. On the other hand, and now from a microeconomic point of view, the constraint on medicine spending imposed on doctors by the British reform accentuates the brokering relationship between doctor and patient, strengthening the position of the former. Therapeutic choices may, in fact, be improperly swayed by administrative considerations which could, if excessive, produce phenomena of patient discrimination. Since doctors have to cope with the constraint of the annual availability of medicines, they may decide to draw up a list of priorities among their patients, thereby creating an implicit hierarchy obviously incompatible with any possible equity criterion and, moreover, concealed from the patients for obvious reasons of information asymmetry. Of course, this problem would diminish if the hierarchy established by the doctor was based exclusively on pathologies and clinical cases (that is, if it was a hierarchy of pathological cases not of patients). Three mechanisms ensure that the latter system predominates over the former: the first is ethical in nature, the second relates to the doctor's motives, and the third obeys the competitive logic envisioned by the reform.

As regards the application of an ethical code governing choices in the allocation of medicines, it seems reasonable to suppose that doctors tend to obey a common moral system from which any extra-clinical consideration should be excluded. This ethical code should be reinforced by the lack of incentives for unjust discrimination (that is, behaviour not guided by the hierarchy of pathologies). The third mechanism is the only one implicitly envisaged by the quasi-markets formula, and it is the weakest. The idea, in fact, is that doctors practising unfair discrimination in the allocation of medicines will be punished by the market because their patients will change doctors. The weakness of this mechanism – which has already been amply discussed – stems from the above-mentioned problem of information asymmetry. And it once again reveals the basic incoherence of the quasi-markets formula, which on the one hand (rightly) considers patients unable to make their own medicine consumption choices, but on the other attributes to them the ability to evaluate their doctor's actions, confirming their trust in him/her or taking their custom elsewhere.

Turning to analysis of the mechanisms which control spending on hospital services – and more in general everything concerning the services supplied by the national health service and in some way decided by the family practitioner – there are differences between the British and Italian cases which resemble those already reported as regards spending on medicine. In the case of hospital services, too, British doctors are subject to an availability constraint which, at least in the government's intentions, should be understood in 'managerial' terms. More specifically, the reform requires that family practitioners should be fully informed about the financing methods prescribed for the various hospital services, and that they should bargain with the hospitals in their district in order to obtain the best price for the type of treatment required by the patient. For example, the doctor may negotiate a portfolio of fixed-price contracts for specialist examinations with the hospitals. Thus patients who require urgent specialist treatment may be sent to a hospital with which their doctor has stipulated a contract. The overall saving of resources by the health system should be guaranteed by the creation of a quasi-market in which the contracting parties are the family practitioner and the hospitals.

In Italy, the hospital services prescribed by the family practitioner are also covered by a 'ticket', and the same logic applies to them as for medicines. In this case too, as we saw in that of medicines, it is the patient who must cope directly with the resource availability constraint, while the doctor's only task is to assess the clinical appropriateness of the patient's choice of health structure.

In Britain, the only difference with respect to the system of medicines allocation is the problem of the varying amounts of 'managerial' skill possessed by doctors, which, because of the system of contract bargaining with the hospitals, may have an effect on the patients' degree of well-being. Extremely able doctors may be able to win the best possible formula for access to hospitals available on the market for their patients. Conversely, doctors unskilled in market research and bargaining techniques may obtain the worst conditions for use of the same services. Once again, at the risk of repetition, the problem is the capacity of patients to compare among the contracting abilities of doctors in order to ensure that they do not receive a second-class hospital service.

The third difference between the reformed British system and the Italian system concerns measures to promote quality. This problem is not formally recognized in Italy; that is, there is no legal device which is explicitly and exclusively intended to improve the quality of the family practitioner service. In Great Britain, as we have seen, this is one of the problems that has attracted the closest government attention, resulting in the creation of the auditing committees and, more in general, the requirement that all health system facilities must produce information. I have already discussed the drawbacks and advantages of these measures; I therefore only point out that they acquire even greater importance in Britain compared with Italy because of the spirit of competition injected into the British system by the reform.

Turning finally to the similarities and differences between the British reformed system and the Italian system, one notes first that there are certainly more similarities between the two systems than there are differences. In particular, both systems adopt a quite similar mechanism of payments to doctors mainly based on the number of patients, with no corrective available to reward those who cater to a particularly demanding clientele. In this connection, one notes that doctors in both Italy and Britain must respect fixed surgery hours. They must therefore be indifferent to the characteristics of their patients, given that the amount of service to be supplied is predetermined. This applies mostly to the Italian case, less so to the British one because of the effects of the budget constraint that I have repeatedly mentioned above. On the other hand if we consider the relationship that ties the surgery access time to the patients' degree of clinical difficulty, we can suppose that some form of perverse incentive toward users selection exists also in the case of the Italian model. It is in fact reasonable to believe that a patient afflicted with a complex pathology should require longer and more frequent medical examinations than a healthy one. This means that an increase in the percentage of the 'high effort patients' should increase the ratio between the total number of patients and the average waiting time, producing a deterioration in the quality of the service offered by the surgery and a consequent loss of competitiveness. On the contrary, an increase in the percentage of the 'low effort patients' should improve the quality of the surgery and its competitiveness, allowing the practitioner to obtain a greater number of patients and consequently also an higher wage.

Another feature common to both systems is the almost perfect planning of supply. Both in Italy and in Britain, the number of doctors is centrally fixed; which amounts to the formative determination of the maximum quantity of service delivered. In this case too, the consequences of this feature of the two systems are more significant in Britain than in Italy. There is no need to reiterate the undesirable effects that may arise in the British quasi-market as a result of the oligopolistic structure artificially imposed on the service.

The final feature common to both systems relates to procedures for selection of a doctor by patients. In both systems in fact, patients are formally free to choose any family practitioner[12] they wish, and they may also change doctors if they are dissatisfied.

5   AN EMPIRICAL SURVEY ON MICRO DATA: THE PROVINCE OF TRENTO CASE-STUDY

The large number of analogies between the Italian and the British systems allows Italian data to be used in empirical verification of some of the questions raised in previous sections. The following main issues will be analysed:

1.   Do differences among patients really influence practitioners' salaries?
2.   Is expenditure on medicines really influenced by patient characteristics?
3.   Does some form of patient selection exist?

In Italy, at the national level, micro-data on the family practitioner market are not available, but some local authorities have created quite interesting databases on this service. I shall illustrate the case of the province of Trento, which is interesting not only because of the good quality of the data available but also because this region can be considered representative of quite a large part of the north of Italy.

The data refer to 1992 and concern 284 practitioners[13] who were distributed among 11 local health authorities (USL) and 49 health precincts (*ambiti*).[14] The distribution of practitioners per local health authority and the average number of patients per practitioner is given in Table 16.1.

Table 16.1 shows that there are great differences in the number of practitioners per USL and also that the average number of patients is rather non-homogeneous: the difference between the maximum average number of patients (USL5) and the minimum (USL4) is in fact 312, which means that there is a difference of about 20 per cent between these two local authorities.

Female patients amount to around 52 per cent of the total population, while female practitioners represent only 12 per cent of the practitioner population. Apart from sex, the only variable in the database that discriminates among patients is age.[15]

Table 16.1   Average number of patients per practitioner per USL

Local health authorities	Avg. number of patients	Std. Dev.	Number of GPs
USL1	1496	190	9
USL2	1434	163	7
USL3	1521	166	15
USL4	1211	348	29
USL5	1523	296	81
USL6	1320	352	22
USL7	1310	238	11
USL8	1366	288	26
USL9	1363	325	25
USL10	1303	404	53
USL11	1356	330	6

Table 16.2   Patients distributed by age group (means and percentages per GP)

Ages	Mean	%	Std. Dev.	Min.	%	Max.	%
from 0 to 3	8.48	0.61	16.72	0	0.00	106	7.44
4–14	91.41	6.61	54.08	7	0.51	294	20.63
15–25	228.05	16.32	65.45	54	8.93	390	22.65
26–60	739.73	53.14	191.07	174	38.33	1069	67.18
over 61	323.77	23.32	106.19	62	8.66	659	45.15

Table 16.2 comprises a possible scattering of patients' age intended to take into account the fact that older patients are usually characterized by more complex and frequent pathologies and therefore require a stronger effort by practitioners and more medicines. Table 16.2 relates to both our first and second questions, which were to verify the existence of a causal relationship between patients' characteristics and, respectively, practitioners' salaries and expenditure on medicines. In order to address the first question we must first of all measure practitioners' salaries. A simple way to do this is to consider the total number of patients actually served, because, as we have just seen, the Italian National Health Service pays a fixed amount of money per patient actually served by a general practitioner.[16] In recalling the argument of the

previous section, the main hypothesis on which to ground explanation of the level of practitioners' pay is the following:

H_1 = the larger the number of high effort patients, the greater the amount of time and effort required of the practitioner and the lower the total number of patients that can actually be served.

Note that this assumption is based on the idea that when the average number of high effort patients increases then so too does access time to the surgery; that is, patients must wait longer to be seen by the doctor. This phenomenon should diminish the competitiveness of the practitioner, reducing her/his real users stock and her/his effective salary.

The generic model chosen to explain practitioners' salaries (measured as total number of patients) is the following:

$$w = f(Z, \Psi, 1/k) \qquad\qquad [1]$$

where Z and Ψ are respectively the vector of the factors that build the practitioner's professional profile and competitiveness, and the environment characteristics vector, while k is the percentage of high effort patients served. The main hypothesis embodied in model [16.1] is that the value of the dependent variable is not solely influenced by the degree of patient 'difficulty' but also by the practitioner's therapeutic choices and by the characteristics (socio-economic and epidemiological) prevalent in each health precinct. Unfortunately, the variables that can be used to fit the model are rather naive:

Z vector: z_1 = practitioner's age;
z_2 = maximum number of patients that the practitioner is allowed to serve;[17]
z_3 = signals whether the practitioner is also a medical officer[18] (a dummy variable which takes value 1 if the practitioner is also a medical officer).
Ψ vector: $\psi_{(m)}$ = set of 49 dummy variables taking value 1 for the given precinct and value 0 for all other precincts, $((m)$ is the identification code for the precinct).
k = percentage of elderly patients (patients older than 61).

It is should be stressed that most of the independents just illustrated can be considered as weak proxies for the true factors that should influence the dependent. In particular, variables z_1 and z_3 imply the following strong assumption:

H_2 = the practitioner's age and her/his formal role are assumed as proxies of her/his professional experience and market competitiveness; it is hypothesized in particular that a qualification as a medical officer increases recruitment potential.

The variables included in vector Ψ entail only one concise but crucial assumption:

H_3 = the dummy variables used to specify each precinct are assumed to summarize all the important environmental differences among individual practitioners' markets.

Finally a last assumption is required by k:

H_4 = the greater concentration of the high effort patients is in the elderly patients group.

This assumption requires little specification since it is evident that, within a given population, the percentage of illnesses normally increases with patients' age. The results of the OLS regression are as follows:

Model 16.1 Dependent variable: total number of patients

Variable	B	SE B	Beta	T	Sig T
Ψ_9	−833.7656	252.7562	−0.1484	−3.299	0.0011
Ψ_{24}	184.5731	56.7111	0.1513	3.255	0.0013
z_1	0.2057	1.8360	0.0057	0.112	0.9109
z_2	0.9986	0.0857	0.5879	11.649	0.0000
z_3	98.5361	44.3447	0.1030	2.222	0.0271
k	−7.6991	2.8763	−0.1251	−2.677	0.0079
(Constant)	−23.5771	136.3119		−0.173	0.8628

Note:

Multiple $R = 0.6654$, $R^2 = 0.4427$, Standard Error = 251.8916, $F = 36.55$, Signif. $F = 0.0000$

For the sake of conciseness, only the values of the dummies included in the Ψ vector with a t-statistics significance higher than 0.05 are reported. On the same criterion, variable z_1, i.e. practitioner's age, could be eliminated from the model. The percentage of the dependent's variance explained by the model is about 44 per cent. The significance level of the F statistics allows rejection of the null hypothesis of absence of correlation between the dependent and the explicatives. The overall quality of the model is quite good, although not excellent. Therefore every statement made must be weighted by paying attention to the real explanatory power of the model.

Inspection of the values of the t-statistics and of the beta coefficients – subject to the well-known statistical limitations to the second of these indicators[19] – we may assign the highest role in the hierarchy of the independents to z_2, followed by ψ_9, ψ_{24}, k, and finally z_3.

The most interesting finding is that, as was to be expected, the total number of patients is in inverse ratio to the percentage of elderly patients. Also coherent with our assumptions is the sign of the coefficients calculated for all the Z vector variables.

It is more difficult to account for the influence of the environmental variables. Unfortunately, the information available on the characteristics of the people belonging to these precincts does not suggest any convincing explanation. Nor do the epidemiological data (number of old people, percentage of people belonging to high-risk groups) or the limited socio-economic data (e.g. per-capita income) give plausible explanations for the role played by these variables.

It seems reasonable to conclude from these results that a reduction in the percentage of the elderly patients is to the advantage of the practitioner, because it should increase the total number of patients and consequently also his/her level of pay.

Answering the second of our initial questions requires examination of average spending on medicines per user. The model used in this case is very similar to the previous one, apart from the exclusion of z_2 (maximum number of patients that the practitioner is allowed to serve) and the inclusion of the number of patients younger than 61 actually served by the practitioner (variable z_k).

The new model accordingly becomes:

$$\tau = f(Z_2, \Psi, 1/k) \qquad [2]$$

where τ is the average spending on medicines per user and Z_2 is the new vector of the practitioners' individual characteristics.

The assumptions for k and for the variables included in vector Ψ are the same as those in the previous model, while the assumptions for the Z_2 vector become:

   $H_5 =$ a practitioner's personal and professional profile can influence
          therapeutic choices; it can therefore be assumed as a (weak) proxy

for the therapeutic style (average number of prescriptions and average spending medicines) of each practitioner;

H_6 = by issuing a larger number of medical prescriptions, practitioners can enhance their competitiveness, thereby increasing the number of users actually served.

While assumption H_5 requires little comment, hypothesis H_6 requires brief explanation. Bearing in mind the quite complex problems of information asymmetry that characterize the general practitioner market, it seems plausible that one of the more understandable information signals available to a user concerning the quality of the service offered is the number of medicines that her/his doctor prescribes for her/him. It is also reasonable to assume that this phenomenon is well known to practitioners who use prescriptions as a means to attract more patients.

The model yields the following results:

Model 16.2 *Dependent variable: average spending on medicines per patients;*

Variable	B	SE B	Beta	T	Sig. T
ψ_{12}	−86141.0072	38157.9665	−0.1184	−2.257	0.0248
ψ_{31}	−34250.6691	17177.7162	−0.1038	−1.994	0.0472
ψ_{41}	51100.1876	16406.3174	0.1621	3.115	0.0020
z_1	−302.1323	362.9872	−0.0461	−0.832	0.4059
z_3	−2848.7426	9238.1413	−0.0162	−0.308	0.7580
z_k	40.0584	17.6444	0.1255	2.270	0.0240
k	5528.8140	621.3296	0.4916	8.898	0.0000
(Constant)	86109.6065	23163.6654		3.717	0.0002

Note:

Multiple R=0.5098, R Square=0.2599, Standard Error=53152.3989, F=13,8023, Signif F=0.0000

The overall quality of the model is poorer than that of the previous one. The t-statistics significance indicates that variables z_1 and z_3 should both be removed, and therefore that their role in explanation of the dependent is negligible. By contrast, both z and z_k are significant and positively correlated with spending on medicines, in accordance with our assumptions. Note that the influential environmental variables have changed, although, in this case too, their role is not clear.

The results appear to confirm the most important of our initial assumptions. In particular, it appears that a larger number of elderly patients increases average expenditure on medicines. This largely predictable result should not reflect on the recruitment strategy of Italian practitioners, but it could be influential on British practitioners in that it has important effects on drug budget flexibility.

The results so far described can be of help in answering the last of our initial question: that is, whether it is possible to observe any real form of user selection within the sample. Assuming that the best strategy to maximize pay and to minimize spending on medicines is to accept only young patients, i.e. avoid elderly ones, is there any practitioner in our sample with a list of patients comprising a percentage of old people significantly lower than the average?

In our sample, the average percentage of patients older than 61 per practitioner is 23 per cent, and the standard deviation is about 5 per cent. One way to verify whether a form of 'cream-skimming' exists, is to select sub-samples with a special composition of the number of elderly patients. Table 16.3 gives the figures for four arbitrary sub-samples:

1. practitioners less than 15 per cent of whose patients are elderly;
2. practitioners less than 18 per cent of whose patients are elderly;
3. practitioners more than 26 per cent of whose patients are elderly;
4. practitioners more than 33 per cent of whose patients are elderly.

Table 16.3   Average spending, prescriptions, practitioners' age and number of patients (sub-samples)

	N	Average expense (It. liras)		Average receipts		Average practitioner age		Average total patients	
		Mean	Std. Dev.	Mean	Std. Dev.	Mean	Std. Dev.	Mean	Std. Dev.
For Entire Pop.		229838	61699	6.67	1.65	46.09	9.32	1391.44	333.29
>15% elderly	270	232557	61650	6.74	1.65	46.35	9.47	1397.08	331.39
<15% elderly	14	177407	33353	5.24	0.84	41.21	2.75	1282.71	363.77
>18% elderly	244	236376	61593	6.83	1.64	46.57	9.71	1400.83	331.27
<18% elderly	40	189956	45688	5.69	1.33	43.20	5.69	1334.15	344.04
<26% elderly	200	218295	57115	6.33	1.45	45.02	8.41	1397.41	329.44
>26% elderly	84	256864	63886	7.45	1.81	48.64	10.81	1377.47	343.69
<33% elderly	267	225388	58323	6.55	1.53	45.80	9.08	1398.94	320.58
>33% elderly	17	299742	72526	8.54	2.23	50.59	11.92	1273.71	490.38

Inspection of Table 16.3 reveals that an increase in the percentage of elderly patients produces, as expected, an increase both in average spending on medicines per patient and in the average number of prescriptions per patient. Less predictable, however, were the values for average practitioner age and for the average number of patients served by each practitioner. The data in Table 16.3 seem to show the existence of a positive relationship between the patients' age and the practitioner's age, at least within the sub-samples considered here. More precisely, and looking at extreme situations, there exists some form of relationship between young doctors and young patients as well as between old practitioners and elderly patients. A possible and reasonable explanation for this phenomenon is that young doctors are building their practices and therefore find it easier to recruit 'new' patients, that is, young people. Similarly, old practitioners have their longstanding patients, probably recruited many years previously and growing old with their practitioner.

Confirmation for this intuition is provided by the average number of patients, which is lower in both the two extreme sub-samples and higher in the middle ones. This finding may be due to different practitioner recruitment strategies, which are presumably intense but only initially for younger practitioners and progressively decrease for older ones, who feel less motivated to increase or even to maintain their number of patients.[20]

Figure 16.3 Distribution of percentages of elderly patients

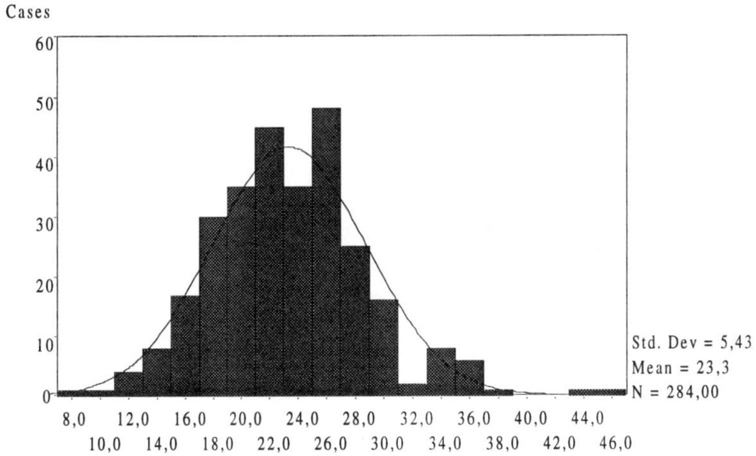

The general conclusion to be drawn from the foregoing analysis, therefore, is that no significant patient selection was conducted in 1992 by practitioners in the province of Trento. On the other hand, it is not possible entirely to exclude the existence of 'cream-skimming' in the sample. This suspicion can be checked by considering a further, very restricted, sub-sample consisting of practitioners older than the average but with a small number of elderly patients.

This sub-sample could include practitioners at least older than 47 (bearing in mind that average practioner age is 46.09) and with a small percentage of elderly patients, which also in this case can only be arbitrarily chosen. On inspecting the distribution of the percentages of elderly patients reported in Figure 16.3, we can fix this second arbitrary threshold at 20 per cent, which is slightly less than average and fits a reasonable number of practitioners.

The figures for this new sub-sample, which comprises only 13 practitioners, are given in Table 16.4.

Table 16.4   Practitioners older than 47 with less than 20% elderly patients

Variable	Mean	Std. Dev.	Minimum	Maximum
Avg. receipts	6.05	1.05	4	8
Percentage elderly users	18.05	1.53	15.94	19.98
Avg. total patients	1627.08	303.80	712	1815
Avg. spending (It. lire)	201175.69	40364.64	122.051	270.534

The crucial information contained in Table 16.4 is the average total number of patients served by the practitioners in this small sub-sample. Recalling the value of this variable for the entire population, i.e. 1391, one notes that the practitioners belonging to the reduced sub-sample have about 17 per cent more patients than the average practitioner (i.e. 17 per cent higher earnings). Furthermore, this advantage, even if reduced, persists if we make a comparison with the sub-sample of practitioners aged more than 47: for this sample the average total number of patients is in fact 1515.

Can we conclude that the thirteen practitioners in the micro-sample really indulge in patient selection? Obviously we cannot, although there are good grounds for suspecting that they do. It is also worth noting that we have considered only one among the various possible 'critical' sub-samples (for example, we could have analysed sub-samples within each health precinct). However, if analysis had been extended to include local pecularities it is reasonable to suppose that other situations would arise in which some form of cream-skimming was suspected.

6 CONCLUSIONS

The main conclusion to emerge from the foregoing analysis of the quasi-markets model applied to the family practitioner service concerns the difficulty of reconciling the 'paternalistic' principle of the superimposition of public decisions on private consumption decisions with the endeavour to improve efficiency by introducing the market mechanism. The compromise solution of the British quasi-markets system raises a number of doubts concerning the possible perverse effects that may derive from the pursuit of efficiency based on competition among doctors and bargaining between doctors and hospitals. This said, some of the innovations introduced by the British reform – in particular, that of appointing the doctor as the actor responsible for the management, financial too, of health resources – seem in many respects as being more rational than those implicit in the Italian health-care system. The device of the Italian 'ticket', in fact, is highly questionable, especially as regards spending on medicines, the growth of which seems almost entirely due to increases in prices, not in consumption.

The lack of applied studies of at least some of the perverse effects that the quasi-market of the family practitioner service may produce precludes any firmer conclusion than those tentatively set out in this study.

NOTES

1. An earlier version of this paper appeared as 'Quasi-Markets and Uncertainty: The Case of General Practice Service', Discussion Paper, no. 3, Università di Trento, Dipartimento di Economia, 1993. It was presented at a seminar at the Department of Economics of the University of Trento and it has been discussed with members of the Department of Economics of the University of Bristol. In particular I have benefited from extensive discussions with John Broome, Ian Jewitt and Carol Propper. Responsibility for errors or omissions remains mine alone.

2. Most notably: the Education Reform Act of 1988; the Griffiths Report on Personal Social Services of 1988, the recommendations of which led to publication of a White Paper by the Department of Health in 1989; the studies carried out in 1988–89 by the Ministry of Health which led to a radical project for reforming the health system; the Housing Act of 1988; the Housing and Local Government Act of 1989.

3. An example of this mechanism is given in the Education Reform Act of 1988 which allows parents to enrol their children at any school they wish, even outside their local government area. Schools then receive financing according to the number of their enrolments.

4. Among examples relative to the public sector perhaps the most important is the American health system and social welfare system. As regards the former, one can cite the home

nursing service whereby the state acts as both financial mediator and guarantor between the client and the body providing the service. An example in the private sector is the distribution by companies of luncheon vouchers to their employees, rather than provide a canteen service.

5. Amongst other things, doctors are required to be fully informed concerning the financing methods used by the hospital services which they suggest their patients.

6. The Family Practitioner Committee is a body which intermediates between the family doctor and his/her patients as well as monitoring the doctor's work. Each committee is responsible for a particular district. After the reform, the number of members was reduced from thirty to eleven, comprising four professionals (a doctor, a dentist, a pharmacist, and a professional nurse), five non-professional members appointed by the Regional Health Authority, a government representative, and a executive director chosen by the government representative and by the non-professional members of the committee.

7. Apart from the number of patients served, the only other incentive envisaged by the reform is the awarding of bonuses to doctors who carry out specific clinical programmes, for example, a vaccination campaign. Fixed 'bonuses' are also available for medical surgeries located in depressed urban areas or in rural areas with extremely low population densities.

8. The problem of patient selection is widely reported in the literature. See for example Glennester (1991) who provides a survey of the main writings on the subject, notably Akerlof (1970), Pauly (1986), Barr (1987) and Summers (1989).

9. The nature of the service provided by the family practitioner has already been discussed. More specifically, it can be conceived as divided among several outputs which are only partly interconnected. These outputs included diagnostic and prognostic activity, directing patients to other health-care structures, direct therapy, the prescribing of medicine, etc.

10. On the problems involved in assessment of the quality of the service supplied by the family practitioner see the brief bibliography attached to this article. More specifically, one may imagine a continuum ranging from Lancaster's original definition of goods as a sum of 'characteristics' to works which more specifically address the case of health services.

11. It is worth stressing that the increase in spending on medicines seems due, not to a growth of consumption but to price increases. In Italy, the consumption of medicines between 1980 and 1987 remained practically constant while between 1980 and 1989 the annual increase in prices was 17 per cent – that is, 7 percentage points higher than the inflation trend. Thus the introduction of the ticket in Italy was intended more to re-equilibrate spending on medicines than to curb it.

12. Of course, the patients' freedom of choice is restricted to doctors practising in their catchment area. For example, in Italy this area corresponds to the so-called 'ambito territoriale' (health precinct), which is usually smaller than the area covered by the USL (local health authority). The only exception to this rule is when the user resides in a municipal district that includes more than one health precinct, in this case the user can choose a practitioner belonging to every precincts included in the area of her/his municipal

district. On this and more in general on legal aspects of the Italian family practitioner service, see D.P.R., 28 September 1990, no. 260.

13. Excluded from the total number of general practitioners active in the province of Trento in 1992 are the 16 cases of practitioners with fewer than 300 patients. This is because below this minimum number of patients we find only very young practitioners (first year of practice) or very old ones (last year) whose characteristics cannot be considered 'normal' for the sample.

14. The ambiti are geographical areas whose size is fixed by law. The criteria followed in determining the size of an ambito is exclusively the number of inhabitants, which must be at least 1500.

15. The database comprises another interesting variable concerning patients, namely the number of low-income users exempt from payment of the ticket. Unfortunately, this information has not been yet checked and therefore has not been used for obvious reasons of quality.

16. The Italian National Health Service payment system for the general practitioners is made up of two main components: a fixed component which is determined by professional seniority (number of years of service) and a variable one given by the number of patients actually served.

17. The maximum number of patients that a practitioner is allowed to accept is fixed by the Health Authority at either 1800 or 1500. The theoretical minimum number of patients is decided by each practitioner, but it cannot be lower than 500. Obviously the minimum effective number can be lower.

18. In Italy, general practitioners can also simultaneously work as medical officers.

19. The beta coefficients are calculated from the regression coefficients in the following standard way:

$$B_k = \beta_k \left(\frac{S_k}{S_y} \right)$$

where Sk is the standard deviation of the kth independent variable. As is well known, the beta values are contingent on the other independent variables in the equation, and they are affected by the correlation between the dependents. For these reasons, the beta coefficients cannot be considered to be good indicators of the individual importance of the given variable in determining the dependent.

20. In the Italian health system, the practioner's pay increases automatically with professional seniority. Therefore, the marginal advantage deriving from an increase in patient numbers presumably decreases.

REFERENCES

Akerlof, G. (1970), 'The Market for Lemons: Qualitative Uncertainty and the Market Mechanism', *Quarterly Journal of Economics*, **84**, pp. 488–500.

Barr, N. (1987), *The Economics of the Welfare State*, London: Weidenfeld.

Bartlett, W. (1991), 'Quasi Markets and Contracts: A Markets and Hierarchies Perspective on NHS Reforms', *Public Money and Management*, **11** (3), pp. 53–61.

Bös, D (1986), *Public Enterprise Economics*, Amsterdam: North Holland.

Coase R.H. (1937), 'The Nature of the Firm', *Economica*, **4**, pp. 386–405.

De Ste Croix, R. (1992), *Can Quality be Assured in an Uncertain World?*, Studies in Decentralization and Quasi-Markets, Working Paper no. 10, Bristol: SAUS Publications.

Elster, J. and J.E. Roemer (eds) (1991), *Interpersonal Comparisons of Well-Being*, New York: Cambridge University Press.

Fisher, F.M. and K. Shell (1971), 'Taste and Quality Change in the Pure Theory of the True Cost of Living Index', in Z. Griliches (1971).

Glennester, H. (1991), 'Quasi-Markets for Education?', *The Economic Journal*, **101** (408), pp. 1268–76.

Griliches, Z. (ed.) (1971), *Price Indexes and Quality Change: Studies in New Methods of Measurement*, Cambridge, Mass.: Harvard University Press.

Lancaster, K.J. (1966a), 'A New Approach to Consumer Theory', *Journal of Political Economy*, **74**, pp. 132–57.

Lancaster, K.J. (1966b), 'Change and Innovation in the Technology of Consumption', *American Economic Review*, **56**, pp. 14–23.

Le Grand, J. (1990), 'Quasi-markets and Social Policy', *Studies in Decentralization and Quasi-Markets*, Working Paper no. 1, Bristol: SAUS Publications.

Musgrave, R.A. (1959), *The theory of public Finance*, New York: McGraw Hill.

Pauly, M.V. (1986), 'Taxation, Health Insurance and Market Failure in the Medical Economy', *Journal of Economic Literature*, **24**, pp. 629–75.

Propper, C. (1992), 'Quasi-Markets, Contracts and Quality', *Studies in Decentralization and Quasi-Markets*, Working Paper no. 9, Bristol: SAUS Publications.

Stone, J.R.N. (1956), *Quantity and Price Indexes in National Accounts*, Paris: Organization for European Economic Cooperation.

Summers, L.H. (1989), 'Some Simple Economics of Mandated Benefits', *American Economic Review*, **79** (2), pp. 177–83.

The Health Service (1989), *Working for Patients*, London: HMSO.

17. Privatization, Non-Profit Trusts and Contracts for Healthcare Services in the UK[*]

Will Bartlett

One of the most important and long lasting institutions which formed part of the social-democratic welfare state created in the UK at the end of the Second World War was the National Health Service (NHS). This was a system of health care provision based upon the socialist principle of distribution according to need, free at the point of delivery and universal in coverage.

From its inception in 1948 the NHS was organized as a centralized administrative system of health care delivery financed by the state. Funds flowed down through the administrative hierarchy from the Ministry of Health to reach individual hospitals in the form of block grants. A parallel system of primary care was organized through the network of family doctors known as General Practitioners (GPs).

The degree of centralization should not be over-emphasized, however. There were variations in the implementation of health policies at local levels, and the professional clinical autonomy of hospital doctors was a powerful countervailing influence against central state control. In addition, GPs have all along been self-employed professionals, or organized in professional partnerships, contracted to work for the NHS. Indeed, a central issue has been the creation of suitable mechanisms to ensure that policies formulated by government would be converted into effective action by lower levels of the administrative hierarchy and by doctors in their daily clinical practice. This struggle between policy-makers and practitioners, akin to the classical principal–agent relationship between shareholders and management in private businesses (see for example Milgrom and Roberts, 1992), has provided a major impetus to continual reform and reorganization in the NHS.

When the NHS was first established, the majority of hospitals in England were put under the administration of fourteen Regional Hospital Boards. These boards employed hospital doctors, and appointed 400 Hospital

375

Management Committees to run groups of hospitals at a local level. The only exception was the teaching hospitals, which were managed by separate boards of governors directly accountable to the Ministry of Health. In 1974 this structure was extended by the creation of 90 Area Health Authorities as a second tier of administration under Regional Health Authorities (which took over from the Regional Health Boards). Doctors' employment contracts were still held at the regional level. The Areas were in turn divided into Districts which became the lowest tier of management. However, it was soon realized that this structure extended the span of control too far, and led to greatly increased administrative costs with little practical improvement in control over policy implementation. Further reorganization led to the abolition of the Area Health Authorities and the transformation of their subordinate Districts into 192 full District Health Authorities in 1982 (Ham, 1985).

Nevertheless, one of the main problems with these arrangements remained unsolved, namely the lack of effective control by policy-makers over the independent decisions of doctors. Although doctors were employees of the Regional Health Authorities, they retained full clinical autonomy, and were effectively in control of decisions over use of resources. According to a recent study, they held effective ownership of the use of beds in their own departments, and had the power to veto change (Harrison, 1994). In addition, they were able to influence the decisions of the Health Authorities, which were run on the principle of consensus management. The Griffiths report of 1983 criticized the administrative structure of the NHS on the grounds that it lacked an effective and clearly defined management function. The report recommended the appointment of general managers at all levels of the NHS to speed up decision making, and to reduce the autonomous influence of doctors over the use of resources. Implementation of the report led, in the mid-1980s, to the first moves towards increasing the role of cost-minded management in the NHS.

However, no amount of administrative reform appeared capable of overcoming the fundamental dilemma involved in the attempt to reconcile the conflicting interests of policy-makers and practitioners within a single administrative structure. As long as hospital doctors continued to exert autonomous influence and control over resource use from within the administrative hierarchy, the exercise of management power would inevitably be subject to clinical veto, given the existence of soft budget constraints. A radical solution to the problem was introduced by the NHS and Community Care Act of 1990. A key feature of these most recent measures has been a decentralization of the structure of production of secondary health services, and the establishment of a competitive 'quasi-market' for health services (Le Grand, 1991).

This decentralization has involved a variety of distinct processes including devolution of managerial responsibility to individual operating units (the 'purchaser–provider split'), and accompanying processes of marketization and privatization. There was also a parallel process of decentralization of finance for purchasing through the creation of devolved budgets held by individual GP 'fund-holders' (GPFH). Secondary health services have remained largely publicly funded, but they are now provided by a new set of autonomous NHS Trusts, led by their own general managers (Chief Executives). These Trusts remain under state ownership, but are independently managed and are in competition with one another for contracts from a variety of purchasers which include District Health Authorities, GPFHs and the private sector insurance companies.

The main ostensible objectives of the reforms were to improve the efficiency of health care delivery, increase the range of consumer choice, widen the responsiveness of the system to consumers' needs and ensure that improvements in the efficiency with which health services are delivered are not gained at the expense of equity. Whether the reforms achieve these goals depends largely upon whether the quasi-market can deal with the principal–agent relationship between policy-makers and medical practitioners. This in turn depends upon how well the quasi-market can mimic the classic conditions for efficiency of markets. Le Grand and Bartlett (1993) identify the conditions for the efficient operation of quasi-markets in terms of the degree of competition in the market structure, the quality of the information available to the market agents, the absence of offsetting transactions costs, and the development of an appropriate motivation structure and set of incentives facing individual agents and provider units. These conditions are especially problematic in the case of the new NHS owing to the nature of property rights arrangements, since although the NHS Trusts are now independently managed they remain under state ownership (see section 6 below). Equity considerations relate primarily to the possible development of opportunities for 'cream-skimming' (i.e. discrimination by providers against more expensive users) which are likely to arise where purchaser–provider contracts are based on capitation principles (as in the case of GPs) or are organised as block contracts (as in the case of many contracts signed by NHS Trusts with DHA purchasers).

In this paper I focus attention on the process of decentralization and the role of NHS Trusts, which have become the main providers of secondary health care services in the new NHS. The key question which the paper addresses this: to what extent can the decentralized institutions of NHS Trusts be expected to contribute to the success of the quasi-market reforms? In developing an answer to this question I examine the extent to which they have genuine managerial autonomy and their status as non-profit organizations; and I develop some of the building blocks of a new economic model of NHS Trusts. I also look at the way NHS Trusts as key providers interact with, and respond to, the developing and changing structure of purchasing organizations through the mechanism of purchaser–provider contracts. Finally, the paper turns to the issue of privatization. This section examines the extent to which the existing structure of partially privatized independent NHS Trusts is able to meet the requirements of a decentralized quasi-market structure. If not, is there a need for further developments involving greater private sector participation, or a even deeper degree of privatization of NHS Trusts themselves? One of the conclusions which will be derived from the analysis is that there is as yet an insufficient empirical basis for a definitive answer to these questions. The concluding section ends by suggesting a number of directions for further research.

1   DECENTRALIZATION AND NHS REFORMS

Decentralization of the NHS has involved changes in two main areas. Firstly District Health Authorities have been split into purchaser and provider units, with DHAs retaining responsibility only for purchasing health services on behalf of their resident population. Secondly, selected larger GP practices have received locally-managed budgets with which they can make decentralized purchasing decisions for patient services from NHS Trusts or private sector hospitals. These two contrasting processes have been distinguished by Glennerster and Matsaganis (1993) as respectively 'top-down' and 'bottom-up' approaches to decentralization.

The separation of DHA purchasing and providing functions was implemented in April 1991, as individual hospitals were converted into decentralized provider units. The DHA itself was split into a purchaser and a provider arm.[1] Initially, provider units (i.e. hospitals, ambulance services, community health services, etc.) remained under the management and control of the DHA (they were renamed 'Directly Managed Units' or DMUs). The purchaser–provider split took its full effect, however, as individual hospitals were transformed into organizations which were independent of the DHA, through a process of conversion of individual hospitals, or groups of hospitals and other services, into 'self-managing' NHS Trusts.

The introduction of GP fund-holding was a more gradual process. The first wave of GP fund-holders was set up on the 1st April 1991 and covered 1720 GPs in 306 practices, covering 7.5 per cent of the population. Gradually, more and more GPs are achieving fund-holding status, and in some areas they are becoming the dominant form of purchasing organization.

The essence of the decentralization is that finance of the health service remains a public responsibility, and access to health care services remains free at the point of delivery. Services are no longer provided through a system of state-owned enterprises, organized and directed centrally by the Ministry of Health through the RHAs and DHAs, but by independent NHS Trusts. Moreover, within this new system, resources are secured by provider units on a competitive basis. Independent decentralized providers enter competitive bids for contracts with decentralized purchasers. The intention of the reforms is that a decentralized quasi-market system of resource allocation should be established in the field of health care.

2   THE CREATION OF NHS TRUSTS

2.1   The legal framework

NHS Trusts are essentially public corporations. They are not charitable voluntary organizations, as can be found in other areas of social welfare such as personal social services (Bartlett, 1993). The legal framework for NHS Trusts is contained in the 1990 Health and Community Care Act, which set out their financial and other obligations. When a Trust is established it issues a prospectus dealing with various areas over which the Trust has discretion, including its overall aims, progress in arranging contracts, the way it will develop services, the quality that will be assured, its leadership and management arrangements, personnel issues, information systems and management of estates. These areas of discretion are sometimes called 'freedoms'. Most importantly, the Trust can decide upon the range and quality of services provided, the number, mix and remuneration of staff. In the early phase of development it was also expected that Trusts would be able to retain their operating surpluses for reinvestment, growth and improved staff remuneration. In practice, the Minister of Health has restricted and regulated many of these freedoms. In particular, Trusts are no longer permitted to retain their surpluses, or make investment decisions independent of government control. In fact, any surpluses that are reinvested are likely to trigger a corresponding reduction in the amount of money the government is willing to lend to the Trust for capital expenditure.

In the search for additional ways to fund expansion, Trusts are likely to turn increasingly to the private sector, and to enter into conflict with government over the range and extent of their autonomy and freedoms.

2.2   The transition: four waves of Trusts

The first wave of NHS Trusts was established on April 1st 1991; it accounted for 46000 (12 per cent) of the total number of beds in the NHS and for £1.8 billion (13.5 per cent) of total NHS revenue expenditure. A further 105 'second wave' Trusts were established in April 1992, and a third wave of 168 Trusts was established in April 1993.

The growth in the number of Trusts and the extent to which they have become the dominant providers of secondary health care in the UK has exceeded most early expectations. The extent of the transition is shown in Table 17.1:

Table 17.1   Development of NHS Trusts in the UK

	1st Wave	2nd Wave	3rd Wave	Cumulative % of total
Beds	34596	59930	92071	77%
Employees	106531	138974	242289	61%

Source:
The Third Newchurch Guide to NHS Trusts, London: Newchurch & Co. Ltd., 1993; Health and Personal Social Services Statistics for England, 1993 edition, London: HMSO.

A fourth wave of NHS Trusts was established in April 1994 which includes a further 99 Trusts. Following this possibly final phase of transition, the majority of hospital services in the UK will be provided by more than 400 NHS Trusts, providing around 95 per cent of all hospital and community health services. Only a small minority of units will remain under the direct management of District Health Authorities. The number, composition and structure of NHS Trusts is likely to change further over the coming years, more through combined processes of merger, acquisition and specialisation than through further new conversions.

2.3   The effect on DHAs: purchasing agents

In several DHAs there will no longer be any directly managed units. These DHAs will then become essentially only purchasing agents. And they will be in competition with GPFHs in their areas for the services provided by NHS Trusts for the range of services which the fund-holders can buy themselves. The new style DHAs will be searching for a new role. Some, such as the

Gloucester Authority, are already anticipating the loss of even their commissioning role, as a larger number of GPFHs come on stream. Gloucester is pioneering new services such as the development of a sophisticated intelligence, information and IT function to provide market research and information to the new purchaser and provider organizations. In some areas, the new style DHAs are also beginning a process of merger with the FHSAs to form super-purchaser organizations.

3 DECENTRALIZATION AND NHS TRUSTS: THE ISSUES

It is clear that NHS Trusts are set to become the lynchpin of the provider side of the NHS reforms. If the reforms are to be successful and to meet the criteria which have been established for their success, then it will be very largely through the way the NHS Trusts behave. This paper identifies aspects of the decentralization process which are crucial in this respect.

Firstly, there is the issue of managerial autonomy. Will the new autonomy given to independent provider units and to their management provide effective incentives for improved performance? Will they be motivated to respond to the new quasi-market opportunities as reflected through the financial provisions embodied in contracts? In other words, will the NHS Trusts become effective agents of the policies which the state seeks to implement in the provision of health services?

Secondly, there is the issue of marketization. The new NHS Trusts will be operating as public corporations in a quasi-market environment. Three questions are pertinent here. Will this environment be competitive; will it be subject to problems of transactions costs; and will the new quasi-market contracts provide opportunities and incentives for Trusts to engage in cream-skimming?

Thirdly, there is the issue of privatization. The government has denied that the creation of NHS Trusts can formally be regarded as a process of privatization, since the major shareholder remains the state. Indeed the state is the only shareholder. It holds the liabilities of the Trusts in the form of 'Public Dividend Capital' (PDC) and Interest Bearing Debt (IBD). These forms of liabilities have been created on conversion to Trust status, usually in a 50:50 proportion. There is no provision for private shareholding or for borrowing from the private sector. In this sense the Trusts remain public sector organizations. In another sense, though, a process of partial privatization has taken place. The Trusts are autonomous independent corporations, which are in theory able to dispose of and acquire assets, even though this freedom is in practice limited, as sales of assets in excess of a certain amount need the approval of the Minister.

Nevertheless, as reported in section 6 below, opportunities are emerging for the involvement of private sector finance in the further development of the NHS Trusts. But will the further involvement of the private sector help to overcome the defficiencies of the new system? Or will the encroachment of the private sector lead to the creation of further inequities in the delivery of health services?

4   S TRUSTS AND DECENTRALIZATION: MANAGERIAL AUTONOMY

4.1   The management structure of NHS Trusts

The executive board of an NHS Trust is composed of five executive directors, five non-executive directors appointed by the Minister of Health and the RHA, and a chief executive appointed by the Minister of Health. Below this level of management are the administrative departments and the medical departments. The organization of the NHS Trust at this level is heavily influenced by the legacy of the institutional structures inherited from the past. One could say, in the spirit of the work of Granovetter (1985), that the institutional structure of the NHS Trusts is socially embedded. However this is not to deny that it is subject to continuing processes of change as the effects of the reforms work themselves through. As in the past, the peculiarity of the organizational structure of NHS hospitals is the generally high degree of autonomy enjoyed by the medical departments. The almost syndicalist nature, and autonomous influence, of the medical profession in NHS hospitals has been emphasized by Strong and Robinson (1990) in their study of the institutional and organizational development of NHS hospitals.

What is new in the context of NHS Trusts is that the whole issue of who manages and controls hospitals and other provider units is now much more important than in the past. To some extent, the influence of clinicians has been extended and formalized through their representation on the Executive Board. But the administrative departments are also represented on the Executive Board. And the key areas of decision-making are probably found at the lower levels within the administrative and clinical departments.

Here two separate models seem to be in the process of development (Fitzgerald, 1991). One is the model of the clinical directorate. This is a specialty-based clinical department headed by a senior clinical consultant who is the key decision-maker with managerial responsibility. The clinical directorate has a devolved budget and has extensive autonomy in the use of surpluses. The second model is that of speciality management. In this version, the clinical department is administered by a non-clinical general manager, or speciality manager. The speciality manager is the budget-holder who agrees activity targets with clinicians who otherwise have little direct involvement in managerial decision-making. General management extends down to the point of service delivery, and general managers directly manage clinical professionals.

Whilst considerable research has been carried out on the composition and activity of the NHS Trusts Executive Boards (Ashburner, 1993; Cairncross and Ashburner, 1992), thus far there seems to be no direct research on the internal organizational structure and associated patterns of control over key business decisions at the level of operational departments. In the absence of this research, one is forced to rely on some rather speculative foundations for the development of hypotheses concerning the economic behaviour of NHS Trusts in the new quasi-market setting of purchaser–provider contracts and decentralized health care delivery.

4.2 Are NHS Trusts non-profit firms?

The first issue in developing an analysis of the effects of managerial autonomy and decentralization is the categorization of the type of institutions which NHS Trusts are. One characterization likely to be fruitful is that of the NHS Trust as a non-profit firm (Bartlett and Le Grand, 1994). Non-profit firms are distinguished from other types of firms mainly by the characteristic that they face a non-distribution constraint: any surpluses must be ploughed back into the firm and not used to reward individuals who exercise control over the firm (trustees, officers, directors, members, etc.). This characteristic seems to apply in the case of NHS Trusts. Trusts are only permitted to borrow money for capital expenditure from the Treasury. And the amount they are allowed to borrow is tightly controlled. The Treasury fixes the amount, which is known as an External Financing Limit (EFL). Should the Trust earn a surplus and use this to finance capital expenditure then there is a corresponding reduction in the amount that can be borrowed from the Treasury, so that the Trust must remain within its agreed EFL. The fact that NHS Trusts are in effect not permitted to retain their operating surpluses suggests that it would be appropriate to model them as non-profit firms, i.e. as firms which face a non-distribution constraint.

This is likely to have two consequences. Firstly, to the extent that non-profits are more likely to be motivated by considerations of quality of service than for-profits, purchasers may be more willing to offer contracts to them. In the absence of good information about the quality of service, purchasers may fear that for-profits would seek to win contracts by cutting costs and quality. This may give the NHS Trusts a competitive advantage over private for-profit hospitals. Secondly, the disadvantage is that the tight control over the reinvestment of surpluses is likely to provide incentives to NHS Trusts to develop very short-term business strategies. If this occurs there would be adverse consequences for the dynamic efficiency of the quasi-market system.

4.3 Models of hospitals as non-profit firms

However, this characterization does not do much to provide a behavioural model of such firms. Bartlett and Le Grand (1994) review a number of models of the non-profit hospital firm. These have been based on a variety of behavioural assumptions. One set of models emphasizes the role of the hospital manager as the key decision-maker. In this tradition, Newhouse (1970) and Joseph (1974) have suggested a model based on the idea of service maximization subject to a budget constraint.

Others emphasize the role of the chief medical officers as the key decision-makers and have drawn on the literature of the labour-managed firm to model the hospital as a partnership of doctors. Thus Pauly and Redisch (1973) present a model in which the hospital is akin to a producer cooperative in which clinicians with fixed hours of work maximize net per capita income.

These two contrasting views have been reconciled in a constructive approach developed by Harris (1977), who argues that the interests of both managers and clinicians should be taken into account in developing an appropriate model of a non-profit hospital. He views the hospital as a composite of two distinct firms: a management firm and a medical firm. The management firm supplies the medical firm with inputs, whilst the medical firm demands inputs from the management firm on behalf of the patients.

4.4 A model of the NHS trust

The approach developed by Harris seems to be suitable to begin to develop a model of an NHS Trust. However, rather than characterizing the Trust as being composed of two separate firms, one could think in terms of divisions within the firm. According to a recent account, clinicians and health-care managers have very different roles within the NHS Trust hospital (Welsby, 1992). In this view, clinicians seek to maximize individual patient benefit, whilst managers seek to organize clinical services to maximize throughput. Welsby argues that since clinicians will ask management for more and more resources to improve the quality of care, current financial constraints mean that clinical and management roles are bound to conflict.

My own interviews with managers in NHS Trusts suggest that this view may not quite capture the main conflicts involved. These seem to concern the desire of clinicians, rather than managers, to maximize throughput. Clinicians often appear to interpret their concern for patient benefit by admitting more patients than management would like. Management struggles to contain the demands made by the clinical specialities for resources, not so much because more resources are requested per patient, but because clinicians are engaged in an almost competitive race to maximize the number of patients treated, with little regard for management's cash-limited budgets.

As an initial hypothesis, I suggest that it would be fruitful to model the NHS Trust as a system in which labour-managed clinical directorates hold devolved budgets. The directorates pursue an objective of utility maximization with income and patient benefit as arguments of the utility function. But because of competition within the Trust among the clinical directorates for resources, the income of the directorate is linked to the number of patients treated, i.e. to its size and growth. Clinical directors compete for patients because the larger the directorate *vis-à-vis* other directorates in the hospital, the larger their budget and the greater their incomes, surpluses and prestige.

There does indeed seem to have been an apparent increase in activity in terms of in-patient referrals since the reforms were introduced (NHSME, 1992a, 1992b). This can be explained in part by the attempts of clinical directors to boost the throughput of patients. Increased throughput is reflected in a reduction in the average length of stay in hospitals which has been brought about by changes in clinical practice leading to earlier discharge of patients from hospital. Early discharge seems in turn to have boosted the rate of readmission of patients who suffer a relapse of symptoms. And since readmissions are counted as new cases, the increase in referral rates takes place without any real corresponding increase in the actual delivery of health care.

In many cases, managers are unable directly to control the rate of patient throughput in the hospital. And, since they face a hard budget constraint dictated by the block contracts that they have signed with their purchasers, a situation can easily arise in which the budget is exhausted before the end of the financial year. At this point, clinicians are told to suspend operations, wards are closed, and excess capacity develops in the system. In other cases, managers may have more direct control over the activity of clinicians, and clinicians are told to slow down their rate of throughput for patients on block contracts, and to boost their throughput of patients on cost-per-case contracts (often the patients of GPFHs).

This behaviour appears to be widespread amongst NHS Trusts. A recent survey of 243 surgeons by the Royal College of Surgeons found that between April and November 1993 as many as 44 per cent of surgical units had been told by their managements to reduce or stop some activities. Almost one third (30 per cent) of surgeons had been asked to work less hard, and 5 per cent of units had stopped treating elective surgery cases altogether. One-third of surgeons had also been told only to treat patients of GP fund-holders (Mihill, 1994).

5   NHS TRUSTS AND DECENTRALIZATION: MARKETIZATION

A key feature and purpose of the decentralizing NHS reforms has been to introduce elements of market-like competition into the provision of health services, without however abandoning the essentially socialist nature of the NHS: that health services should be provided free at the point of delivery. The reforms therefore resemble the introduction of a form of market socialism on a sectoral level within the UK. The essence of this process is the creation of a quasi-market based upon the purchaser–provider split. The instrument through which this market is made to work is the purchaser–provider contract.

Contracts can basically be of two types: the block contract and the cost-per-case contract. A mixed form of contract is also available: the cost-and-volume contract. And there are also examples of other hybrid types of contract emerging, such as the block contract with floors and ceilings. The essential difference among different types of contract, however, is in the amount of price information for individual treatments which they contain.

Block contracts are cheap to establish but contain little information, as they specify little more than a fixed global sum to be paid by the purchaser to the provider. Initially, they represented little more than the reproduction of the pre-reform pattern of activity. Typically, they specify an 'indicative volume' of cases to be treated in each specialty broken down between in-patient stays, day cases and out-patient attendances. Action to be taken when the indicative volume is exceeded or not met is subject to further bargaining and agreement between the Trust and the purchasing Authority. Block contracts are problematic for the provider if they do not contain ceilings on activity levels, because they expose the provider to the risk of cost over-run if more than the forecast number of cases are admitted and treated. According to one recent study (Cairns, 1993), there are already cases in which providers are finding that they are treating many more patients compared to previous years without a corresponding increase in revenue from purchasers. Providers, however, sometimes appear to be overstating the actual increase in services provided. The volume of services is measured by 'completed consultant episodes' and as patients are passed from one consultant to another within a hospital a single course of treatment can sometimes count for more than one unit of volume.

Cost-per-case contracts avoid some of the problems of block contracts, but they are costly to write, implement and enforce for large volumes of activity, precisely because they contain more information than block contracts. They also make the purchaser vulnerable to the risk of budget over-run where the number of cases which are admitted at the stated price cannot be controlled by the purchaser directly. They are more likely to be promoted by smaller purchasers such as GPFHs, who can control the rate of referral.

Elsewhere I have explored the risk-sharing properties of various types of contracts (Bartlett, 1991). The formal analysis of the optimal risk-sharing contract has also been elegantly set out by Levaggi (1994). However, it has become apparent that the more important issue relates to the development of inequalities. These arise because of the different types of contracts signed by different purchasers. DHAs sign block contracts. But part of their budget is transferred to GPFHs who sign cost-per-case contracts. These cost-per-case contracts are very attractive to providers (Trusts) because they provide additional income over and above their basic core funding through the block contract with the DHA.

Moreover a GPFH tends to have more to spend per patient than the effective amount of resources triggered by a referral from a non-GPFH. This is because the budgets allocated to GPFHs are calculated on the basis of the previous years' activity levels measured in terms of the number of patients referred to hospital. Knowing this, prospective GPFHs have attempted, usually successfully, to boost their rates of patient referral in the year prior to becoming fund-holders. There is some evidence, based on a careful study of fund-holder budgets in one regional health authority area, that this has given rise to a situation where the resources backing up a referral from a GPFH exceed the available resources backing up referrals from non-fundholding GPs (Dixon, 1994). Glennerster et al. (1994) argue that this effect in part merely represents previously existing differences in referral patterns. They also report a Department of Health study which apparently showed that GPFHs received less than would have been allocated if a standard national formula had been applied. Nevertheless, despite these cautions, the Dixon study shows that at least in the initial phases of the fund-holding experiment, many GPFHs were able to extract a favourable allocation of resources to their budgets in comparison with the resources available to non-GPFHs.

This, together with the desire of hospital managers to attract patients on cost-per-case contracts, means that patients from GPFHs are able to queue-jump. In this way a two-tier system may develop as a result of decentralizing reforms and the way contracts are structured, leading to inequalities in the provision of health services.

In addition, there has been a gradual increase in the extent to which purchasers have put out contracts to the private sector. GPFHs are reported to be making increasing use of the private sector to carry out simple procedures such as cataract operations. This gives rise to the development of new forms of cream-skimming (or 'cherry-picking'), this time by the private sector. The private sector takes on the relatively easy, low-risk cases, leaving high-cost high-risk treatments to the NHS (Timmins, 1993).

DHAs have also increased the amount of services they have commissioned from the private sector from £160 million to £187 million. And NHS Trusts themselves often buy care services in from the private sector. The amount involved tripled between 1991/2 and 1992/3, rising from £12 million to £44.5 million.

6   NHS TRUSTS AND DECENTRALIZATION: PRIVATIZATION

Are NHS Trusts privatized organizations? Formally not, since the main and only shareholder is the state. But they do have extensive managerial autonomy, although this is much more closely regulated and circumscribed than had originally been intended. The NHS Trusts have certain freedoms, and in particular are able to buy and sell assets up to a certain limit. They are free to develop their own employment and labour relations policies, and to make their own decisions about the type, quality and mix of services that they provide. Moreover, they can set up trading companies on their own initiative which engage directly on the market for profit: the so-called 'income generating' activities. In a sense, then, they are partially privatized enterprises. However, they remain circumscribed in their freedom of activity and are ultimately responsible to the Minister of Health for their performance.

But the fact of their formal autonomy suggests that NHS trust managers will not rest content with the existing limitations on their freedoms. And there are a number of areas in which one can envisage a developing relationship and opening-up to the private sector. These areas of 'opportunity' have recently been given prominence in a pamphlet by Willets produced by the right-wing think tank, the Social Market Foundation (Willetts, 1993).

Willetts has identified six ways in which private finance can be involved in the provision of health services alongside or through the new structure of the NHS. These are: leasing, turnkey projects, building and operating NHS units, private hospitals contracting to NHS purchasers, private initiatives in the areas of primary and community care, and shared facilities. These areas for private sector involvement have been opened up by recent changes in policy which have raised the threshold of private finance schemes requiring Treasury approval from £250000 to £10 million announced in January 1993 (Salter and Douglas, 1994).

A number of recent developments illustrate that many Trusts are already beginning to explore the possibilities of involving the private sector in financing and operating extensions to their activities, or generating private sector activity themselves to generate additional income.

The first example of a leasing arrangement has emerged in Darlings. The Darlings Memorial Hospital submitted a bid for conversion to Trust status in April 1994, and as part of its business plan proposed to lease a number of surplus wards and an operating theatre to a private health company, Independent British Healthcare (IBH). IBH already operates fourteen private hospitals in the UK, and has proposed a profit-sharing lease in Darlings. The arrangement would include opportunities for NHS consultants to operate privately on the patients of GPFHs. This is a test case which, if successful, could open the doors for leasing arrangements of a similar nature elsewhere (Brindle, 1994)

Elsewhere, Trusts have begun to develop their own private-sector activities. (In Eastern Europe this might be called 'wild privatization'.) One example came to light in the case of the Northumbria Ambulance Service Trust because the private activities made a loss of £83000. They included the activities of a company set up by the Trust to sell security services, the provision of training services to foreign ambulance crews, transporting donor organs within the UK, and a vehicle service and maintenance operation based in Newcastle (Donegan, 1993).

The implications for the operation of quasi-markets are serious. Since Trusts cannot engage in long-term capital spending outside their EFLs, they are forced to look to private-sector schemes to carry out their expansion plans. The patients associated with private-sector initiatives are likely to receive preferential treatment as a result, compared to those who are waiting in the NHS queue. Once again, opportunities for the development of inequities abound.

7 NHS TRUSTS AND THE PERFORMANCE OF THE NEW NHS: WHAT WE NEED TO KNOW

The new quasi-market in health service provision in the UK is in its infancy. But already a fundamental and radical transformation of the system of health-care delivery in the UK has been carried through. Non-profit organizations in the form of NHS Trusts have become the most important type of supply-side provider organization in the area of secondary health care. An extensive decentralization of managerial autonomy has taken place, and the provision of health care is becoming marketized through the mechanism of purchaser–provider contracts.

It is not clear, however, whether the processes of change and transformation have come to an end. Will NHS Trusts prove to be stable institutional forms, or do they represent a transitional phase on a path towards full privatization of the NHS?

This paper has explored some of the problems facing the existing system of NHS Trusts in its infancy. Firstly, I considered the issue of managerial autonomy. It was initially expected that more complete autonomy for decentralized provider institutions in the context of a competitive quasi-market would present them with high-powered incentives to improve their efficiency and performance. These incentives were expected to provide the basis for Trusts to become effective agents of health policies determined by the state.

However, since the early stages of the reform, the state (perhaps fearful of the instabilities of an unregulated market) has introduced extensive powers of control and regulation over the new providers. This policy development is especially counter-productive in the area of control over the Trusts' ability to make decisions about the level of reinvestment of surpluses. This leads to a short-term approach to business strategy which may eventually undermine the competitive position of NHS Trusts. It also opens up opportunities for the further encroachment of private capital into the financing of expansion programmes in the NHS. And it encourages NHS managers to seek out income-earning opportunities for Trusts outside the regulated areas by setting up 'income generating' private companies, diversifying and diluting the Trusts' purposes as health-care providers.

Relaxation of this area of regulation would provide a greater stability to the institutional structure and organizational form of the NHS Trusts.

In the second section of the paper, I explored the issue of marketization through the introduction of the new mechanism of purchaser–provider contracts. Since there is incomplete information about costs and prices throughout the NHS, purchasers are relying mainly on forms of incomplete contracts known as block contracts to govern their transactions with providers. These have the advantage of relatively low *ex ante* transaction costs, but impose heavy *ex post* costs due to a requirement for an increased level of monitoring, the possibility of cost over-runs which may fall on providers where activity exceeds the predicted levels, and expose the purchaser to the costs of opportunistic behaviour by providers. One example of this is the over-counting of activity by providers in terms of completed consultant episodes. Another example is the increase in readmission rates due to the incentives facing clinical directors to boost throughput. Block contracts also open up the potential for cream-skimming (and the associated inequities) wherever Trusts can selectively admit patients who are less likely to be costly to treat, and refuse or limit treatment to others (the elderly, smokers). In addition, it is becoming increasingly clear that in many cases managers are instructing clinicians to selectively admit only the patients of GPFHs. This is partly to do with the increased resources which GPFHs may have available to support their referrals compared to non-fundholders; and partly it is to do with the fact that GPFHs are more likely than DHAs to have negotiated cost-per-case contracts for their patients and so be seen as sources of 'additional' income over and above the core funding provided by DHA block contracts.

What are the implications for the performance and stability of NHS Trusts? Firstly, some of these problems are probably temporary, and will disappear as experience with operating and negotiating contracts increases, alongside an increase in the amount of information available about costs and prices. Already, more sophisticated approaches to contract pricing are being developed (such as some initiatives in banded price contracts which have been reported recently in the professional press). Secondly, some of the problems are linked to the existence of a dual structure of purchasing. NHS Trusts are able to discriminate between DHA purchasers operating block contracts and GP fund-holder purchasers operating cost-per-case contracts. One solution to this problem will develop as the system gravitates towards one or other type of purchasing as the norm. The current trend is towards heavier reliance on GP fund-holding. This has some advantages in the areas of competition among purchasers, closer links between purchasers and users, and some information advantages in that GPs can more readily assess the quality of outcomes than can DHAs. On the other hand, recent proposals by the Labour Party argue in favour of DHAs as the dominant form of purchaser, partly out of a concern for the apparent inequities in treatment of patients of fund-holders and non-fundholders. In fact the problem of inequity will disappear as soon as the duality of purchasing agents disappears, by whatever route this is achieved. Finally, NHS Trusts may have some inbuilt competitive advantages on the quasi-market in relation to for-profit providers, due to the preferences of purchasers to negotiate contracts with non-profit firms on grounds of quality assurance.

In conclusion, the analysis presented in this paper has demonstrated that much more needs to be known about the economic behaviour of NHS Trusts as key providers on the NHS quasi-market. In particular we need to know about the internal organizational structure of Trusts: is the clinical directorate model more widespread than the speciality manager model? Linked to this we need more direct information about the objectives of the key decision-makers on the Trust boards and at the level of department heads, in both administrative and clinical activities.

Another main area to which further research should be directed is the development of new private-sector initiatives by NHS Trusts, and the degree and types of involvement of private capital in the development of Trusts capital programmes, and operating activities.

One key question for the further development of quasi-markets in health care in the UK will be the extent to which the problems identified in this paper and elsewhere in the emerging literature on quasi-market reforms open up opportunities for the further involvement of the private sector in the financing of the provision of secondary care services. Recent reports suggest that the private sector is indeed already encroaching increasingly on what has for many years been exclusively public sector territory. But although the increasing involvement of the private sector may overcome some problems of weak incentives for efficiency facing provider units (themselves partly a result of over-regulation of capital budgeting decisions), it is likely also to further open up possibilities for the further development of market-related inequalities in the provision of health services. This seems to be an emerging dilemma in the quasi-market provision of health services in the UK.

NOTES

*   This paper has been written with the financial support of the ESRC as part of a project on 'Providers, Purchasers and Contracts: the Economic Effects of Institutional Reform in the NHS'. The project forms part of the ESRC Contracts and Competition Research Programme. I am grateful for helpful comments received from Julian Le Grand and Deborah Wilson, and have benefited greatly from discussions about the whole area of NHS reform with Lyn Harrison and Carol Propper.

1. For a case study of this process see Bartlett and Harrison (1993).

REFERENCES

Ashburner, L. (1993), 'The Composition of NHS Trust Boards', unpublished, University of Warwick.

Bartlett, W. (1991), 'Quasi-Markets and Contracts: A Markets and Hierarchies Perspective on NHS Reforms', *Public Money and Management*, pp. 53–61.

Bartlett W. (1993), 'Riduzione dell'intervento pubblico, sviluppo dell'offerta non profit e forme di contrattazione nei servizi sociali in Gran Bretagna', in C. Borzaga and A. Matacena (eds), *Il futuro dei servizi sociali in italia: il ruolo della cooperazione sociale nei processi di depubblicizzazione*, Istituto Italiano di Studi Cooperativi 'Luigi Luzzati', pp. 107–20.

Bartlett, W. and L. Harrison (1993), 'Quasi-Markets and the National Health Service Reforms', in J. Le Grand and W. Bartlett (eds), *Quasi-Markets and Social Policy*, London: Macmillan.

Bartlett, W. and J. Le Grand (1994), 'The Performance of Trusts', in R. Robinson and J. Le Grand (eds), *Evaluating the NHS Reforms*, London: The King's Fund Institute.

Brindle, D. (1994), 'Health Firms in Lease Deal at NHS Hospital', *The Guardian*, 17 February.

Cairncross, L. and L. Ashburner (1992), *NHS Trust Boards: the First Wave. Research for Action: Authorities in the NHS*, 6, Warwick: University of Warwick: Centre for Corporate Strategy and Change.

Cairns, J. (1993) 'Contracts: Problems and Prospects', *Health Policy*, **25**, pp. 127–40.

Dixon, J. (1994), 'Why Funding GP Fundholders is Leading to Tiers', paper presented to the Health Economists' Study Group, London School of Hygiene and Tropical Medicine, 5–7 January 1994.

Donegan, L. (1993), 'Ambulance Trust loses £83,000', *The Guardian*, 9 September.

Fitzgerald, L. (1991), 'This Year's Model', *Health Service Journal*, pp. 26–7.

Glennerster, H. and M. Matsaganis (1993), 'The UK Health Reforms: The Fundholding Experiment', *Health Policy*, **23**, pp. 179–91.

Glennerster, H., M. Matsaganis, P. Owens and S. Hancock (1994), 'GP Fundholding: Wild Card or Winning Hand?', in R. Robinson and J. Le Grand (eds), *Evaluating the NHS Reforms*, London: The King's Fund Institute.

Granovetter, M. (1985), 'Economic Action and Social Structure: The Problem of the Embeddedness', *American Journal of Sociology*, **91** (3), pp. 3–11.

Ham, C. (1985), *Health Policy in Britain: The Politics and Organisation of the National Health Service*, (2nd edn), London: Macmillan.

Harris, J. (1977), 'The Internal Organisation of Hospitals: Some Economic Implications', *Bell Journal of Economics*, **8**, pp. 467–82.

Harrison, S. (1994), *National Health Service Management in the 1980s*, Aldershot: Avebury.

Joseph, H. (1974), 'On Economic Theories of Hospital Behaviour', *Journal of Economics and Business*, **27**, pp. 69–74.

Le Grand, J. (1991), 'Quasi-Markets and Social Policy', *Economic Journal*, **101**, pp. 1256–67.

Le Grand, J. and W. Bartlett (eds) (1993), *Quasi-Markets and Social Policy,* London: Macmillan.

Levaggi, R. (1994), 'The Purchaser–provider Optimal Contract', paper presented to the Health Economists' Study Group, London School of Hygiene and Tropical Medicine, 5–7 January 1994.

Mihill, C. (1994), 'Cash Squeeze Puts Clamp on Operations', *The Guardian*, February.

Milgrom, P. and P. Roberts (1992), *Economics, Organisation and Management*, London: Prentice-Hall International.

Newhouse, J. (1970), 'Toward a Theory of Non-Profit Institutions: An Economic Model of a Hospital', *American Economic Review*, **63**, pp. 64–74.

NHSME (1992a), *NHS Reforms: The First Six Months*, London: NHS Management Executive.

NHSME (1992b), *NHS Trusts: the First 12 Months*, London: NHS Management Executive.

Pauly, M.V. and M. Redisch (1973), 'The Not-For-Profit Hospital as a Physicians Cooperative', *American Economic Review*, **63**, pp. 87–99.

Salter, B. and G. Douglas (1994), 'Private Money and Public Health: Managing the Risks', *Health Services Management*, April, pp. 10–11.

Strong, P. and J. Robinson (1990), *The NHS: Under New Management*, Milton Keynes: Open University Press.

Timmins, N. (1993), 'NHS Trusts Buy in more Care from Private Sector', *The Independent*, 22 December.

Welsby, P.D. (1992), 'Should Clinicians Accept Management Responsibilities?', *Postgraduate Medical Journal*, **68**, pp. 671–72.

Willetts, D. (1993), 'The Opportunities for Private Funding in the NHS', Occasional Paper, 3, London: Social Market Foundation.

Index